Stephan Aier   Mathias Ekstedt
Florian Matthes   Erik Proper
Jorge L. Sanz (Eds.)

W0036997

Trends in Enterprise Architecture Research and Practice-Driven Research on Enterprise Transformation

7th Workshop, TEAR 2012
and 5th Working Conference, PRET 2012
Held at The Open Group Conference 2012
Barcelona, Spain, October 23-24, 2012
Proceedings

 Springer

Volume Editors

Stephan Aier
University of St. Gallen
St. Gallen, Switzerland
E-mail: stephan.aier@unisg.ch

Mathias Ekstedt
Royal Institute of Technology
Stockholm, Sweden
E-mail: mathiase@ics.kth.se

Florian Matthes
Technische Universität München
Garching bei München, Germany
E-mail: matthes@in.tum.de

Erik Proper
CRP Henri Tudor, Luxembourg
Radboud University Nijmegen, The Netherlands
E-mail: erik.proper@tudor.lu

Jorge L. Sanz
IBM Research
San Jose, CA, USA
E-mail: jorges@us.ibm.com

ISSN 1865-1348   e-ISSN 1865-1356
ISBN 978-3-642-34162-5   e-ISBN 978-3-642-34163-2
DOI 10.1007/978-3-642-34163-2
Springer Heidelberg Dordrecht London New York

Library of Congress Control Number: 2012948779

ACM Computing Classification (1998): J.1, H.3.5, H.4, K.6.3

Typesetting: Camera-ready by author, data conversion by Scientific Publishing Services, Chennai, India

Printed on acid-free paper

Springer is part of Springer Science+Business Media (www.springer.com)

Preface

The 7th Trends in Enterprise Architecture Research (TEAR 2012) Workshop and
the 5th Practice-Driven Research on Enterprise Transformation (PRET-5) Working Conference were co-located with The Open Group's Conference on Enterprise
Architecture, Cloud Computing, Security, taking place in Spain, Barcelona,
October 22–26, 2012.

TEAR 2012 and PRET-5 were organized as an integrated event as a parallel
track to The Open Group Conference, where the TEAR and PRET tracks were
tightly integrated. This is also why it was decided to produce an integrated
proceedings volume.

The Events

The TEAR workshop series brings together enterprise architecture (EA) researchers from different research communities and provides a forum to present
EA research results and to discuss future EA research directions.

The field of EA has gained considerable attention over the last years. For
defining the term architecture, most agree on the ISO/IEC 42010:2007 Standard,
where architecture is defined as the *"fundamental organization of a system, embodied in its components, their relationships to each other and the environment,
and the principles governing its design and evolution."* For EA the focus is on
the overall enterprise in contrast to partial architectures such as IT architecture
or software architecture. EA explicitly incorporates business-related artefacts
in addition to traditional IS/IT artefacts. By providing an enterprise-wide perspective, EA is a means for organizations to coordinate their adaptations to
increasingly fast-changing market conditions which influence the entire chain of
activities of an enterprise, from business processes to IT support.

TEAR 2012 was the seventh in an increasingly successful series of workshops,
previously held in Hong Kong, Switzerland, Australia, Sweden, The Netherlands,
and Finland.

The *PRET working conference* series brings together researchers and practitioners interested in enterprise transformation. More specifically, the PRET
events aim to build a bridge between theory and practice, between researchers
and practitioners.

Modern day enterprises are in a constant state of flux. New technologies,
new markets, globalization, mergers, acquisitions, etcetera are among the 'usual
suspects' that require enterprises to transform themselves to deal with these
challenges and new realities. Most information systems practitioners will find
themselves working in a context of enterprise transformation. One could even go
as far as to claim that a business-oriented perspective on information systems is
really about enterprise transformation, where enterprise transformation involves
the use of methods and techniques from enterprise engineering, enterprise modelling, enterprise architecture, and information systems engineering. As a field
of study, enterprise transformation requires a close interaction between practice

and academia. What works and does not work requires validation in real-life situations. Conversely, it is in industrial practice where challenges can be found that may fuel and inspire researchers.

PRET-5 was the fifth in an increasingly successful series of working conferences, previously held in The Netherlands (twice), Luxembourg, and Poland.

The Open Group Conference

The Open Group Conference provides a venue to practitioners and academics to gain valuable knowledge and to participate in The Open Group's Forums and Work Groups that are developing the next generation of open, vendor-neutral standards and certifications. Those who attend The Open Group Conferences benefit from the opportunity to leverage the expertise of other experts, learn from others' experiences, and delve into content most relevant to their jobs and organizations.

Conferences also present an opportunity for attendees to access a wide range of experts, practitioners, and specialists in a non-sales environment, and build professional relationships. The Open Group hosts four quarterly conferences as well as regional conferences hosted by our local partners around the globe.

Why Join Forces?

The TEAR and PRET workshops already joined forces before, during the Enterprise Engineering Week in 2010, in Delft, The Netherlands. At that time, the visitors of the two workshops, as well as the organizers, saw a clear benefit for future collaboration between the two events. Even though both events have a distinct identity, their topics and audience show an overlap that makes them natural partners.

Joining forces with The Open Group Conference also provides a unique opportunity to build a bridge between practitioners, standardization efforts, and academic research, in the areas of enterprise transformation and enterprise architecture.

The Program

We received a total of 24 high-quality papers. After an extensive review process by a distinguished international Program Committee, with most papers receiving three reviews, we accepted the 18 papers that appear in these proceedings. Of these 18 papers, 5 papers were PRET papers and 13 were TEAR papers.

No further distinction was made between these types of paper, leading to an integrated program of PRET and TEAR, involving six sessions covering: EAM Effectivity, Languages for EA, EAM and the Ability to Change, Advanced Topics in EA, Governing Enterprise Transformations, and EA Applications.

August 2012

Stephan Aier
Mathias Ekstedt
Florian Matthes
Henderik A. Proper
Jorge L. Sanz

Organization

TEAR-2012 Workshop Co-chairs

Stephan Aier	University of St. Gallen, Switzerland
Mathias Ekstedt	Royal Institute of Technology Stockholm, Sweden
Florian Matthes	Technische Universität München, Germany

TEAR Steering Committee

Stephan Aier	University of St. Gallen, St. Gallen, Switzerland
Mathias Ekstedt	Royal Institute of Technology Stockholm, Sweden
Marc M. Lankhorst	Novay Enschede, The Netherlands
Henderik A. Proper	Public Research Centre Henri Tudor, Luxembourg and Radboud University Nijmegen, The Netherlands
Robert Winter	University of St. Gallen, St. Gallen, Switzerland

PRET-5 Working Conference Co-chairs

Frank Harmsen	Ernst & Young IT Advisory and Maastricht University, The Netherlands
Henderik A. Proper	Public Research Centre Henri Tudor, Luxembourg and Radboud University Nijmegen, The Netherlands
Jorge L. Sanz	IBM, USA
Khaled Gaaloul	Public Research Centre Henri Tudor, Luxembourg

PRET Steering Committee

Frank Harmsen	Ernst & Young and Maastricht University, The Netherlands
Birgit Hofreiter	Vienna University of Technology, Austria
Henderik A. Proper	Public Research Centre Tudor, Luxembourg and Radboud University Nijmegen, The Netherlands
Stefan Strecker	University of Hagen, Germany
José Tribolet	Technical University of Lisbon, Portugal

Reviewers

The organizers would like to thank the following reviewers for providing reviews of the papers submitted of the TEAR 2012 and PRET-5 events:

Agnes Nakakawa	Radboud University Nijmegen, The Netherlands and Makerere University, Uganda
Andreas L. Opdahl	University of Bergen, Norway
Antonia Albani	University of St. Gallen, Switzerland
Barbara Pernici	Politecnico di Milano, Italy
Barbara Weber	University of Innsbruck, Austria
Bas van Gils	BiZZdesign, The Netherlands
Birgit Hofreiter	Vienna University of Technology, Austria
Brian Cameron	Penn State University, USA
Carlos Pascoa	Technical University of Lisbon, Portugal
Christian Huemer	Vienna University of Technology, Austria
Christian Schweda	Iteratec GmbH, Germany
Christine Legner	HEC Lausanne, Switzerland
Colette Rolland	University Paris 1 Pantheon Sorbonne, France
Daniel Möller	European Business School, Germany
Elmar J. Sinz	University of Bamberg, Germany
Eric Dubois	Public Research Centre Henri Tudor, Luxembourg
Frederik Ahlemann	European Business School, Germany
Gil Regev	EPFL and Itecor, Switzerland
Giuseppe Berio	LabSTICC, University of South Brittany, France
Gottfried Vossen	University of Münster, Germany
Graham McLeod	Promis Ltd & Inspired.org, UK
Hans Mulder	VIA Groep and University of Antwerp, Belgium
Hans-Georg Fill	University of Vienna, Austria
Hervé Panetto	University of Lorraine, France
Jaap Gordijn	VU University Amsterdam, The Netherlands
Jan Mendling	Vienna University of Economics and Business, Austria
Janis Grabis	Riga Technical University, Latvia
Janis Stirna	Royal Institute of Technology, Sweden
Joachim Schelp	Helsana, Switzerland
Johan Ullberg	Royal Institute of Technology Stockholm, Sweden
Johan Versendaal	Utrecht University of Applied Science, The Netherlands

Stefanie Rinderle-Ma	University of Vienna, Austria
Stijn Hoppenbrouwers	Radboud University Nijmegen, The Netherlands
Sudha Ram	University of Arizona, USA
Sybren de Kinderen	Public Research Centre Henri Tudor, Luxembourg
Thomas Hess	LMU München, Germany
Tim O'Neill	University of Technology Sydney, Australia
Ulrich Frank	University of Duisburg-Essen, Germany
Ulrike Lechner	Universität der Bundeswehr München, Germany
Volker Wiemann	Bielefeld University of Applied Sciences, Germany
Waldo Rocha Flores	Royal Institute of Technology Stockholm, Sweden
Wilhelm Hasselbring	University of Kiel, Germany
Wolfgang Keller	objectarchitects, Germany
Wolfgang Molnar	Public Research Centre Henri Tudor, Luxembourg
Xavier Franch	Universitat Politecnica de Catalunya, Spain
Yves Pigneur	University of Lausanne, Switzerland

Table of Contents

TEAR: Advanced Topics in Enterprise Architecture

PRET: Governing Enterprise Transformation

TEAR: EA Management Effectivity

A Framework for Creating Pattern Languages
for Enterprise Architecture

Paula Kotzé[1], Motse Tsogang[2], and Alta van der Merwe[3]

[1] CSIR Meraka Institute, PO Box 395, Pretoria, 0001, South Africa; and School of ICT Nelson Mandela Metropolitan University, Port Elizabeth, South Africa
[2] School of Computing, University of South Africa, Pretoria, 0003, South Africa
[3] Department of Informatics, University of Pretoria, Private Bag X20, Hatfield, 0028, South Africa
paula.kotze@meraka.org.za, mtsogang@gmail.com, alta@up.ac.za

Abstract. The use of patterns and pattern languages in enterprise architecture (EA) is a relatively novel concept. Although both the concepts of patterns and EA are over 30 years old, the notion of design patterns is hardly applied to EA. There is a lack of pattern collections specifically devoted to EA: only a small number of patterns and pattern collections specifically aimed at enterprise architecture can be found in the public domain. Furthermore no framework or method exist that would assist enterprise architects in creating patterns and pattern languages for EA. This paper aims to bridge this gap by proposing a pattern framework for enterprise architecture (PF4EA), which can guide the development of well-grounded patterns and pattern languages for the EA domain. The components of the frameworks are described as well as a method for its use.

Keywords: Enterprise architecture, design patterns, pattern languages, pattern collections.

1 Introduction

Patterns are an attempt to describe solutions to problems or practices in a specific context, and which are harvested from 'best practices' and working solutions [18]. A *design pattern* is an approach to abstracting and capturing the knowledge for reuse on what made a solution, or paradigm, successful in relation to the problems identified in a particular context [35]. A design pattern can be thus be seen as "a piece of literature that describes a design problem and a general solution for the problem in a particular context" [14:2]. Design patterns originated in the field of building architecture, when Christopher Alexander invented the idea of capturing design guidelines in the form of design patterns [2]. Although the basic design pattern concept spans domains, the purpose, presentation and level of abstraction vary according to the domain and even within the domain [22]. Patterns are usually grouped into a *pattern collection*, either into a pattern catalogue or pattern language [6, 32, 35, 54]. This paper primarily focuses on pattern languages. A pattern language "is a collection of patterns that build on each other to generate a system" [14:17]. A pattern on its own solves a disjoint design problem, while a pattern language builds a 'system'.

S. Aier et al. (Eds.): TEAR 2012 and PRET 2012, LNBIP 131, pp. 1–20, 2012.

The idea expressed in a pattern should be general enough to be applied in to a variety of systems within its context, but still specific enough to give constructive guidance. Design patterns are therefore often put forward as a way to assist novices in mastering a new domain [5, 12]. Patterns could likewise thus be put forward as a way to assist novice enterprise architects (and provide support for experienced enterprise architects) in the task of doing enterprise architecture.

An enterprise is a socio-technical organization or entity that functions on a relatively continuous basis to achieve a common set of goals and objectives, and has a mission and vision that guides how it should operate at all times [29, 37, 47]. An understanding of an enterprise's components and how they are related to one another can be obtained from its underlying architecture. *Enterprise architecture* (EA) "is the continuous practice of describing the essential elements of a socio-technical organization, their relationships to each other and to the environment, in order to understand complexity and manage change" [19].

Patterns and pattern languages for EA is a fairly novel domain. Although both the concepts of patterns and EA are over 30 years old, the notion of design patterns is hardly applied to EA and there is a lack of pattern collections specifically devoted to EA. To assist in bridging this gap, the aim of this paper is to propose a framework that can be followed to guide the development of well-grounded pattern languages for the EA domain. Although the framework is EA specific, the arguments on which the framework is based are fairly generic and can equally be applied to other domains (i.e. by replacing the EA-prefixed steps with a generic <topic>-prefix).

Section 2 provides the theoretical background for the paper by introducing the concept of patterns and pattern languages in more detail. Section 3 presents the Pattern Framework for Enterprise Architecture (PF4EA), whilst section 4 describes the method for using PF4EA. Section 5 provides examples of the use of PF4EA, whilst section 6 concludes.

2   Background

2.1   Patterns and Pattern Languages

Patterns are harvested from best practices on what has worked well in the past for a particular problem in a particular context, and is an attempt towards a description of successful implementation of a solution for that problem in the specific context [2, 32]. A pattern context is the preconditions under which a pattern is applicable, or a description of the initial state, before the pattern is applied to its intended problem [46]. From a usage perspective, patterns provide the guidelines for the description of solutions to analysis, design and architecture related problems [14, 18, 26]. In a practical sense, each pattern describes a problem that occurs repeatedly in a particular context, and then describes the core solution underpinning the problem, in such a way that one can use the solution many times over, without ever having exactly the same end result [2].

For any pattern to be legitimate, it must adhere to several general pattern characteristics [6, 14, 17, 54]:

— A pattern is grounded in a domain by being associated to a context as well as other patterns, and has no meaning outside the design domain or the pattern language it forms part of.
— A pattern implies an artefact.
— A pattern bridges many levels of abstraction.
— A pattern is both functional and non-functional, and should include the reason(s) and rationale why the solution is recommended, and what trade-offs are involved when such a pattern is used.
— A pattern is both a process and a thing, relating the design process and structure of the end product.
— A pattern is validated by use and cannot be verified or validated from a purely theoretical framework, without its practical application in its relevant context.
— A pattern captures a big idea and is meant to focus on key problems within a context and implies maximum reusability (whenever the problem emerges again, the pattern gets reapplied).
— A pattern conforms to a particular template.
— A pattern should be part of a pattern language where different patterns work together to solve a recurring complex problem in a particular context.

The next two sections discuss the pattern templates and pattern collections in more detail.

2.2   Pattern Forms and Templates

All patterns in the same language should have the same format [2]. A pattern form or template is a structure describing the essential elements and format of a pattern. Pattern templates vary between and even within application domains. For example, templates for building architecture (e.g. the Alexandrian Form for building architecture [41]), would differ from those for software engineering (e.g. the Portland Pattern Form (PF) [16], the canonical / Coplien form [3], the compact form (CF) [50], the Gang of Four Form (GoFF) [25], the Beck Form (BF) [44], etc.). In the EA domain the Enterprise Architecture Management (EAM) Pattern Catalog [21] supports a light-weight, organization-specific approach to EA management based on best practices, and distinguishes between three types of patterns: methodology (EA management) patterns, viewpoint patterns and information patterns. The pattern form are similar to the Buschmann's [9] software engineering form and includes the following elements: name, short description, example, context, problem, solution, implementation, variants, known uses, consequences, 'see also' (reference to associated patterns) and credits.

2.3   Pattern Collections

Patterns are usually grouped into a *pattern collection*, either into a pattern catalogue or a pattern language [6, 32, 35, 54]. A catalogue is a list or a collection of items usually organized in alphabetical order [48], where the patterns do not necessarily have to be related. When several related patterns are combined to solve a recurring complex problem in a specified context, the grouping of associated patterns is referred to as a *pattern language* [2, 7, 14, 18, 20, 35]. A pattern language is a structured method of describing good design practices within a particular domain. A pattern language is characterized by noting the common problems in a field of interest, describing the most effective solutions for meeting some stated goal, helping the designer move from problem to problem in a logical way, and allowing for many different paths through the design process.

2.4   Searching and Creating Individual Patterns

Patterns are discovered and not invented. There are basically two ways in which pattern collections can be discovered or formed [24]: through crafting/creating new patterns and through searching/harvesting patterns from existing pattern libraries or through automated processes (e.g. [45]). Patterns are discovered through observation and discrimination [24]. Observation reveals the underlying pattern and discrimination allows for selecting beneficial patterns that would advantage the specific domain. To craft a pattern, the problem to be solved must identified and the forces in tension discovered and documented. This is followed by a resolution of the forces, where the practitioner observes what solutions have been fashioned by other practitioners, and what is the best practice solution matching the forces that lead to the problem. The discovered solution is expressed as a pattern of action, which substantiates the solution in a general.

2.5   Creating Pattern Languages

Although patterns and pattern language collections abound, literature on the actual process of creating pattern languages are sparse. Cunningham [15], for example, suggested a few steps to get a pattern language writer going:

— Pick a whole area of focus, not just one idea. The area must practical and linked to the task that needs to be completed.
— Make a list of all the little things you have learned through the years about the area or document someone's experience in solving a particular problem.
— Cast each item on your list as a solution, and include the reasons for doing so (i.e. record the forces that bear on a solution).
— Write each item as a pattern making use of a pattern form (template).
— Organize the patterns into sections. Write an introductory paragraph to each section listing the patterns by name. Study the higher level structure of the patterns and write linking paragraphs when associations exist.
— Write an introduction to the patterns language, including the forces addressed.

In another example, Meszaros and Doble [40] defined a pattern language for writing patterns consisting of: context-setting patterns, pattern structuring patterns, pattern naming and referencing patterns, patterns for making patterns understandable and pattern language structuring patterns. The latter sets out a few guidelines for creating pattern languages:

— Identifying a set of patterns as a pattern language and writing a summary to introduce the larger problem and the patterns which contribute to solving it.
— Describe the overall context.
— Use a running example throughout.
— Highlight common problems, i.e. the common threads found in more than one pattern, and how the patterns can be used together to do something useful.
— Use distinctive headings to convey structure.
— Provide a problem/solution summary to help the reader find the pattern(s) that solve their specific problems
— Provide a glossary.

2.6   Patterns and Pattern Languages for Enterprise Architecture

Using the TOGAF architecture development process [47] as an example (but with no claim to representing the entire EA domain as such), the scope of the enterprise architecture development process is said to involve architecture vision development, business architecture development, information systems architecture development, technology architecture development, opportunity and solutions, migration planning, implementation governance, as well as the architecture change management. Enterprise architecture patterns should therefore include 'organizational' patterns that involve the full scope of enterprise architecture concerns, including people, processes, technology and facilities.

There are only a small number of pattern collections specifically focused on aspects of the EA development process, or claiming to focus on EA. Two existing examples, with individual patterns that are closely related to enterprise architecture from a primarily architecture management perspective, include:

— The EAM Pattern Catalog [21, 43] focusing on EA management to complement existing EA frameworks to provide a holistic and generic view on the problem of EA management, and to provide additional detail and guidance needed to systematically establish EA management in a step-wise fashion within an enterprise.
— A pattern catalogue for multichannel management described by Lankhorst and Oude Luttighuis [38], which they consider as a constituent of EA, to assist organisations to manage and align the various information channels they use in communicating with their customers.

Although limited specific EA patterns can be found, individual patterns can be found in disjoint pattern collections for other domains, which could be used in various enterprise architecture domains (but not specifically identified as such), for example organizational architecture [13], business modelling patterns [52], workflow patterns [51], software development patterns [25], etc. We also analysed a representative set of EA frameworks and none supports the concept of design patterns in any substantive way. Design patterns are, however, briefly mentioned in TOGAF V8 [46], FEAF [11],

The Zachman Framework for Enterprise Architecture [55] and GERAM [30]. There is therefore a lack of recorded research and guidelines on developing patterns for EA, and specifically pattern languages. In the case of pattern languages this is not the case for only the EA domain, but also in general. This paper attempts to address this gap in research by proposing a pattern framework for the development of patterns and pattern languages for EA, but which could also be used as guide to pattern language development in other domains.

3   The Pattern Framework for Enterprise Architecture (PF4EA)

Following an intensive literature study on the aspects that influence the development and maintenance of EA (combined with practical experience in these aspects), as well as an in-depth study and experience with the practices of patterns and pattern languages over an extended period of time, the Pattern Framework for Enterprise Architecture (PF4EA) was developed. PF4EA integrates the fundamental aspects related to patterns and pattern languages, as well as their associated processes and procedures, with the fundamental aspects related to enterprise architecture and its associated processes and procedures. Fig. 1 presents PF4EA graphically.

The components of PF4EA are organized into five construct layers, each addressing a specific aspect related to *patterns and pattern languages* and/or *enterprise architecture*:

1. *Theoretical context*: The theoretical context and best practices of both patterns and pattern languages and enterprise architecture, providing the theoretical foundation for PF4EA.
2. *Context specific rules and properties*: Determining and specifying the specific best practices, rules and properties related to patterns and pattern languages, which will be used in the patterns and pattern language to be developed, the specific enterprise architecture aspects for which the patterns and pattern language is to be developed, and the specific enterprise architecture framework(s) that will be supported by the patterns and pattern language to be developed in PF4EA.
3. *Context specific pattern relationships*: Specifying the context specific pattern relationships that will apply to the pattern language under development, including the *generic pattern relationships,* the *EA specific pattern relationships* and the related *EA framework specific pattern relationships.*
4. *Pattern search / creation*: Searching/creating individual patterns to support the aspects identified in the pattern context specific rules and properties making use of the EA processes and methodologies and EA framework rules and properties.
5. *Pattern language creation*: Applying the context specific pattern relationships to the set of standalone patterns created to develop a pattern language based on coherent principles. The output is the target pattern language for the specific enterprise architecture aspect under consideration. Each construct layer has an associated action that describes the action of use applicable to the construct layer, namely contextualize,

consider, conform, create, and connect, respectively. These actions are described in more detail in section 4.

As indicated in Fig. 1, PF4EA comprises of 11 different components, which present the framework with various functionalities:

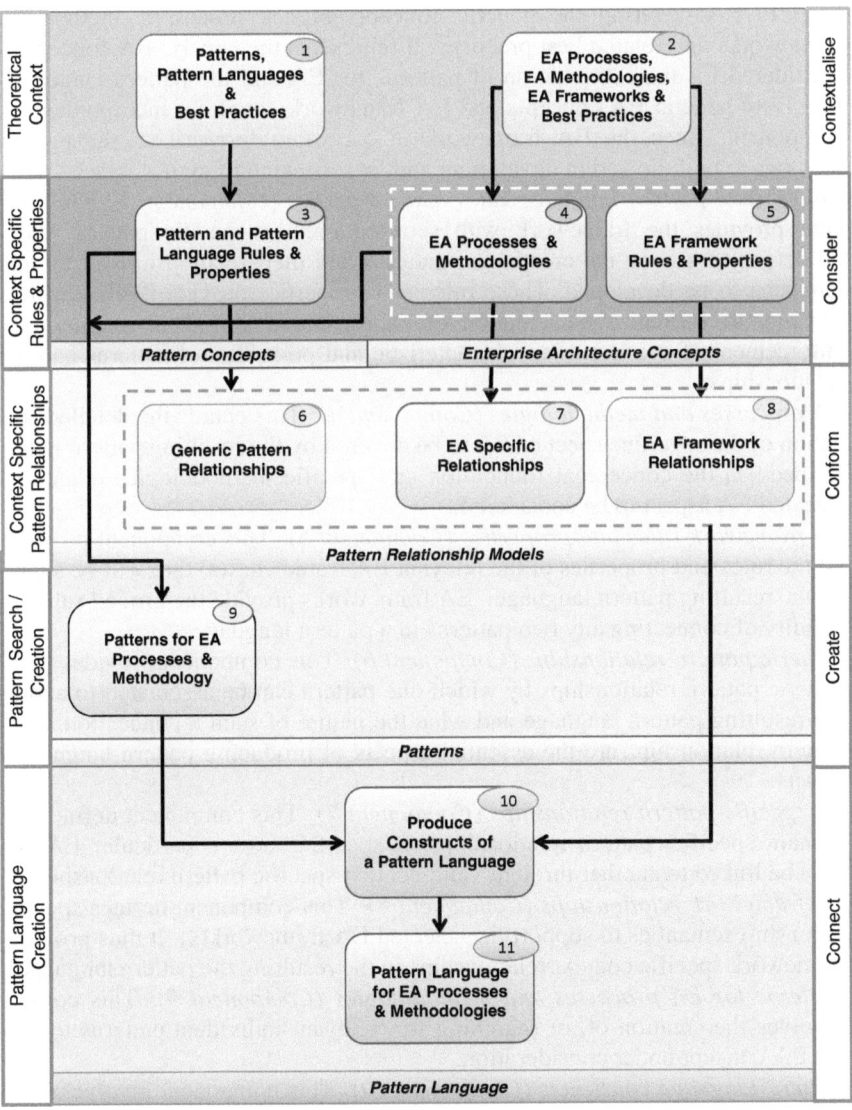

Fig. 1. The Pattern Framework for Enterprise Architecture (PF4EA)

1. *Patterns, pattern languages and best practices (Component 1):* This component represents the theoretical foundation and the best practices related to patterns and pattern languages in general. It represents the generic pattern concepts to be considered for the composition of patterns for EA and the pattern languages for EA.

2. *EA Processes, methodologies, frameworks and best practices (Component 2):* This component represents the theoretical foundation and the best practices related to EA covering the generic concepts of EA processes, methodologies, frameworks and related best practices. It represents the generic EA concepts to be considered for the composition of patterns for EA and the pattern languages for EA. Both general EA concepts and EA framework detail are incorporated in this component, since the EA framework in use often 'prescribes' the process or methods to be followed in developing and EA or maintaining it.

3. *Pattern and pattern language rules and properties (Component 3):* This component provides the framework with selected context specific pattern rules and properties to govern the creation of patterns and their relationships in the pattern language to be developed. These rules and properties provide PF4EA with functionality to formalize the creation of patterns in a consistent manner through enforcement of specific rules, characteristic and properties of patterns and pattern relationships.

4. *EA processes and methodologies (Component 4):* This entails the detailed specification of the specific aspect of EA to be covered by the resulting pattern language. It specifies the conceptual foundation and specific methodologies related to the selected EA aspect to be considered.

5. *EA framework rules and properties (Component 5):* This component provides for all the rules and properties of the relevant EA framework(s) that will be supported by the resulting pattern language. EA frameworks provide the ground rules on the validity of connecting any two patterns in a pattern language.

6. *Generic pattern relationships (Component 6):* This component provides the valid generic pattern relationships by which one pattern can be associated to another in the resulting pattern language and what the nature of such a connection is. These pattern relationships are the essential aspects of producing pattern language constructs.

7. *EA specific pattern relationships (Component 7):* This component defines EA, or domain specific, pattern relationships. It specifies how a particular EA pattern may be linked to another through valid context specific pattern relationships.

8. *EA framework relationships (Component 8):* This component defines specific relationship semantics to support the selected EA framework(s). It thus provides for framework specific context relationships in the resulting the pattern language.

9. *Patterns for EA processes and methodologies (Component 9):* This component involves the creation of, or searching for, relevant individual patterns to support the EA concept under consideration.

10. *Pattern language constructs (Component 10):* This component involves identifying the relationships that exists between the individual patterns (identified in Component 9), using the generic pattern relationships (Component 6), the EA specific pattern relationships (Component 7), and the EA framework relationships (Component 8). This creates the individual pattern language pieces that when combined forms the pattern language for EA.

11. *Pattern language for EA processes and methodologies (Component 11):* This component integrates all of the patterns and the relationships that exists between them into a pattern language, and identifies any orphan patterns and gaps that may require the development of additional patterns or pattern relationships. In also includes a description of the overall context of the pattern language and provide a problem/solution summary and glossary.

4   Method to Use PF4EA

For any framework to be complete, a method must be provided outlining the process to use the framework for its intended purpose. The use of PF4EA is categorized into five action stages, as indicated in Fig. 1:

1. *Contextualize*: Establishing the theoretical foundations and best practices supporting PF4EA.
2. *Consider:* Establishing and specifying the relevant pattern and EA aspects supporting, or to be supported by, the resulting pattern language.
3. *Conform:* Specifying how individual pattern components are allowed to relate to each other.
4. *Create:* Creating patterns for the EA concepts under consideration.
5. *Connect:* Connecting individual patterns into a pattern language.

Fig. 2 depicts the flow between these five actions and the steps through the related components when applying PF4EA to create a pattern language for the selected EA aspects. Each step is described briefly below.

1. *Contextualise*:
   - Step 1: Study fundamental patterns and pattern language theoretical concepts and best practices (if not familiar with this theoretical context already).
   - Step 2: Study the fundamental EA theoretical concepts (if not familiar with it already).
2. *Consider*:
   - Step 3: Use the knowledge obtained in Step 2 to determine the EA aspects for which a pattern language are to be created.
   - Step 4: Use the outcome of Step 3 to decide on the EA concept for which to create a pattern language. If the concept is not fully developed / specified generically, develop / refine the concept.
   - Step 5: Use the knowledge obtained in Steps 3 and 4 to decide on the EA framework that will be supported by the pattern language under development. If the EA framework rules and properties are not fully developed / specified generically, develop/refine the rules and properties.
   - Step 6: Use the knowledge obtained in Step 1 to decide on the general pattern rules and properties that must be adhered to by the pattern language to be developed, and which would be appropriate for the EA concepts identified in Steps 3 to 5.

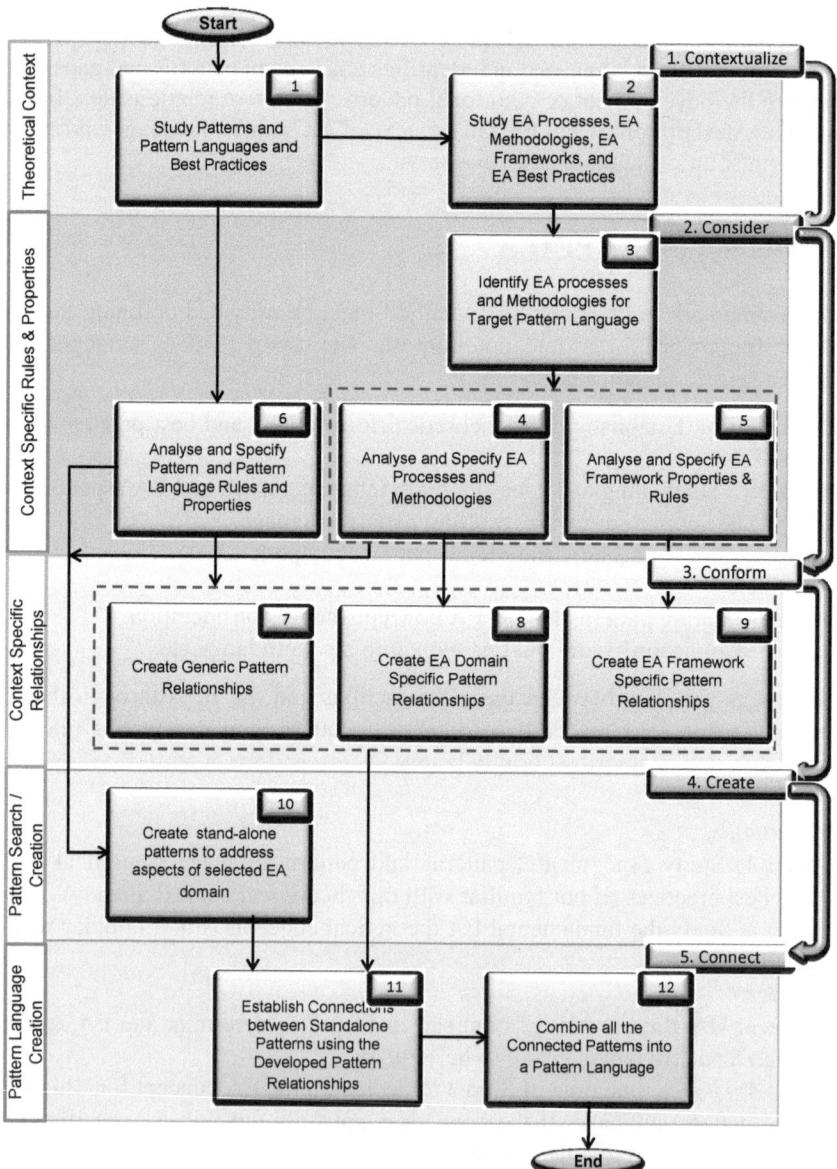

Fig. 2. Method to apply PF4EA

3. *Conform*:

- Step 7: Use the outcome of Step 6 to specify the conditions for the generic pattern specific relationships that are to be used to connect individual patterns into a pattern language.
- Step 8: Use the outcome of Step 4 and Step 6 to establish the EA specific pattern relationships matching the EA concept for which to create a pattern language.

- Step 9: Use the outcome of Step 5 and Step 6 to establish the pattern relationships for the specific EA framework that will be supported.

4. *Create*:
- Step 10: Search for existing patterns that support the EA concept identified in Step 4 and the EA framework identified in Step 5. If the patterns do not exist, develop/derive the patterns using the outcome of Steps 4, 5 and 6 using a pattern development method, such as the one described by Cunningham [15].

5. *Connect*:
- Step 11: Using the outcome of Steps 7, 8 and 9 to establish relationships between the patterns identified or developed in Step 10.
- Step 12: Use the outcome of Step 11 to combine all the patterns and graphically represent the resulting pattern language adhering to both pattern and EA fundamentals. If any orphan patterns exist, use steps 4 to 11 above to develop additional patterns enabling connections between all the patterns in the pattern language. Add a preamble to the resulting pattern language, describing the overall context of the pattern language, a problem/solution summary and a glossary.

5   Example – Towards a Pattern Language for Enterprise Architecture Development and Maintenance

To illustrate the components and use of PF4EA we present a number of examples. These examples, however, do not present the components of a complete pattern language, but are merely for illustrative purposes.

5.1   Contextualise

Steps 1 and 2
We have studied patterns and pattern languages in various domains in the past and are familiar with the basic concepts related to these aspects (see for example [33-35]). We are all experienced in EA and all have multiple of EA certifications and have published various papers on the topic (see for example [31, 39]). If this was not the case we would have had to study the basic concepts related to both the domains of EA and patterns and pattern languages in detail, prior to embarking on the pattern building exercise.

5.2   Consider

Step 3: Step 3 uses the knowledge obtained in Step 2 to determine the EA aspects for which a pattern language are to be created. Our aim was to develop a pattern language that could assist novice enterprise architects in the development and maintenance of enterprise architecture. We briefly introduce some of the concepts used in the remaining sections.

EA development focuses on establishing and specifying an understanding all of the socio-technical elements in an enterprise, including people, processes, business, organization and technology and how these elements interrelate [19, 53]. EA maintenance is a process of managing change to existing architecture models to accommodate changes that might have emerged due to change in process, technology, people and business [47].

Architectures have a cycle through which they evolve. According to Lankhorst [37], the architecture design process life cycle plays in important role in the evolution of any type of architecture. The architecture process consists of the steps that take an original idea through to the design and implementation phases, and eventually the management of architecture [4, 10, 27, 28, 37].

A *baseline architecture* is part of overall enterprise architecture and is an *as-is* overall architecture prior to entering a cycle of architecture review, redesign, development and maintenance [TOGAF, 2009]. A *target architecture* defines the *to-be-built* enterprise architecture and comprises of a complete description of the vision, scope, and partial high-level descriptions of the business's information systems models and design architectures reflecting the future view of aspects relating to business processes, data, applications, information systems and the technical infrastructure within an enterprise [11, 42, 49].

Zachman [55] defines EA as the total set of descriptive representations (models) relevant for describing an enterprise, that is, the descriptive representations required to create (a coherent, optimal) enterprise and to serve as a baseline for changing the enterprise once it is created. The total set of relevant descriptive representations would necessarily have to include all the intersections between the abstractions and perspectives. The Zachman Framework for Enterprise Architecture [56] do not formally define a process to use the Framework, but its use is implicated by the process to compile the descriptive representations mentioned.

Step 4: Step 4 uses the outcome of Step 3 to decide on the EA concept for which to create a pattern language. If the concept is not fully developed / specified generically, develop / refine the concept. An in depth study of EA concepts revealed that when referring to EA development and maintenance most authors refer to the TOGAF ADM [47], but that no generic set of steps for the development and maintenance of enterprise architecture exists. We therefore, as a first step, studied various publications and best practices to develop a set of generic steps for EA development and maintenance. An extract of these steps is presented in Fig. 3.

Step 5: Step 5 uses the knowledge obtained in Steps 3 and 4 to decide on the EA framework that will be supported by the pattern language under development. If the EA framework rules and properties are not fully developed / specified generically, develop/refine the rules and properties. The Zachman Framework for Enterprise Architecture [56] was, due to its ontological nature and its ability to guide the development of applicable models, selected as an example to illustrate the concepts. The decision was made to use this framework for the first version of the pattern language. As a future endeavour a more comprehensive example using TOGAF is envisaged.

S#	Step Domain	Brief rule description
Architecture Vision And Planning		
STP01	Architecture vision	Establish the architecture target vision for the current development.
STP02	Architecture vision	Establish resource plan for accomplishment of the vision.
STP03	Architecture vision	Select an appropriate enterprise architecture framework.
Baseline Architectures		
STP04	Baseline Architecture	Create inventory for current IT infrastructure.
STP05	Baseline Architecture	Create inventory of current business processes.
STP06	Baseline Architecture	Create inventory of people, roles and responsibilities.
STP07	Baseline Architecture	Create inventory of current business objectives.
Target Architectures		
STP08	Target Architecture	Craft IT infrastructure target models.
STP09	Target Architecture	Craft business process target models.
STP10	Target Architecture	Craft people resource target models.
STP11	Target Architecture	Craft business objective target models.
Architecture Transition and Integration		
STP12	Transition and Integration	Assess the gap between target and baseline architectures.
STP13	Transition and Integration	Ensure every architecture artefact contributes target architecture.
STP14	Transition and Integration	Ensure alignment of the enterprise architecture to business objectives.
Architecture Maintenance		
STP15	Architecture Maintenance	Every architectural change is documented and updating of baseline architecture.
STP16	Architecture Maintenance	Ensure a periodical update of the architecture models
Architecture Reviews		
STP17	Architecture reviews	Ensure effective communication channels about the enterprise architecture.
STP18	Architecture reviews	Ensure the reviews of architecture by relevant committees.

Fig. 3. Extracts from EA development and maintenance process steps example

Step 6: Step 6 uses the knowledge obtained in Step 1 to decide on the general pattern rules and properties that must be adhered to by the pattern language to be developed and which would be appropriate for the EA concepts identified in Steps 3 to 5. Amongst other rules and properties, we decided on the use of the following pattern (expandable) template, derived from studying several other pattern templates:

— *Pattern Name*: A unique name to identify a pattern.
— *Problem*: The design problem which is addressed the creation of a pattern.
— *Context*: In which circumstances and domain is this pattern applicable?
— *Forces*: The various forces that impact the creation or existence of a pattern.
— *Solution*: Describe what needs to be done as a solution that resolves forces from strongest in this context in relation to addressing the recurring problem.
— *Related Patterns*: What enterprise architecture patterns are closely related to this one?
— *Rationale*: Is a description of why the solution is an appropriate one and not another.
— *Example*: An artefact (e.g. a graphical model, an algorithm, a formula, a structured rule (text), etc.), which illustrates how the pattern operates.

5.3   Conform

Step 7: Step 7 uses the outcome of Step 6 to specify the conditions for generic pattern specific relationships that are to be used to connect individual patterns into a pattern language. We specified a number of generic pattern relationships using a semi-formal notation. These relationships include the *is made of* relationship, *is equivalent of* relationship, *is alternative of* relationship and *is variant of* relationship [1, 8, 36].

For example, the *is equivalent of* relationship was specified using the following statements:

$\forall$ x:1..n, $Pattern_x$: PATTERN $\bullet$ $Pattern_x \Rightarrow Problem_x \wedge Solution_x \wedge Context_x$

(Given any pattern $Pattern_x$, there exist a problem $Problem_x$, being addressed by that pattern, and a solution $Solution_x$, produced by that pattern, and a context $Context_x$, in which such a pattern is applicable. The set PATTERN to represents the set of all valid patterns.)

$\forall$ i,j:1..n, $Pattern_i$, $Pattern_j$: PATTERN

if (($Problem_i \equiv Problem_j$) $\wedge$ ($Solution_i \equiv Solution_j$) $\wedge$ ($Context_x \equiv Context_x$))

then $Pattern_i \equiv Pattern_j$

$\Rightarrow Pattern_i$ = is-equivalent-of $Pattern_j$

(If the problems associated with $Pattern_i$ and $Pattern_j$ are equivalent, their solutions are and their contexts are also equivalent, then $Pattern_i$ and $Pattern_j$ are equivalent and said to be equivalent patterns of each other.)

Step 8: Step 8 uses the outcome of Step 4 and Step 6 to establish EA specific pattern relationships for the EA concept for which to create a pattern language.

We specified several EA specific relationships, one of which is the *is baseline2target of* pattern relationship. In this relationship, one pattern is used to produce a solution to a problem in the baseline architecture, whilst the second pattern is used to advance the baseline architecture into a target architecture solution.

$\forall$ i,j:1..n, $Pattern_i$, $Pattern_j$: PATTERN

if (($Pattern_i \Rightarrow Solution_{baselineArchitecture}$) $\wedge$ ($Patternj \Rightarrow Solution_{targetArchitecture}$)) $\wedge$
(($Context_i \equiv Context_j$) $\wedge$ ($Problem_i \equiv Problem_j$)) $\wedge$
(($Solution_i$ « $Solution_j$) $\square$ ($Solution_i$ » $Solution_j$) $\square$ ($Solution_i \equiv Solution_j$))
then $Pattern_i$ = is-baseline2target-of($Pattern_j$)

if $Pattern_i$ = is-baseline2target-of ($Pattern_j$)
then $Solution_i$ = is-baseline2target-of ($Solution_j$)
(« means the baseline architecture pattern solution remain unchanged whilst target architecture solution changes; » means the baseline architecture pattern solution changes into target with additional alterations, whilst $\equiv$ means the baseline architecture pattern remains the same in the target architecture pattern solutions)

Step 9: Step 9 uses the outcome of Step 5 and Step 6 to establish pattern relationships for the specific EA framework that will be supported. We specified relationships for all the framework rules of The Zachman Framework for Enterprise Architecture [56]. These relationships include, amongst others: *diagonal, non-diagonal, is transformation of, is identification of, is definition of, is representation of, is specification of, is configuration of.*

For example, in The Zachman Framework for Enterprise Architecture, moving from one perspective to another in a vertical manner is referred to as transformation. The two patterns involved in an *is transformation of* type of relationship are associated with two adjacent perspectives ('rows' and abstractions (columns) in The Zachman Framework for Enterprise Architecture.

$\forall$ i,j:1..n, $Pattern_i$, $Pattern_j$: *PATTERN*
if (($Problem_i \neq Problem_j$) $\wedge$ ($Abstraction_i \equiv Abstraction_j$)) $\wedge$
   (($Perspective_i \neq Perspective_j$) $\wedge$ ($Solutioni \neq Solutionj$)) $\wedge$
   (($Perspective_i \wedge Perspective_j$) = adjacent)
then $Pattern_i$ = is-transformation-of($Pattern_j$)

if $Pattern_i$ = is-transformation-of ($Pattern_j$)
then : $Solution_i$ = is-transformation-of ($Solution_j$)

Although this approach is appropriate to The Zachman Framework for Enterprise Architecture, the approach of specifying the pattern relationships will have to be adapted for other frameworks, according to the rules of such frameworks.

5.4   Create

Step 10: Step 10 searches for existing patterns that support the EA concept identified in Step 4 and the EA framework identified in Step 5. If the patterns do not exist, develop/derive the patterns using the outcome of Steps 4, 5 and 6. We created a (incomplete) set of patterns for the set of EA development and maintenance steps in Fig. 3. The set of patterns is indicated in Fig. 4. Fig. 5 illustrates an example of such a pattern.

EAP {Pattern language for enterprise architecture}	
EAP1=Architecture Vision Statement	EAP15=Target Enterprise Data
EAP2=Expert Resource Acquisition	EAP16=Target Information Systems Architecture
EAP3=Enterprise Architecture Framework Selection	EAP17=Target Technology Architecture
EAP4=Baseline Business Objectives Inventory	EAP18=Architecture Gap Examination
EAP5=Baseline Business Process Inventory	EAP19=Architecture Solution
EAP6=Baseline Enterprise Information Inventory	EAP20=Integration Implementation
EAP7=Baseline Human Capital	EAP21=Post Integration Architecture Examination
EAP8=Baseline Enterprise Data	EAP22=Architecture Change Management
EAP9=Baseline Information Systems Inventory	EAP23=Architecture Periodic Maintenance
EAP10=Baseline Technology Architecture Inventory	EAP24=Architecture Communication Glossary
EAP11=Target Business Objectives	EAP25=Architecture Communication Channel
EAP12=Target Business Process	EAP26=Architecture Committee Formation
EAP13=Target Enterprise Information	EAP27=Architecture Review Time Table
EAP14=Target Human Capital	

Fig. 4. Patterns for EA development and maintenance

Pattern EAP4

Pattern Name: _Enterprise Architecture Framework Selection_
Problem: How do you ensure that an appropriate enterprise architecture framework is selected for enterprise architecture development?
Context: you are doing enterprise architecture in which case you have to choose an appropriate and effective framework to use in the development of enterprise architecture.
Forces:
- The selection of a framework can be very challenging due to many existing and competing frameworks.
- The selection of a framework is dependent on its effectiveness in doing enterprise architecture and the experience of using such a framework.
- Select a good framework that is understood by all participants.
- Framework selection can be biased due to favouritism of one framework over another.

Solution:
Select an appropriate enterprise architecture framework that your expects have used and have experience in it. The framework will be used to create necessary enterprise architecture artefacts in accordance with desired architecture futuristic state.
Related patterns: In this pattern language, there is no specific related _enterprise architecture framework selection._
Rationale:
It is crucial to have an inventory of where an enterprise is, in relation to available business objectives implementing any business objective to establish where the new objectives are going to fit in the baseline business objectives.

Fig. 5. EA Framework selection pattern

5.5   Connect

Step 11: Step 11 uses the outcome of Steps 7, 8 and 9 to establish relationships between the patterns identified or developed in Step 10. Each individual pattern is compared to each of the other patterns to determine whether any relationship exists between the patterns. All the relationships are recorded. Although this may become a cumbersome process as the pattern language grows, the step is essential in establishing a valid pattern language. Further research would be required to streamline the process.

Step 12: Step 12 uses the outcome of Step 11 to combine all the patterns and graphically represent the resulting pattern language adhering to both pattern and EA fundamentals. The various perspective of The Zachman Framework for Enterprise Architecture [56] are used to guide the representation, e.g. the business architecture patterns are mapped to the business perspective, etc. The pattern relationships are then applied to all the patterns across all the perspectives to create meaningful associations between patterns mapped on the same perspective, and those with valid relationships in adjacent perspectives.

The process of connecting patterns to form the language involves the application of context pattern relationships, which associate one pattern to another via the type of relationship they share. If any orphan patterns exist, use steps 4 to 11 above to develop additional patterns enabling connections between all the patterns in the pattern language. Fig. 6 provides an example of how such a graphical representation of a pattern language for EA could be presented. The colour and shape of the connecting lines represent the various types of relationships that exist (e.g. = represents _is transformation of_). In addition to this representation a preamble to the resulting pattern language must be compiled (not shown here), describing the overall context of the pattern language, and provide problem/solution summary and glossary.

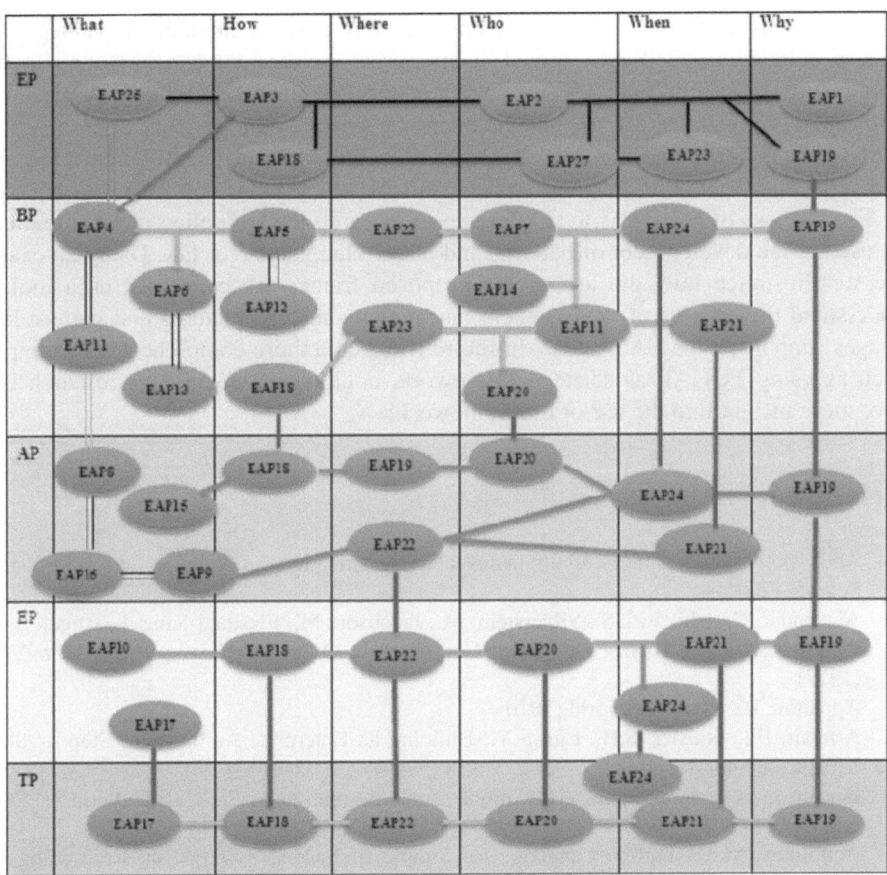

Fig. 6. Example of mapping a set of patterns for EA into a pattern language and graphically presenting the language using the abstractions and perspective of the Zachman Framework for Enterprise Architecture as canvas

6   Conclusion

The rapid growth of the field of information and communications technology imposes change as the only constant faced by most enterprises. The biggest challenge that enterprises are facing currently is how to keep track of their internal and environmental changes as and when such occur. When an enterprise explicitly keep track of changes in its internal components and how these components interrelate to one another, as well as environmental change, it is said to have done its EA explicitly [23].

There are many approaches towards implementation of EA to assist enterprises to overcome their challenges relating to managing change and complexity. However the existing approaches do not explicitly include patterns as an approach to EA development and maintenance. The use of patterns and pattern languages in enterprise architecture is a relatively novel concept and only a small number of patterns and pattern collection specifically aimed at enterprise architecture can be found in the public domain. In this paper we presented a pattern framework for enterprise architecture (PF4EA), making use of, and augmenting some of the existing approaches to developing patterns and pattern languages (e.g. the work of Cunningham [15] and Meszaros and Doble [40] on creating patterns and pattern languages, respectively).

The purpose of PF4EA is to fill the gap in research for a baseline method that can be used in the development of patterns and pattern languages for EA. Using an example we illustrated how the use of the proposed framework can assist as a tool to understand the process of development and maintenance of patterns and pattern languages supporting the EA process. In future research a more comprehensive example, such as using TOGAF as selected framework, could complement this research and give more insight into the use of the framework.

References

1. Abel, A.: Design pattern relationships and classifications. Computer and Information Science (2001)
2. Alexander, C., Ishikawa, S., Silverstein, M., Jacobson, M., Fiksdahl-King, I., Angel, S.: A Pattern Language: Towns, Buildings, Construction. Oxford University Press, New York (1977)
3. Appleton, B.: Cononical Form (2010)
4. Armour, F.J., Kaisler, S.H., Liu, S.Y.: Building an Enterprise Architecture Step by Step. IEEE Computer Society 1520-9202, 31–38 (1999)
5. Bergin, J.: A pattern language for initial course design. ACM SIGCSE Bulletin 31, 282–286 (2001)
6. Bottomley, M.: A Pattern Language for Simple Embedded Systems. In: Proceedings of PLOP 1999 - Pattern Languages of Programs 1999, Hillside (1999)
7. Buschmann, F., Henney, K., Schamidt, D.: Past, Present, and Future Trends in Software Patterns. IEEE Software 24, 31–37 (2007)
8. Buschmann, F., Henney, K., Schamidt, D.C.: Past, Present, and Future Trends in Software Patterns. IEEE Digital library (2007)
9. Buschmann, F., Meunier, R., Rohnert, H., Sommerlad, P., Stal, M.: Pattern-Oriented Software Architecture: a system of patterns, vol. 1. John Wiley & Sons, Chichester (1996)
10. Callas, G.: Process Based Enterprise Architecture Building. IEEE Xplore Digital Library 1, 239–244 (2006)
11. CIO-Council: Federal Enterprise Architecture Framework Version 1.1 (1999)
12. Clancy, M.J., Linn, M.C.: Patterns and pedagogy. ACM SIGCSE Bulletin 31, 37–42 (1999)
13. Coplien, J.: A generative development-process pattern language. In: Pattern Languages of Program Design, pp. 183–237. Addison-Wesley Publishing Co., New York (1994)
14. Coplien, J.: Software Patterns. SIGS Books & Multimedia, New York (1996)
15. Cunningham, W.: Tips for writing pattern languages (1994)
16. Cunningham, W.: About the Portland Form (2011)
17. Dearden, A., Finlay, J.: Pattern Languages in HCI: A Critical Review. Lawrence Erlbaum Associates, Inc. 21, 49–102 (2006)

18. Devedzic, V.: Software Patterns. In: Handbook of Software Engineering and Knowledge Engineering (2004)
19. EARF: Definition for enterprise architecture as defined by the Enterprise Architecture Research Forum (2009)
20. Ellison, M.: A Pattern Language for Information Architecture (2009)
21. Ernst, A.: Enterprise Architecture Management Patterns. In: PLoP 2008: Proceedings of the 15th Conference on Pattern Languages of Programs. ACM, New York (2008)
22. Faridul, I.: Investigating XML as Language for HCI Patterns Representation. Secondary Investigating XML as Language for HCI Patterns Representation. Master Thesis. Concordia University (2003)
23. Finkelstein, C.: Enterprise Architecture for Integration: Rapid Delivery Methods and Technologies. Artech House (2006)
24. Fortino, A.: A Pattern Language for Innovation Management. In: Proceedings of PICMET 2008, pp. 415–419. IEEE, Cape Town (2008)
25. Gamma, E., Helm, R., Johnson, R., Vlissides, J.: Design Patterns, Elements of Reusable Object-oriented Software. Addison Wesley Professional, Boston (1995)
26. Griffiths, R.N., Pemberton, L.: Don't write guidelines write patterns! (2005)
27. Gur, N.: Steps to create enterprise/system. Architecture (2004), http://weblogs.asp.net/ngur/articles/194704.aspx
28. Harmon, P.: Developing enterprise architecture, white paper, business trends (2003)
29. Hoogervorst, J.A.P.: Enterprise Architecture: Enabling Integration, Agility and Change (2003)
30. IFIP–IFAC Task Force on Architectures for Enterprise Integration: GERAM: Generalised Enterprise Reference Architecture and Methodology, Version 1.6.3 (1999)
31. Jacobs, D., Kotzé, P., van der Merwe, A., Gerber, A.: Enterprise Architecture for Small and Medium Enterprise Growth. In: Albani, A., Dietz, J.L.G., Verelst, J. (eds.) EEWC 2011. LNBIP, vol. 79, pp. 61–75. Springer, Heidelberg (2011)
32. Kerievsky, J.: Refactoring To Patterns. Addison-Wesley, Boston (2005)
33. Kotzé, P., Renaud, K.: Do We Practise What We Preach in Formulating Our Design and Development Methods? In: Gulliksen, J., Harning, M.B., van der Veer, G.C., Wesson, J. (eds.) EIS 2007. LNCS, vol. 4940, pp. 566–585. Springer, Heidelberg (2008)
34. Kotzé, P., Renaud, K., Koukouletsos, K., Khazaei, B., Dearden, A.: Patterns, anti-patterns and guidelines – effective aids to teaching HCI principles? In: Hvannberg, E.T., Read, J.C., Bannon, L., Kotzé, P., Wong, W. (eds.) Inventivity: Teaching Theory, Design and Innovation in HCI, pp. 115–120. University of Limerick (2006)
35. Kotzé, P., Renaud, K., Van Biljon, J.: Don't do this – Pitfalls in using anti-patterns in teaching human–computer interaction principles. Computers & Education 50, 979–1008 (2008)
36. Kumar, K., Prabhakar, T.V.: Design Decision Topology Model for Pattern Relationship Analysis (2008)
37. Lankhorst, M. (ed.): Enterprise Architecture at Work: Modelling, Communication, and Analysis. Springer, New York (2005)
38. Lankhorst, M., Oude Luttighuis, P.: Enterprise Architecture Patterns for Multichannel Management. Lecture Notes in Informatics (Software Engineering 2009) P-150, 1–17 (2009)
39. Mentz, J., Kotzé, P., van der Merwe, A.: A Comparison of Practitioner and Researcher Definitions of Enterprise Architecture using an Interpretation Method. In: Moller, C., Chaudhry, S. (eds.) Advances in Enterprise Information Systems. CRC Press, Balkema (2011)

40. Meszaros, G., Doble, J.: A pattern language for pattern writing. In: Pattern Languages of Program Design, vol. 3, pp. 529–574. Addison-Wesley Longman Publishing Co., Boston (1997)
41. Noyes, D.: Alexandrian Form (2007)
42. Pavlak, A.: Enterprise Architecture: Lessons from Classical Architecture (2006)
43. Sabine, B., Matthes, F., Schweda, C.M.: EAM Pattern Catalog Software Engineering for Business Information Systems, Faculty for Informatics, TU München (2010)
44. Silver, S.: Beck Form (2007)
45. Spinellis, D., Raptis, K.: Component mining: A process and its pattern language. Information and Software Technology 42, 609–617 (2000)
46. The Open Group: TOGAF 8.1.1 Online: Architecture Patterns. The Open Group (2006)
47. The Open Group: TOGAF Version 9. Van Haren Publishing, United States (2009)
48. Thompson, D.: The Concise Oxford Dictionary of current English. In: Flowler, H.W., Flowler, F.G. (eds.) The Concise Oxford Dictionary. Clarendon Press, Oxford (1995)
49. TOGAF: Definitions (2009)
50. Tremblay, B.: Compact Form (2003)
51. van der Aalst, W., ter Hofstede, A., Kiepuszewski, B., Barros, A.: Workflow Patterns (2003)
52. Veryard, R.: Component-Based Business Background Material. Business Patterns (2000)
53. Wang, X., Zhao, Y.: An Enterprise Architecture Development Method in Chinese Manufacturing Industry. In: Ninth International Conference on Hybrid Intelligent Systems, pp. 226–230. IEEE Computer Society (2009)
54. Winn, T., Calder, P.: Is this a pattern? IEEE Software 19, 59–66 (2002)
55. Zachman, J.A.: Z101 MasterClass: Framework Foundations (Presented as part of Zachman Certification training at CSIR's Meraka Intitute, February 15, 2010). Zachman International, Pretoria, p. 151 (2010)
56. Zachman, J.A.: The Zachman Framework for Enterprise Architecture - The Enterprise Ontology Version 3.0 (2011)

Challenges for Automated Enterprise Architecture Documentation

Matheus Hauder, Florian Matthes, and Sascha Roth

Technische Universität München (TUM)
Chair for Informatics 19 (sebis)
Boltzmannstr. 3, 85748 Garching bei München, Germany
{matheus.hauder,matthes,roth}@tum.de

Abstract. Currently the documentation of an Enterprise Architecture (EA) is performed manually to a large extent. Due to the intrinsic complexity of today's organizations this task is challenging and often perceived as very time-consuming and error-prone. Recent efforts in research and industry seek to automate EA documentation by retrieving and maintaining relevant information from productive systems. In this paper major challenges for an automated EA documentation are presented based on 1) a practical example from a global acting enterprise of the German fashion industry, 2) a literature review, and 3) a survey among 123 EA practitioners. The identified challenges are synthesized to four categories and constitute the foundation for future research efforts and pose new questions not yet considered.

Keywords: Enterprise Architecture (EA), automated EA documentation, challenges, literature survey, model transformation, practitioner survey.

1 Motivation

Decision makers need to be supported with sound and up to date information about the EA [26]. This includes the organizational structure, processes, application systems, and technologies [15]. Existing EA documentation approaches struggle with the information volume and rapidly changing requirements within organizations. A study conducted by Winter et al. [27] reveals a high degree of manual work with very little automation during the documentation and maintenance of EA models. This high degree of manual work combined with the increasing information volume of organizations results in very time-consuming, error-prone and expensive maintenance of EA information. Next to meeting these information demands of organizations, the EA documentation also needs to achieve and sustain a high quality in the collected data [9].

Motivated by these problems recent research activities propose processes for automated EA documentation [8] and investigate possible information sources to retrieve relevant EA information from productive systems [6,7]. These initial research efforts reveal a substantial amount of relevant EA information that can

S. Aier et al. (Eds.): TEAR 2012 and PRET 2012, LNBIP 131, pp. 21–39, 2012.

be gathered from productive systems and provide guidance for maintaining EA models using these information sources. While first steps towards an automated EA documentation in organizations were investigated, to the best of the authors' knowledge existing literature did not investigate major challenges for automated EA documentation. Literature regarding automated EA documentation is still very scarce, so that identifying current challenges for this field requires additional quantitative and qualitative analyses of current practices in organizations in order to receive a thorough list of relevant challenges. In this paper we illustrate model transformations to collect relevant EA information from three different information sources, conduct a survey among EA practitioners, and investigate current literature.

In the next section the applied research methodology to identify challenges for automated EA documentation is presented. In Section 3 a prototypical model transformation from an enterprise of the German fashion industry is provided to identify transformation challenges. The results from a survey among EA practitioners are shown in Section 4. Section 5 presents the identified challenges for automated EA documentation before the paper concludes with a summary.

2   Research Methodology

The research methodology to identify challenges for automated EA documentation is based on three different sources that are illustrated in Figure 1. The selection of these sources was performed to provide a thorough list of challenges. A prototypical model transformation for three potential EA information sources is provided to identify challenges regarding the transformation of the collected information into a central EA repository. Within a literature review major challenges for automated EA documentation are identified. Furthermore, a survey among EA practitioners is conducted including questions on EA documentation and automation in particular. In the following the individual parts of the approach are presented more detailed.

In previous work we have investigated an Enterprise Service Bus (ESB) from an enterprise of the German fashion industry as one particular information source [6]. With this information source entities of the ArchiMate meta-model could be covered with up to 50% on the infrastructure layer, 75% on the application layer and 20% on the organizational layer. In this paper we build on these findings and investigate further productive systems from this enterprise in order to integrate them into a central EA repository. We argue that considering several information sources is necessary in order to reach a high model coverage since these productive systems provide information on different layers of the EA. While an ESB can be used to retrieve information on the application level, a network monitor tool for instance might provide more technical information from the infrastructure layer. Therefore, an integration of several information sources is an essential challenge to achieve an automated EA documentation. Based on this prototypical implementation we identify challenges for the model transformation and integration of information sources.

Model Transformation	Literature Review	Practitioner Survey
▪ Model transformation for three EA information sources from an organization of the fashion industry ▪ Data model extracted for all three EA information sources ▪ Challenges for the transformation of automatically retrieved EA information identified	▪ Database-driven literature review from relevant conferences and journals ▪ Identification of literature referring to automated EA documentation issues ▪ Identified issues aggregated to concepts regarding challenges in automated EA documentation	▪ Survey on automated EA documentation among 123 EA practicioners ▪ Questions related to EA documentation and automation in particular ▪ Explorative survey on EA documentation challenges

identification of 16 challenges

Automated EA Documentation Challenges

identification of 4 categories

Transformation Challenges	Data Challenges	Business and Organizational Challenges	Tooling

Fig. 1. Research methodology to identify automated EA documentation challenges

According to Glaser et al. [11] we performed a content analysis of relevant literature. This literature was identified with a database-driven review using the AIS Electronic Library and IEEE Xplore [25]. Regarding the relevance of this topic for organizations in practice the research efforts are still very scarce (cf. e.g. [1]). Nevertheless, we identified several publications dealing with different aspects of automated EA documentation. In previous work we have investigated a model transformation and data quality aspects of an ESB from an organization of the fashion industry [6,12]. Another concrete implementation using a security network scanner can be found in [7]. A process and its requirements for automated EA documentation is presented in [8,9]. Next to these recent publications on automated EA documentation we identified adjacent publications that deal with related research questions.

Furthermore, we conducted a global explorative survey to analyze the status-quo of EA documentation and investigate quality aspects of possible information sources within organization. Within this survey over 1100 invitations were sent by e-mail to EA experts for an online questionnaire. We received 123 answers in total with organizations from, e.g., Canada, Germany, Great Britain, India, New Zealand, South Africa, Switzerland, and USA. Among the participants were 68 Enterprise Architects (55.28%), 22 Enterprise Architecture Consultants (17.89%), as well as 8 Software Architects (6.50%). The Enterprise Architecture Consultants in this survey were asked to answer on behalf of one specific organization. Largest industry sectors of the participating organizations are Finance with 37 (30.08%), IT and Technology with 23 (18.70%), and Government with 11 (8.94%). Main goal of this survey is to answer research questions on the status-quo of EA documentation, relevant productive systems containing EA information, data quality attributes of these systems, and typical integration problems for the identified information sources. First findings of the survey show that documentation of EA information is a major challenge for organizations since it is regarded as very time consuming and the achieved data quality is not sufficient. Furthermore, some organizations have already implemented automation in their EA documentation processes. In this paper we summarize the questions as well as free text answers on automated EA documentation challenges organizations are currently faced with or are considered to be relevant for the future.

3   Model Transformation

In this section we exemplify the combination of three models, namely 1) Iteraplan that can be assigned to the business layer 2) SAP Process Integration (PI) which is an Enterprise Service Bus (ESB) as a representative for the application layer, and 3) Nagios, an infrastructure monitoring tool that gathers data from the technology layer. Presented models have been reverse engineered from the respective information source whereas semantics of the entities therein are inferred through exegesis of respective documentation [14,22,20].

In practice, semantic concepts of those systems strongly depend on concrete instance data. As reference to an existing and established standard, they are

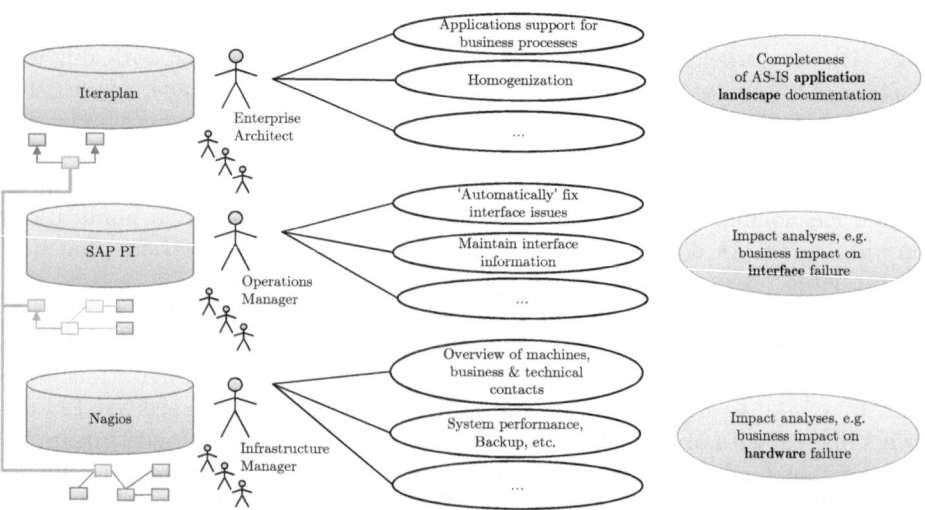

Fig. 2. Data model integration, use cases and sample concerns of stakeholders

compared the ArchiMate 2.0 specification [24] where appropriate. Our industry partner's vision of an automated EA documentation, data should not only be imported to a common repository, but also (vertically) integrated. As shown in Figure 2, the systems we utilize as an illustrating example serve different stakeholders and, thus, are especially suited for respective use cases. However, when integrating these information sources vertically, i.e. by connecting these information silos, impact analyses from top-down (e.g. 'Which parts of my infrastructure is business critical?') and bottom-up (e.g. 'Which business process are influenced by server downtimes?') are facilitated and each individual stakeholder gets a more holistic view (for viewpoints see e.g. [2,5,3,23,13]). Moreover, connecting an EA tool with operative systems also can be utilized to double-check manually collected data, i.e. facilitate data correctness, completeness, or detect white-spots.

3.1   Iteraplan

At the Business Layer Iteraplan covers concepts like *Business Domains* that group *Business Processes, Business Functions, Business Objects, Business Units* and, via the *Business Mapping*, also *Products. Business Processes* of Iteraplan "have a Name and a Description, and may also have Attributes [...]. You can also specify one or more subordinate Business Processes and the sequence of these subordinate processes" [14]. In contrast, ArchiMate defines it as "[...] a behavior element that groups behavior based on an ordering of activities. It is intended to produce a defined set of products or business services" [24]. In addition, we found that a *Business Function* of Iteraplan has a respective entity in the ArchiMate specification, namely *Business Function*. Thereby, the former is documented as "Business Functions have a Name and a Description, and may also have attributes[...]" [14] whereas the later separates the meaning of Business Functions and Business Processes and describes a *Business Function* as "[...] a behavior element that groups behavior based on a chosen set of criteria (typically required business resources and/or competences) [...and] while a business process groups behavior is based on a sequence or 'flow' of activities that is needed to realize a product or service, a business function typically groups behavior based on required business resources, skills, competences, knowledge, etc." [24].

Business Objects of Iteraplan are also defined as an entity with name and description whereas the ArchiMate specification defines a *Business Object* "as a passive element that has relevance from a business perspective" [24]. Moreover, the ArchiMate specification details Business Objects "represent the important 'informational' or 'conceptual' elements in which the business thinks about a domain. [...] Business objects are passive in the sense that they do not trigger or perform processes" [24]. *Product* refers to the ArchiMate concept *Product*, where a "[...] product is defined as a coherent collection of services, accompanied by a contract/set of agreements, which is offered as a whole to (internal or external) customers" [24]. In Iteraplan, the entity *Product* does not cover contracts or agreements, but may include several *Business Functions* for this *Product* in a *Business Domain*.

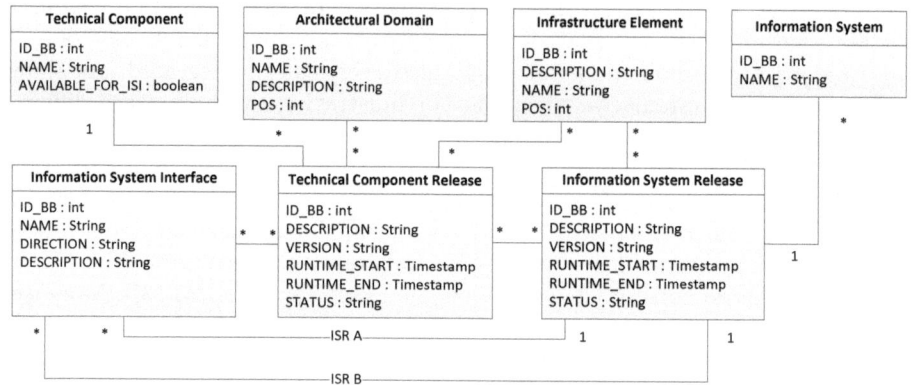

Fig. 3. Simplified excerpt of the Iteraplan data model at the application layer

At the Application Layer, detailed in Figure 3, Iteraplan contains data about *Information Systems* whereby "most work with Information Systems is done by creating or modifying their releases" [14]. Thereby, each Information System Release is a version of a particular Information System. Besides name and description, an *Information System Release* has two timestamps to indicate the period in which a release is productive.

Information System in the sense of Iteraplan fall close to the Application Component of ArchiMate. "An application component is defined as a modular, deployable, and replaceable part of a software system that encapsulates its behavior and data and exposes these through a set of interfaces" [24]. Iteraplan also contains information about *Information System Interfaces* which can be directly mapped to *Application Interface* of ArchiMate "defined as a point of access where an application service is made available to a user or another application component" [24]. In Iteraplan, an *Information System Interface* "has moreover relationships with the Business Objects it is transporting, and with the Technical Components on which it is based" [14].

At the Infrastructure Layer Iteraplan uses a *Technical Component* to describe for instance programming languages or frameworks, databases, or application servers use by an *Information System*. A *Technical Component* can be compared with a *Node* of ArchiMate "[...] defined as a computational resource upon which artifacts may be stored or deployed for execution" [24]. Such a Node can be a device, system software, or even a network element. Thereby a device is "a hardware resource upon which artifacts may be stored or deployed for execution" [24]. In this vein, Iteraplan also uses *Infrastructure Elements* that "describe the operating platform (servers etc.) on which the Information System Release is running" [14].

The Iteraplan documentation describes the remaining entities from a technical view, i.e. they all have a name and a description field and may or may not be hierarchically organized. As a consequence, it strongly depends on a concrete instance of Iteraplan whether its data refers to above outlined concepts.

Iteraplan uses *Attributes* and *Attributes Values* to extend concepts by means of key value pairs.

3.2 SAP PI

Figure 4 details the data model of SAP PI utilized as information source to map a tool entirely used as knowledge management tool, namely Iteraplan, to the real world, i.e. operative IT.

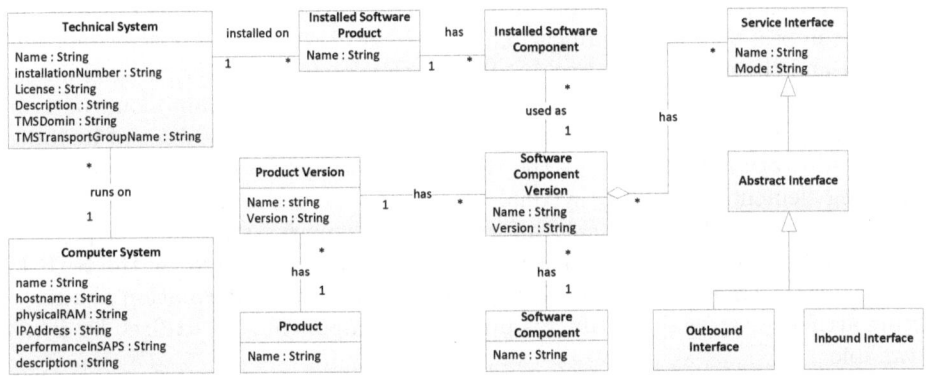

Fig. 4. Simplified excerpt of the SAP PI data model

At the Business Layer, SAP PI only implicitly contains relevant information. Considering the entire SAP PI data model, information about underlying, pursued goals is completely absent. Even though business objects, i.e. "a unit of information relevant from a business perspective" [24], are not directly included in SAP PI, data types may indicate their existence (cf. SAP PI best practice data naming conventions [21]). As a consequence, it strongly depends on a concrete instance [6,12] whether the SAP PI system contains information about business objects.

Central to the Application Layer is the *Application Component* specified as a "[...] modular, deployable, and replaceable part of a system [...]" [24]. While SAP PI introduces two similar concepts, software components and software products whereas the former are not deployable. Products involved in message exchange processes form an application collaboration. Access to the underlying services provided by application components as well as their groupings is modeled by application interfaces, semantically equivalent to SAP PIs enterprise service interface. Which application component invokes which interface is implicitly included in SAP PIs routing information (receiver determination and interface determination) defining the message exchange between enterprise service interfaces and software products. While internal functionality of application components remains invisible to SAP PI, first indications on external visible functionality (application services) exist. Behavioral information in SAP PI is available rather indirectly in interfaces and the included descriptions of operations. However, even though the operations contain all service information, it is questionable whether the operations can be automatically aggregated to specify the service forming the combined functionality.

At the Technology Layer, SAP PI comprises information about the underlying infrastructure. This begins with ArchiMate's *node*, modeling a computational resource which corresponds to SAP PI's computer system. As the provided and needed interfaces of infrastructure components are not essential for the coordination of applications, none of this information appears in SAP PI's data. While the underlying physical mediums are abstracted in SAP PI each invocation of a service comprises two communication paths, one between the service client and SAP PI and the other between SAP PI and the service provider. In ArchiMate, system software ("software environment for specific types of components and objects" [24]) belongs to the behavioral concepts. In SAP PI, a subset of installed system software is registered at the System Landscape Directory including the following elements: operating systems, database systems, and technical systems. In ArchiMate, artifact, the sole informational element, represents "a physical piece of information" [24]. With the exception of files imported by the SAP PI components such as WSDL files for specifying interfaces, information about existing artifacts, especially artifacts application components are realized by, is not available.

3.3 Nagios

A simplified version of the data model for Nagios is shown in 5. As an infrastructure monitoring tool, Nagios does not contain any data referring to Business or Application Layer. Nagios is able to actively and passively monitor infrastructure elements and thus contains manifold information about hosts, services, and network elements. At the Infrastructure Layer Nagios uses the *Downtime History* to manually store (planned) downtimes of hosts or services. If downtimes are defined assigned hosts and services are not checked anymore and no notifications are sent to the contact person during defined periods, because the downtime is scheduled.

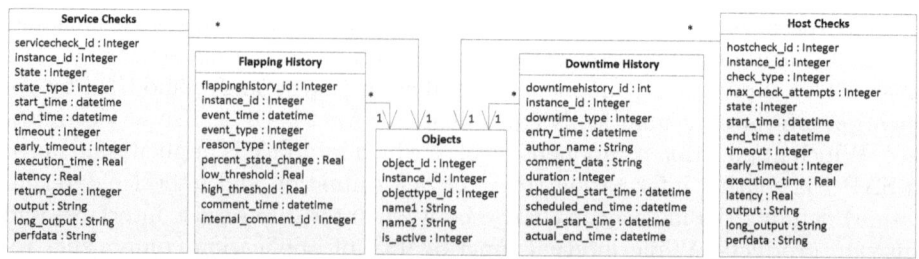

Fig. 5. Simplified excerpt of the Nagios data model

Nagios uses a client/server architecture and saves responses of acknowledgment requests in the *Acknowledgments* class. For hosts, these acknowledgments are up, down, or unreachable whereas for services, they can be either ok, warning, critical, or unknown. This data is stored together with a timestamp. The *Flappinghistory* stores the flapping data of services or hosts, i.e. it saves the event when one state of a service or host is changed. Nagios saves the periodical checks of hosts in *Host Checks* whereas periodical checks of services are stored as *Service Checks* whereby the state (up, down, or unreachable) is also captured. Via the *start_time* and *end_time* attribute, the period of a certain state can be calculated.

Since ArchiMate does not include such fine grained information, a mapping may embrace nodes or devices (cf. above). However, monitoring tools can be employed to map the 'real world' to an EA model to facilitate its completeness and correctness. Mapping such fine grained information to an EA model refers to the challenge of Data Granularity detailed below.

3.4 Vertical Model Integration

Figure 6 shows an example for a model mapping of the three above introduced data models. As illustrated, transformation rule φ is required to perform a semantically and syntactically correct mapping.

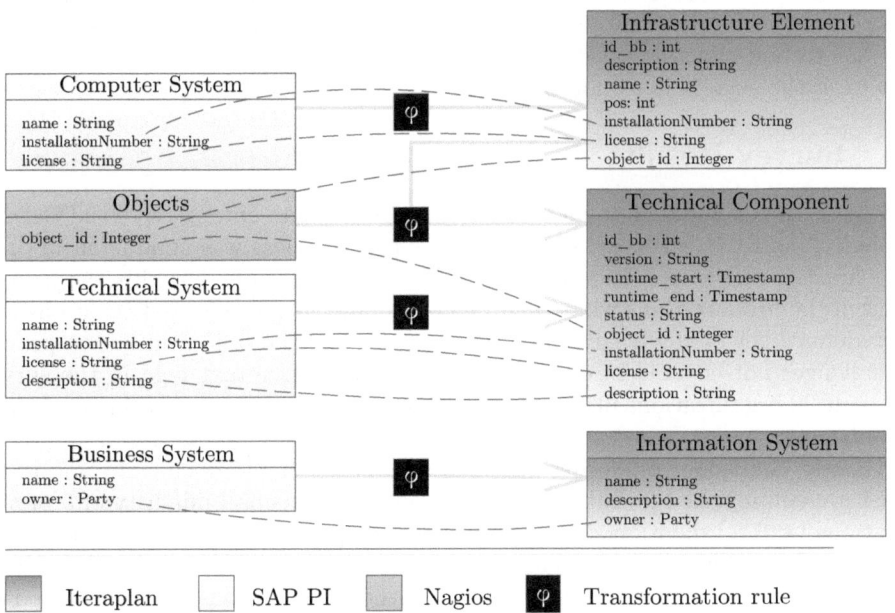

Fig. 6. Data model mapping of SAP PI and Nagios to Iteraplan

As illustrated, SAP PI's *Computer Systems* can be mapped to *Infrastructure Elements* of Iteraplan. In our vertical integration scenario, Iteraplan's Infrastructure Elements gets licensing information and installation numbers. In this vein, the Nagios model element *Objects* contains an enumeration of `objecttype_id` which can either indicate that the object is a host or an infrastructure service. In this case, a mapping table has to be provided that maps *Objects* in Nagios to *Infrastructure Elements* or *Technical Components* of Iteraplan by applying a filter (`objecttype_id == 1`) ensuring only hosts are mapped. Another filter (`objecttype_id == 0`) can be used to identify services which subsequently could be mapped to *Technical Components*. Thereby, φ first has to search for a matching object (e.g. similar or even equal hostname or IP address). If a matching object has been found, φ has to align data if a source attribute already corresponds to a target attribute, e.g. validating or invalidating data.

Otherwise, φ could add/fill non-existing attributes or append values. Again, attributes contained in the source model (Nagios) are transfered to the target model (Iteraplan) to enable vertical integration. Thereby, fields contained in both models need to be synchronized, e.g. the field description. *Technical Systems* of SAP PI can be mapped by φ to *Technical Components* of Iteraplan. In this vein, naming conventions [21] are essential since φ needs an identifier for each *Technical System* or *Technical Component* and a respective mapping table. Commonly, IP addresses for instance are not maintained in an EA tool, possibly in an ESB, but definitely in an infrastructure monitoring tool or Configuration Management Database (CMDB). This becomes more critical when harmonizing or vertically integrating three different data sources. Finally, SAP PI's *Business Systems* can be directly mapped to Iteraplan's *Information Systems*. Thereby, φ has to find the relevant *Information Systems* in Iteraplan first, or insert new data, if the system does not exist.

4   Survey Results

Next to the exemplified model transformation from an enterprise of the German fashion industry, a survey among 123 EA practitioners was conducted in order to identify challenges for automated EA documentation. For this purpose we asked the organizations what their current challenges in this context are using a predefined set of challenges. In addition, we asked the organizations to provide challenges not covered in our selection by using a free text field in the survey. About 20 organizations utilized this option and provided information on further challenges.

These challenges hindering automated updates in the documentation of the EA are summarized in Table 1, whereas only a very small minority of 5 organizations (4.07%) mentioned that they have no specific challenge in their organization. A total number of 123 organizations answered this question with at least one of the provided answers. 91 (73.98%) of the organizations have mentioned the abstraction gap between the EA and the information source as challenge. This challenge has also been identified within the model transformation from Section 3. The cost of integration for the EA tool was stated by 74 (60.16%) of the

Table 1. What hinders updates in the context of EA?

Answer	Count	Percentage
Abstraction gap to EA model	91	73.98%
Cost of integration for EA tool	74	60.16%
Low data quality at information sources	55	44.72%
Low return of investment	35	28.46%
Security when using network scanners	17	13.82%
Other	20	16.26%
Nothing specific	5	4.07%

organizations indicating a missing support of existing solutions. Almost half of the organizations (44.72%) also highlighted low data quality at the information sources as challenging. Since organizations typically have multiple information sources containing relevant EA information, further research is necessary to identify possible information sources and their data quality attributes. Automating the EA documentation requires large initial investments in the organizations due to the missing tool support. In our survey 35 (28.46%) organizations stated a low return of investment as an obstacle. Around 17 (13.82%) organizations foresee security when using network scanners as challenging. Usually these tools require administrative rights since that have to be executed on the machines to monitor.

Table 2. Do you plan to use automated EA model updates in the future?

Answer	Count	Percentage
Yes	25	20.33%
No	24	19.51%
Not yet considered	31	25.20%

Table 3. Why do you not plan to use automation?

Answer	Count	Percentage
Too difficult	11	8.94%
Too expensive	9	7.32%
Not enough ROI	9	7.32%
Not enough tool support	8	6.50%
Other	6	4.88%

One organization stated within the free text field the definition of roles and responsibilities for the collected data as challenging. Since a complete automation of the EA documentation is probably not achievable, manual activities will be necessary in future. Therefore, appropriate roles and responsibilities are necessary to coordinate the data collection and ensure a high data quality of the imported information. Another organization mentioned the effort to transform data from the information sources to the EA repository as challenging. Similarly, the lack of standardization and the inclusion of all appropriate information sources are related to this challenge. Many of these issues already have been investigated in the exemplified model transformation in Section 3. Several organizations also mentioned the general acceptance and a low degree of upper management awareness of EA management as challenge. This is a critical challenge although it is not directly related to automated EA documentation.

The organizations were also asked if they plan to use automated EA model updates in the future. The results are shown in Table 2 with 25 (20.33%) organizations planing to use automation. At the same time 31 (25.30%) organizations have not yet considered to use automated EA model updates. Therefore, almost half of the organizations might apply techniques for automated EA documentation in the future. The 24 (19.51%) organizations not planing to use automation were also asked give a reason for this decision that are shown in Table 3. 11 (8.94%) organizations envision automation as too expensive to implement in their organization, while 9 (7.32%) organizations think it is too difficult to acquire and it provides not enough return on investment. Around 8 (6.50%) of the organizations mentioned that enough tool support for automated EA documentation is available.

5   Challenges for Automated Enterprise Architecture Documentation

In this Section challenges from the above presented model transformation from an enterprise of the German fashion industry as well as the practitioner survey are identified and grouped into three high-level categories. In addition, a literature review was performed to identify new challenges and align them with the findings from this paper. An overview of all categorized challenges found in this paper is shown in Table 4 containing a reference to the identified sources for every challenge.

5.1   Data Challenges

The collection of appropriate data is the foundation to enable automated EA documentation in organizations. Data challenges result from collecting data utilizing productive systems that contain relevant EA information within organizations. Main reasons for these challenges are the multitude of possible productive systems in organizations and the quality as well as actuality of the retrieved information.

DC 1 - Overload of productive systems due to large volume of transactions for automated data collection. Productive systems may be influenced in the daily operation when the entire data store or parts thereof are collected during the data collection step. As a result these these outlined mechanisms could lead to unexpected peak loads in the productive systems. This can be quite a challenge due to causal relationships in the infrastructure of the organization, especially if the productive system used as information source is essential for the business. In our illustrating example (cf. Section 3), the ESB can be considered as the nervous system of an enterprise interconnecting business applications and processes [6].

DC 2 - Selection of the right productive systems as information sources for EA documentation. Automated EA documentation requires the integration of several information sources in the organization. The selection of the information sources need to assessed according to several categories as already identified by Farwick et al. [8]. For this purpose the selection has to consider the content of the information sources with respect to the relevance for EA. Another issue in this context is the necessary effort to build an interface for exporting the data from the information source. In many cases the productive systems have no interface provided and their meta model needs to be reverse engineered in an additional step [6]. Further examples are the data quality attributes and the level of security that can be achieved for the exchange of the data.

DC 3 - Detection of changes in the real world EA and their propagation to the EA model in the repository. Automated EA documentation consists of two major steps, which are the documentation of the existing EA as well as the maintenance of an appropriate data actuality of the repository. Maintaining the EA repository requires an automatic detection of changes in the real world EA from different sources. This includes for instance the detection of new information systems, infrastructure elements, projects, as well as changes of these elements as highlighted by Farwick et al. [9]. Furthermore solutions are necessary to propagate these changes to the EA repository.

DC 4 - Data quality in the productive systems not sufficient for the documentation of EA information. Automated EA documentation requires sufficient data quality at the productive systems. However, 55 (44.72%) of the participating organizations in the survey envision the data quality of the information sources as too low for EA documentation. At this point further research is necessary to evaluate possible information sources in organizations and their quality attributes. Possible quality attributes for information sources that need to be investigated are for instance actuality, completeness, correctness, and granularity. Next to this evaluation of possible information sources in organizations, quality assurance mechanisms are necessary to ensure the data quality using manual checks.

5.2   Transformation Challenges

Once the data could be collected from information sources of the organization a transformation step needs to align this information with the target model of the EA repository. To achieve this goal the transformation has to deal with several challenges resulting from different models between information source and the target repository.

TC 1 - Model transformation for the exchange of EA information necessary due to missing interfaces and standards. As exemplified above, customized model transformations are necessary to map the different information sources to a target model. Major reason for these individual model transformations are missing standards or non-conformance to standards of enterprises. Conformance to standards, e.g. to ArchiMate 2.0 [24], could simplify such a mapping for instance when a semantically and syntactically correct mapping is required. The transformation rules become more complex when adding new information sources. In our case, additional mapping tables where provided. Thereby, a mapping function commonly first has to search for a matching object and, if found, align data only if a source attribute already corresponds to a target attribute, e.g. validating or invalidating data. Otherwise, strategies like adding new attributes, filling unset attributes, or appending values have to be chosen individually for each transformation rule.

TC 2 - Ambiguous concepts imported from the productive systems in the organization require a consolidation. Our examples already indicate that rigorous data migration mechanisms like table merging and data cleansing (see [17]) must be provided for such a vertical integration. We conclude that frequent model changes of the target model are necessary when adding new information sources. Thus, a non-rigid typed model could be beneficial to some extent. Moser et al. [18] address the challenge of inaccurate data in the EA repository. Data gathered from different information sources tends to be inhomogeneous [17], i.e. different data formats or simply different lengths of fixed-character fields. Regardless data is entered manually or automatically via import mechanisms, data has to be consolidated. For instance, synonyms and homonyms have to be cleared. In the worst case, ambiguous concepts are imported and have to be cleaned afterwards. For manual data collection, Fischer et al. propose data quality contracts [10] between different parties. However, for automation, this remains a challenge after all and data migration mechanisms like a staging area (see [17]) might be necessary.

TC 3 - Administration of collected data from the productive systems is required to ensure actuality and consistency. A meta-model as mentioned by [8] is necessary to automatically trigger activities to increase the quality of the collected information. Such a meta-model needs to consider attributes for expiry time of imported data elements, the date of last change, data responsibilities, data sources, etc.

TC 4 - Duplicate EA elements imported from different productive systems of the organization. Once imported in an EA repository, data can be analyzed. During the analysis process, the actual source of an information piece could matter [8,9], e.g. if information is wrong or bad data quality is detected. Identity reconciliation also is a necessity to synchronize changes in the EA repository with the original source.

TC 5 - Abstraction between the EA model and the imported information from productive systems of the organization. Major challenge for organizations is the abstraction gap between the EA model and the provided elements from the information sources. 91 (73.98%) organizations rated this as the most important challenge for automation. This confirms our findings from Section 3. If our industry

Table 4. Categorization of automated EA documentation challenges

ID	Challenge	Source
	Data Challenges	
DC 1	Overload of productive systems due to large volume of transactions for automated data collection.	Model Transformation
DC 2	Selection of the right productive systems as information sources for EA documentation.	[8,6]
DC 3	Detection of changes in the real world EA and their propagation to the EA model in the repository.	[9]
DC 4	Data quality in the productive systems not sufficient for the documentation of EA information..	Survey
	Transformation Challenges	
TC 1	Model transformation for the exchange of EA information necessary due to missing interfaces and standards.	Model Transformation, [18]
TC 2	Ambiguous concepts imported from the productive systems in the organization require a consolidation.	[10,17,18], Model Transformation
TC 3	Administration of collected data from the productive systems is required to ensure actuality and consistency.	[8]
TC 4	Duplicate EA elements imported from different productive systems of the organization.	[8,9]
TC 5	Abstraction between the EA model and the imported information from productive systems of the organization.	[9], Survey, Model Transformation
	Business and Organizational Challenges	
BC 1	Security vulnerability through monitoring tools in the infrastructure of the organization.	[7], Survey
BC 2	Not enough return on investment due to large initial investment efforts.	Survey
BC 3	Involvement of data owners for the maintenance of imported EA information.	Survey, [18]
	Tooling	
T 1	Synchronization of changes in the EA model to the underlying productive systems.	[4,19], Model Transformation
T 2	Collection of information not relevant or too fine-grained for decision makers in the EA.	[8]
T 3	Analyses have to be decoupled from the meta-model.	[13,16], Survey
T 4	Not enough tool support for automated EA documentation available.	Survey, Model Transformation

partner did not chose an integrative approach, elements imported from productive systems (SAP PI and Nagios) are too fine-grained for mere EA purposes. To overcome the abstraction gap, EA documentation may be facilitated by human tasks in a semi-automated manner.

5.3   Business and Organizational Challenges

Next to rather technical issues resulting from the information extraction and transformation of this information, there are further challenges regarding the added business value of automation as well as the organization. Since it requires large initial investments in organizations and proven solutions are missing in industry, automation is not feasible in some situations.

BC 1 - Security vulnerability through monitoring tools in the infrastructure of the organization. Network scanners provide information about the network architecture of an organization regarding all devices that are communication over TCP or UDP. This includes computers, firewalls, printers, and application information [7]. In the survey conducted in this paper 17 (13.82%) organizations foresee security as a critical challenge when using these network scanners for EA documentation. Since applications are actively observed within the machines, these tools usually need to be executed directly on the observing infrastructure with privileged access rights. As a result, tools monitoring infrastructure information about the EA pose security vulnerabilities for an organization.

BC 2 - Not enough return on investment due to large initial investment efforts. The initial effort to develop interfaces for the considered information sources and the cost for adapting existing EA tools to support automated documentation is regarded as very high. As a result 35 (28.46%) of all organizations that participated in the survey mentioned concerns about a low return of investment for automated EA documentation. Among the 24 (19.51%) organizations not planning to use automated EA model updates this issue was also raised as one of the main reasons. 9 (7.32%) do not plan to use automation since it is too expensive and does not guarantee any ROI.

BC 3 - Involvement of data owners for the maintenance of imported EA information. Within the survey another organization stated the definition of roles and responsible persons for the collected data as challenging. Defined roles are necessary to coordinate the maintenance of EA models on a coarse-grained level. Further responsibilities on the detail level of single applications, infrastructure elements, and processes are required to maintain the EA model information. These responsibilities are necessary since a complete automation of the EA documentation is not possible and manual quality assurance is necessary.

5.4   Tooling

Automated EA documentation is only feasible with the appropriate support of tool vendors. However, available tools are not capable to support importing, editing, and validating model data for automated EA documentation [16]. Existing solutions only support simple import mechanisms that are mainly limited to Excel or CSV files.

T 1 - Synchronization of changes in the EA model to the underlying productive systems. The exemplified model transformation presented in Section 3 processes data from the information sources to a target EA model by mapping the concepts and attributes. The managed evolution of an EA requires architects to adapt certain parts of the model, e.g., remove unused interfaces [4,19]. These changes in the EA model need to be synchronized with the underlying information sources that were used to import the information automatically. Ideally, this information could be directly applied to a CMDB for instance to avoid multiple updates in several applications that might create inconsistencies.

T 2 - Collection of information not relevant or too fine-grained for decision makers in the EA. One of the main goals of automated EA documentation is to provide as many as possible concepts of the EA model by gathering the information from productive systems to avoid time consuming and error prone manual data collection. At the same time the EA model needs to omit information that are too fine-grained for decision makers in order to keep the model as lean as possible. Therefore mechanisms are necessary to tailor the target EA model and define concepts that should not be automatically imported [8]. A tool for automated EA documentation needs to support these requirements sufficiently.

T3 - Analyses have to be decoupled from the meta-model. An automated EA documentation endeavor is an ongoing process and, thus, it is not very likely to be realized with a big-bang strategy. Consequently, it is very likely that the meta-model of the target model (EA repository) has to be extended over time. Current EA tools [16] offer analysis mechanisms to analyze the EA meta-model with respect to some extension mechanisms. Thus, it might happen these analyses have to be altered when the EA model changes. As discussed in [13] by Hauder et al. analyses of a frequently changing meta-model is a challenging task. We conclude that analyses cannot be directly bound to the meta-model but the subject to be analyzed (models) must be interchangeable.

T4 - Not enough tool support for automated EA documentation available. A majority of 74 (60.16%) organizations stated that the necessary tool integration is very expensive to extend existing tools for EA management. Among the 24 (19.51%) organizations not planing to use automated EA model updates in future around 8 (6.50%) organizations mentioned not enough tool support as a reason for this. Due to the lack of available solutions for automated EA documentation, existing tools require a customized adaption to import EA information from productive systems. In our example, we implemented the model transformations individually.

6   Conclusion

In this paper, we have identified challenges for automated EA documentation. Therefore we have investigated model transformations from three information sources, presented our findings from a survey among 123 EA practitioners, and combined it with a literature study. Major challenges identified in this paper are synthesized and grouped along the categories *data, transformation, business and organization* as well as *tooling*. Within data challenges main aspects are the data quality and the selection of appropriate information sources. Transformation challenges deal with the mapping from different information sources to a central repository and the maintenance of this repository. Business and organization challenges address the added value of automation and the impact on the organizational structure. As the last category, tooling contains challenges for tool aided realization of automated EA documentation and the integration with existing EA repositories. The present paper is the first contribution elaborating challenges for automated EA documentation. These challenges constitute the foundation for future research efforts dealing with the applicability and effectiveness of automated EA documentation in organizations. We intent to discuss identified challenges as well as solutions at TEAR and to critically reflect automated EA documentation when put into practice with the audience.

References

1. Berneaud, M., Buckl, S., Diaz-Fuentes, A., Matthes, F., Monahov, I., Nowobliska, A., Roth, S., Schweda, C.M., Weber, U., Zeiner, M.: Trends for enterprise architecture management tools survey. Technical report, Technische Universität München (2012)
2. Buckl, S., Ernst, A.M., Lankes, J., Matthes, F.: Enterprise Architecture Management Pattern Catalog (Version 1.0). Technical report, Chair for Informatics 19 (sebis), Technische Universität München, Munich, Germany (2008)
3. Buckl, S., Matthes, F., Monahov, I., Roth, S., Schulz, C., Schweda, C.M.: Enterprise architecture management patterns for enterprise-wide access views on business objects. In: European Conference on Pattern Languages of Programs (EuroPLoP) 2011, Irsee Monastery, Bavaria, Germany (2011)
4. Buckl, S., Matthes, F., Roth, S., Schulz, C., Schweda, C.M.: A conceptual framework for enterprise architecture design. In: Workshop Trends in Enterprise Architecture Research (TEAR), Delft, The Netherlands (2010)
5. Buckl, S., Matthes, F., Roth, S., Schulz, C., Schweda, C.M.: A method for constructing enterprise-wide access views on business objects. In: Informatik 2010: IT-Governance in verteilten Systemen (GVS 2010), Leipzig, Germany (2010)
6. Buschle, M., Ekstedt, M., Grunow, S., Hauder, M., Matthes, F., Roth, S.: Automated Enterprise Architecture Documentation using an Enterprise Service Bus (2012)
7. Buschle, M., Holm, H., Sommestad, T., Ekstedt, M., Shahzad, K.: A Tool for automatic Enterprise Architecture modeling, pp. 25–32 (2011)
8. Farwick, M., Agreiter, B., Breu, R., Ryll, S., Voges, K., Hanschke, I.: Automation processes for enterprise architecture management. In: Proceedings of the 2011 IEEE 15th International Enterprise Distributed Object Computing Conference Workshops, EDOCW 2011, pp. 340–349. IEEE Computer Society, Washington, DC (2011)
9. Farwick, M., Agreiter, B., Breu, R., Ryll, S., Voges, K., Hanschke, I.: Requirements for automated enterprise architecture model maintenance - a requirements analysis based on a literature review and an exploratory survey. ICEIS (4), 325–337 (2011)

10. Fischer, R., Aier, S., Winter, R.: A federated approach to enterprise architecture model maintenance. In: Reichert, M., Strecker, S., Turowski, K. (eds.) EMISA. LNI, vol. P-119, pp. 9–22. GI (2007)
11. Glaser, B.G., Strauss, A.L.: The Discovery of Grounded Theory, Aldine, vol. 20 (1967)
12. Grunow, S., Matthes, F., Roth, S.: Towards Automated Enterprise Architecture Documentation: Data Quality Aspects of SAP PI. In: Morzy, T., Härder, T., Wrembel, R. (eds.) Advances in Databases and Information Systems. AISC, vol. 186, pp. 103–113. Springer, Heidelberg (2013)
13. Hauder, M., Matthes, F., Roth, S., Schulz, C.: Generating dynamic cross-organizational process visualizations through abstract view model pattern matching. In: Architecture Modeling for Future Internet enabled Enterprise (AMFInE), Valencia, Spain (2012)
14. iteratec GmbH. iteraplan documentation home (2012), `http://www.iteraplan.de/wiki/display/iteraplan/iteraplan+Documentation+Home`
15. Lankhorst, M.: Enterprise Architecture at Work: Modelling, Communication and Analysis, 2nd edn. Springer, Berlin (2009)
16. Matthes, F., Buckl, S., Leitel, J., Schweda, C.M.: Enterprise Architecture Management Tool Survey 2008 (2008)
17. Matthes, F., Schulz, C.: Towards an integrated data migration process model. Technical report, Technische Universität München, München, Germany (2012)
18. Moser, C., Junginger, S., Brückmann, M., Schöne, K.: Some process patterns for enterprise architecture management. In: Proceedings, Workshop on Patterns in Enterprise Architecture Management (PEAM 2009), Bonn, pp. 19–30 (2009)
19. Murer, S., Bonati, B., Furrer, F.J., Murer, S., Bonati, B., Furrer, F.J.: Managed Evolution. Springer, Heidelberg (2011)
20. Nagios Enterprises. Nagios documentation (2012), `http://www.nagios.org/documentation`
21. SAP AG. PI Best Practices Naming Conventions (2012), `http://www.sdn.sap.com/irj/scn/go/portal/prtroot/docs/library/uuid/40a66d0e-fe5e-2c10-8a85-e418b59ab36a`
22. SAP AG. SAP help portal (2012), `http://help.sap.com`
23. Schaub, M., Matthes, F., Roth, S.: Towards a conceptual framework for interactive enterprise architecture management visualizations. In: Modellierung, Bamberg, Germany (2012)
24. The Open Group. Archimate 2.0 Specification. Van Haren Publishing (2012)
25. Vom Brocke, J., Simons, A., Niehaves, B., Riemer, K., Plattfaut, R., Cleven, A.: Reconstructing the giant: on the importance of rigour in documenting the literature search process, pp. 1–13. Hampton Press (2009)
26. Weill, P., Ross, J.: IT Savvy: What Top Executives Must Know to Go from Pain to Gain. Harvard Business Press (2009)
27. Winter, K., Buckl, S., Matthes, F., Schweda, C.M.: Investigating the state-of-the-art in enterprise architecture management method in literature and practice. In: 5th Mediterranean Conference on Information Systems, MCIS 2010 (2010)

Building Strategic Enterprise Context Models with *i*: A Pattern-Based Approach[*]

Juan Pablo Carvallo[1] and Xavier Franch[2]

[1] Universidad del Azuay
Av. 24 de Mayo 7-77, Cuenca, Ecuador
jpcarvallo@uazuay.edu.ec
[2] Universitat Politècnica de Catalunya (UPC)
c/Jordi Girona 1-3, 08034 Barcelona, Spain
franch@essi.upc.edu

Abstract. Modern enterprise engineering (EE) requires deep understanding of organizations and their interaction with their context. Because of this, in early phases of the EE process, enterprise context models are often built and used to reason about organizational needs with respects to actors in their context and vice versa. However, far from simple, this task is usually cumbersome because of knowledge and communication gaps among technical personnel performing EE activities and their administrative counterparts. In this paper, we propose the use of strategic patterns expressed with the *i** language aimed to help bridging this gap. Patterns emerged from several industrial applications of our DHARMA method, and synthesize knowledge about common enterprise strategies, e.g. CRM. Patterns have been constructed based on the well-known Porter's model of the 5 market forces and built upon *i** strategic dependency models. In this way technical and administrative knowledge and skills are synthesized in a commonly agreeable framework. The use of patterns is illustrated with an industrial example in the telecom field.

Keywords: enterprise pattern, enterprise context model, market forces, strategic dependencies, *i** framework, iStar.

1 Introduction

Modern enterprises largely rely on information systems specifically designed to manage the continuously increasing complexity of interactions with actors in their context. Architecting such systems requires deep understanding of the enterprise context and strategies. Because of this, early phases of the enterprise engineering (EE) process are usually oriented to model the enterprise context. Enterprise context models, as part of a wider enterprise architecture model, include environmental actors (i.e., actors in the context of an enterprise that interact with it) and descriptions of the relationships among them. Resulting models help understanding the purpose of enterprises on their

---

[*] This work has been partially supported by the Spanish project TIN2010-19130-C02-01.

S. Aier et al. (Eds.): TEAR 2012 and PRET 2012, LNBIP 131, pp. 40–59, 2012.

environment, what is required from them, and to reason about the way in which they will respond to the specific needs generating value.

Enterprise context models are therefore a fundamental piece that helps enterprise decision-makers to design and refine their business strategies and enterprise architects to understand what will be required from the resulting socio-technical system. However, far from easy, the construction of such models is usually a cumbersome task, mainly due to:

- Communication gaps among technical personnel, who usually lacks knowledge about business strategies, modeling, planning, and administration skills; and their administrative counterparts, with similar limitation in relation to methodological business processes and requirements elicitation, and systems modeling techniques.
- Limited knowledge of the enterprise structure, operations and strategy, which forces technical staff to spend important amounts of time studying and understanding business, to be reconciled with time constraints resulting from internal and external pressures and narrow windows of opportunity, which increases the risk of misunderstandings or misinterpretations.

One strategy to mitigate this situation is to foster knowledge reuse, designing some artifacts that may be used as templates for both technical and managerial personnel in order to improve understanding. In this paper we propose the use of patterns with this purpose. A pattern has been defined as a solution to a recurring problem in a particular context [1]. Patterns collect relevant knowledge that appears consistently throughout several similar experiences, which has been systematized and stored in an appropriated structure for its future use in analogous settings.

In our particular case, we are interested in storing enterprise context knowledge, which has been identified and systematized in the domain of business analysis and strategy. In order to make it accessible to enterprise architects, we represent this knowledge by means *i* strategic dependency* (SD) models [2]. Therefore, patterns include environmental actors and their strategic dependencies. Patterns emerged from several industrial and academic applications of the first activity of our DHARMA method [3], which requires the construction of *i**-based context models.

For building the catalogue of patterns, we distinguish two levels of abstraction. At the highest level, we make an analysis of enterprise behavior guided by the theory and the elements described in Porter's model of the 5 market forces [4]. This analysis is applicable in general to any kind of enterprise. At the lowest level, we consider enterprise strategies which describe how a particular enterprise operates, e.g., Enterprise Resource Planning (ERP), Customer Relationship Management (CRM) and Supply Chain Management (SCM) [5].

2   Background

2.1   Porter's Model of the Five Market Forces

Porter's model of the five market forces is designed to help organizations analyze the influence of 5 forces on their business and to reason about the strategies potentially available to make them profitable. Although subject of some criticism from its retractors, Porter's model remains wildly accepted, studied and used in the practice [6].

According to Porter [4], "the essence of formulating competitive strategy is relating a company to its environment". Although the environment is very broad encompassing social and economic forces, from the business point of view a key aspect in the environment of an enterprise is the industry or industries in which it competes. The state of competition in the industry depends on five competitive forces (see Fig. 1): threat of new entrants; threat of substitution; bargain power of customers; bargain power of suppliers; and rivalry among current competitors. Lately, some authors have proposed a sixth force, the government, not only because of its regulatory power, but also because it may become a potential competitor in some industries e.g. public vs. private schools. We do not consider this force in this paper.

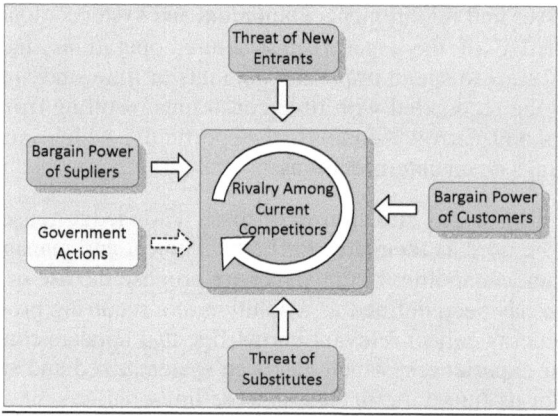

Fig. 1. Porter's model of the five market forces

2.2   The *i** Framework

The *i** framework [2] was formulated for representing, modeling and reasoning about socio-technical systems. Its modeling language is constituted basically by a set of graphic constructs which can be used in two models: the Strategic Dependency (SD) model, which allows the representation of organizational actors, and the Strategic Rationale (SR) model, which represents the internal actors' rationale. Since our patterns are defined as SD models, we focus the explanation on SD constructs.

Actors in SD models are classified in DHARMA as human, organizational, software or hardware. They can be related by *is-a* (subtyping) relationships and may have social dependencies. A *dependency* is a relationship among two actors, one of them, named *depender*, who depends for the accomplishment of some internal intention from a second actor, named *dependee*. The dependency is then characterized by an *intentional element* (*dependum*) which represents the dependency's element. The primary intentional elements are: *resource*, *task*, *goal* and *softgoal*. A softgoal represents a goal that can be partially satisfied, or a goal that requires additional agreement about how it is satisfied. They are usually introduced for representing non-functional requirements and quality concerns. Fig. 2 presents an *i** SD model in the Ecuatorian Etapatelecom company, introduced in Section 6.1.

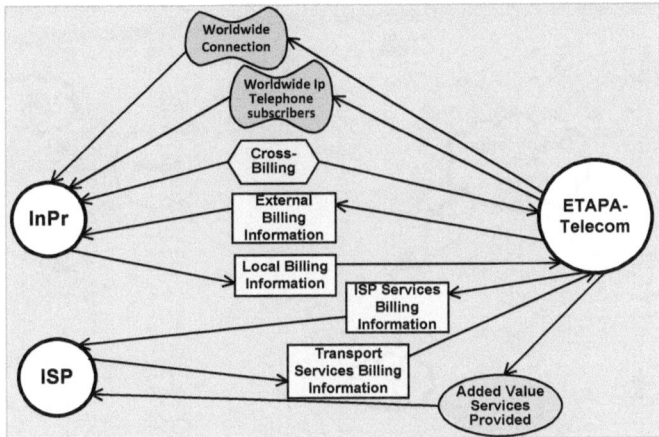

Fig. 2. An *i** SD model for the Etapatelecom case

2.3 The DHARMA Method

The DHARMA method has been used in the context of this work. It aims at the definition of enterprise architectures using the *i** framework [3]. The process resulting from the method (see Fig. 3) is initiated by modeling the enterprise context (1), then introducing the system in the organization (2), analysing its impact in detail (3) and identifying its generic enterprise architecture (4), i.e. actors that form the system, the services that must be covered by each of them and the relationships among them. It is clear, thus, that improving the initial construction of the enterprise context model would be of great help for the method applicability.

2.4 Patterns in the *i** Framework

Several approaches about the definition and use of patterns in *i** have been proposed. Among them, the closest proposals to ours are the works on social structures presented in [7][8], where the authors propose a set of social patterns, drawn from research on cooperative and distributed architectures. Several differences with our approach:

- Formalization. We will provide a formal definition of pattern instantiation and a couple of metrics to measure coverage.
- Size. In their work, patterns are intended to model different types of cooperation settings among organizations, e.g., Structure-in-5 and Joint Venture. In our approach, patterns are much more detailed and intended to model the context of particular organization instead of the relation among groups of them.
- Background. Our approach is based on theory of business administration and marked strategy whilst these approaches are based on organizational theory.

The aim of these works is to propose ontology for information systems, inspired by social and organizational structures. Our work is intended to provide guidance in early phases of the EE process, providing artifacts to bridge communication gaps among technical EE staff and administrative staff.

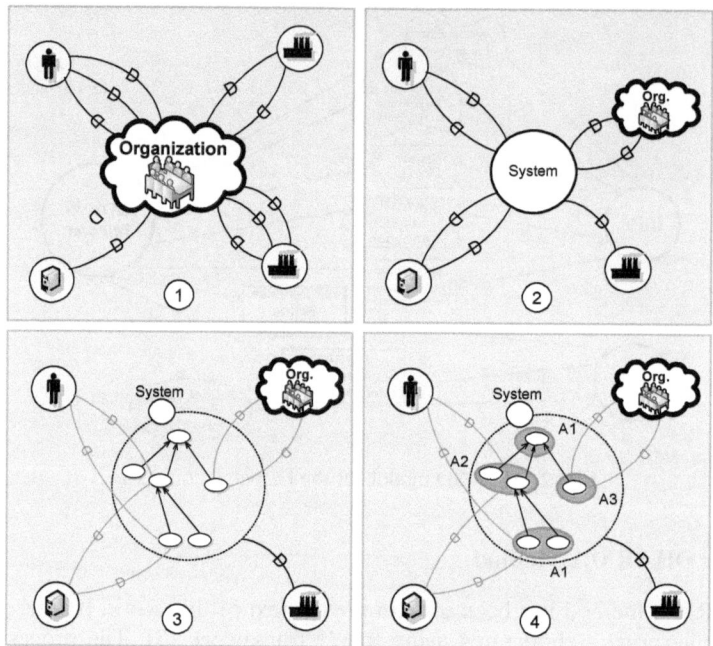

Fig. 3. The DHARMA method

3   Formal Definition of Patterns

Being aware that Alexander's definition of pattern includes several parts that may play a fundamental part in a reuse strategy, in this paper we focus on the expression of the solution part expressed as an *i** SD model. Although cumbersome, we consider this formalization a necessary step in order to be able to rigorously define the patterns and make possible some future work on analysis techniques and measures' definition.

3.1   *i** SD Models

Definition. *i** SD Model.

An *i** SD model M is a tuple M = (A, D, L) being A the set of actors, D the set of dependencies and L the set of actor specialization links.

Definition. Set of actors.

Given the *i** SD model M = (A, D, L), the set of actors A = {A_i} is such that each A_i is a pair (name, type), with type = (Human, Organizational, Software, Hardware).

Definition. Set of dependencies.

Given the *i** SD model M = (A, D, L), the set of dependencies D (over A) is a set D = {d_i} such that each d_i is a tuple (name, dpr, dpe, type), with dpr, dpe∈ A such that dpr ≠ dpe, and type = (Goal, Softgoal, Task, Resource).

Definition. Set of actor specialization links.

Given the *i** SD model M = (A, D, L), the set of actor specialization links L is a set L = {l$_i$} such that each l$_i$ is a pair (superactor, subactor), with superactor, subactor∈ A such that superactor ≠ subactor (in fact, cycles are not allowed).

We remark again that these definitions present some simplifications over the complete definition of the *i** SD models as available e.g. in the *i** wiki [9], but the concepts introduced here are enough for the patterns identified so far. As mentioned above, these changes align with previous work on the use of *i** in industrial settings (see e.g. [3]) which points to the fact that in practice some constructs create some confusion and act as an adoption barrier for practitioners. Also, as we will see in the next sections, we adopt three graphical conventions: first, we allow for a tabular representation of *i** models, especially useful when models grow; second, we represent direction of dependencies by arrowheads instead of the "D" convention of *i**; third, given two dependencies d1 = (n, a1, a2, t) and d2 = (n, a2, a1, t), we can draw these two dependencies using just a single graphical dependency with arrowheads in both directions. Bidirectional dependencies are useful to express mutual collaboration in actors.

3.2   Patterns and Their Application

In our proposal a context model patterns is nothing else than a plain *i** SD model defined as in Section 3.1.

Definition. Context model pattern.
Any *i** SD model M is a context model pattern.

In Fig. 4 we show an excerpt of the context model pattern for our CRM case study, that will be introduced in more detail in Section 5.

The key concept around patterns is that of instantiation. Instantiation is defined upon the notion of model correspondence, that defines how actors and dependencies of a pattern are assigned to other actors and dependencies that are defined on a different space (i.e., the actors and dependencies of the enterprise, *ent*).

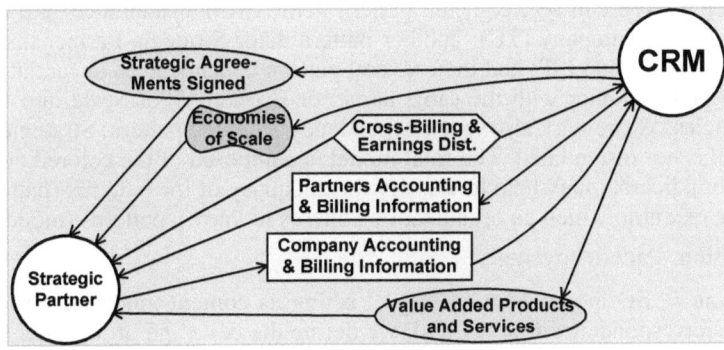

Fig. 4. Example of context model pattern (excerpt)

Definition. Model correspondence. Domain, rank.

Given the $i*$ SD model $M = (A, D, L)$, and given the sets A_{ent}, D_{ent} and L_{ent}, being A_{ent} a set of actors, D_{ent} a set of dependencies (over A_{ent}) and L_{ent} a set of actor specialization links, $A_{ent} \cap A = \varnothing$ (thus $D_{ent} \cap D = \varnothing$), a model correspondence C from M to $(A_{ent}, D_{ent}, L_{ent})$ is a pair of correspondences, $C = (c_A, c_D)$, $c_A \subseteq (A \times A_{ent})$ and $c_D \subseteq (D \times D_{ent})$. Correctness conditions are:

- Actors appearing in dependencies must be aligned:
  $((n, a1, a2, t), (m, b1, b2, w)) \in c_D \Rightarrow (a1, b1) \in c_A \wedge (a2, b2) \in c_A$
- If a subactor is part of the correspondence, its superactor must be too:
  $(a, b) \in c_A \Rightarrow (\forall x: (x, a) \in L: (\exists y: (x, y) \in c_A))$

Given a correspondence $c \subseteq (X \times Y)$, we define its domain and rank as:

- $dom(c) = \{ x \in X: (\exists y \in Y: (x, y) \in c)$
- $rnk(c) = \{ y \in Y: (\exists x \in X: (x, y) \in c)$

The correspondence is not a function, since every pattern's actor and dependency can be assigned to a zero, one or several actors and dependencies of the enterprise model.

The instantiation of a pattern consists of an application of that pattern to the model's actors and dependencies in order to create a new $i*$ SD model, the context model of the enterprise. That is, starting from the pattern, the actors and dependencies that are part of the correspondence are substituted by the corresponded elements, whilst actor links from the pattern are correctly preserved and new actor links are added.

Definition. Pattern instantiation. Enterprise context model.

Given an $i*$ SD model $M = (A, D, L)$ acting as context model pattern, and given a model correspondence $C = (c_A, c_D)$ as above, we define the pattern instantiation of M by C as an SD model M_{inst}, the enterprise context model, $M_{inst} = (A_{inst}, D_{inst}, L_{inst})$, as:

$A_{inst} = rnk(c_A)$, $D_{inst} = rnk(c_D)$, $L_{inst} = corresponded(L, c_A) \cup L_{ent}$

where *corresponded* maps actors appearing in actor links according to the correspondence defined among actors:

corresponded$(L, c_A) = \{ (x, y): (a, x) \in A \wedge (b, y) \in A \wedge (a, b) \in L \}$

Fig. 5 shows an example of instantiation involving the pattern presented in Fig. 4 and the organization model presented in Fig. 2. Pattern elements are shown semi-transparent. We can see, e.g., the pattern actor CRM instantiated into one actor the Etapatelecom company (TC); another pattern actor Strategic Partner instantiated into two actors InPr and ISP; and then several pattern dependencies instantiated, e.g. Cross-Billing into another with the same name, or Economies of Scale into two other dependencies. We remark also that a dependency from the pattern, Strategic Agreements Signed, is not instantiated. The final model is composed of the colored elements.

Two indicators may help to classify the adequacy of the patterns (pattern coverage) and the extent to which an organization adheres to known patterns (model coverage).

Definition. Pattern coverage.

Given an $i*$ SD model $M = (A, D, L)$ acting as context model pattern, and given a model correspondence $C = (c_A, c_D)$, we define the coverage of M under C, $cov(M, C)$ as the percentage of elements of M that have a correspondence defined in C:

$cov_{pat}(M, c) = (\|dom(c_A)\| + \|dom(c_D)\|) / (\|A\| + \|D\|) * 100$, $\|S\|$ being the size of S.

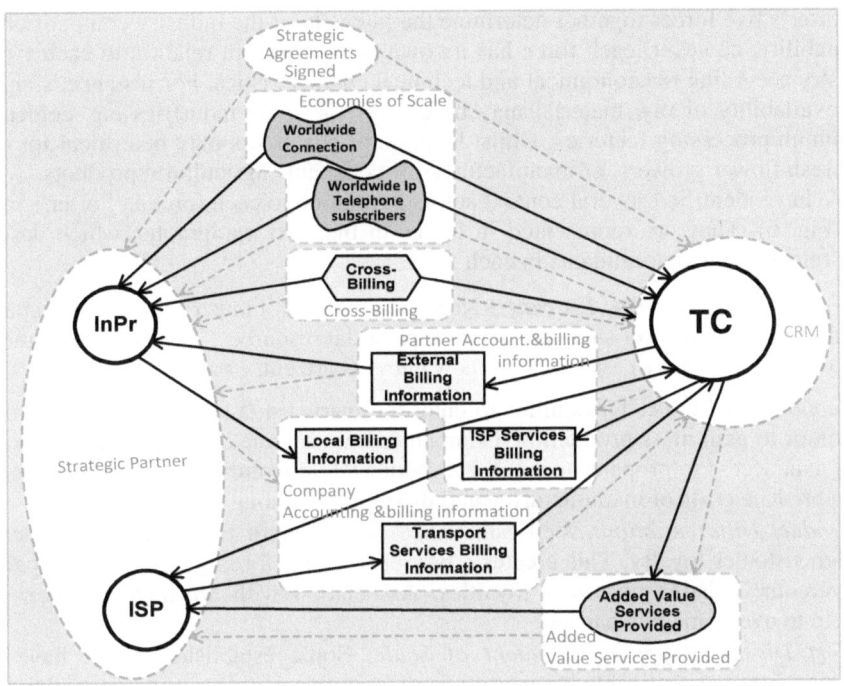

Fig. 5. Example of pattern instantiation

Definition. Model coverage.

Given an *i** SD model $M_{ent} = (A_{ent}, D_{ent}, L_{ent})$ and given a set of *i** SD models M = $\{M_k = (A_k, D_k, L_k)\}$ acting as context model patterns, and given the set of model correspondences over them C = $\{C_k = (c_{A[k]}, c_{D[k]})\}$, such that $c_{A[k]} \subseteq (A_k \times A_{ent})$ and $c_{D[k]} \subseteq (D_k \times D_{ent})$, we define the coverage of M_{ent} under M and C, $cov(M_{ent}, M, C)$, as the percentage of elements of M_{ent} that have a correspondence defined in C:

$$cov_{mod}(M, c) = \|\{a \in A_{ent}: (\exists k: a \in rnk(c_{A[k]}))\| + \|\{d \in A_{ent}: (\exists k: d \in rnk(c_{D[k]}))\|$$
$$/ (\|A_{ent}\| + \|D_{ent}\|) * 100$$

In the example above, we obtain $cov_{pat}(M, c) = 87,5\%$ and $cov_{mode}(M, c) = 100\%$.

4 Patterns for Generic Perspective of Enterprises

Porter's model of the five market forces can be used as basis to construct enterprise context models. Each of the forces has a set of *determinants* associated to them, which describe the way in which various external agents interact with the enterprise. External agents can be modeled as actors in the context of the enterprise and their interaction with the enterprise by means of strategic dependencies, describing the intentionality between them and the enterprise. In the rest of this section, we introduce the forces in detail and propose the *i** SD pattern that describes them. For space reasons, we provide thorough details just in the first force and then an overall description for the rest of forces.

Porter's five forces together determine the intensity of the industry competition and profitability, however, each force has its own prominence in relation to each type of industry according to economical and technical characteristics. For instance, suppliers and availability of raw material may be critical for some industries e.g. cement, or aluminum processing factories, whilst location of customers may be critical for other e.g. fresh flower growers, or manufacturers of perishable agricultural products.

We have identified several context actors in relation to each force in Porter's model (see Fig. 6). They are represented in italics in the next paragraphs, which describe their relation with determinants in each force.

1st. Force - Potential New Entrants: New entrants to an industry bring new capacity, the desire to gain market share and some substantial resources. The main determinants (listed in Porter's work) associated to new entrants are entry barriers:

- *Economies of scale:* Difficulties to enter the market due to higher cost of production or to gain mass production. Companies may associate with *Strategic Partners* to gain access to property technology, reduce learning curves, expand its coverage, and reduce costs of manufacturing and distribution among other.
- *Product Differentiation:* Well established firms benefit from brand identification and customer loyalty. This creates a barrier to entry, forcing entrants to expend to overcome existing customer loyalties. Association with *Strategic Partners* may help to overcome this barrier.
- *Cost Disadvantages Independent of Scale*: Some established firms have cost advantages not replicable by entrants, e.g. favorable access to raw materials. Association with *Strategic Partners* is a way to overcome cost disadvantages e.g. by providing access to raw materials.
- *Capital Requirements*: Need of *financial* resources to compete in the market, e.g. for covering start-up losses. To satisfy capital requirements 3 actors have been identified: *Owners, Financial Institutions* and *Shareholders*.

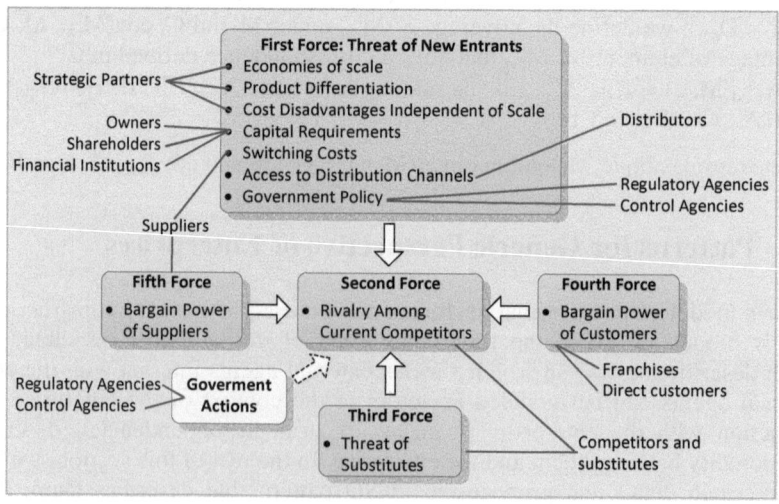

Fig. 6. Generic context actors in relation to the five market forces

- *Government Policy.* Government regulations may limit entry of new competitors, by e.g. requiring licenses or limiting access to some raw materials. We identified two actors in the environment: *Regulatory Agencies* and *Control Agencies.*
- *Access to Distribution Channels*: New *entrants* need to secure distribution of their products. In other to do so, they need to persuade channels to accept their products through price breaks and cooperative advertising, which reduces their profits. To access distribution channels companies sought to relate to *Distributors*, responsible for making product or services accessible to customers.

2ⁿᵈ· Force - Industry Competitors: Rivalry among existing competitors consists in the use of tactics to gain a better position in the market. Tactics may include price competition, advertising battles, new products introduction, and increased customer service or warranties. The force of the competition depends of several factors, e.g., number of equally balanced competitors, slow industry growth, etc.

A new actor in the environment has been identified in relation to this force, *Competitors*. They influence company's strategy and the decisions to be taken. Any change in the competition strategy will have an impact in the preferences of the customers; companies must be informed to react accordingly and maintain market share.

3ʳᵈ Force - Substitutes: Two goods are substitutes if one of them can replace the other under some circumstances, e.g., cable TV can be replaced by internet streaming services if there is enough bandwidth available. In some sectors, products or services can impose price limits if they are considered good substitutes. Substitute availability drives customers to continuously compare offers against changing costs.

In this work, we consider substitutes part of the competition. They provide alternative products and services and influence company's strategy in a similar way than competitors. Thus, the *Competitors* SCA is renamed as *Competitors and Substitutes.*

4ᵗʰ· Force - Customers: Buyers compete with the industry by forcing down prices, bargaining for higher quality or more services, and playing competitors against each other at the expense of industry profitability. Bargain strength of customer's increases under some circumstances, e.g., an important buyer group concentrates or purchases large volumes relative to seller sales.

In relation to the fourth force we identify two actors *Franchises* and *Direct Customers*. These actors are indispensable for the sustainability of a company.

5ᵗʰ· Force - Suppliers: Suppliers can exert bargaining power over an industry by threatening to raise prices or reduce the quality of purchased goods and services. Suppliers bargain strength increases when offered products or services are scarce and buyers generate large demand, bringing them to a weaker negotiation position, particularly when there are not substitutes available or the cost of replacing them is high. On the contrary, bargain power of suppliers reduces when offered goods or services are standard, there are substitutes available or there are several suppliers offering similar products or services.

In relation to this force, we identified the environment actor *Suppliers*. Companies depend on them for the provision of row materials, machinery, means of transport or infrastructure needed for their operation, product manufacture and service provision.

Table 1 describes some dependencies identified in relation to each of these actors, represented in tabular form. The table includes the description of the dependencies, their type and the direction with respect to the organization. The list of identified dependencies does not pretend to be exhaustive, but rather to reflect the dependencies that repeatedly appeared in several industrial experiences.

5   Enterprise Strategies: The CRM Case

In order to confront and balance market forces and to generate a profit, enterprises adopt several strategies. Not only differentiation and prices are considered, but also operational strategies, which allow them to focus in some market segments whit particular products and services. Well-known strategies, which categorize organizations in relation to the name of their core information systems, include ERP, CRM and SCM. For the sake of brevity, we are going to focus on one particular case, the CRM enterprise strategy. An excerpt of its *i** graphical representation is shown in Fig. 7 and dependencies in Table 2.

The CRM strategy is usually related to service enterprises [10]. These enterprises thrive and because of their importance, they have gained an increasingly prominent position. In pure service enterprises: the commercial function is carried without products; there is not direct human contact with clients; services are not storable; there are only user, operator and way to do; services are tailored to client needs; and the perceived quality is more malleable.

One of the most decisive issues is the treatment of all matters relating to staff, because of its intimate relationship with the process. CRM enterprises must be very careful whit personnel selection and training, but also of the conception of the services and the technologies required to support them.

Globalization, diversification and deregulation have increased competition. Today's customers have more options and enterprises must ensure that best clients remain loyal, at the time that new prospects begin to be loyal and profitable. This requires an intensive analysis of the front end applications used to interact with customers, such as billing, order recording and market segmentation, among others.

CRM enterprises usually handle three phases designed to bring them closer to customers; each of them having a different impact in the relationship:

- *Acquisition of new customers*: New customers are attracted by promoting services. Differential aspects shall be made evident for customers to purchase them. The value proposition must be backed up by excellent service and after-sales support.
- *Increase profitability of existing customers*: Improving existing relationship promotes cross-selling of services, increasing sales of services previously acquired by the client and thus profitability. The value of the proposition lies in an offer of convenience and lower cost.
- *Lifetime retention of good customers*: retention focuses on the adaptability of the services by not offering what the general market wants, but what existing customers need. The value of the proposition is to offer a service or product to the best interest of the client through a proactive relationship. Currently the leading companies focus more on retention than the attraction of new clients.

All phases of CRM are interrelated and provide the basis for a new organizational architecture, where business processes revolve around the needs of the client.

Table 1. Generic Context Dependencies

Generic Actor	Dependency Type	Dependency	Direction	Degree of Dependency
Strategic Partners	Goal	Strategic agreements signed	←	Critical
	Resource	Strategic agreements	←	Critical
	Soft Goal	Economies of scale achieved	←	Committed
	Soft Goal	Proprietary technology accessed	←	Committed
	Goal	Business knowledge and training Provided	←	Committed
	Goal	Product differentiated	←	Committed
	Goal	Value added to products and services	→	Critical
	Resource	Company accounting and cross-billing information	←	Critical
	Resource	Partners accounting and cross-billing information	→	Critical
	Task	Cross-billing and earnings distribution	←	Critical
Owners	Goal	Business started	←	Critical
	Resource	Opening capital	←	Critical
	Resource	Performance, accounting and management information	→	Critical
	Goal	Strategic decisions	←	Committed
	Goal	Strategic actions performed	→	Critical
Share-holders	Goal	Shares acquired	←	Critical
	Resource	Shares documents	→	Critical
	Resource	Performance Information	→	Critical
	Resource	Investment capital	←	Critical
	Soft Goal	Profit earned	→	Critical
Financial Institutions	Goal	Financial services provided	←	Committed
	Goal	Loans and mortgages provided	←	Committed
	Soft Goal	Convenient interest rates	←	Committed
	Soft Goal	Adequate payment terms	←	Committed
	Goal	Investments, Savings and checking accounts managed	←	Critical
	Resource	Financial Statements	←	Critical
	Goal	Financial services acquired	→	Critical
	Resource	loans and mortgages information	→	Critical
	Soft Goal	Timely payment	→	Committed
Distributors	Goal	Distribution channels accessed	←	Critical
	Goal	Products and services accessed by customers	←	Critical
	Soft Goal	Locations always supplied	←	Committed
	Resource	Products and services	→	Critical
Regulatory Agencies	Goal	Promulgation of laws and regulations	←	Critical
	Goal	Permits and licenses Issued	←	Critical
	Resource	Laws, regulations	←	Committed
	Resources	Operation licenses and permits	←	Critical
Control Agencies	Resource	Operation information	→	Critical
	Resource	Auditing information	←	Critical
	Goal	Compliance of laws and regulations validated	←	Critical
	Goal	Operation licenses and permits maintained	←	Critical
Competitors and substitutes	Resource	Information of products and strategy	←	Committed
	Resource	Market conditions	←	Committed
Franchises	Goal	Franchises granted	→	Critical
	Soft Goal	Quality of products and services preserved	←	Critical
	Goal	Massive access to customers	←	Committed
	Resource	Operation resources	→	Critical
Direct Customers	Goal	Products and services acquired	←	Critical
	Soft Goal	Quality of products and services	→	Critical
	Soft Goal	Convenient prices	→	Critical
	Resource	Products and services	→	Critical
Suppliers	Goal	Access to Specialized technology, products and services	←	Critical
	Resources	Especialiced technology, products and services	←	Critical
	Soft Goal	Costs and conditions kept stable	←	Committed
	Soft Goal	Quality of products and services	←	Committed
	Soft Goal	Timely payments	→	Committed

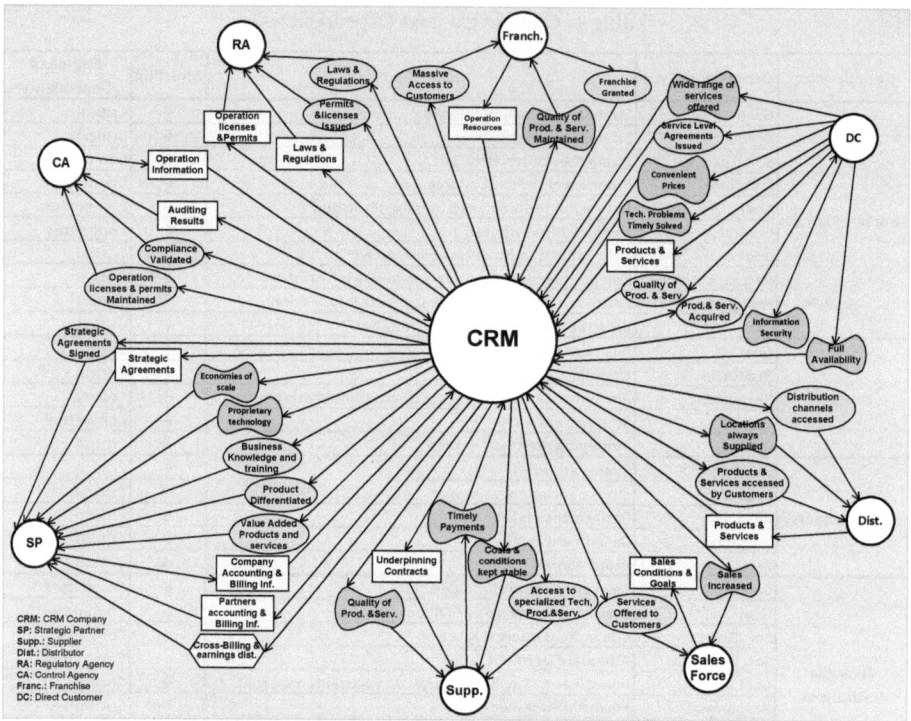

Fig. 7. Excerpt of the CRM Enterprise Context Model Pattern

The CRM patterns in built upon the actors and dependencies identified in Section 4 for Porter's model (i.e., enterprise strategy patterns are designed as an extension of Porter's *i** SD model). New actors have been identified for CRM organizations: *Market Research and strategy Organizations* and *Sales Force*. The first one helps CRM organizations to study and analyze the market, to identify specific market segments and potential services required by their customers. These organizations also help in the evaluation of customer's satisfaction and perception of quality of services. Sales forces help to promote and advertise services, to close sales and thus to increase sales.

6   The Patterns in the Practice

The patterns resulting from our work have emerged from a post-mortem analysis of two large industrial experiences related to the CRM strategy, and later validated in some academic exercises. We are currently using the ERP pattern in an ongoing industrial project. In this section, we will focus on the CRM case. The two projects are the Etapatelecom company case described in more detail in Subsection 6.1, whilst the second project was the formulation of an IT Strategic Plan for an airport. In both cases we applied the DHARMA method. We involved in the post-mortem analysis some selected stakeholders that participated in the use of DHARMA.

Table 2. CRM specific context dependencies

Generic Actor	Dependency Type	Dependency	Direction
Strategic Partners	Goal	Services packaged and offered as combos	←
	Goal	Complementary services provided	←
	Soft Goal	Quality of services improved	←
	Soft Goal	Access to new locations	←
Control Agencies	Resource	Customers support and complains reports	←
Direct Customers	Soft Goal	Wide range of services offered	→
	Soft Goal	Appropriated rates and fees	→
	Soft Goal	Information kept secure	→
	Soft Goal	Full availability	→
	Soft Goal	Customers fidelity	←
	Goal	Service level agreements issued	→
	Resource	SLAS	→
	Soft Goal	Timely attention and solution to Problems	→
Suppliers	Goal	Underpinning contracts established	←
	Resources	Underpinning contracts	←
Sales Force	Goal	Service offered to customers	←
	Soft Goal	Service sales closed	←
	Soft Goal	Sales Increased	←
	Resource	Sales conditions & Goals	←
Market research and strategy	Goal	Market surveys issued	←
	Goal	Marked analyzed	←
	Soft Goal	Marked segmentation	←
	Goal	Customers satisfaction evaluated	←
	Soft Goal	Customer needs and requirements identified	←

Concerning academic validation, we remark a project conducted by university students under our direction, in which the context of the institution was modeled guided by the elements in the pattern. The validation was successful, meaning that the resulting context model for the institution was completely obtained from the CRM pattern (in other words, its model coverage was 100%).

6.1   The Telecom Company Case Study

In order to illustrate the practical use of the patterns, the Etapatelecom company (TC) case has been selected. The company provides broadband Internet access and fixed telephone services in Ecuador.

To fulfill its deployment strategy, the TC had to face the selection and adoption of several technologies, and the DHARMA method was used to define its enterprise architecture. Being a utility company, the TC aligns with the CRM strategy. The context model constructed for that case (together with other cases outlined in subsection 6.3) was later used to define the patterns described in this paper. Therefore, it provides good examples to support the practical application of the patterns described in the next literal.

6.2   Applying Patterns to the TC Case

In Section 3, we have provided the formalization of the pattern concept. On top of this formalization, we need to have a casuistic that facilitates their use. Practical application of the patterns is conducted in a systematic way. Each actor and then each dependency in the pattern are reviewed in order to identify their particular instances in the context of the organization under analysis. In this way some typical cases may appear. In this subsection, we illustrate this casuistic using the TC case as if it had been defined as an instance of the CRM pattern.

When analyzing actors, three instantiation cases may emerge (see Figure 8a for the definition and Figure 9 for the examples). In the case of actors, we apply definitions of Section 3 over concrete instances of the following models:

- CRM pattern: $CRM = (A_{crm}, D_{crm}, L_{crm})$
- Elements of TC: (A_{tc}, D_{tc}, L_{tc})
- Correspondence to be defined: $C_{tc} = (c_A, c_D)$

1) *One-to-one actor's instantiation.* An actor in the pattern is instantiated by an actor in the context of the organization. This is the case of the *Franchise* actor included in the CRM pattern that has been instantiated by the *Telecenter Franchise* actor from TC

$$Franchise \in A_{crm} \wedge TelecenterFranchise \in A_{tc} \wedge (Franchise, TelecenterFranchise) \in c_A$$

2) *One-to-many actor's instantiation.* An actor in the pattern is instantiated by many actors in the context of the organization. This may happen in two different situations: a) several actors need to collaborate together to provide the intention of the pattern actor; b) the enterprise actor related to the GCA is very generic and is subtyped into several others using is-a. As an example of b), the *Direct Customers* actor in the CRM pattern has been instantiated by *Subscriber* which at its turn is subtyped into *Public Telephone User* and the *Home Telephone User* actors in the context of ETP.

$$DirectCustomers \in A_{crm} \wedge HomeTelephoneUser \in A_{tc} \wedge$$
$$PublicTelephoneUser \in A_{tc} \wedge Susbscriber \in A_{tc} \wedge$$
$$(Subscriber, PublicTelephoneUser) \in L_{tc} \wedge (Subscriber, HomeTelephoneUser) \in L_{tc} \wedge$$
$$(DirectCustomers, Subscriber) \in c_A \wedge (DirectCustomers, PublicTelephoneUser) \in c_A \wedge$$
$$(DirectCustomers, HomeTelephoneUser) \in c_A$$

3) *Null actor's instantiation.* One actor in the pattern cannot be instantiated by any actor in the context of an organization. This is the case of the Sales Force CRM actor, which has not instances in the TC context. Sales force of this organization is internal, thus no relation exist with other organizations.

$$SalesForce \in A_{crm} \wedge SalesForce \notin dom(A_{tc})$$

Table 3 sums up the relation among actors in the CRM Pattern and their instances identified in the TC case (actors with no instances have been omitted due to space limitations). Fig. 9 presents an excerpt of the instantiation of the CRM organization Pattern in the TC case.

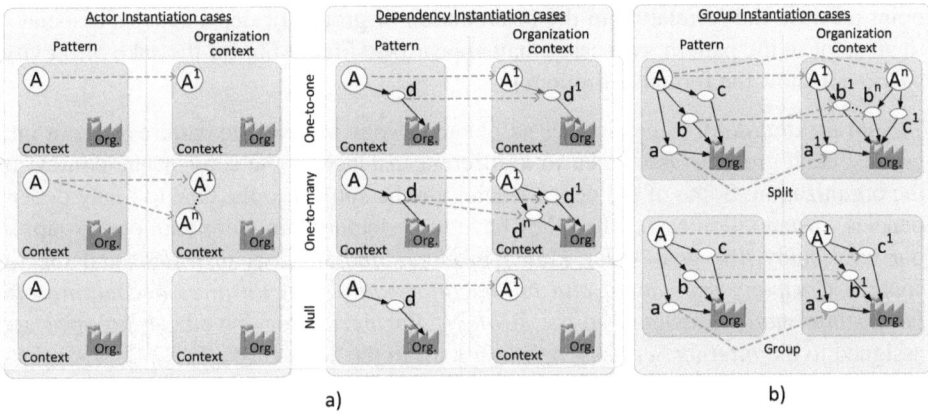

Fig. 8. (a) Actors and Dependency instantiation cases; b) dependency group instantiation cases

Similarly to actors, when analyzing individual dependencies associated to an actor in the pattern, three instantiation cases have been identified (see Figure 8a).

4) *One-to-one dependency instantiation.* A dependency associated to one actor in the pattern is instantiated by one dependency associated to an instance of the actor in the context of the enterprise. So, the softgoals *Full availability*, *Information Security*, and *Wide range of services offered* associated to the *Direct Customers* actor in the pattern, have been instantiated by the soft goals *Full availability*, *Information Security* and *World Wide Connection* associated to the *Subscriber* actor in the context of TC.

$$d1=(WideRangeOfServicesOffered,DirectCustomer,CRM,softg)\in D_{crm} \wedge$$
$$d2=(WorldWideConnection,Subscriber,TC,softg)\in D_{tc} \wedge (d1, d2)\in c_D$$

(Correctness condition on actors holds, e.g. $(CRM, TC)\in c_A$).

5) *One-to-many dependency instantiation.* A dependency associated to one actor in the pattern is instantiated by many dependency associated to an instance of the actor in the context of the organization. In this case, the pattern dependency is considered too coarse for its use in the enterprise context model and thus it is assigned to several dependencies that altogether provide the required intentionality. This is the case of the soft goal *Economies of scale* associated to the *Strategic Partner* actor in the pattern, which has been instantiated by the soft goals *Worldwide connection* and *Access to worldwide IP telephone subscribers* associated to the *Interconnection Provider* actor in the context of *TC*. (The formal definition is similar to the case 2) and is not included for the sake of brevity.)

6) *Null dependency instantiation.* A dependency associated to one actor in the pattern has no instances associated to an instance of the actor in the context of the organization. This is the case of the goal *Strategic Agreements Signed* associated to the *Strategic Partner* actor in the pattern, which has no instances in the case of *Interconnection Provider* actor. Interconnection is mandatory among telephone service providers in the country where TC operates, therefore this goal was not considered. From the structural

point of view and in relation to the instantiation of groups of dependencies associated to an actor in the pattern, two cases may appear (see Figure 6b; for the sake of brevity, we do not show the formal definitions).

7) *Split instantiation.* Dependencies associated to one actor in the pattern are split into groups; each group is associated to a different instance of the actor in the context of the organization. Some of the dependencies can be subject to the One to many dependencies' instantiation case, when they have to be included in more than one group. In our case study, the goal *Value added products and services provided*, and the resources *Company accounting and billing information* and *Partners accounting and billing information*, assigned to the *Strategic Partners* actor, have been grouped and assigned to the *Internet Service Providers* actor in the context of *TC*.

8) *Group Instantiation.* All of the dependencies associated to an actor in the pattern (or the ones for which instances exists in the context of the organization), are associated to a single instance of the actor in the context of the organization e.g., the *Direct User* dependencies in the pattern and the *Subscriber* dependencies in the TC context.

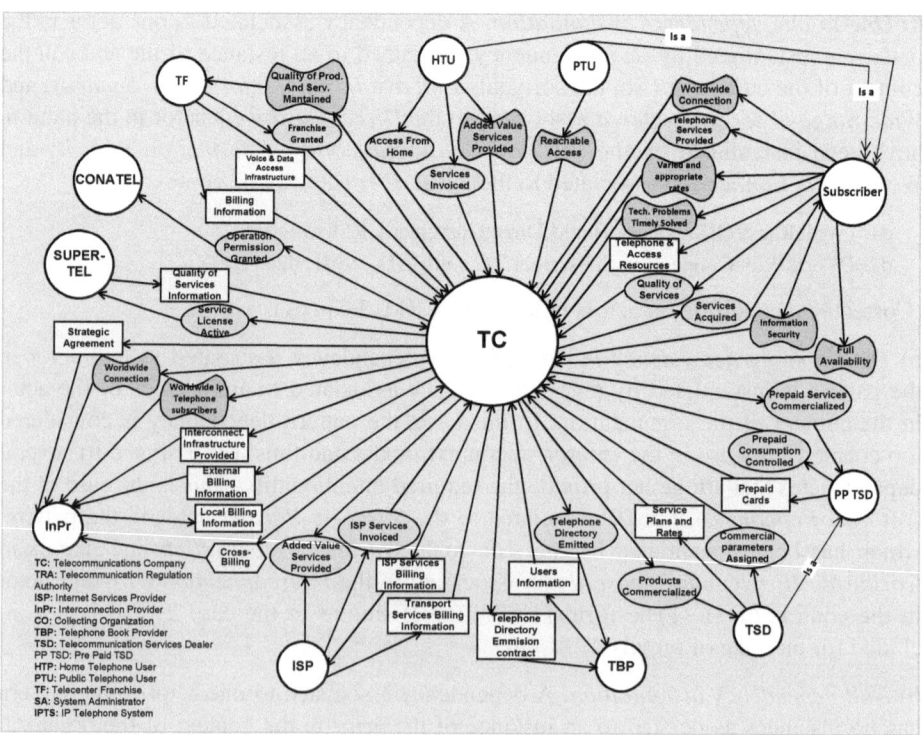

Fig. 9. Excerpt of the instantiation of the CRM organization Pattern in the TC case

Table 3. Actors in the CRM strategy pattern and their instances in the TC case

Actor in Pattern	Instance
Strategic Partners	Interconnection Provider (InPr); Internet Services Provider (ISP); Cable TV Provider (TVP)
Owners	TC Owner
Share-holders	-
Financial Institutions	Banks
Distributors	Telecommunication Services Dealer (TSD); Prepaid TSD (PP TSD)
Regulatory Agencies	National Consul of Telecommunications (NCT)
Control Agencies	Telecommunication Superintendence (ST); Internal Revenue Service; Company's Superintendence
Competitors and Substitutes	Fixed Telephone Companies; Mobile Telecom Companies
Franchises	Telecentre Franchise (TF)
Direct Customers	Subscriber; Home Teleph. User (HTU); Public Teleph. User (PTU)
Suppliers	Telephone Book Provider (TBP)
Sales Force	-
Market Research&Strategy	MR; Deloitte Touche Tohmatsu

6.3   Some Numbers

As mentioned above, the CRM pattern was obtained from two industrial cases and later validated with academic cases, in particular one of the validation cases was of similar size than the two industrial cases and is the one reported here. In Table 4 we present the three cases with the coverage of model and pattern detailed by type of element and the grand total. In the case of the two industrial cases, since this is a post-mortem analysis, it should be interpreted as what could have happen if the pattern would have existed in advance. We may see that the two coverage measures are good enough. From the point of view of the models obtained, most of the actors of the enterprise context model are bound to CRM pattern actors, except for one actor in each context model. Dependencies also are mostly result of instantiation from the pattern. From the point of view of pattern coverage, percentages show that the pattern captures the needs of an enterprise that applies the CRM strategy.

With respect to the academic validation case, we obtained the University model applying directly the CRM pattern, and the fundamental result was that the model obtained from the pattern was good enough as to consider unnecessary to add more elements, so model coverage was 100% (probably an extreme case). The coverage of the pattern was even greater than in the two industrial cases: even if the model in the academic case does not identify dependencies for all 28 actors, the numbers point out to an increase in the number of dependencies identified when using the pattern. However, this fact shall be validated with future experiences.

Table 4. Numbers in relation to the industrial and academic cases

	TC case			Airport case			Academic Case		
	nb. elements	model coverage	pattern coverage	nb. elements	model coverage	pattern coverage	nb. elements	model coverage	pattern coverage
actors	20	95%	90%	26	97%	90%	28	100%	93%
goal dep.	20	85%	83%	56	80%	91%	126	100%	87%
softg dep.	18	73%	90%	38	79%	85%	83	100%	92%
res. dep.	20	80%	84%	32	90%	82%	75	100%	86%
TOTAL	78	83%	87%	152	87%	87%	312	100%	90%

6.4   Applicability Issues

In the case studies conducted so far, we have learned some practical tips that may help in making a winning case when applying the presented approach:

- Define a multidisciplinary team before starting the process, to support the analysis. Include staff at least from financial, legal, marketing and commercial department.
- Provide basic training to participants about the modeling concepts. Conduct the training sessions in short (max. 2 hours) workshops.
- In training workshops, sketch first a simplified version of the *i** SD model representing the pattern and provide sample dependencies to clarify concepts.
- As a first step in the construction of context model of the organization, use actors in the patterns as checklist (one at the time) and identify all of their instances in the context of the organization. Include them in a two columns table: the first column for actors in the pattern and the second one their associated instances in the context of the organization.
- Next, use the dependencies associated to actors in the pattern as checklist to identify their instances in relation to each identified actor instance in the context of the organization. Sketch partial *i** SD models to record and discuss about identified dependency instances with participants.
- When working with stakeholders, as a general rule: do not try to draw perfect *i** models. Just draw quick sketches including 2 or 3 actors maximum (preferable instances of a same actor in the pattern). Graphical conventions as those included in [3] and also in this paper (e.g., tabular representation of models) can be used.
- Add additional columns to the table to include dependency description, type and direction, as shown in Tables 1 to 3. Record in these columns all dependencies identified regarding each actor.
- Do not try to address all actor instances in a single workshop. It is better to conduct several shorter meetings addressing instances of single actor (or groups of actors) in the pattern at the time.
- Draw the final *i** SD context model only when all the dependencies have been identified and tabulated.
- Draw complete *i** context models only when specifically required and with proper justifications. *i** graphic representation is great for brainstorming and discussing with meeting participants, but large models tend to be confusing and costly in terms of time. Partial diagrams are just as good and easier to draw.

7   Conclusions

In this paper, we have presented a pattern-based approach for constructing intentional context models as *i** SD diagrams. To this aim, we have analyzed a general model for enterprises, Porter's model; one particular example of enterprise strategy, the CRM strategy; we have formulated patterns for this strategy; and we have studied the results of applying the patterns to some cases.

The main advantage of our approach is its industrial applicability, in terms of theory, scalability and orientation:

- The patterns synthesize knowledge about business strategies, making it accessible to requirements engineers and helping to close the gap between them and enterprisers since they can be used as communication bridge among technical and administrative staff.
- Being based on solid theories like the Porter's model and enterprise strategies like CRM, they provide a general foundation that applies to a lot of enterprises.
- The level of detail (thanks to the solid foundation) including much more model elements that other existing proposals, makes it feasible to apply to real cases.
- It is also important to remark that the pattern-based approach has been formally defined using an algebraic formulation of *i** as baseline. This is also a differentiating characteristic compared to other pattern-based approaches.

In addition to the context model patterns presented in this work, which resulted from the application of the first activity of the DHARMA method in industrial and academic experiences, we are also working on system context patterns and hybrid systems architectural patterns for generic ERP, CRM and SCM strategies. These patterns resulted from the application of the second, third and fourth activities of the DHARMA method.

References

1. Alexander, C.: The Timeless Way of Building. Oxford Univ. Pr. (1979)
2. Yu, E.: Modelling Strategic Relationships for Process Reengineering. PhD. University of Toronto (1995)
3. Carvallo, J.P., Franch, X.: On the Use of *i** for Architecting Hybrid Systems: A Method and an Evaluation Report. In: Persson, A., Stirna, J. (eds.) PoEM 2009. LNBIP, vol. 39, pp. 38–53. Springer, Heidelberg (2009)
4. Porter, M.E.: Competitive Strategy. Free Press (1990)
5. Steinberg, M.: Enterprise Applications: A Conceptual Look at ERP, CRM, and SCM. Hill Associates Inc. (2006)
6. Coyne, K.P., Balakrishnan, S.: The McKinsey Quarterly 4 (1996)
7. Fuxman, A., Giorgini, P., Kolp, M., Mylopoulos, J.: Information Systems as Social Structures. In: FOIS 2001, pp. 10–21. ACM Press (2001)
8. Kolp, M., Giorgini, P., Mylopoulos, J.: Information Systems Development through Social Structures. In: SEKE 2002, pp. 183–190. ACM Press (2002)
9. The *i** Wiki, http://istar.rwth-aachen.de/tiki-view_articles.php
10. Turban, E., et al.: Information Technology for Management: Transforming Business in the Digital Economy. John Wiley & Sons (2002)
11. Anderson, K., Kerr, C.: Customer Relationships Management. Mc.Graw Hill (2002)

Method Support of Large-Scale Transformation in the Insurance Sector: Exploring Foundations

Nils Labusch and Robert Winter

Institute of Information Management, University of St. Gallen, Mueller-Friedberg-Strasse 8,
9000 St. Gallen, Switzerland
{Nils.Labusch,Robert.Winter}@unisg.ch

Abstract. Many enterprises need to handle programs that impose fundamental changes to the organization as well as the supporting IT systems. While general guidance for such transformations in form of methods, reference models, principles, etc. is available, the specific context of the insurance sector is often not considered. We conducted an interview series with informants from major European insurance companies to explore the specifics of enterprise transformation in the insurance sector. The results suggest amending existing transformation support methods by regarding transformation triggers, transformation program types and core techniques. E.g., transformations that deal with standardization, mergers and acquisitions and internal alignment are not sufficiently covered yet and techniques that deal with soft and social aspects of transformations are less visible in the insurance sector. Our findings create not only the basis for a wider survey to extend and validate initial findings, but also for comparing and discussing concrete enterprise transformation cases.

Keywords: transformation, insurance, techniques, method, empirical study.

1 Introduction

Enterprises need to pass through major transformations. Rouse [1] defines such enterprise transformation (ET) not as routine but "fundamental change that substantially alters an organization's relationships with one or more key constituencies, e.g., customers, employees, suppliers, and investors". ET can involve new value propositions (like products and services) or change the inner structure of the enterprise. Further, ET could involve old value propositions provided in fundamentally new ways [1]. Examples are mergers & acquisitions, detachment of host systems or other efforts that are reflected in strategic planning. Unfortunately, many ETs are not or only partially successful, often because enterprises do not maintain an appropriate transformation capability [2].

The insurance sector is affected by major ETs only recently. In the past, the business model in the sector was very stable [3]. This changed in recent years: ET is induced by changing legislation and regulation (e.g. the Solvency act) [4] as much as increasing cost pressure e.g. induced by the changing situation on the financial markets and the financial crisis. The context of the ETs is difficult for manifold

S. Aier et al. (Eds.): TEAR 2012 and PRET 2012, LNBIP 131, pp. 60–78, 2012.

reasons. First, the inner culture of the insurances is rather traditional – major ETs were not necessary in the past. Second, contracts with customers need to be kept and managed for long periods, even longer than those of banks. This leads e.g. to IT systems that are sometimes many decades in use [5]. Third, national differences need to be considered. On the one hand, the legislation differs, on the other hand market structure and customer demands force the insurance companies to strive away from their traditional business models [3].

In order to deal with these challenges, sound methods can provide guidance and avoid major and expensive failure. Incorporating the industry context proved already valuable to be in other related areas [6] and methods [7]. In order to develop these methods, it is important to understand, which *techniques* (thus, possible ways in which the results e.g. the successful ET can be achieved [8]) are necessary or effective in a certain situation. We concentrate on techniques in the paper at hand, since many of these are already existent in the companies (examples are techniques also applied in program management, like goal definition or milestone planning) and guidance about which techniques to concentrate on during the ET. Because of the complexity of the ET, single solutions cannot be expected to fit all problems, the design and engineering of guidance however needs to consider the specifics of the current problem [9]. As a compromise between (economic) 'one size-fits-all' solutions and (most effective) problem-specific ones, usually a handful of problem situations are differentiated that cluster related design problems [10]. These situations are usually specified by a combination of *context factors* (e.g. size of the industry) with certain *program types* [8]. Depending on the situation, different techniques might be appropriate in order to handle the specific situation.

Because of the specific products, services and the induced challenges and goals in the insurance market that differ from other industries, we assume that effective ET guidance needs to include assistance about where to focus on during an ET. Therefore, in order to provide ET guidance for the insurance industry, we need to investigate the detailed context of the industry and triggers that imply certain types of ET. Further we need to know which techniques are necessary or obligatory in order to conduct successful ET programs in this industry sector. This paper aims at exploring the insurance setting and the identification of aspects that differ from generic ET guidance. Thus we propose the following research question:

RQ: What are context, triggers, program types, core techniques of enterprise transformation in the insurance sector?

We discuss the related work in section two. We go on by presenting our research approach in section three. The results are presented in section four and summarizing propositions are drawn. In section five we discuss these propositions and their influence on the guidance of ET in the insurance sector. Section six provides a summary and outlook.

2   Related Work

Manifold methods and approaches to deal with fundamental changes in organizations have been proposed. We conducted a literature database search including for-and backward search in order to identify approaches that concentrate on fundamentally changing the business and less on an optimization of the day-to-day activities. Findings reveal approaches like total quality management (TQM) which gained attention almost 20 years ago, focusing on aspects like quality awareness, continuous improvement, quality measuring and control [11]. A more recent approach is Six Sigma, a method that deals with the improvement of processes in organizations [12]. However, these approaches focus on continuous improvement and do not include specific techniques relevant for ETs. Six Sigma further is related to industrial application and thus less appropriate for the insurance context [13].

Relevant findings that concentrate on fundamental changes and thus ET are rare. One approach that we identified is the business engineering framework by Oesterle & Winter [14] which proposes the identification of drivers and goals of ETs by explicitly including business as much as IT-related aspects. A more recent approach proposed by SAP is Business Transformation Management Methodology (BTM^2) – a practice driven approach that includes well-known disciplines like strategic management, process management project and portfolio management which are integrated by means of an additional discipline called meta management [15]. Such meta-management offers a cyclic and iterative phase model for ETs (envision, engage, transform and optimize), a structure including roles and activities, provision of measures, skill development support and principles to conduct ET programs. However, the approach does not provide context-oriented guidance like industry specific extensions for the insurance sector.

Another approach is introduced by Baumoel [16, 17]. The author developed a situational method to support ET programs. The approach is based on interviews with informants from different industries, case studies with heterogeneous types of ETs and the analysis of ET-related methods. The approach aims at investigating which techniques were successfully applied in specific situations of ET. In order to identify the specific situations, a list of influence factors was created. Such influence factors for example are the process architecture, the available capabilities, the structure of competition, power structures, existing measures and many more. The analyzed cases are clustered according to these influence factors into five clusters of ET situations: "strategy adaptation", "communication and interaction with customers and business network", "growth strategies and cultural aspects in a technological context", "process engineering and process redesign" and "improvement of agility of the organization". In the next step, the author analyzes whether there is a systematic relationship between the successful application of certain techniques and the ET situation. The analysis yields some techniques that have been successfully applied in every ET, no matter which specific situation is present, while some other techniques have been successfully applied only in specific ET situations. Figure 1 illustrates the concept of situation specific technique application.

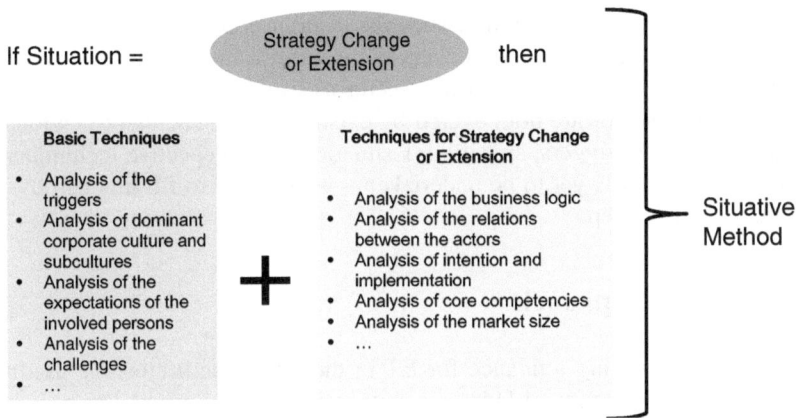

Fig. 1. Basic Concept of the Baumoel Approach (based on [16, 17])

Once a situation is identified (e.g. "Strategy Change or Extension"), Baumoel's method provides guidance on how to deal with such an ET program. This especially includes a list of techniques that should be applied because these techniques have been successfully applied in "similar" ETs, i.e. in the same ET situation. In a concrete ET, the identification of the respective situation together with the choice of appropriate (= generally applicable plus situation specific) techniques constitute a situational ET support method.

Baumoel's approach provides some insights that provide a starting point regarding our research question. It is designed however to deal with ET in general. The underlying interviews and cases were conducted in many industries; the coverage of insurance companies remains unclear.

While Baumoel's approach focuses on the techniques applied during an ET, other approaches focus on capabilities [18], roles of individuals or corporate functions [19, 20] or governance structures [21]. From our point of view, all of them are important since we share the understanding of Purchase et al. [22] who consider the ET activities as occurring in a complex system environment. Each of these perspectives on ET therefore presents an important aspect that together support a holistic view on ET. However, in this paper we narrow down the focus on the techniques perspective for the following reason: Staw & Epstein [23] discuss the impact of different techniques on the firms performance. While not finding a significant influence in the industrial context, Iseri-Say et al. [24] identify positive influences in the context of a more heterogeneous industry mix (e.g. service and production sector). They further show how single techniques differ in their positive business impact. This provides evidence for the importance of the industry sector and motivates the focus on techniques as a general managerial value driver.

Summarized, related work implies that (1) ET is a complex challenge that needs guidance, e.g. by method support, (2) the existing approaches differ in their degree of detail according to the described techniques and situations, and (3) applying such an approach yields techniques that are most relevant in certain situations. Although these findings are widely accepted, some issues for insurance companies remain: None of the discussed approaches explicitly covers the insurance industry at this time. Therefore, the specific detailed context of this sector as well as specific ET situations that exist (only) in this sector are not covered by existing work. The identification of specific context, specific triggers, specific ET situations and respective techniques of ET in the insurance sector is yet to be undertaken – we prepare to fill this gap by exploring the field in a first step.

3   Research Approach

Given the limited existing guidance for ET in the insurance sector, we used the approach introduced by Baumoel [16] as a foundation for our work. The reason is the solid base with identified techniques, program types and the empirical foundation. We conducted a multiple case study approach guided by Eisenhardt [25]. Such an approach usually yields robust and generalizable findings [26].

3.1   Data Collection in Literature and Interviews

In order to gain detailed insight to the context in the insurance industry we conducted literature search by following guidance provided e.g. by vom Brocke et al. [27] and Webster & Watson [28]. Since we wanted to identify as many ET triggers and context factors ahead of the interview phase, we conducted a general database search and did not restrict this search by concentrating on major journals or conferences. However, we restricted the search by filtering research areas in order to keep the focus on the guiding research question (e.g. we excluded medical articles). We further aimed at the identification of case studies related to the topic. We applied the following search terms:

- "Insurance Industry" AND (Challenge* OR defiance*)
- Transform AND "insurance industry"
- Change AND insurance
- Topic=("case study") AND Topic=(change) AND Topic=(insurance)
- Topic=("case study") AND Topic=(transform*) AND Topic=(insurance)

We surveyed the results by reading the abstracts and finalizing the decision if an article was relevant for further inclusion in the research process. We decided to only include articles that deal with ET in the insurance context or such that provide probably relevant context factors. In addition to the structured search, we conducted reverse searches by surveying the references of articles we found during the first search steps. We further added sources that were already known in the research group in order to provide a rich foundation for the preparation of the interviews.

Based on the surveyed literature, we developed the questionnaire for the interviews. The questionnaire starts with biographical questions about the company and the informant's role in that company. We move on with open questions about the market environment of the company (like "Are there dominant strategies that insurance companies execute?). We move on to open, ET related questions (e.g. "If you compare different ET programs, what is important to achieve success?"). We asked the interviewee to think about concrete ET programs he/she is part of and to illustrate these. We related the following questions to these examples in order to allow for a court-room questioning style of interviewing [29]. We asked primarily about the extent, the scope and the success of the ET in the following part of the questionnaire. We further asked for situations by providing and discussing five reference situations based on Baumoel [16, 17] that we slightly modified (concerning the wording) in order to increase their understandability and relevance for the insurance industry. We ended the questionnaire with closed questions like ("Which of those techniques have been necessary in order to be successful in the ET?"). We provided a list of techniques, also based on Baumoel [16, 17] that according to the method are always necessary to be conducted (basic class). We discussed with the interview partners if this is the case or if ET programs have been successful even without considering those techniques.

We conducted the interviews face-to-face or via telephone, depending on the availability of the interviewees or the local distance. For the phone interviews we incorporated guidelines given by Burke & Miller [30] like providing the questionnaire upfront or being aware of the difficulties of the communication channel. We relied on additional data sources like reports offered by the insurances (e.g. the annual reports), publically available information about the interviewees (e.g. social network profiles), press releases, websites, field notes etc. The triangulation of such sources increases the robustness of the resulting findings [31]. Our informants were all highly knowledgeable managers or C-level assistants. We used snowball sampling [32] in order to get in contact with further interview partners in the same case company (thus, we included the question "Do you know colleagues that could provide insight to this topic?"). All interviews were recorded and transcribed in order to allow for further processing by different researchers. We transcribed the interview in the language we discussed with participants. Extracts presented in this paper are translated for understandability reasons. Some informants did not allow full transcripts but only summaries of the interviews. In order to avoid biases of informants, whenever possible we interviewed more than one person for each case. We asked the informants to focus on their own experiences and tried to find examples that are not located too far away in the past. We further tried to avoid questioning that allows informants to speculate [19]. We further promised our informants to keep their and their company`s anonymity in order to allow them for providing honest answers.

3.2   Informants

Our informants are working with three European insurance companies that provide life and non-life insurance for private and business customers. All informants are located in departments that allow for a broad overview of the programs and programs executed and those that belong to ETs. Our informant from INSURANCE1 conducted large-scale IT programs, before changing to the business side of the insurance. Our informant from INSURANCE2 is mostly dealing with transformations from a financial point of view. The informants from INSURANCE3 are located in the C-level offices related to IT (INSURANCE3a) or business operations (INSURANCE3b).

3.3   Data Analysis

We followed recommendations for multiple case studies by Eisenhardt [25] and used within-case and cross case analysis. We used the software Atlas.Ti in order to conduct a first open coding. We used the graphical functions of Atlas.Ti in order to cluster the codes in a purposeful way to get an overview concerning the constructs we were searching for. We used cross-case analysis for the following purposes: First, we aksed our informants about their experience concerning triggers of certain program types. By comparing the answers of different informants, we could combine those into a mapping. Second, we compared the informant's perceptions about the value and necessity of certain techniques we provided them with.

4   Findings

In this section we provide our findings from literature search and case interviews. We especially present triggers for ET programs, context factors, classes of ET programs and techniques concerning the insurance industry.

4.1   Triggers for Enterprise Transformations

The literature analysis revealed several potential driving factors for ET programs. Especially a large-scale study by Fuernthaler et al. [3] provided challenges in the insurance industry that we interpreted as potential ET triggers. However, in the cases we asked the informants about their perception of triggering factors. We could relate most of them to the identified potential factors of the literature analysis. Table 1 provides evidence for the relevant drivers for ET programs.

Table 1. Potential Trigger for ETs in the Insurance Sector

	Evidence Literature	Evidence Case Studies
Regulation	Regulation [3, 4]	"There is the whole insurance contract legislation, the small revision. Right now that is in parliament and will for sure affect us." (INSURANCE1). Legislation imposes changes to the insurances un strategic and operational level (INSURANCE2).
Environmental Risks	Climate change fosters risks [33, 34]	
	Risks induced by terrorism [35]	
New Service & Product Offers	Fee-based advisory services will gain [3]	"If the customer has a fire and needs to interrupt operations, somebody comes and does not just consult about the insurance but also about how to make the company safe. Also for private persons" (INSURANCE1)
	Change of sold service: Awareness of prevention as an alternative to remedying [3]	"Consulting […] what you can do before the damage occurs" (INSURANCE1)
	Growth opportunities e.g. with capital financed retirement products [3]	
		Emerging markets need different services and products (INSURANCE3b)
New Customer Expectations	Changing customer behavior [3]	Customer retention and customer relationships become important (INSURANCE2). Products need to be offered that flexibly adapt to customer's life situation (INSURANCE3b).
	Increasing focus on more differentiated target groups [3]	
	Individualization & Personal marketing is very important [3]	
	Multi-channel sales necessary [3]	
		Social media as new contact channel (INSURANCE3b)
		Demographic change imposes challenges (INSURANCE3b)

Table 1. (continued)

	Evidence Literature	Evidence Case Studies
Pressure to reduce costs	Lower willingness to pay of customers [3]	"Cost pressure – people compare, if too many costs are displayed" (INSURANCE1) Costs need to be reduced (INSURANCE2)
	Banks as major competitors [3]	
	Price more important than brand [36]	
		"Of course there are the deep market interests that are apparent at the moment. The whole single life and collective life business is no longer lucrative, thus, new products are needed" (INSURANCE1)

Summarized, the evidence from the literature search was confirmed in the interviews. However, concerning the aspects of climate change and terrorisms induced risks, those were not mentioned in the interviews. We assume two reasons: First, handling risks is the core business of insurances [37], thus these new risks are not perceived as fundamental change but rather an evolution of the current core business model. Insurances developed a high maturity in dealing with such risks [3]. Some of those risks are difficult or impossible to insure anyway [38]. Second, our informants are located on managerial levels and less in the calculation of risks premiums. Concluding, we do not consider the environmental risks as a reason for ET further on. Summarized, we state the following proposition:

Proposition 1: Potential trigger for enterprise transformation programs are (1) regulation, (2) new service and product offers, (3) new customer expectations and (4) pressure to reduce costs.

4.2   Context of Enterprise Transformations

ETs take place in a certain market and enterprise environment. The insurance market is rather stable concerning to the perceptions of our informants. Especially growth is not a primary goal of the insurance companies [3], e.g. since efficient distribution networks are already in place [39]. However, while not fostering growth in general, selecting the right customers is considered crucial. As an example, our informant from INSURANCE1 explained, that customers are classified into A, B, C and D categories. A-customers a treated with a special high service quality, meanwhile D customers the insurance tries to even get rid of. The insurance that handles the classification of customers in A to D classes in the best manner, will gain the best market revenues.

ET programs are strongly challenged by the availability of resources. Insurances are tackled by an inability to get access to qualified workers [3]. That leads to problems in the programs. While money is not considered to be a major problem, resource scarcity is crucial. Key persons in a program that have know-how are crucial for the success need to be kept in the program from beginning to end and should not be taken away by other programs.

The organizational structure usually is functional or organized in divisions. According to our informants, process oriented organizational structures are appearing more and more. The understanding about the extent of ETs in the insurances is almost the same like in general literature [1]. In INSURANCE1 the first discussed ET program affected three departments; the second discussed program affected seven departments. In INSURANCE2 the program affected also the whole organization. In INSURANCE3a the ETs affected the whole division in the area of IT or strategic development.

A low willingness to innovate that literature reveals [3] could not be confirmed by our informants. At least in the last time, product innovation or the need to change modes of working is seen in the insurances. INSURANCE2 and INSURANCE3 for example introduced new insurance products that in one case combined insurance with financial products; INSURANCE1 shifted the focus of its products to prevention. Because of the long-time stable business model of insurances (INSURANCE3b), the need for such innovation however occurred later than in other industries.

Summarized, the context of the ET is determined by a stable market with surprisingly (compared to the saturated traditional market) low cost pressure, where the actors needed to innovate in in order to gain or keep market share. In such market, highly qualified personnel are key and challenges exist to attract those people. The organizational structures are rather traditional and functional (INSURANCE3b).

Proposition 2: The enterprise transformation context is determined by a rather stable market, resource scarcity concerning qualified personnel, traditional organizational structures.

4.3   Classes of Enterprise Transformations

Based on Baumoel [16, 17] we identified five classes of ET programs that are illustrated in table 2.

According to all informants, these categories cover most of the conducted ET programs. However, many programs could be related to more than one class (INSURANCE3b). The "roll out" class was considered to be rather incremental than fundamental change by one informant (INSURANCE3b). Summarized, this leads to proposition 3a:

Proposition 3a: The stated classes business networking, optimization, roll out, repositioning and flexibility increase cover most of the enterprise transformation programs conducted in insurance companies but not in a one-to-one manner.

Table 2. ET Program Types (based on [16, 17])

Program Type	Description
Business Networking	Programs of this type are about collaboration and communication with customers, partners and the systematic extension of such relations – e.g. in the context of value networks or division of labor/ Specialization.
Optimization	These programs are about the reengineering of existent processes or functions e.g. in order to achieve cost-savings, speed increases or higher quality.
Roll Out	Programs that incorporate new ideas that were developed in single units or processes and transfer them to the whole organization or larger organizational areas.
Repositioning	These programs are about change or extension of the strategy
Flexibility Increase	Programs of this type deal with increasing the entrepreneurial capacity to act.

However, the "repositioning" class of programs was perceived as very generic and almost a cover for the others by one informant (INSURANCE1). Further the question occurred, where to put standardization programs and programs that deal with the internal alignment of processes and information. The latter was brought up concerning the situation that it is often not clear, where relevant information can be found. An example is a claim that comes in and is of course assigned to a certain name. Nevertheless, it is not a simple task to collect all information and contracts about that person in order to provide a good service. The question is not that much how to connect these information sources technically but at first to investigate, who keeps the information where in the company (INSURANCE3a). Further it was not clear to the informants, were to put programs that deal with mergers and acquisitions (INSURANCE3b). This leads to proposition 3b:

Proposition 3b: Programs that deal with standardization, internal alignment or mergers & acquisitions are not properly covered by the presented classes.

We were interested, if drivers discussed above primarily foster programs of specific classes. The informants agreed that drivers can foster basically all of the above program classes. Nonetheless, some tendency is observable that certain drivers rather relate to certain program classes. For example, the pressure to reduce costs leads mainly to optimization programs. Regulation enforces on the one hand optimization but also the establishment of new ideas, since existing ones no longer are permitted. The informant of INSURANCE3b argued that optimized processes can better cope with new regulatory challenges. In INSURANCE1 the necessary new service & product offers lead to cross-linking programs in order to include partners for the service provision. For example in the car insurance, INSURANCE1 works together with car garages in order to provide innovative services. The pressure for cost reductions goes along with optimization programs. Establishment is especially apparent when ideas from local agencies should be transferred to the market in other countries and thus also mostly driven by the need to introduce innovative services and products. Similar the informant from INSURANCE3b mentioned the transfer of best-practices from mature to emergent markets. This leads to proposition 3c:

Proposition 3c: There seems to be a tendency that certain triggers relate to certain types of programs.

4.4   Techniques of Enterprise Transformations

Manifold techniques need to be applied in an ET program/effort/initiative, however, not all are necessary for each type of ET effort. With our informants we discussed the basis class of necessary techniques according to Baumoel [16, 17]. The author claims that this list contains the techniques that should be applied in order to conduct successful ETs. We discussed this list with our informants in order to gain insights about the relevance and prioritization of the items. Most of the techniques were considered important in general. Table 3 shows the techniques that the informants considered especially important.

The analysis of the expectations of involved persons as much as the definition and analysis of the benefits was perceived as very important by almost all informants. Further the important role of communication was highlighted. It became apparent that especially techniques that are emphasized in traditional management literature are perceived as very important. The aspect of management attention was highlighted a lot by the informants, even if the extend may differ. For INSURANCE1, management attention is true buy in and commitment which is reflected by being involved in steering boards and active control with not just one but many managers. The informant from INSURANCE3a highlighted that from an IT perspective not necessarily management attention is the key success factor but attention from the business side.

Summarized, the general techniques stated to be important for every ET mostly apply for the insurance industry, too. There was no technique that all informants consider to be relevant, however some were perceived as being especially important. Some were perceived to cover the same issue and could be condensed in a single item.

Proposition 4a: The provided list of basic techniques in general is relevant for enterprise transformation programs in the insurance sector. Some basic techniques seem to be more important than others.

Table 3. Basic ET Techniques Considered especially Important

Technique	Comments
Analysis of the expectations of the involved persons	"Very important, if this is not done it can become very difficult" (INSURANCE1) Important to be defined (INSURANCE2)
Analysis and definition of decision processes	"Is done and is important" (INSURANCE1)
Analysis and definition of the benefit	Important to get commitment (INSURANCE2) "No matter if the benefit is qualitative or quantitative that needs to be done in order to have measurable goals" (INSURANCE3b)
Definition of the addressees of the ET	"I would consider that as very important in order to include the right parties in the change process" (INSURANNCE3b)
Definition of program goals	"Very important, especially combined with 18 [Analysis and definition of the benefit]"
Definition of vision and mission	"It is crucial, it is a communication tool" (INSURANCE1)
Definition of the program extent	"Very very difficult, especially in large scale projects, the tends to extent the project [...] Control of the extent is a very crucial factor" (INSURANCE3b)
Definition and planning of the kind of communication	"Crucial, if it is not done, it becomes really difficult" (INSURANCE1) "Communication is extremely crucial," (INSURANCE3b)
Determination of stakeholder influences	It is important to identify the interests of all the stakeholders (INSURANCE3b).
Guidance: Ensure management commitment and role model	"Absolut crucial" (INSURANCE1) "Absolutely crucial - commitment, sponsorship, change leadership" (INSURANCE3b)

Some of the techniques in the list have been considered redundant or including each other. Our informant from INSURANCE1 for example would not cover the analysis of consequences in an additional point since such argumentation should be covered in the goals. Explicit analysis of the consequences is not seen as a necessary technique to achieve program success.

For certain techniques, the informants differed in their view. For example our informant from INSURANCE3a considered the technique of defining a vision for the ET as not necessary or even not appropriate. For him, the vision belongs to the corporate level but not to the level of ET programs, in here goals are the relevant aspect. The other informants however, considered having a vision as especially important.

We also asked the informants about techniques they would not consider as absolutely crucial or less important. Table 4 summarizes this discussion.

Table 4. Basic ET Techniques often not Conducted or not Considered to be Crucial

Technique	Comments
Analysis of the dominant corporate cultures and subcultures	"Never saw that this was done [...] you would rather think about how to influence the culture in order to realize the strategy" (INSURANCE1)
Analysis of the history of success	"Never seen, there are success stories but not because of a project" (INSURANCE1) "We maybe do that not enough, we document the findings in the project but we might not have the maturity achieved in that area to analyze it before each new project" (INSURANCE3a)
Analysis of the mentality / mindset	"Done rather seldom but might be more important to do" (INSURANCE1) "That is not done" (INSURANCE3b)
Analysis of employee satisfaction	"We do that in the company but not project-based" (INSURANCE1)
Analysis and definition of drivers	"I have never seen that" (INSURANCE1)
Determination of the process orientation	"We tried to do that but except for projects that deal explicitly with process change we are not doing it any longer" (INSURANCE1)
Determination of resistances	"I never saw that this is done systematically. If resistances occur, you go into those" (INSURANCE1)
Ensure organizational learning	"I never explicitly experienced organizational learning" (INSUARNCE1)

It becomes apparent that many of the techniques that were described as less important or less used, deal with rather "soft" factors. An explanation might be the hierarchical culture in the industry that shifts concentration rather to the "hard" techniques. However, incorporating these factors might be a good idea in order to increase the success probability of the ET.

Proposition 4b: Techniques that deal with "soft" aspects are less used and considered to be less crucial than "hard" ones.

5   Discussion

ETs are a relevant topic in the insurance industry, motivated by different aspects. We identified detailed context, triggers, program types and core techniques that are relevant. In table 5 we summarize the propositions we derived within the findings section.

Table 5. Propositions Summary

	Proposition
1	Potential trigger for enterprise transformation programs are (1) regulation, (2) new service and product offers, (3) new customer expectations and (4) pressure to reduce costs.
2	The enterprise transformation context is determined by a rather stable market, resource scarcity concerning qualified personnel, traditional organizational structures.
3a	The stated classes business networking, optimization, roll out, repositioning and flexibility increase cover most of the enterprise transformation programs conducted in insurance companies but not in a one-to-one manner.
3b	Programs that deal with standardization, internal alignment or mergers & acquisitions are not properly covered by the presented classes.
3c	There seems to be a tendency that certain triggers relate to certain types of programs.
4a	The provided list of basic techniques in general is relevant for enterprise transformation programs in the insurance sector. Some basic techniques seem to be more important than others.
4b	Techniques that deal with "soft" aspects are less used and considered to be less crucial than "hard" ones.

Based on proposition 3c, we identified a first *mapping of triggers and program types* in the insurance context (see illustration in figure 2). We thus extended the Baumoel [16, 17] approach with this part. We identified four classes of potential triggers for ET programs, such as regulation, new service and product offers, new customer expectations and the pressure to reduce costs. These are especially triggers, because the insurance market is rather traditional business (INSURANCE3b), in other markets and branches the triggers might be different or less foster fundamental change. We gained evidence that certain triggers can be mapped to certain program types – this allows to (1) better communicate the necessary ET steps and (2) shows that the existent categories are suitable also for the insurance industry. However, the discussions showed that some programs are not clearly covered or hard to fit in the program classes. For those programs, further research about their guidance is necessary. This is especially the case, since the issue was not just mentioned by one informant but across the different cases. Furthermore, IT related programs seem to have additional needs concerning the applied techniques. No longer management attention but rather attention from the business side was considered to be very important (INSURANCE3a). To cover this, we would extend the approach by a class of techniques especially needed for IT programs.

We further could identify *techniques* that our informants consider to be more or less important for ETs in the insurance sector (see tables 3 and 4 in the results section). ETs are affected by the hierarchical structures that most insurance companies persist of. Evidence for that is provided by the perceived minor relevance of techniques like analysis of mentality, etc. Because of the hierarchical coordination, such aspects might not be considered to be important. However, when it comes to the movement to new emergent markets, those techniques might gain in importance. We would thus propose, to cover this by a class of programs that especially deals with addressing new emergent markets.

Our initial assumption that the insurance context fosters different classes of techniques or prioritizations partially holds true. However, almost all informants did not see specifics to other companies from the financial industry (e.g. banks) since e.g. factors like regulation are also given here. We therefore see a huge potential in increasing the industry context to the financial industry as such. Figure 2 illustrates the findings, proposition 3c is included by the mapping arrows; the context is illustrated by the grey background.

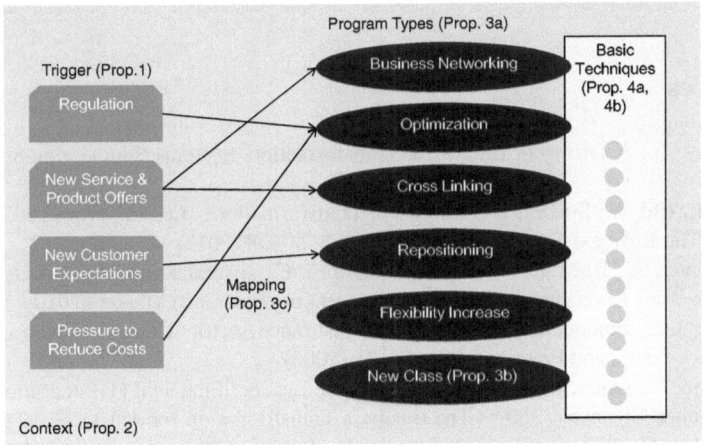

Fig. 2. Summarized Overview

6   Summary and Outlook

In this article we explored context, trigger, ET situation and core technique candidates for the insurance sector. The focus on insurances helps to focus scarce resources on the most promising aspects for ET success. We further identified connection points for further research.

However, the chosen research design implies some limitations. We used a given method for the guidance of ET as a foundation for our work. That implies the following major weakness: A certain bias exists, which classes and techniques exist and might be important. We covered this problem by applying a qualitative research design that allows for deeper discussion than a quantitative evaluation of the techniques. A quantitative approach would have not allowed us to determine that some ETs are difficult to cover with the existing situations and especially which ones not. Another limitation that occurs is about biases of informants. Even if we used methods that avoid such biases, e.g. we cannot be sure that if informants perceive an ET as successful, such ET is also successful in the scientific sense. We further did not conduct an evaluation of the findings presented in the paper so far. However, the chosen approach is well-known for the characteristic of providing stable empirical propositions.

The topic is very complex we were only able to cover a very broad rather than a deep perspective in this paper. However, we gained insights into the context, triggers, program types and core techniques in order to prioritize further in-depth work. The paper at hand is especially important to identify the foundations for the development of usable artifacts in the future. Thus the paper at hand has to be considered as a first exploration of the field, while further more detailed analysis and afterwards design steps will follow. This includes e.g. validation of the interviews by means of a survey and single in-depth case studies including an analysis and evaluation of the adopted methods.

References

1. Rouse, W.B.: A Theory of Enterprise Transformation. Systems Engineering 8(4), 279–295 (2005)
2. Ward, J., Uhl, A.: Success and Failure in Transformation – Lessons from 13 Case Studies. 360° – The Business Transformation Journal 3, 30–38 (2012)
3. Fuernthaler, A., Baettig, V., Burr, B., Stampfli, C.: Insurance in 2015 – Determining the Position: New Coordinates in the German-speaking Insurance Market (2010)
4. Trichet, J.C.: Financial stability and the insurance sector. Geneva Papers on Risk and Insurance-Issues and Practice 30(1), 65–71 (2005)
5. Giordano, G., Lamy, A., Janasz, T.: Who's the Leader? Financial IT Integration at a Global Insurance Company. 360° – The Business Transformation Journal 1, 53–59 (2011)
6. Hawawini, G., Subramanian, V., Verdin, P.: Is performance driven by industry-or firm-specific factors? A new look at the evidence. Strategic Management Journal 24(1), 1–16 (2003)
7. Becker, J., Pfeiffer, D., Räckers, M., Fuchs, P.: Business Process Management in Public Administrations – The Pictrue Approach (2007)
8. Bucher, T., Klesse, M., Kurpjuweit, S., Winter, R.: Situational Method Engineering - On the Differentiation of "Context" and "Project Type". In: Situational Method Engineering - Fundamentals and Experiences, pp. 33–48. Springer, Geneva (2007)
9. Lahrmann, G., Winter, R., Fischer, M.: Design and Engineering for Situational Transformation. In: Harmsen, F., Proper, E., Schalkwijk, F., Barjis, J., Overbeek, S. (eds.) PRET 2010. LNBIP, vol. 69, pp. 1–16. Springer, Heidelberg (2010)

10. Winter, R.: Design Solution Analysis for the Construction of Situational Design Methods. Engineering Methods in the Service-Oriented Context 351, 19–33 (2011)
11. Powell, T.C.: Total quality management as competitive advantage: a review and empirical study. Strategic Management Journal 16(1), 15–38 (1995)
12. Linderman, K., Schroeder, R.G., Zaheer, S., Choo, A.S.: Six Sigma - A Goal-Theoretic Perspective. Journal of Operations Management 21(2), 193–203 (2003)
13. Goh, T.N.: Six Triumphs and Six Tragedies of Six Sigma. Quality Engineering 22(4), 299–305 (2010)
14. Österle, H., Winter, R.: Business Engineering. In: Österle, H., Winter, R. (eds.) Business Engineering - Auf dem Weg zum Unternehmen des Informationszeitalters, pp. 3–19. Springer, Berlin (2003)
15. Stiles, P., Uhl, A.: Meta Management: Connecting the Parts of Business Transformation. 360° – The Business Transformation Journal 3, 24–29 (2012)
16. Baumöl, U.: Strategic Agility through Situational Method Construction. In: Reichwald, R., Huff, A.S. (eds.) Proceedings of the European Academy of Management Annual Conference 2005, pp. 1–34 (2005)
17. Baumöl, U.: Change Management in Organisationen: Situative Methodenkonstruktion für flexible Veränderungsprozesse. Gabler, Wiesbaden (2008)
18. Teece, D.J.: Explicating dynamic capabilities: the nature and microfoundations of (sustainable) enterprise performance. Strategic Management Journal 28(13), 1319–1350 (2007)
19. Beer, M.: The transformation of the human resource function: Resolving the tension between a traditional administrative and a new strategic role. Human Resource Management 36(1), 49–57 (1997)
20. Van Helden, G.J.: Researching Public Sector Transformation: The Role of Management Accounting. Financial Accountability & Management 21(1), 99–133 (2005)
21. Harmsen, F., Proper, E., Kok, N.: Informed Governance of Enterprise Transformations. In: Proper, E., Harmsen, F., Dietz, J.L.G. (eds.) PRET 2009. LNBIP, vol. 28, pp. 155–180. Springer, Heidelberg (2009)
22. Purchase, V., Parry, G., Valerdi, R., Nightingale, D., Mills, J.: Enterprise Transformation: Why Are We Interested, What Is It, and What Are the Challenges? Journal of Enterprise Transformation 1(1), 14–33 (2011)
23. Staw, B.M., Epstein, L.D.: What Bandwagons Bring: Effects of Popular Management Techniques on Corporate Performance, Reputation, and CEO Pay. Administrative Science Quarterly 45(3), 523–556 (2000)
24. Iseri-Say, A., Toker, A., Kantur, D.: Do popular management techniques improve performance?: Evidence from large businesses in Turkey. Journal of Management Development 27(7), 660–667 (2008)
25. Eisenhardt, K.M.: Building Theories from Case Study Research. Academy of Management Review 14(4), 532–550 (1989)
26. Eisenhardt, K.M., Graebner, M.E.: Theory Building from Cases: Opportunities and Challenges. Academy of Management Journal 50(1), 25–32 (2007)
27. vom Brocke, J., Simons, A., Niehaves, B., Riemer, K., Plattfaut, R., Cleven, A.: Reconstructing the Giant: On the Importance of Rigour in Documenting the Literature Search Process. In: Proceedings of the ECIS 2009, Verona, pp. 2206–2217 (2009)
28. Webster, J., Watson, R.T.: Analyzing the Past to prepare for the Future: Writing a Literature Review. MIS Quarterly 26(2), 13–23 (2002)
29. Huber, G.P., Power, D.J.: Retrospective reports of strategic-level managers: Guidelines for increasing their accuracy. Strategic Management Journal 6(2), 171–180 (1985)

30. Burke, L.A., Miller, M.K.: Phone Interviewing as a Means of Data Collection: Lessons Learned and Practical Recommendations. Forum: Qualitative Social Research 2(2), 1–8 (2001)
31. Jick, T.D.: Mixing Qualitative and Quantitative Methods: Triangulation in Action. Administrative Science Quarterly 24(4), 602–611 (1979)
32. Noy, C.: Sampling Knowledge: The Hermeneutics of Snowball Sampling in Qualitative Research. International Journal of Social Research Methodology 11(4), 327–344 (2007)
33. Phelan, L., Taplin, R., Henderson-Sellers, A., Albrecht, G.: Ecological Viability or Liability? Insurance System Responses to Climate Risk. Environmental Policy and Governance 21(2), 112–130 (2011)
34. Thistlethwaite, J.: The ClimateWise Principles: Self-Regulating Climate Change Risks in the Insurance Sector. Business & Society 51(1), 121–147 (2012)
35. Wolgast, M.: Global terrorism and the insurance industry: new challenges and policy responses. In: Brueck, T. (ed.) The Economic Analysis of Terrorism, pp. 146–172. Routledge, Abington (2007)
36. Van Dijk, M., Pomp, M., Douven, R., Laske-Aldershof, T., Schut, E., De Boer, W., De Boo, A.: Consumer price sensitivity in Dutch health insurance. International Journal of Health Care Finance & Economics 8(4), 225–244 (2008)
37. Thoyts, R.: Insurance Theory and Practice. Routledge, Abington (2010)
38. Jaffee, D.M., Russell, T.: Catastrophe Insurance, Capital Markets, and Uninsurable Risks. The Journal of Risk and Insurance 64(2), 205–230 (1997)
39. Kling, G., Ghobadian, A., O'Regan, N.: Organic growth and shareholder value: A case study of the insurance industry. International Journal of Research in Marketing 27(4), 276–283 (2009)

On the Categorization and Measurability of Enterprise Architecture Benefits with the Enterprise Architecture Value Framework

Henk Plessius, Raymond Slot, and Leo Pruijt

Hogeschool Utrecht, University of Applied Sciences,
Information Systems Architecture Research Group,
Nijenoord 1, 3552 AS Utrecht, The Netherlands
{henk.plessius,raymond.slot,leo.pruijt}@hu.nl

Abstract. With the development of Enterprise Architecture (EA) as a discipline, measuring and understanding its value for business and IT has become relevant. In this paper a framework for categorizing the benefits of EA, the Enterprise Architecture Value Framework (EAVF), is presented and based on this framework, a measurability maturity scale is introduced.

In the EAVF the value aspects of EA are expressed using the four perspectives of the Balanced Scorecard with regard to the development of these aspects over time, defining sixteen key areas in which EA may provide value. In its current form the framework can support architects and researchers in describing and categorizing the benefits of EA.

As part of our ongoing research on the value of EA, two pilots using the framework have been carried out at large financial institutions. These pilots illustrate how to use the EAVF as a tool in measuring the benefits of EA.

Keywords: enterprise architecture, EA benefits, value, measurability.

1   Introduction

It has been 25 years since Zachman [1] introduced the concept of architecture as a new approach in reducing the complexity of the information function within an organization. Since those days, the complexity of the IT-landscape has increased manifold and IT has become an integral part of many business processes. To control, or at least to understand, the current state of affairs in an organization and to be able to manage transformations of the business, Enterprise Architecture (EA) plays an important role nowadays as demonstrated by Ross et al. [2] for example. EA can play an important role in decision making as well: Johnson et al. [3] describe how (under certain conditions) EA can clarify and rationalize the decision process.

EA has been defined by the IEEE [4] as *"the fundamental organization of a system embodied in its components, their relationships to each other and to the environment and the principles guiding its design and evolution"*. Following Lange et al. [5] we prefer to emphasize its transformational nature by stating that EA has to *"translate the*

S. Aier et al. (Eds.): TEAR 2012 and PRET 2012, LNBIP 131, pp. 79–92, 2012.

broader goals and principles of an organization's strategy into concrete processes and systems enabling the organization to realize its goals", thereby contributing to the organization's continuity and profit.

In recent years, the question if EA can do what it promises has become relevant. Stated differently: what exactly are the benefits of EA and which activities contribute to its value? A comprehensive and recent overview of the literature on this topic has been given by Tamm et al. [6] who give the following classification of EA benefits, based on a systematic literature review of 50 studies:

(1)   increased responsiveness and guidance to change;
(2)   improved decisionmaking;
(3)   improved communication & collaboration;
(4)   reduced (IT) costs;
(5)   business-IT alignment;
(6)   improved business processes;
(7)   improved IT systems;
(8)   re-use of resources;
(9)   improve integration;
(10) reduce risk;
(11) regulatory compliance;
(12) provides stability.

By the definition given above, EA is active on the tactical and strategic level of an organization, rather than on the operational level. It has many characteristics in common with the policies of the organization and as such is generally deemed valuable, but not measurable. Hence, as summarized in [7], the literature on EA value tends to focus on the benefits of EA, rather than on value itself: the (quantifiable) result of benefits and costs involved. In our ongoing research we are interested in the value of EA as the EA should direct its efforts on maximizing this value and thereby its contribution towards the goals of the organization. More authors support this position, see for example [8] and [9]. One of the authors of this paper has demonstrated in previous work a positive correlation between Solution Architecture and project results [10]; the effect of EA on the performance of an organization is however still an open question.

As business goals are unique to an organization, so are the (possible) benefits from EA for that organization and a lot of research has gone into classifying these benefits. So far, proposed classifications are mainly one-dimensional. Examples, apart from the one given above, are the classification into the categories of the strategy map by Boucharas et al. [9] and that of van der Raadt [11] using agility and alignment as principal categories. Foorthuis et al. [12] focus on the mutual interference between a dozen or so categories of benefits, an approach that has been extended by Lange et al. [5] into a benefit realization model and by Tamm et al. [6] in an EA benefits model. There are some multi-dimensional approaches toward the value of architecture as well. For example, Schelp and Stutz [13] use the perspectives of the balanced scorecard on one dimension and organizational scope on the other one. However, organizational scope is not necessary independent from the perspectives of the balanced scorecard. Our approach is similar to theirs, but – following Wideman's suggestions for improving project management [14] - we use the time as a second dimension, thereby ensuring two independent axes in our model.

From these two dimensions, we have created an EA value framework which, as we will show in the next paragraph, covers the entire "value-universe". A further contribution, based on the framework, is the development of a measurability maturity scale to express the level of measurability of EA benefits.

This study results from the research question: *"How can EA benefits be classified and how can these benefits be measured?"* This question is part of our broader research on measuring the value of EA. To address our current research question we first conducted a review of EA benefits as outlined before. From there we used the approach of design-science research [15], [16] in developing the framework and its derived questionnaire (see par. 3).

Closely related to our research is the work of our colleague Pruijt on the effectiveness of EA [17].

In this paper, we present in par. 2 the framework and the design decisions behind it. In the next paragraph, additional instruments for assessments are introduced followed by an overview of the results of the assessments in two pilot organizations in par. 4. In par. 5, we summarize and discuss our findings and give an outlook to our future research.

2 The Enterprise Architecture Value Framework

As stated before, the final goal of EA is to create value (financial and non-financial) for the organization. To assess if the EA function in an organization succeeds in creating value, it is necessary to state exactly what we mean by value. Bowman and Ambrosini [18] distinguish between (perceived) *use value* (subjective, defined by the customers based on their perception of usefulness; the price the customers are prepared to pay) and *exchange value* (objective, the price actually paid). For our purposes the use value, i.e. the value as perceived by the clients (here: the organization) in relation to their needs (here: the organizational goals) seems most appropriate. As this is a perceived concept, an assessment of this use value is subjectively related to the individual organization and care should be taken in generalizing results to other organizations.

To be able to measure value, we adopt an operational definition of value: *"value is the contribution to the goals of the organization"*. By this definition value can be a contribution to the profit of the organization, but also a growth in customer satisfaction or in agility of the organization. It may even be a decrease in productivity (which, when the goal is to increase productivity, is an example where value is negative).

From this definition it follows that organizational goals should be included in measuring value. For our model, we decided to use the original classification of Kaplan & Norton's balanced scorecard [19], [20], [21]. Our rationale behind this choice is that it is not too complicated (only four categories or perspectives) and generally well known to decision makers in organizations. Hence, our value measurements will be carried out in respect to the following four perspectives:

- *Financial*: the financial perspective can be characterized as the shareholders' view on the organization. The keywords here are money (revenues as well as costs), risk and compliance.
- *Customer*: the customer perspective is the externals' view on the organization. Customer satisfaction and market share are generally important questions here.
- *Internal*: the internal perspective is the way the organization is perceived by its managers and employees. The focus is normally on internal efficiency and productivity, but work satisfaction or sustainability may be taken into account as well.
- *Learning & growth*: the perspective of learning and growth is the long-term view. The central question is the continuity of the organization in the long term. Typical keywords here are innovation and change.

As explained in the introduction of this paper, it is very difficult, if not impossible, to measure directly the contribution of EA to the organizational goals. So we decided to use a detour (as sketched in figure 1) and first establish to what extent the EA is able to implement its goals in the operations of the organization, followed by an assessment of the difference in value stemming from these changes (in terms of the organizational goals).

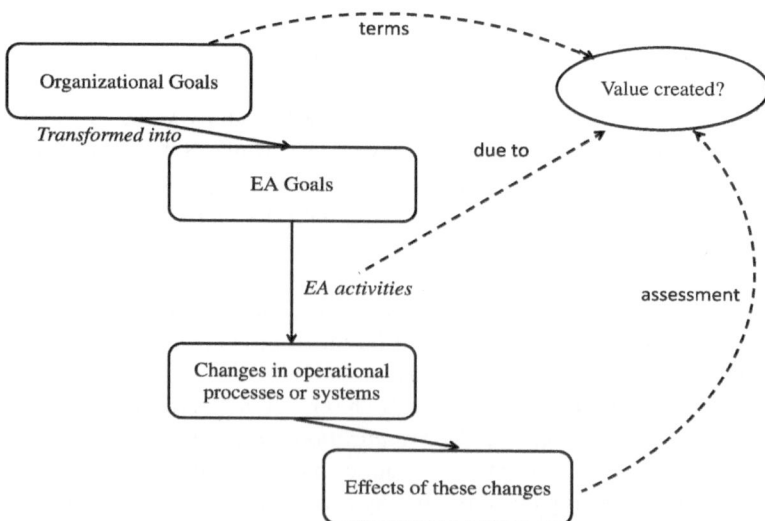

Fig. 1. Measuring the value of EA in an indirect way

In practice these changes in the operations result from EA goals from the past, so we have to go back in time and 'follow' the goals which were important some years back towards their implementation now and derive the difference in value of the resulting products as created by EA activities.

So, apart from being related to the goals of the organization, value evolves in time. As we are interested in value as created by EA activities, figure 1 suggests that this can take place during the development and implementation of EA in the operations (step 1) as well as after the operational changes are implemented (step 2). For the first step – towards the implementation of the EA – two logical phases can be discerned: the architecture development process, resulting in the target architecture, and the realization process aimed at implementing this target architecture. In the second step, when (parts of) the target architecture are implemented in operational processes and systems, we differentiate, based on reported benefits[1], between the value resulting from plain use of the results and the re-use of these results, as stimulated by the EA, in different environments.

These considerations have resulted in four phases in our model, which below are summarized and related to the familiar phases in the Architecture Development Method (ADM) of TOGAF-9 [22] as well:

- *Development*: in the development phase, the EA is developed and maintained. This phase corresponds with the ADM phases Architecture Vision, Business Architecture, Information Systems Architectures and Technology Architecture.
- *Realization*: the realization phase is where programs are defined and projects are carried out to implement the changes defined in the EA. This phase corresponds with the ADM phases Opportunities and Solutions, Migration Planning and Implementation Governance.
- *Use*: After the implementation, changes have been implemented in the organization and the time to collect the promised benefits has come. Monitoring the new architecture (Architecture Change Management in ADM) is a continuing activity in this phase.
- *Re-use*: the Re-use phase is a seamless continuation of the Use phase and as such part of the phase Architecture Change management in ADM. However, after implementing parts of a new architecture, re-use of these parts may have a big influence on the next parts and thus yield value.

While the second axis of our model is defined by time, it is loosely coupled with organizational responsibilities as well. In general, the architecture function in an organization is responsible for the development phase while for the realization phase the change function (program and project leaders, portfolio managers, etc.) has the responsibility. In the use phase, the operational function takes over the responsibility and for the re-use phase the architecture and change function should both be responsible.

Since in our model the two dimensions (perspectives and phases) are mutually independent, we can combine them in a framework: the *Enterprise Architecture Value*

---

[1] As an example see benefit #8: re-use of resources, in the classification from Tamm et al. as quoted in the Introduction of this paper.

Framework (EAVF) as shown in figure 2. In the framework, we use a dashed line between the phases Use and Re-use to emphasize that these phases are not strictly separated.

As has been shown by various authors (see for example [5], [9], [13]), every value-construct, i.e. every construct that contributes to the goals of the enterprise, can be placed in one of the columns (perspectives of the Balanced Scorecard) of the framework. Moreover, whenever a change in value occurs in a value-construct, it can be attributed to one of the rows (the phases) of the framework. This guarantees that our framework is complete and covers all of the "value-universe". It follows that it is possible (but not always trivial) to map another categorization into the framework; an example has been given in figure 2 where three of the categories of Tamm et al. (see the Introduction of this paper) have been placed in the framework.

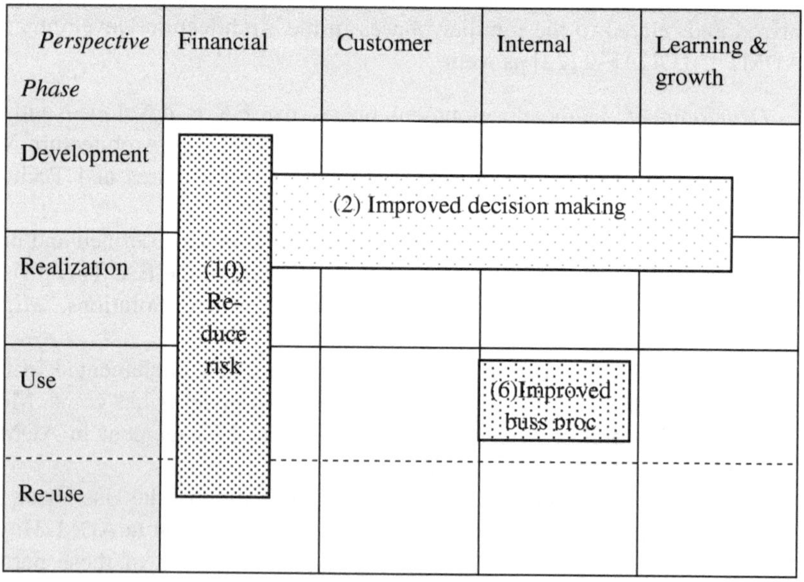

Perspective / Phase	Financial	Customer	Internal	Learning & growth
Development				
		(2) Improved decision making		
Realization	(10) Re-duce risk			
Use			(6) Improved buss proc	
Re-use				

Fig. 2. The Enterprise Architecture Value Framework with horizontal the four perspectives of the Balanced Scorecard and vertical the four phases where value may be created

The primary strength of a complete framework is that it subdivides the value-universe. For example, in our framework each cell is focused on a specific aspect and timeframe which makes it easier to identify where benefits and costs may originate and who are the stakeholders. The difficult question remains however if the changes in value are (at least partly) the result of the EA. We will discuss this "traceability of EA" later on in this paper (see par. 5).

3 Instruments Based on the EAVF

3.1 The Questionnaire

As discussed in the introduction of this paper, many authors have published about the benefits of EA. Therefore, in our research on the value of EA, we decided to build on the work of others and focus on the benefits of EA as a first step.

In order to measure these benefits, enough data must be gathered and made available in the organization. To identify which data sources are available and appropriate in an organization, we decided to conduct structured interviews [23] with stakeholders in the organization. For these interviews we developed, based on the EAVF, a questionnaire. The questions in this questionnaire are constructed using a cascade of universal questions (as depicted in figure 3) and we made certain that the benefits as reported in the literature (see [5], [6], [7], [8], [9], [11], [12], [13]) were covered by mapping these benefits into the EAVF.

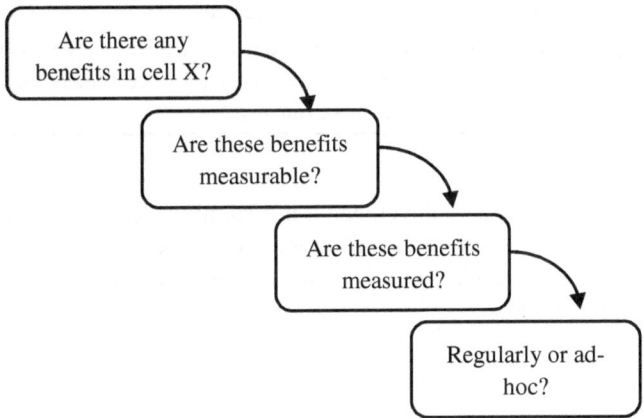

Fig. 3. A cascade of universal questions for measuring, used in the construction of a questionnaire for the EAVF

For example: in the Customer perspective we focus on the interaction between the organization and the outside world. This may be done regarding individual external entities (customers) or a group of external entities: a market. In the Use-phase, benefits therefore may be found in increased customer satisfaction and/or a greater market share, both of which are measurable. To support in maximizing these benefits, market research or usability testing can be carried out in the Realization phase[2] to reduce uncertainty, likely leading to better decisions and from there to a better implementation and to the intended benefits.

With our questionnaire, we assess the actual situation in an organization: are all relevant benefits measured and if so, how and to what extent. As an illustration some questions from the questionnaire as used in interview sessions, have been depicted in table 1.

---

[2] The importance of this testing should of course be determined in the Development phase.

Table 1. Part of the questionnaire (not all question from the Customers' perspective shown)

Phase	Customer's Perspective
Development	In developing the architecture, have the consequences for the customers and the market been taken into account? Where? How is this translated to the realization phase?
Realization	Has the impact of the migration on the customers and the market been established? Are there any analyses and/or scenarios developed and if yes, what were the expected results?
Use	Has the market share increased as a result of the changes? How is this measured?
	Has the customer satisfaction changed as a result of the changes? How is this measured?
Re-use	Has a strategic advantage in the market been reached by virtue of the architecture? How is this evaluated?
	Has the ability of the organization to react on changes in the environment (like market changes, changes in customers' needs, etc.) increased? How is this evaluated?

Along with the questionnaire, we developed a measurability scale for assessing the measurability of the benefits and a set of indicators to evaluate the actual value of the benefits as perceived by the organization. Both the questionnaire and the set of indicators are available via the authors.

3.2   Measurability

From a first pilot with the framework (as described in [24]) we learned that it is important to establish if there is enough factual documentation to quantify the benefits of EA. In order to do so, we defined a *"measurability maturity scale"*. This scale informs the organization about its value-awareness and makes a comparison with other organizations possible. This scale is developed in accordance with the familiar stages used by most maturity models (see for example the work of Kohlegger et al. [25]) and should be applied to every cell of the matrix. The scale consists of four levels:

1. *Ad-hoc*: measuring relevant aspects of value is sometimes done, but not systematically; information comes in the form of examples
2. *Measurable*: systematic measurements of value aspects are available, but not every relevant aspect is fully covered.

3. *Measured*: systematic measurements are made to such an extent that a value can be derived.
4. *Managed*: value is used as an instrument in managing the EA activities.

The measurability level is assessed by scoring what is documented for the benefits in every cell of the EAVF. Only in cells where the measurability is at least *"measured"*, quantitative statements on the value of the benefits can be made. When this level is not reached, only qualitative statements can be made, which by their very nature are subjective so different interviewees may give different answers, depending on their viewpoint.

3.3 Evaluating Benefits

To be able to evaluate the benefits of EA even when the measurability is low, we developed a set of indicators for the benefits in every cell of the EAVF. With these indicators, we assess the opinion of the interviewees on the benefits. As these indicators ask for a judgment, they are scored by the researchers on a 5-point Likert scale (table 2), where possible supported by examples or data.

Table 2. 5-point Likert scale used in the evaluation of benefits

score	1	2	3	4	5
meaning	totally disagree	disagree	neutral	agree	agree totally

In table 3 some of these indicators are shown as an example. Note that in these indicators the traceability of architecture is taken into account.

Table 3. Example of indicators used in evaluating the benefits of EA (not all indicators from the Customer's perspective are shown)

Phase	Indicators in the Customer's perspective
Development	The role of the market in the architecture is in accordance with the importance of the market for the organization
	The role of the customer in the architecture is in accordance with the importance of the customer for the organization
Realization	Due to the architecture analyses and/or scenarios of the impact on the market are made
	Due to the architecture analyses and/or scenarios of the impact on the customer are made
Use	The market share increased due to the architecture
	The customer satisfaction increased due to the architecture
Re-use	Due to the architecture the ability to react on external changes has increased

4   Pilots with the EA Value Framework

Before any actual assessment can take place we have to make a decision on the scope of the assessment as measuring every goal over longer timeframes will in most cases be practically impossible. We have to choose: will the assessment represent a certain period or will the focus be on a couple of representative EA goals which will be followed throughout? To answer questions like this, we start an assessment with a preparation phase. In this preparation phase, we determine with the head of the architectural department the scope of the assessment, which stakeholders will be interviewed and we collect relevant documentation. After the preparation phase, we carry out the interview sessions with the identified stakeholders, using the questionnaire. In these interviews, we usually focus on one or two rows in the framework and we emphasize the importance of measurements and documentation. In this way, a complete as possible picture can be build showing where benefits are realized in the architectural process.

We have applied the EAVF and the derived questionnaire in two pilot organizations. In both organizations, we set out to measure the benefits realized by the EA function. The first organization that we assessed is a governmental institution. For that organization, we established that the measurability of the benefits created by EA was low. This case has been extensively reported in [24].

The second pilot organization is a large non-governmental financial company. This organization started some 3 years ago with EA and developed a target architecture around a central data warehouse. The implementation of this data warehouse was not very fortunate and only a small part of the intended data warehouse was implemented at the time of the assessment (spring 2012). In this organization, the measurability of EA benefits was low too, but, using the indicators described in the previous paragraph (par 3.3), we were able to evaluate the benefits of EA as perceived by the stakeholders. Figure 4 shows, based on the evaluation of the interviews and the documentation gathered, the summary of the results in the EA Value Framework. In figure 4a the measurability level is given, showing that in this organization reliable data (i.e. a score of at least 3) are available almost only in the realization phase. In the Re-use phase and in the Learning and Growth perspective hardly any documentation is available which explains the low scores in the figure.

Measurability	Finan-cial	Cus-tomer	Inter-nal	Lear-ning
Development	1,7	2,4	2,2	2
Realization	3,2	3	3,1	1,3
Use	2,9	3	2,6	1
Re-use	2	1	1,2	1

Legend:
1 – Ad-hoc
2 – Measurable
3 – Measured
4 – Managed

Fig. 4a. Results of the assessment of the measurability level in the pilot organization

Evaluation of benefits	Finan-cial	Cus-tomer	Inter-nal	Lear-ning
Development	3,3	3,4	3,3	2,5
Realization	1,2	2,5	3,4	2,4
Use	2,2	1,6	2,1	2
Re-use	3,4	2	2,7	2,3

Legend:
1 – totally disagree
2 – disagree
3 - neutral
4 – agree
5 – agree totally

Fig. 4b. Results of the assessment of the benefits in the pilot organization

In figure 4b, the scores on the perceived benefits are plotted. Due to the low scores on measurability, the scores on these benefits are based on the interviews mainly. Figure 4b shows there is a slight 'plus' (score above 3) in the Development phase which can be traced back tot the increased maturity of the EA function. In the Realization phase the scores are low, with the exception of the Internal perspective (from the interviews we learned that this was by virtue of the insight created by the architecture), meaning that hardly any benefits of EA were perceived by the stakeholders. However, a much more serious cause for concern for the architects is that "the business" hardly did perceive any value from EA (low scores in the Use-phase): "it has cost too much and [results] came too late". In other words, the architecture function has a major credibility problem with the operational function in that organization. Finally, re-use just started and higher scores may be expected here in time.

Based on the framework and the more detailed results from the interviews and the documentation, we were able to advise this organization which direction their EA should take: more business, less IT-oriented.

5   Discussion and Future Research

In this paper, we presented a framework, the Enterprise Architecture Value Framework (EAVF), which can be used to categorize the value aspects of EA. The EAVF builds on earlier research in this field as shown in the introduction of this paper. The framework covers the value universe of EA and it supports researchers to understand what types of value may be discerned in EA and when value is created.

Based on the framework we developed a questionnaire to assess the measurability and the benefits of EA. The framework and its derived questionnaire have been tested in a couple of pilot organizations. From these pilots we learned that the EAVF can be used in assessing the benefits of EA, but some reserve should be taken in this conclusion as the measurability level in both organizations was low and as a consequence the scores on the benefits as realized by EA were quite subjective. But these scores do reflect the general opinion on EA (perceived use value) in those organizations and as such give important feedback to the architecture function.

A key finding of the pilots is that we were able to assess, in a short period of time, the level of measurability of EA in the organization. The pilot organizations were interested in measuring the benefits of architecture, but did not have a clear understanding of the type of information that was needed to measure it. Because of the results achieved in the pilot, we were able to provide the organizations with a clear overview of the information that is needed to assess this value and to help them understand which part of the required information is already available. Following our assessment, we were able to express the availability of information on a measurability maturity scale, linked to the cells of the EAVF. This result allows the pilot organizations to start initiatives for acquiring the required information, in order to improve the measurability of the benefits of EA in the future.

In the second pilot, we were able to give an evaluation of the benefits stemming from EA as well, albeit that this evaluation reflects strongly the (subjective) judgments of the stakeholders. In this organization the EA did not succeed in delivering what was promised so very little real benefits for the daily operations were created, which is clearly reflected in the EAVF (as shown in fig. 4).

It is quite difficult to establish without doubt the traceability of EA. Changes in business processes and IT are started to deliver value to the organization. Our aim is to understand if we can trace back (part of) this value to results which are based upon, or initiated by, EA principles and guidelines. We found that benefits created in the first two phases of the EAVF (Development and Realization) can well be traced back to the EA, as these phases are closely related to the work of the architects. Traceability is more difficult in later phases as in most organizations many of the projects are started on initiative of the business and architectural principles are applied afterwards. Therefore, benefits can be accredited to the business departments as well as to the EA. We consider introducing a scope-factor in future pilots to express the proportion of EA in the measured value. In this way, it would become possible to express that a certain result can be attributed to the activities of the EA for say 40%.

In the second pilot organization, the followed project was quite clearly "EA induced", but the results in the Use-phase were not very convincing to the business.

The results presented in this study are based on two pilots only. To validate our findings, more organizations need to be considered, preferably with a higher measurability level resulting in more demonstrable benefits due to EA (or lack thereof). However, considering the first results obtained with the value framework as presented in this paper and although a lot of research still has to be done, we expect that the EAVF will become a central tool in our research.

References

1. Zachman, J.: A Framework for Information Architecture. IBM Systems Journal 26(3) (1987)
2. Ross, J.W., Weill, P., Robertson, D.C.: Enterprise Architecture As Strategy: Creating a Foundation for Business Execution. Harvard Business School Publishing, Boston (2006)
3. Johnson, P., Ekstedt, M., Silva, E., Plazaola, L.: Using Enterprise Architecture for CIO Decision-making: on the Importance of Theory. In: Proceedings of the 2nd Annual Conference on Systems Engineering Research, CSER (2004)

4. IEEE. The IEEE 1471-2000 standard - Architecture Views and Viewpoints. IEEE (2000)
5. Lange, M., Mendling, J.: An Experts' Perspective on Enterprise Architecture Goals, Framework Adoption and Benefit Assessment. In: Proceedings of the 15th IEEE International Enterprise Distributed Object Computing Conference Workshops (EDOCW), pp. 304–313 (2011)
6. Tamm, T., Seddon, P.B., Shanks, G., Reynolds, P.: How Does Enterprise Architecture Add Value to Organizations? Communications of the Association for Information Systems 28, Article 10, 141–168 (2011)
7. Townsend, S.: The Value of Enterprise Architecture, part 1 – 6. Series start (2011), http://www.sdn.sap.com/irj/scn/weblogs?blog=/pub/wlg/22948
8. van Steenbergen, M., Brinkkemper, S.: Modeling the contribution of enterprise architecture practice to the achievement of business goals. In: Papadopoulos, G.A., Wojtkowski, W., Wojtkowski, W.G., Wrycza, S., Zupancic, J. (eds.) Information Systems Development: Towards a Service Provision Society. Springer, New York (2008)
9. Boucharas, V., van Steenbergen, M., Jansen, S., Brinkkemper, S.: The Contribution of Enterprise Architecture to the Achievement of Organizational Goals: Establishing the Enterprise Architecture Benefits Framework. Technical Report UU-CS-2010-014, Utrecht (2010)
10. Slot, R.: A method for valuing Architecture-Based Business Transformation and Measuring the value of Solutions Architecture. PhD Thesis, Utrecht (2010)
11. van der Raadt, B.: Enterprise Architecture coming of Age. Increasing the Performance of an Emerging Discipline. PhD Thesis, Amsterdam (2011)
12. Foorthuis, R., van Steenbergen, M., Mushkudiani, M., Bruls, W., Brinkkemper, S.: On course but not there yet: Enterprise Architecture Conformance and Benefits in Systems Development. In: ICIS 2010 Proceedings. Paper 110 (2010)
13. Schelp, J., Stutz, M.: A Balanced Scorecard Approach to measure the Value of Enterprise Architecture. Journal of Enterprise Architecture 3(1), 5–12 (2007)
14. Wideman, M.: Improving PM: Linking Success Criteria to Project Type (2008), http://www.maxwideman.com/papers/improvingpm/intro.html
15. Hevner, A., March, S., Park, J., Ram, S.: Design Science in Information Systems Research. MIS Quarterly 28(1), 75–105 (2004)
16. Peffers, K., Tuunanen, T., Rothenberger, M.A., Chatterjee, S.: A Design Science Research Methodology for Information Systems Research. Journal of Management Information Systems 24(3), 45–78 (2008)
17. Pruijt, L., Slot, R., Plessius, H.: The Enterprise Architecture Realization Index. In: Archivalue, Portfolio Management with Enterprise Architecture, Novay, Enschede, pp. 72–81 (2012)
18. Bowman, C., Ambrosini, V.: Value Creation Versus Value Capture: Towards a Coherent Definition of Value in Strategy. British Journal of Management 11, 1–15 (2000)
19. Kaplan, R.S., Norton, D.P.: The balanced scorecard—measures that drive performance. Harvard Business Review, 71–79 (January-February 1992)
20. Kaplan, R.S., Norton, D.P.: Transforming the balanced scorecard from performance measurement to strategic management. Accounting Horizons, part I, 87–104 (March), Part II, 147–160 (June) (2001)
21. Norreklit, H.: The balance on the balanced scorecard - a critical analysis of some of its assumptions. Management Accounting Research 11, 65–88 (2000)

22. TOGAF. The Open Group Architecture Framework, Version 9.1. TOGAF (2011), http://www3.opengroup.org/
23. Bryman, A., Bell, E.: Business Research Methods, 2nd edn. Oxford Press Inc., New York (2007)
24. Plessius, H., Slot, R.: Valuing Enterprise Architecture. In: Archivalue, Portfolio Management with Enterprise Architecture, Novay, Enschede, pp. 94–99 (2012)
25. Kohlegger, M., Maier, R., Thalmann, S.: Understanding Maturity Models Results of a Structured Content Analysis. In: Proceedings of IKNOW 2009 International Conference on Knowledge Management and Knowledge Technologies, pp. 51–61 (September 2009)

The Application of Enterprise Reference Architecture in the Financial Industry

Wijke ten Harmsen van der Beek[1], Jos Trienekens[2], and Paul Grefen[2]

[1] Capgemini, Papendorpseweg 100, P.O. Box 2575, 3500 GN Utrecht, The Netherlands
wijke.ten.harmsenvanderbeek@capgemini.com
[2] School of Industrial Engineering, Information Systems, Eindhoven University of Technology,
Den Dolech 2, P.O. Box 513, 5600 MB Eindhoven, The Netherlands
{j.j.m.trienekens,p.w.p.j.grefen}@tue.nl

Abstract. Financial institutions are facing enormous challenges in business / IT alignment. Enterprise architecture (EA) is seen as key in addressing these challenges. Major issues still exist in EA design and realization. The concept of reference architecture is explored as one of the elements that are essential to improve the quality of architectural work. In this paper we describe the research agenda to ERA. First we provide a working definition for the concept of Enterprise Reference Architecture (ERA). Second we provide a conceptual model wherein ERA is positioned. The research is based on Design Science and is now in the first explorative phase. Pilot interviews were held with the objective to validate the model. Preliminary results show that the model is recognized and give also insight in current needs for ERA.

Keywords: enterprise architecture, reference architecture, architecture framework, design science, financial market.

1   Introduction

This paper describes the research agenda to enterprise reference architecture, which will be executed in joint collaboration between an academic institute and business partners. The aim of the research is to provide solutions in the area of enterprise reference architecture in order to support enterprise architects in their architectural activities. To this end ERA will be positioned in a conceptual model. This paper will also present the (partial) validation of the conceptual model in practice.

There is an increasing tension between the needs of business and the capabilities of their IT landscapes. At the one hand business management is more demanding to flexibility, functionality and robustness of IT, on the other hand business management is limiting the budgets for IT investments in view of cost control. The costs for IT are in some branches enormous, e.g. financial institutions [9], due to costly legacy systems and the introduction of new technology trends. Organisations are pushed to act as quick as possible on these trends in view of severe competition, high expectations of more IT aware customers sharing their opinions in social media. New legislation requires changes to be made in business processes and information systems.

S. Aier et al. (Eds.): TEAR 2012 and PRET 2012, LNBIP 131, pp. 93–110, 2012.
© Springer-Verlag Berlin Heidelberg 2012

Furthermore there is an increased need for risk management, due to the economical unpredictable context. Organisations are challenged to explore new business models. Hence, all these developments pose high requirements to the business services, processes and the supporting IT.

In particular the financial industry is facing significant challenges. The financial crisis that started in 2007 and the subsequent Euro-crisis that emerged since 2011 have even intensified the need to address these challenges. Banks and insurance companies have to manage their costs, their positions and their risks carefully. Legislation, regulations and accounting standards (e.g. Basel III, SOX, IFRS, and Solvency II) require more stringent and transparent reporting. However, the IT landscapes of banking and insurance companies are still scattered, and characterized by monolithic platforms, expensive inflexible legacy systems, and core systems with limited flexibility layered up by add-ons of supporting systems [9]. Stove-piped systems, business silos, duplication of functionality, information inconsistency and long lead times for implementing changes in processes and IT are commonly found.

Enterprise architecture is key to cope with these challenges of business/IT alignment. Enterprise architecture is recognized as the well-accepted discipline that can provide guidance to business management in choices for the business process and application landscape [11, 24] in such way to operate as efficient as possible (costs) and to enable business benefits by providing more value and enabling new business. This enterprise architecture discipline claims to provide the capabilities to design the target architecture and to set out the transformation map to the always changing future and to provide handles for decision making and realization: 'Enterprise architecture guides managers in designing business processes, and application developers in building business applications in a way that matches with business mission, vision, strategy and goals' [5, 19]. Also in the financial industry, enterprise architects have the challenge to define the future target state. In order to do so, they use generic architecture frameworks, methods and language. In addition they are in need of more specific reference architectures to support them in design and realization, but at this moment there is not much available.

The aim of the research described in this paper is to provide solutions in the area of ERA that have a methodological foundation. The structure of the paper is as follows. In section 2 we describe the observed need for enterprise reference architecture in the financial industry. In section 3 we describe various related concepts: architecture, enterprise architecture, reference architecture and we give a working definition for enterprise reference architecture. In section 4 we present the research agenda including the conceptual model for the research, the research goal, the research questions, the research deliverables and the research approach. In section 5 we describe the preliminary results of a validation of (part) of the conceptual model in practice, i.e. a small set of interviews with experienced architecture practitioners. In section 6 we end with conclusions and further work to be done.

2   The Need for Enterprise Reference Architecture in the Financial Industry

In the past decades, the architecture profession has matured in the sense that there are more commonly accepted methods and frameworks and that there are certification requirements to the architecture professionals. Examples are TOGAF9 as architecture framework provided by The Open Group [7] and ArchiMate as architecture modelling method [5], also adopted by The Open Group [8]. The profession matured with these practice oriented methods and tools, however from scientific point of view there are still unanswered questions regarding these methods and frameworks. Still architects in several markets, e.g. the financial industry, have adopted these methods and frameworks to improve their architectural capabilities, and   to apply these in their daily practice. Architecture frameworks and architecture modelling methods are instruments introducing a common vocabulary and way of working to construct models for the as-is situation and the to-be situation in information system design. However, no-one is ever sure whether the designed enterprise architecture is of the required quality and will meet the expectations. No scientifically based instruments are available to get this insight. There is no single comprehensive view of the ways enterprise architecture might add value to an organization [11]. The architecture discipline is still not able to explain clearly whether the architectural models provide indeed the adequate answers to the problems posed [17]. The practical application of enterprise architecture is still in its infancy [20].

In spite of the available methods, financial companies still experience a gap between the practical urgent issues they need to cope with and the available architectural methods. As craftsmen, the architects apply the generic architecture methods for analyzing issues and designing the target solution. There is not a measure or norm they can refer to, in order to determine whether the proposed solutions will indeed lead to the expected business / IT alignment level and as such, to the foreseen business results.

In recent studies [1, 2, 3] the concept of 'reference architecture' is explored as one of the elements that are essential to improve the quality of the architectural work. The usage of reference architecture is perceived as important to improve the quality of the designed enterprise architectures [14, 16].

Not only in academic literature the concept of reference architecture is identified as essential for architectural work, but also in the empirical practice the need for reference architecture for the financial industry is expressed [24]. For the banking industry reference architecture is now under development by the Banking Industry Architecture Network (BIAN), founded in 2008: the so-called BIAN Service Landscape. The BIAN Service landscape can be used as a reference to benchmark architectural documentation and for identifying gaps. The support for such BIAN Service landscape as reference architecture for banking is quite broad, noticing the number of leading members (ABN AMRO, Commonwealth Bank of Australia, Credit Suisse, Deutsche Bank, Banco Galicia, ING, Kutxa, Postbank Systems AG, Rabobank Group, Scotiabank, Standard Bank of South Africa, UniCredit Group, Zurcher

Kantonalbank, SWIFT). The banks that are participating in BIAN all have complex IT environments and have very demanding requirements [25].

Reference architectures are urgently needed to cope with the challenges posed to the enterprise architects, especially in the financial industry. Reference architecture for a typical financial enterprise (e.g. a bank or an insurance company) can be used as guidance and reference point during the design, realization and maintenance of the enterprise architecture. The purpose of such enterprise reference architecture – we abbreviate it to ERA – is three-fold. With regard to the architecture product, the purpose of ERA is to enhance the quality of the resulting enterprise architecture, in the sense that it meets the expectations of the stakeholders. With regard to the architecture process, the purpose of ERA is to speed up the enterprise architecting process and delivery of enterprise architecture results. With regard to the architecture context, the purpose of ERA is to provide improved support to the business in decision making regarding the business/IT alignment, design, realization and maintenance.

3   Definition of Concepts

In this paragraph the concepts of architecture, enterprise architecture and reference architecture are defined, followed by a working definition for enterprise reference architecture. We will refer to academic literature and practitioners' literature. The concepts of architecture, enterprise architecture and reference architecture are described in a number of academic studies [1, 2, 3, 4, 5, 10, 13, 20, 28, 29, 30]. Practitioners' literature [6, 7, 14, 16, 27, 29] provides also quite some descriptions of these concepts.

3.1   Architecture

According to the standardization organization ANSI architecture is defined as the fundamental organization of a system, embodied in its components, their relationships to each other and the environment, and the principles governing its design and evolution [27]. The Open Group further elaborates on this resulting in the following definition [7]: 'Architecture is: 1. a formal description of a system, or detailed plan of the system at component level to guide its implementation; 2. the structure of components, their interrelationship, and the principles and guidelines governing their design and evolution over time.

It is important to determine the location of the architecture description at the aggregation dimension [13] as shown in figure 1.

Fig. 1. Aggregation Levels for Architecture Description

3.2   Enterprise Architecture

Enterprise architecture is located on the two highest aggregation levels for architecture. The Open Group [7] defines enterprise in their TOGAF9 edition as any collection of organizations that has a common set of goals. The term 'enterprise' in the content of 'enterprise architecture' can be used to denote both an entire enterprise – encompassing all of its information and technology services, processes and infrastructure – and a specific domain within the enterprise. In both case, the architecture crosses multiple systems, and multiple functional groups within the enterprise.' The Open Group also recognizes that enterprise architecture can be located at the highest level of the aggregation dimension. Lankhorst et.al [5] define enterprise architecture as "a coherent whole of principles, methods and models that are used in the design and realization of an enterprise's organizational structure, business process, information systems and infrastructure'. Dietz [20] defines enterprise architecture theoretically and practically. Theoretically 'enterprise architecture is understood as the whole set of design principles that an enterprise applies in (re-) designing itself, basically in all its aspects. Operationally enterprise architecture is the whole set of design principles that are applicable to the (re-) designing and (re-) engineering of an enterprise. Three partial architectures are distinguished: the business architecture, the application architecture, the technical architecture." The three partial architectures are also distinguished in the architecture modelling method called ArchiMate [5], which offers a modelling language to make enterprise architecture representations. This ArchiMate method is adopted by The Open Group [8], with the motivation to mobilize the enterprise architecture practitioners to design enterprise architecture models for the three partial architectures in a service oriented way in a formal language that is understandable and readable for all architects. TOGAF9 seems already to be embraced by architects in the financial market, and it is expected that also ArchiMate will be received warmly; especially because there is tooling support available for ArchiMate modelling (examples are BizzDesign

Architect, IDS Scheer Aris ArchiMate Modeller, IBM Rational System Architect and OpenSource Archi ArchiMate Modelling). As result, the Open Group definition seems to be workable in the current architecture practice [29], as it is based on the joint best practices as collected and described by The Open Group and is freely available.

3.3   Reference Architecture

Grefen [13] defines reference architecture as "a general design (abstract blueprint) of a structure for a specific class of information systems. A reference architecture can in general be descriptive or prescriptive." A descriptive reference architecture is based upon the existing best practices in a specific context. Elsinga et al [6] define a reference architecture as 'a reusable architecture model to be used as guideline and starting point for engagements'; engagements in the sense of a programme of projects, wherein a future IT architecture will be realized. The IT world uses the term often for infrastructural concepts [30]. According to [30] a broader view on reference architecture is needed: there are reference architectures for an architecture for a particular domain - software architecture and enterprise architecture. For both cases the reference architecture provides a template solution for architecture (respectively software – or enterprise architecture) for a particular domain. A reference architecture also provides a common vocabulary with which to discuss implementations, often with the aim to stress commonality.

The concept of reference architecture in the field of enterprise architecture (ERA) is less investigated than software reference architecture (SRA) [1, 2, 3, 4, 10]. Angelov gives the following definition of SRA [1, 28]: 'reference architecture as a generic software architecture for a class of software systems that is used as a foundation for the design of concrete architectures of systems from this class.' A concrete architecture is the architectural description of a concrete software system.

This definition regarding SRA is not applicable for the concept of Enterprise Reference Architecture (ERA), being too much focused on software elements, software systems and data flows.

3.4   Enterprise Reference Architecture

Fattah [16] defines ERA as 'the blue print for the Solution Architecture of a number of potential projects within an organization that embodies the EA principles, policies, standards and guidelines. In other words, an ERA is a Solution Architecture with some of the Architectural Decisions already made and others left open.' The ERA of Fattah should be comprehended as an organization-specific enterprise architecture that is used as reference/standard for the program of projects and will be further specified in concrete solution architectures. An architecture can be labelled as reference architecture only if it is defined to abstract from certain contextual specifics [1]; this is also valid for ERA. An ERA should be abstracted from the contextual, organization- / technology specifics in order to be used for several organizations in a specific class of enterprises. 'A reference architecture is a generic architecture for a class of systems, based on best practices' [14). We conclude that an ERA should not be organization-specific, but generic for a specific class of enterprises. An ERA is used for the design of concrete enterprise architectures, belonging to a certain class of enterprise, in multiple contexts, affecting different stakeholders in each context. Furthermore an ERA can be used in combination of any architecture process framework and architecture notation language. A number of elements of the described definitions for EA and RA need to be combined to come to a working definition for Enterprise Reference Architecture. The elements are shown in figure 2.

	Enterprise Architecture Elements
EA1	Partial Architectures for Business, Application and Technology
EA2	Coherent whole of principles, methods and models
EA3	Design and realization purpose
	Reference Architecture Elements
RA1	Generic template or abstract blueprint
RA2	For an architecture for a particular class, i.e. enterprise class
RA3	provides a common vocabulary and structure
RA4	to support design and implementations

Fig. 2. Elements in EA and RA Definitions

3.5   Working Definition of Enterprise Reference Architecture

We propose the following working definition for ERA: An ERA is a generic EA for a class of enterprises, that is a coherent whole of EA design principles, methods and models which are used as foundation in the design and realization of the concrete EA that consists of three coherent partial architectures: the business architecture, the application architecture and the technology architecture.

4   Research to Enterprise Reference Architecture for the Financial Industry

4.1   Research Goal

The goal of the research program is to deliver a scientific grounded theory about ERA that explains why an ERA is needed, what it is and how it can be used. The ERA theory will explain the position of ERA in relation to abstract architecture frameworks and concrete organization specific enterprise architectures. The ERA theory will deliver a coherent set of models, each with its own purpose and function in the practical work area of EA design, transformation and maintenance. By this research we will embed the concept of ERA in a theoretical framework so that it will have much more rigor than in case it is only based upon best practices. The research program is in the first stage, which has an explorative nature. Some preliminary results of the research is described in this paper.

4.2   Research Approach

The research is done on basis of Design Science. Design Science Research is motivated by the desire to improve the environment by the introduction of new and innovative artefacts and the processes for building these artefacts. The research is set up along the following Design Cycles as described by Hevner [21, 22, 23]: Relevance cycle, Rigor cycle and Design cycle. The research is now in the first phase of research to enterprise reference architecture (ERA). In the first phase the cycles of Relevance and Rigor are executed. The objectives of the first phase are:

1. to gain insight in the enterprise reference architectures (ERAs) for the financial industry that currently exist in literature;
2. to gain insight in the practical usage and application of ERAs in the financial industry;
3. to identify the characteristics of ERAs that determine their applicability to support the enterprise architecture design and management;
4. to identify the characteristics of ERAs that determine their applicability to support decision making regarding enterprise architecture.

This first phase consists of three research strategies: a literature review, a set of semi-structured interviews and a survey. Each research strategy will be executed via a research project with its own approach. The literature review and the interviews will be done in parallel projects.

• The literature review is performed in view of the Rigor Cycle: to get insight in the current body of knowledge about ERAs in the scientific domain.
• The interviews are done in view of the Relevance cycle: to get insight in the needs, problems and opportunities experienced in practice with applying ERAs.
• The survey will be done in later instance to validate the conclusions derived from the results of literature research and the interviews.

The outcome of the three research strategies will be used as basis of the second phase. In the second phase the Design Cycle will be performed aiming to design four artefacts.

4.3   Conceptual Model for Research

The concepts that are defined in section 2 have been positioned in a conceptual model (Figure 3). On the vertical axis at the lower end concrete concepts are positioned and at the higher end abstract concepts. On the horizontal axis at the left hand structural concepts in the real world are positioned and at the right hand mental concepts in a world of representations. On the middle of the horizontal axis transformational process concepts are positioned: architecting activities are transforming the real world to representation, and can also be used to transform representations to the real world. In this model the concepts 'Enterprise' and 'Class of Enterprises' are present in the real world (visualized as rounded rectangle symbols). The concrete, real enterprise belongs to a specific class of enterprises. 'EA' and 'ERA' (visualized by the cloud symbols) are created by architecting activities to represent the concepts 'Enterprise' and 'Class of Enterprises'. EA is a representation of a specific, real enterprise. ERA is a representation of the commonalities in enterprises of a specific class. 'Architecture Framework' is independent of any class of enterprise, and has a common accepted format and structure (visualized by the rectangle symbol); it is on a higher abstraction level than ERA, because it can be used for any class of organization, not only for a specific class. 'Architecture Framework' and 'ERA' are actively applied during the architecting activities, which is expressed by the arrows.

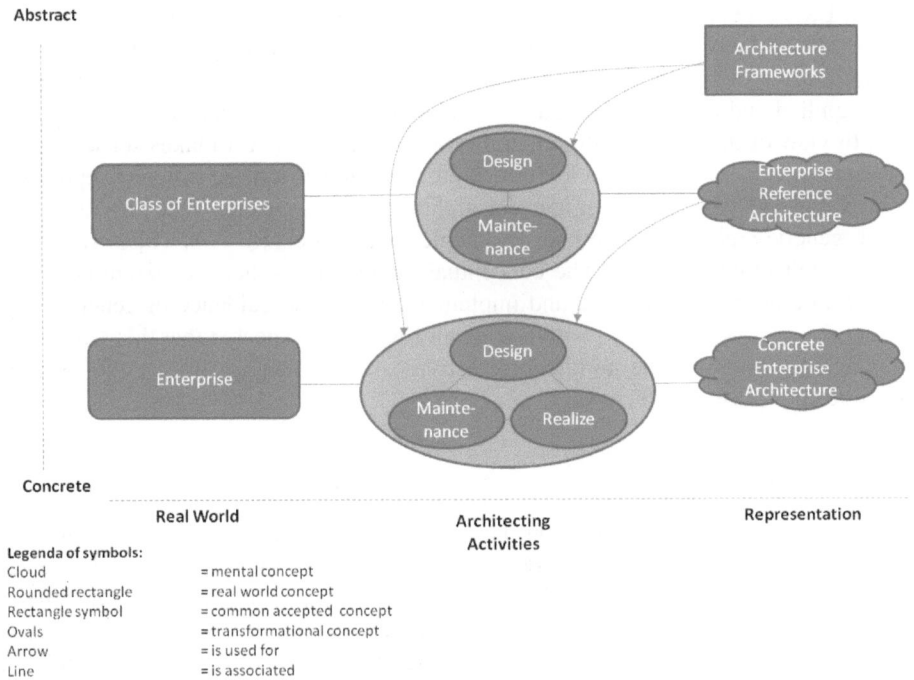

Fig. 3. Conceptual Model: Overview of the Concepts

For this research we will focus on the class of enterprise in the financial industry. To cope with the challenges in the real world, architecting activities are performed leading to a concrete enterprise architecture. Still a concrete enterprise architecture is a representation (e.g. design principles and models) of the baseline and/or the envisioned target state of the enterprise. Even when the concrete EA is realized, i.e. business services, processes, application landscape and technology are implemented, the concrete EA is a representation that will be used for monitoring and maintenance reasons. The nature of ERA is to be a foundation to be specified further for a concrete enterprise architecture of a specific enterprise class, and as such ERA will not be realized for its own purpose; it will always be a reference for the concrete EA.

At this moment enterprise architects apply the available architecture frameworks that support them in the architecting activities. Architecture frameworks provide guidelines and meta models for the EA product and process models. Examples of architecture frameworks [6, 7, 26] that provide a metamodel for structuring the business, application and technology concepts are the Integrated Architecture Framework (IAF), Common Open Reference Architecture (CORA) and the Architecture Content Framework. TOGAF9 provides also a process model: the Architecture Development Method (ADM) including guidelines and techniques that can be applied during the several stages in the ADM. Although the available frameworks and process models offer improved support, there are long lead times for architecture design and (partially) unfulfilled expectations in the realization of the EA. By introducing the concept of ERA – i.e. the representation of a typical enterprise (in other words a blueprint for the EA of the related class of enterprises), **there** is more support and guidance for the architecting activities. For each class of enterprise an ERA needs to be designed, to be applied and to be maintained, in order to keep the relevance for future application. In view of the required alignment between ERA and EA it makes sense to apply the same architecture frameworks for design. An ERA is a more concrete representation of the real world than the current architecture frameworks that provide us abstract, generic architecture methods, principles and models [5, 7, 8, 18] to support us in the architecting activities. The conceptual model shows that a concrete enterprise architecture need to be realized and implemented with the guidance of generic architecture frameworks combined with a relevant ERA. It is expected that this will lead to shorter lead times for the architecting activities and better quality of the resulting concrete enterprise architectures.

4.4   Research Questions

The emphasis in this research is on the 'object-side' of ERA (structure of ERA and application of ERA during activities for EA) and less on the 'development-side' activities for ERA itself (design and maintenance of ERA). The choice to limit the research to the 'object'-side is that firstly current architecture frameworks already offer guidance and support for architecting activities for EA and ERA, and secondly the 'object-side' of ERA is very relevant for the financial industry and is a rather unexplored research area. In our research we have split the research up in four research areas in order to have a set of focused research questions:

1. Foundation: Basic questions regarding ERA
    What is an ERA? What are the requirements to an ERA? Are ERA's already available and how are they used?
2. Product area: ERA as used for the enterprise architecture product
    Can an ERA enhance the quality of the enterprise architecture products in the sense that expectations of stakeholders are fulfilled?
3. Process area: ERA as used for the enterprise architecting process
    Can an ERA speed up the enterprise architecting design process and delivery of enterprise architecture results?
4. Context area: ERA as used to support decision making

Can an ERA provide improved support to the business in decision making regarding the business/IT alignment and during the EA design, realization and maintenance?

The research areas are positioned in the conceptual model leading to a coherent set of questions (figure 4).

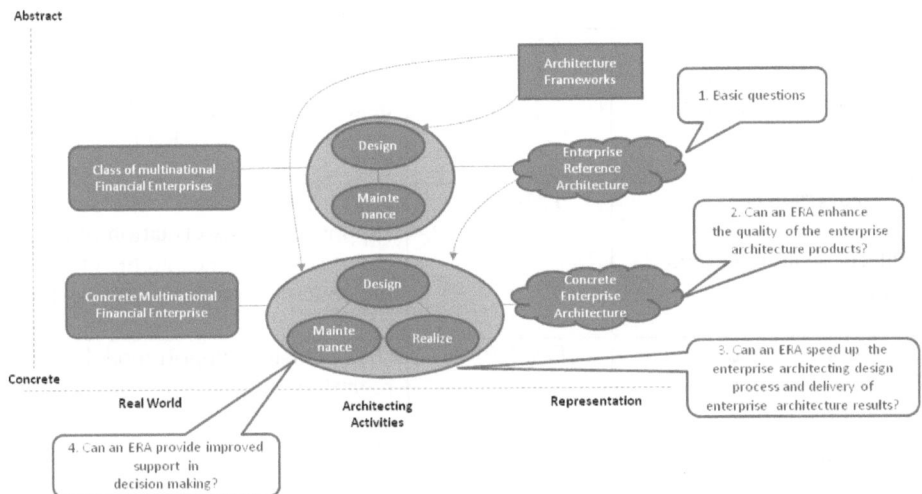

Fig. 4. Research Areas

4.5   Research Deliverables

The objective of the research is to provide solutions for the questions in the distinguished four research areas. This will be done by the design of the following artefacts.

A. A set of norms to be given by enterprise reference architecture (NORM-ERA), which guides architects in analysis of the concrete enterprise.
B. An assessment model to assess the concrete enterprise architecture against the enterprise reference architecture (AM-ERA).
C. A transformation model to support the transformation of the enterprise reference architecture to the concrete enterprise architecture (TM-ERA).
D. A decision support model (DSM-ERA) regarding the concrete enterprise architecture that is under design, realization or maintenance. DSM-ERA is addressing the needs of decision makers and will make use of elements of NORM-ERA, AM-ERA and TM-ERA.

Each artefact is the answer on corresponding research area (table 1).

Table 1. Research Areas and corresponding Artefacts

Research area	Artefact name	Artefact description
Foundation: Basic questions regarding ERA	NORM-ERA	A set of norms given by enterprise reference architecture that guides architects in analysis of the concrete enterprise
Product area: ERA as used for the enterprise architecture product	AM-ERA	An assessment model to assess the concrete enterprise architecture against the enterprise reference architecture (AM-ERA)
Process area: ERA as used for the enterprise architecting process	TM-ERA	A transformation model to support the transformation of the enterprise reference architecture to the concrete enterprise architecture
Context area: ERA as used to support decision making	DSM-ERA	A decision support model regarding the concrete enterprise architecture that is under design, realization or maintenance.

5   Results of First Research Project

This section describes first results of the research project in the relevance cycle: to get insight in the needs, problems and opportunities experienced in practice with applying ERAs.

5.1   Research Strategies

The first phase in the research program to ERA consists of three research strategies: a literature review, a set of semi-structured interviews and a survey. Each research strategy will be executed via a research project with its own approach, so three research projects will be done during the first phase. The main objective of this research project is to validate the ERA concept as positioned in the conceptual model, and to seek for first answers to the coherent set of questions as presented in figure 4. In view of this validation, we have defined the following objectives for the research project using interviews:

1. to identify enterprise reference architectures (ERAs) that are used in the existing architecture practice;
2. to identify users of enterprise reference architectures, and what their needs are regarding enterprise reference architectures;

3. to discover how ERAs are used (or can be used) by architecture practitioners in the design, realization and decision making about concrete enterprise architectures for the financial industry;
4. to identify the requirements for an ERA to be supportive for enterprise architects;
5. to discover the benefits that ERA can bring to enterprise architecture design, realization and decision making.

5.2   Research Decisions for Interviews

The following research decisions are made regarding the interviews. Due to the explanatory nature of this study the interviews are done in a semi-structured manner. The interviews are held with experienced enterprise architects with at least 15 years of working experience in IT and have now a formal job position as architect in the organization. The enterprise architects are certified according to TOGAF specification. The interviews are held with architects that have worked for organizations in the financial market. Each interview is done at the working location of the architect. Duration per interview is 1 hour.

The interviews are set up along the conceptual model (figure 3). At the start of the interview the conceptual model is shown to the interviewee in order to see whether this conceptual model is recognized, and whether the concepts as positioned in the model are clear to the interviewee. The research objectives and the conceptual model are the basis for the formulation of four interview questions.

1. Which enterprise reference architectures do you use in the existing architecture practice?
2. Who do you consider (potential) users of enterprise reference architectures, and what are their needs regarding enterprise reference architectures?
3. How are enterprise reference architectures used (or can be used) by you in your work to design and realization of concrete enterprise architectures?
4. Why are ERAs used or should be used? In other words, what are the benefits that ERA can bring to enterprise architecture design, realization, maintenance and decision making?

During the interview the conceptual model will be placed in front of the interviewee on the table as well as the definitions.

5.3   Results of Pilot Interviews

A limited number of pilot interviews were held to validate the interview format and the conceptual model. Total number of interviewees was 5. In later instance a second larger sample of interviews will be held. All interviewees matched the criteria as decided for the interview sample. Average working experience in the IT is 27 years. Average working experience as enterprise architect is 7 years. All interviewees are member of an architecture unit. They were all employed by an international firm in

IT services; their experience in architecture work was built up through projects done for client organizations, mainly in the financial market. Architects employed by financial organizations were not selected in this small sample because of the pilot nature of this stage of interviewing. In the planned larger sample to be interviewed later also architects employed by financial organizations and having internal architecture roles will be included.

The answers on the questions are described hereafter.

1. *Question 1: Which enterprise reference architectures do you use in the existing architecture practice?* All interviewees could name one or more ERAs. The following ERAs were mentioned: IBM Industry models for banking and insurance companies (IFW, IAA), ERAs for other industries (e.g. the eTOM model provided by the Telemanagement Forum), RAs for specific technology or tooling (e.g. ESB, BPM tooling, ERP tooling), RAs for specific processes (.e.g. Order2Cash, Call Centre). Also BIAN was mentioned once. The IBM Industry models were mentioned mostly. The interviewees also identified technology reference architectures; these are RAs for the implementation of specific technology and are enterprise class independent. The technology reference architectures are mostly delivered by tool suppliers. Although interviewees could name ERAs, the majority of the interviewees (60%) had hardly any practical experience with ERAs. They also mentioned that the financial organizations where they worked for do not make use of ERAs, although these organizations had all developed their own EA that was used indeed as reference for the projects. The interviewees also told that they use mainly a lot of their own architecture models collected during their career.

2. *Question 2: Who do you consider (potential) users of enterprise reference architectures, and what are their needs regarding enterprise reference architectures?* The interviewees identified the following (potential) users of ERA: enterprise architects, project architects, solution architects, architecture governance boards, business managers, program managers, business consultants, information managers, CIOs and suppliers. One interviewee mentioned also external audit organizations as potential users of ERA. Neither software developers nor end-users of the architecture were considered to be users of ERA. The following needs were mentioned that can be fulfilled by the application of ERA. Generic needs are in communication and validation. All stakeholders can use ERA as instrument to provide support in communication and teamwork. Furthermore there is a general need for support in validation of choices that are made during architecting activities. Specific needs are expressed for the several ERA users. The answers make clear that four categories of ERA users can be distinguished: firstly the category of ERA users that are performing the architecting activities, secondly the category of ERA users that are involved in management, thirdly the category of ERA users that are focusing on review and auditing, fourthly the category of ERA users that are providing commercial IT solutions. The first category consists of business consultants, enterprise architects, project architects and solution architects; the first category has specific needs for support in scoping, analysis and design of

processes, applications and IT. The second category consists of business managers, CIOs and program managers; they have specific needs for support in impact analysis of consequences of choices for the total organization and for transformation programs. The third category consists of architecture governance boards and external organizations; the third category has a need for support in auditing and reviewing activities. The fourth category consists of suppliers with the need to have an overview of the requirements to their solutions for a specific class of enterprises.

3. *Question 3: How are enterprise reference architectures used (or can be used) by you in your work to design and realization of concrete enterprise architectures?* The following functions of ERAs were identified: provide support for communication between stakeholders, provide support for scoping and design, provide support for selection of IT tooling and packages, provide support for review. In general an ERA can serve as a checklist that provides guidelines and solution directions. Also an ERA can be used for training and knowledge transfer regarding the specifics of an enterprise class.

4. *Question 4: Why are ERAs used or should be used? What are the benefits?* The interviewees mentioned the following three major benefit areas of ERAs: in the first place communication, in the second place quality, in the third place time reduction. ERA can serve as a communication instrument because it provides the insight of the unique areas of the enterprise class. This communication benefit can only be achieved if the ERA is not too detailed. An ERA will increase the quality of the concrete EA because it is based on best practices of architecture experiences within an enterprise class. 80% of the respondents stated that it is expected that ERA can contribute to reduce the required time for design of EA because ERA shows the focus areas to be worked out.

5.4   Observations

The results of the pilot interviews lead us to the following observations regarding the conceptual model:

- There is good recognition of the conceptual model wherein the distinct concepts of 'architecture framework', 'enterprise reference architecture' and concrete 'enterprise architecture' are positioned and related to concepts as 'class of enterprises' and concrete 'enterprise'.
- There is an additional concept identified that is not present in the presented conceptual model: technology reference architecture (TRA). This TRA is seen as enterprise class independent, and seen as valuable for the concrete EA in addition to the ERA.
- There is hardly any practical experience with ERAs although all interviewed enterprise architects could name examples of ERA.
- ERA is seen as an important instrument that can fulfil a generic need for support in communication and teamwork.

- There is a generic need for ERA in order to validate choices made during architecting activities.
- There are four categories of (potential) ERA users that can be supported with ERA in their specific needs.
- Major benefit areas are expected to be in communication, quality and time reduction.

6   Conclusions

The current available architecture frameworks, models and architecture modelling languages are not sufficient to support architects in coping with the challenges in business/IT alignment. There is a need for additional support and guidance, especially by the financial industry. This can be given by the concept of enterprise reference architecture (ERA).

In this paper we have specified a working definition for ERA and have presented a conceptual model to clarify the concepts of EA and ERA. An ERA is a more concrete representation of the real world than the current architecture frameworks that provide generic architecture methods, principles, models and notation languages. We have chosen to limit our research in the conceptual model to the 'object-side' of ERA because of its relevance for the enterprise architects in the financial Industry. So we decided not to focus on questions regarding the design and maintenance of the ERA itself but to focus on the ERA structure and the application of ERA: what is ERA about, how can ERA be used to assess the concrete EA, how can ERA be applied during architecting processes and how can ERA be applied in decision making by management? We have located these major questions in the conceptual model.

The research to the answers on these questions will deliver a coherent set of artefacts: a set of norms to be given by ERA, an assessment model to assess concrete EA to ERA, a transformation model to support the transformation of ERA to concrete EA and finally a decision support model for management regarding the concrete EA that is under design, realization or maintenance. We have positioned the artefacts in the conceptual model and have put them on our research agenda. The described research agenda is challenging for this rather unexplored research domain. We have described results of a small set of pilot interviews that are held in the first phase of the research. Purpose of the pilot interviews was to validate the conceptual model. The preliminary results show the relevancy of the research. Current data show that there is good recognition of the conceptual model wherein the distinct concepts of 'architecture framework', 'enterprise reference architecture' and concrete 'enterprise architecture' are positioned and related to concepts as 'class of enterprises' and concrete 'enterprise'. ERA is seen as a relevant instrument that can fulfil a generic need for support in communication, teamwork and validation of choices. Although the interview results show that there is hardly any practical experience with ERA, the interview results also show that the architects expect that ERA can bring benefits in three major areas: in the first place improved communications between stakeholders, in the second place higher quality of the concrete enterprise architecture, in the third place reduction of time needed to start up the scoping and design activities. This needs to be validated in the next round of interviews done with more architects. On basis of the current interview results we have identified four categories of (potential) ERA users that can be supported with ERA in their specific needs. In the future research we need to sharpen their requirements for ERA, also in view of the artefacts to be delivered in this research. The interview results also show that there is an additional concept that is not present in the conceptual model: technology reference architecture (TRA). This TRA is seen as enterprise class independent, and seen as valuable for the concrete EA in addition to the ERA. We need to define the concept of TRA and position it in the conceptual model. We need to make clear how it relates to ERA and EA. Furthermore our future research will work on the provision of guidelines how to use ERA and how to apply ERA during architecting activities.

We expect that the results of this research will contribute to the rigor and relevance of ERA. We conclude that ERA is the next step in maturing the enterprise architecture discipline.

References

[1] Angelov, S., Grefen, P., Greefhorst, D.: A Classification of Software Reference Architectures: Analyzing Their Success and Effectiveness. In: Joint Working IEEE/IFIP Conference on Software Architecture & European Conference on Software Architecture (WICSA/ECSA), pp. 141–150. IEEE Computer Society, Cambridge (2009)

[2] Angelov, S., Grefen, P., Greefhorst, D.: A Framework for Analysis and Design of Software Reference Architectures. Information and Software Technology 54(4), 417–431 (2012)

[3] Angelov, S., ten Harmsen van der Beek, W., Trienekens, J.: Software Reference Architectures – A Forgotten Baby? IEEE Software (in press, 2012)

[4] Guessi, M., de Oliveira, L.B.R., Nakagawa, E.Y.: Representation of Reference Architectures: A Systematic Review, Department of Computer Systems, University of São Paulo, SP, Brazil (2011)

[5] Lankhorst, M., et al.: Enterprise Architecture at Work – Modelling, Communication, and Analysis. Springer (2005)

[6] Elzinga, T., van der Vlies, J., Smiers, L.: The CORA Model. SDU (2009)

[7] The Open Group, TOGAF™ Version 9, VanHaren Publishing (2009)

[8] The Open Group, ArchiMate® 2.0, VanHaren Publishing (2012)

[9] Bonney, P., Delmarcelle, P.P., Obitz, T., Peters, G.: TOGAF® BIAN White Paper. The Open Group and Banking Industry Architecture Network (2012), http://www.bian.org

[10] Avgeriou, P., Galster, M.: Empirically-grounded Reference Architectures: A Proposal. In: Proceedings of the Joint ACM SIGSOFT Conference, pp. 153–158. ACM, New York (2011)

[11] Bouchara, V., Brinkkemper, S., Jansen, S., Steenbergen, M.: The Contribution of Enterprise Architecture to the Achievement of Organizational Goals: A Review of the Evidence. In: Proper, E., Lankhorst, M.M., Schönherr, M., Barjis, J., Overbeek, S. (eds.) TEAR 2010. LNBIP, vol. 70, pp. 1–15. Springer, Heidelberg (2010)

[12] Greefhorst, D., Grefen, P., Saaman, E., Bergman, P., van Beek, W.: Referentie-Architectuur: Off-the-Shelf Architectuur. In: Landelijk Architectuur Congres 2008, NAF & SDU, Nieuwegein, The Netherlands (2008) (in Dutch)
[13] Grefen, P.: Business Information System Architectures. Eindhoven University of Technology, Eindhoven (2012)
[14] Greefhorst, D., Grefen, P., Saaman, E., Bergman, P., van Beek, W.: Herbruikbare Architectuur. In: Informatie, pp. 8–14 (September 2009) (in Dutch)
[15] de Boer, R., Oord, E., Schijvenaars, T.: Referentie-architecturen in de Praktijk (October 2011) (in Dutch), http://www.via-nova-architectura.org
[16] Fattah, A.: Enterprise Reference Architecture – Adressing Key Challenges facing EA and Enterprise-Wide Adoption of SOA (June 2009), http://www.via-nova-architectura.org
[17] Johnson, P., Ekstedt, M., Silva, E., Plazaola, L.: Using Enterprise Architecture for CIO Decision-Making: on the Importance of Theory. In: The Proceedings of the 2nd Annual Conference on Systems Engineering Research (2004)
[18] Bernus, P., Nemes, L.: A Framework to Define a Generic Enterprise Reference Architecture and Methodology. Computer Integrated Manufacturing Systems 9(3), 179–191 (1996)
[19] Op't Land, M., Proper, H.A.E., Waage, M., Cloo, J., Steghuis, C.: Enterprise Architecture – Creating Value by Informed Governance. Springer, Berlin (2008)
[20] Dietz, J.L.G.: Architecture, Building Strategy into Design, SDU, Academic Service (2008)
[21] March, S.T., Storey, V.C.: Design Science in the Information Systems Discipline: An Introduction to the Special Issue on Design Science Research. MIS Quarterly 32(4), 725–730 (2008)
[22] Hevner, A., March, S., Park, J., Ram, S.: Design Science in Information Systems Research. MIS Quarterly 28(1), 75–105 (2004)
[23] Hevner, A.: A Three Cycle View of Design Science Research. Scandinavian Journal of Information Systems 19(2), 87–92 (2007)
[24] BIAN (2012), http://www.bian.org
[25] Knox, M., Free, D.: Gartner's Viability Assessment of BIAN. Gartner Industry Research (December 2010)
[26] van 't Wout, J., Waage, M., Hartman, H., Stahlecker, M., Hofman, A.: The Integrated Architecture Framework Explained. Springer (2010)
[27] ANSI, IEEE Standards Organization, IEEE Standard Glossary of Software Engineering Terminology IEEE 1471 (2000)
[28] Angelov, S., Grefen, P., Trienekens, J.: Extending and Adapting the Architecture Tradeoff Analysis Method for the Evaluation of Software Reference Architectures (2011) (in press)
[29] van Bommel, P., Nakakawa, A., Proper, H.A.E.: Quality Enhancement in Creating Enterprise Architecture: Relevance of Academic Models in Practice. In: Proper, E., Harmsen, F., Dietz, J.L.G. (eds.) PRET 2009. LNBIP, vol. 28, pp. 109–133. Springer, Heidelberg (2009)
[30] Muller, G., Hole, E.: Reference Architectures: Why, What and How - White Paper Resulting from Architecture Forum Meeting, Embedded Systems Institute and Stevens Institute of Technology, Hoboken, NJ (2007)

Two Speeds of EAM—A Dynamic Capabilities Perspective

Ralf Abraham, Stephan Aier, and Robert Winter

Institute of Information Management, University of St. Gallen, Mueller-Friedberg-Strasse 8,
9000 St. Gallen, Switzerland
{Ralf.Abraham,Stephan.Aier,Robert.Winter}@unisg.ch

Abstract. We discuss how enterprise architecture management (EAM) supports different types of enterprise transformation (ET), namely planned, proactive transformation on the one hand and emergent, reactive transformation on the other hand. We first conceptualize EAM as a dynamic capability to access the rich literature of the dynamic capabilities framework. Based on these theoretical foundations and observations from two case studies, we find that EAM can be configured both as a planned, structured capability to support proactive ET, as well as an improvisational, simple capability to support reactive ET under time pressure. We argue that an enterprise can simultaneously deploy both sets of EAM capabilities by identifying the core elements of EAM that are required for both capabilities as well as certain capability-specific extensions. We finally discuss governance and feedback mechanisms that help to balance the goals of flexibility and agility associated with dynamic and improvisational capabilities, respectively.

Keywords: Enterprise Transformation, Enterprise Architecture Management, Dynamic Capabilities.

1   Introduction

Enterprises face an increasingly complex environment which forces them to undergo fundamental change, in other words transform themselves [1, 2] The causes for such transformation efforts range from business- or IT-driven initiatives inside the enterprise to external events such as the emergence of new technologies or changing regulatory requirements.

Literature uses different terms to describe fundamental change in the context of organizations, ranging from "organizational transformation" [3, 4] or "business transformation" [5] to "enterprise transformation" [1]. While transformation is usually regarded as fundamental, radical change (second-order change) in contrast to small-scale, incremental (first-order) change, there is some discrepancy whether transformation occurs suddenly and purposefully [1, 3], or whether it results from a continuum of emergent, smaller changes [4, 6]. In this paper, we will follow the definition of Rouse [1] and use the term "enterprise transformation" (ET) to describe change that fundamentally alters an enterprise's relationship with one of its key constituencies,

S. Aier et al. (Eds.): TEAR 2012 and PRET 2012, LNBIP 131, pp. 111–128, 2012.
© Springer-Verlag Berlin Heidelberg 2012

such as employees, suppliers, customers or investors. We understand ET in contrast to routine change as a purposeful steering intervention into an enterprise's evolution, with its purpose being to respond to perceived opportunities, deficiencies or threats [7].

ET affects multiple domains and layers within an enterprise [8] and is eventually performed simultaneously in different projects, which form the basic unit of change. Since these projects exhibit mutual dependencies, ET needs to be coordinated [9]. In order to support and coordinate ET, the field of enterprise architecture management (EAM) is frequently put forward. EAM is regarded as supporting ET by providing alignment between different partial architectural layers, such as business and information technology (IT) [10]. It is also seen as ensuring coherence of individual projects with the overall enterprise strategy, i.e. aiming for global optimization [11]. Yet, the kind of support required for different ET projects varies. Rouse [1] indicates that ET projects performed as reactions to external pressures (such as competitor's initiatives) lead to higher failure rates than proactive ET projects aimed at exploiting internal or external opportunities. He points out the shorter reaction time in the case of reactive transformation as a cause for this difference in failure rates.

In order to assess EAM support for different types of ET projects, we conducted a focus group with enterprise architects in Switzerland in the fall of 2011. Discussing EAM support of different ET projects, the group arrived at two main findings: (1) EAM is able to support proactive, strategy-driven ET projects when it has positioning on corporate levels instead of IT—a finding that is also reflected in literature [12]. (2) When enterprises need to transform swiftly in response to external pressures, EAM is perceived as being too slow and is often bypassed by the business side.

Especially the second finding indicates that EAM needs to provide its services in a leaner, more responsive way to be actually useful in situations of time pressure. Yet, since enterprises face both types of ET projects [1], EAM needs to support both strategic, proactive change while also being able to provide swift assistance when enterprises are forced to react to external pressures. The research question we intend to answer is the following:

1. RQ: How can EAM be configured into variants that provide specific support for proactive and reactive ET projects?

In this paper, we will take a look at a major framework in strategic management literature that emphasizes changing environments and how enterprises configure their capabilities accordingly: The dynamic capabilities framework. By conceptualizing EAM as one instance of a dynamic capability, we are able to build upon the rich vocabulary and findings from the dynamic capabilities framework, in order to show how the nature of a capability changes in response to different types of environmental dynamics.

The rest of this paper is organized as follows. In chapter 2, we review the foundations of the dynamic capabilities framework and EAM before subsuming EAM under the dynamic capabilities framework. In chapter 3, we show how EAM is able to address different types of environmental change. Chapter 4 provides and compares two case studies. Chapter 5 discusses the challenges involved with an EAM function that has to support different configurations. The paper ends with a conclusion.

2   Foundations

2.1   Dynamic Capabilities

In strategic management literature, the dynamic capabilities framework has become a major topic of research in recent years, with its impact also stretching to the domain of information systems [13].

The ultimate goal of the dynamic capabilities framework is "to explain the sources of enterprise-level competitive advantage over time" [14]. The dynamic capabilities framework can thus be seen as an extension of the resource-based view (RBV), which strives to answer the same question. However, the RBV has been criticized for underestimating environmental dynamics [15]. The RBV takes an inward-looking perspective on enterprises by regarding them as resource bundles. If these resource bundles exhibit the so-called VRIN attributes (i.e., if they are valuable, rare, inimitable and non-substitutable), they are seen as explaining the company's sustained competitive advantage. The dynamic capabilities framework, on the other hand, emphasizes the role of environmental changes: The ability to change existing resource configurations is regarded as the source of sustained competitive advantage. The key argument is that the VRIN attributes of an enterprise's resource bundle erode over time as the environment changes. Superior resource configurations may explain short-term competitive advantage, but to achieve sustainable competitive advantage, dynamic capabilities stress the re-configuration of existing resources in order to achieve and maintain alignment with the environment, i.e. the market [13, 16, 17].

What the RBV considers as resources, the dynamic capabilities framework sees as operational capabilities, alternatively referred to as "zero-level" [18], "zero-order" or "ordinary" [17] capabilities. Operational capabilities enable firms to make a living by conducting day-to-day business [19]. Collis [20] defines operational capabilities as "those that reflect an ability to perform the basic operational activities of the firm". Concrete examples of operational capabilities are production processes, information and communication infrastructure, sales or marketing functions. These operational capabilities are the object of interest of dynamic capabilities.

In this paper, we will follow the definition of dynamic capabilities provided by Barreto [13] that is based on an extensive literature review on dynamic capabilities research: "A dynamic capability is the firm's potential to systematically solve problems, formed by its propensity to sense opportunities and threats, to make timely and market-oriented decisions, and to change its resource base." This definition indicates the two key processes of a dynamic capability: (1) Search and selection (identifying opportunities and threats and making decisions), and (2) reconfiguration (changing its operational capabilities or resource base). In a similar vein, Teece [14] breaks dynamic capabilities down into "sensing and seizing" and "reconfiguration" capabilities. The definition indicates that dynamic capabilities help enterprises reconfigure their resource base (i.e., their operational capabilities) in a planned, systematic way. This hierarchy is also indicated by the description of dynamic capabilities as "first-order" [17], "reconfiguration" [17] or "higher level" [18] capabilities.

Dynamic capabilities require significant investments in specialized resources and personnel in order to establish and maintain them [14, 18]. To actually exercise reconfiguration via dynamic capabilities, sufficient time for planning processes and execution is required [16, 17]. Management literature provides various examples of dynamic capabilities, including research and development [19], product development [17], alliancing [16, 19], acquisition [16, 19], knowledge management [14, 19] or activities aimed at "restructuring" [19] or "re-engineering" [19] such as business process management [21].

In order to reconfigure operational capabilities, an enterprise does not necessarily require dynamic capabilities. As Winter [18] notes, "[i]t is quite possible to change without having a dynamic capability". The advantageousness of dynamic capabilities depends on the degree of turbulence in the environment. In relatively stable environments with infrequent changes, occasional reconfiguration can be achieved more cost-efficiently by "ad hoc problem solving" [18, 19]. Winter [18] defines ad hoc problem solving as individual, spontaneous, and non-repetitive acts of creativity to address suddenly occurring problems. Maintaining dynamic capabilities in these environments may well constitute unnecessary overhead. Reconfiguration of operational capabilities with the help of dynamic capabilities is more advantageous in dynamic environments. In turbulent environments, dynamic capabilities are likely to enable superior performance by providing an institutionalized, planned and patterned approach to changing operational capabilities. As Cohen [22] point out, "fortune favors the prepared firm". The overall degree of stability in the environment is frequently referred to as the level of "environmental turbulence" [17, 23]. Three dimensions of environmental turbulence are proposed [23, 24]:

1. Frequency, as experienced by the time span between environmental changes
2. Amplitude, meaning the degree of difference involved in environmental changes
3. Predictability, meaning the amount to which a pattern is recognizable in environmental changes.

Based on these three dimensions, Eisenhardt and Martin [16] as well as Pavlou and El Sawy [17] distinguish two types of environmental turbulence and their effects on the nature of dynamic capabilities. Table 1 describes these two types.

Table 1. Conceptualization of two types of environmental turbulence

Type of environmental turbulence	Frequency	Amplitude	Predictability
"Waves" [17], "Moderately dynamic markets" [16]	High	High	High
"Storms" [17], "High-velocity markets" [16]	High	High	Low

While both "waves" and "storms" may exhibit high frequencies and amplitudes of change, the important difference lies in the predictability of change. Changes may be frequent and wide-ranging, yet if they occur in a context of stable industry structures, identifiable competitors and clear business models, they still follow a certain pattern and therefore fall in the category of waves [16]. On the other hand, unanticipated market moves by aggressive competitors, shifting and unidentifiable competitors and suddenly changing market needs trigger unpredictable change and thus fall in the category of storms [17].

When environmental turbulence falls into the category of waves, dynamic capabilities are materialized as planned, stable processes that are able to exploit past experiences. However, in the event of storms, dynamic capabilities become simple and emergent activities that rely on improvisation rather than planning [16]. Pavlou and El Sawy [17] introduce the term "improvisational capabilities" in addition, i.e. as complements to dynamic capabilities to describe reconfiguration capabilities that are able to address environmental turbulences marked by unpredictable change (storms). Improvisational capabilities are defined as "the ability to spontaneously reconfigure existing resources to build new operational capabilities to address urgent, unpredictable, and novel environmental situations" [17]. Improvisational capabilities as introduced by Pavlou and El Sawy [17] are explicitly distinguished from Winter's [18] notion of ad hoc problem solving. They are seen as collective, patterned, purposeful and repeated capabilities that can be learned and improved with frequent practice. Pavlou and El Sawy [17] stress the importance of real-time information and communication for improvisational capabilities. On the other hand, too strong a reliance on past knowledge and routines is seen as hindering improvisational capabilities [17] while considered an important element for dynamic capabilities [16]. Given their simpler structure, improvisational capabilities can be exercised considerably faster than dynamic capabilities that often rely on a lengthy planning process [17]. In table 2, the most important differences between dynamic and improvisational capabilities are summarized.

Table 2. Improvisational vs. dynamic capabilities (based on Pavlou and El Sawy [17])

	Dynamic capabilities	Improvisational capabilities
Environmental situation	Anticipated environmental events ("waves")	Unanticipated environmental events ("storms")
Nature of activities	Detailed, planned, structured	Simple, emergent, (largely) unstructured
Time requirements	Sufficient time for formal planning and execution required	Faster reconfiguration possible by enabling spontaneous reactions to environmental changes
Role of information	Heavy reliance on existing knowledge, memory from past change projects helps reconfiguration	Real-time information is critical, creation of new knowledge
Type of ET project	Proactive ET	Reactive ET

Summarizing, both dynamic and improvisational capabilities can be considered instances of first-level reconfiguration capabilities, i.e. they both aim at reconfiguring zero-level operational capabilities. When change is predictable (waves) and can be planned, as in the case of proactive ET, dynamic capabilities are more effective than improvisational capabilities [17, 22]. In unpredictable environments (storms) or reactive ET, when change must be brought about swiftly, improvisational capabilities "fully dominate" [17].

2.2   Enterprise Architecture Management

According to the ISO/IEC/IEEE Standard 42010, architecture is defined as "the fundamental organization of a system, embodied in its components, their relationships to each other and the environment, and the principles governing its design and evolution" [25]. This definition of architecture involves two aspects: The first part of the definition ("the fundamental organization of a system, embodied in its components, their relationships to each other and the environment [...]") forms a descriptive aspect, concerning the structure of the system's building blocks and the relationships between them. The second part ("[...] the principles governing its design and evolution") forms a prescriptive aspect, effectively restricting the design and evolution space of the system under consideration.

Following this definition of architecture, we will adopt The Open Group's definition of enterprise architecture (EA) as (1) the fundamental structure of a public or private organization, i.e. a governmental agency or a company, and (2) the principles that guide its design and evolution [26]. Enterprise Architecture Management (EAM) is concerned with establishing, maintaining and purposefully developing an enterprise's architecture [12, 27]. EAM is a continuous management process that addresses EA as its management object [12] and that serves a purpose: achieving business-it-alignment and supporting ET [12, 28, 29, 30].

Addressing the descriptive aspect of architecture, EAM is concerned with establishing transparency. EAM serves as a decision support function by "taking the overwhelming amount of information available and presenting it in a manner that enables effective decision-making" [31]. Capturing the current state of EA and keeping this information up-to-date is therefore seen as one of the EAM team's core tasks [12].

Concerning the prescriptive aspect of architecture, EAM is concerned with maintaining consistency. Principles guide enterprise evolution by restricting design freedom [32] in order to maintain consistency between the enterprise strategy and its implementation (i.e., the actual EA). In this paper, we will follow the argumentation of Buckl et al. [33] and define architectural principles as either taking the form of guidelines (i.e., recommendations), or restrictions. Standards, on the other hand, provide an operationalization of principles.

The EAM goals of transparency and consistency are not independent: Transparency has to be achieved first, in order to maintain consistency (e.g., to prevent principles on different architectural layers from contradicting each other). Once the goals of transparency and consistency are achieved, the EAM goals of flexibility and agility that support changing an enterprise's architecture can be addressed [12, 30]. Since this paper is concerned with EAM support of ET, we will focus on the goals of flexibility and agility.

2.3   EAM in the Dynamic Capabilities Framework

A bundle of dynamic capabilities is required to achieve reconfiguration of operational capabilities. EAM may be seen—amongst several other capabilities as provided in section 2.1—as one specific first-order reconfiguration capability supporting ET. The dynamic capabilities framework stresses the reconfiguration of operational capabilities in order to achieve alignment with the market [13]. EAM stresses the purposeful development (or reconfiguration) of EA building blocks to achieve alignment between architectural layers within the enterprise in order to support transformation [11, 12, 34].

Following a similar argumentation, Aleghehband and Rivard [34] consider "enterprise IT architecture dynamic capability" the "capacity of an organization to purposefully extend, create or modify its IT competencies for tight alignment with the firm's business strategy to support/initiate current/future changes in the business or enable a firm to capitalize on a current/future opportunity." We see the term "enterprise IT architecture" as corresponding to our notion of EAM, since both terms emphasize an enterprise-wide focus with the goal of maintaining alignment between architectural layers: Alaghehband and Rivard [34] stresses that "IT architecture should be analyzed at the enterprise level with the connection to business requirements", citing Ross' [28] definition of enterprise IT architecture as "the organizing logic for applications, data, and infrastructure technologies, as captured in a set of policies and technical choices, intended to enable the firm's business strategy".

The building blocks forming an enterprise's architecture, e.g. its processes, information systems and technical infrastructure, may thus be considered part of its operational capabilities. EAM manages the evolution of EA and thus acts as a reconfiguration capability, depending on the type of environmental turbulence. Figure 1 depicts the conceptualization of EA and EAM in the capabilities framework proposed by Pavlou and El Sawy [17].

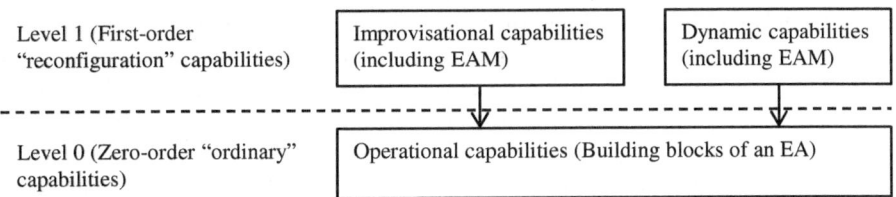

Fig. 1. EA and EAM in the context of ordinary and reconfiguration capabilities (based on Pavlou and El Sawy [17])

Like other dynamic capabilities, establishing and maintaining EAM involves investments that pay off only in environments with a sufficient degree of turbulence. In stable environments with infrequent changes, an enterprise's building blocks could be changed ad hoc, in the sense of Winter's [18] notion of "ad hoc problem solving".

3   EAM Capabilities in Environmental Turbulence

As discussed earlier, the predictability of change is the major determinant whether operational capabilities are to be reconfigured via dynamic capabilities or improvisational capabilities. In the context of EAM, the predictability of change is also distinguishing between two EAM goals: Flexibility and agility [35].

Flexibility is understood as "built-in" configurability, a notion of flexibility also found in production management [36]. In early phases of a design process, a range of possible configurations is determined. The final artifact may then be configured within this pre-considered range. For example, with component based design, end products are configured from individual components, yet the range of components and their configuration rules (which limit the range of possible end products) must be considered at design time. Building configurability into products incurs additional costs; however these initial costs facilitate later changes, since reconfiguration is usually less costly than new development. This is analogous to the situation discussed in dynamic capabilities, which are most advantageous when reacting to frequent yet predictable changes.

In order to address unpredictable changes, i.e. changes that cannot be anticipated at design time, the concept of agility is introduced [35]. Flexibility is considered a sub-goal of agility [35, 36], but agility involves, next to adapting to unexpected change, also the dimension of "speed" in the sense of time-to-market [37]. This is especially valuable in highly turbulent environments ("storms"). We therefore see the goal of agility in EAM as analogous to improvisational capabilities.

3.1   EAM as a Dynamic Capability

Concerning the descriptive aspect of EA, EAM as a dynamic capability may support planning by providing transparency: Based on as-is models of an enterprise, different to-be models can be derived and discussed in order to arrive at a common vision of the future state of the enterprise. Additionally, the discussion process may be supported by different model analyses such as dependency, coverage or heterogeneity analyses. Finally, a roadmap detailing the planned transition may be derived.

Concerning the prescriptive aspect of EA, existing principles and the standards derived from them may efficiently guide ET. Aier and Schelp [35] see standards as contributing positively to flexibility by increasing the interoperability of EA building blocks (e.g., via the provision of common interfaces). This eventually contributes to the goal of consistency by reducing redundancy and preventing local at the expense of global optimization [11].

A concrete example of EAM in this case would be an insurance company offering customers to buy insurance contracts and manage them online (e.g., report mileage for car insurance or make claims). This would be an example of a planned, proactive ET out of strategic considerations (widen distribution channels). Since this new distribution process involves both existing processes (insurance contracts, claim handling) and existing software systems (existing backend-systems complemented by a new web frontend), EA models and dependency analyses provide important information for project management support. Additionally, since the ET is pre-planned, roadmaps, to-be models as well as principles (e.g., on selecting technologies to concentrate know-how or outsourcing to preferred suppliers) can provide support.

3.2 EAM as an Improvisational Capability

In the case of unexpected changes, improvisational capabilities involve spontaneous reconfigurations of existing operational capabilities. EAM cannot plan or prescribe improvisational action: It can only aim at providing conditions that support organizational actors' initiative.

Addressing the descriptive aspect of EA, EAM needs to be concerned with transparency as well, yet the focus is on current rather than future information. Pavlou and El Sawy [17] stress the need of real-time information and communication as important foundations of improvisational capabilities. By providing transparency in the form of as-is models, EAM enables a quick assessment of the status quo as the basis for improvisational capabilities. Analyses on as-is models such as dependency and heterogeneity analyses may provide further information input. Additionally, EAM models aim at fostering shared understanding between stakeholders. Since improvisational capabilities are regarded as collective activities, shared understanding as a basis for communication is especially critical. On the other hand, EAM artifacts like to-be models and roadmaps that rely on planning processes and a sufficient time frame are of lesser value in environments of unpredictable change.

In the prescriptive aspect of EA, principles may provide some structure for improvisation, e.g. by coordinating access to resources. Vera and Crossan [38] emphasize the management of existing resources as a foundation for improvisation. However, existing standards are also likely to hinder improvisation by over-restricting design freedom. Literature suggests that relying too much on past knowledge and structures limits creativity and thus hinders improvisation [17, 38]. Pavlou and El Sawy [17] empirically corroborate the importance of real time information and the problem of relying on past knowledge by examining the effect of different IT systems on improvisational capabilities. They conclude that project management systems and collaborative work systems (i.e., systems that focus on transparency and communication) have a significant effect on improvisational capabilities, while organizational memory systems (i.e., systems that store experiences and lessons from past projects) do not. EA standards may be regarded as incorporations of past knowledge, since they are based on past experiences that may no longer be valid. While the intention behind a principle may still be sensible (e.g., to concentrate technological know-how), a concrete standard (e.g., limiting the set of programming languages to be used) may be no longer appropriate. Therefore a feedback loop checking on the validity of standards and eventually principles is important.

Given the shorter time span and the possible side-effects of over-restricting design freedom, EA standards play a less prominent role in improvisational capabilities than in dynamic capabilities. Instead, mechanisms to handle violations of standards need to be in place, in order to circumvent them in a fast yet disciplined way. Thereby, the risk of past knowledge limiting improvisational actions is mitigated, while at the same time addressing the issue of implementation speed. Finally, enabling exceptions from standards in a planned way (e.g., merely documenting these exceptions is an important first step) forms the basis for restoring consistency at a later point in time.

Case studies also suggest that active involvement of enterprise architects in projects increases implementation speed [39, 40]. For example, decision times on architectural issues such as exceptions from standards may be shortened, and project members are provided with a global view of the enterprise (e.g., making them aware of certain dependencies outside project scope). Moreover, the involvement of architects also serves as a feedback loop concerning the validity of principles. While this feature of EAM is likely to provide benefits for both dynamic and improvisational capabilities, the effects on improvisational capabilities are likely to be more pronounced due to the shorter time frames involved.

A scenario for improvisational capabilities would be an insurance company that is forced by upcoming regulations to amend key components of existing contracts (e.g., mandatory unisex rates in health insurance), implying changed risk assessments and changed premiums. While the overall context may be clear early on (laws passed by legislature), the subsequent implementation requirements may be subject to final specification by various regulatory bodies, leaving insurance companies with very little time to react. In this case, having an overview on current EA elements and their dependencies can be critical to achieve regulatory compliance in the short time frame. In order to speed up implementation projects, architects could be assigned to projects in a consulting function. In this role, they can offer advice on existing dependencies beyond the project scope, as well as make quick decisions on overruling general principles and document exceptions.

In table 3, a summary of the configuration of EAM both as a dynamic and improvisational capability is provided.

Table 3. EAM configurations in environmental turbulence

	Predictable change	Unpredictable change
Reconfiguration capabilities	Dynamic capabilities	Improvisational capabilities
EAM goal	Flexibility	Agility
EA descriptive aspect	Models (As-is, to-be) Analyses Roadmaps	As-is models Analyses
EA prescriptive aspect	Reliance on existing principles	Exceptions from existing standards
Additional measures		Active project support by enterprise architects

4   Case Studies

4.1   Company A

The following case study is reported by Aier and Schelp [35]. Company A is a large telecommunication services provider in Germany. The telecommunication industry is characterized by a high level of environmental turbulence due to a large number of competitors, the unpredictability of their moves and price-sensitive customers. In particular, this leads to frequently changing pricing models, which are—next to the emergence of new technology—the main components of product innovation. Fast time-to-market is vital, especially when Company A has to react to one of its competitor's initiatives. In order to cope with these frequent changes, EAM has been introduced with a focus on technological change projects. Defining an architectural framework has facilitated assessing the impact of change projects. Ultimately, EAM is seen by the management board of Company A as a change-regulating function to ensure enterprise consistency in a highly dynamic environment.

To provide transparency, Company A has created models on different partial architectures. Model creation and maintenance is still managed locally, but integration into a centralized repository is intended. A main advantage of this integration will be the automated creation of dependency models between artifacts from various partial architectures.

Additionally, principles in the form of technological standards are used to maintain interoperability between the overall architecture and individual change projects. These principles are reviewed bi-annually to ensure continuing relevance. In order to check project results' conformance with architectural principles, Company A has a dedicated review process in place. Assessments are conducted throughout the project phase, so that corrective measures can be invoked quickly. Minor deviations from principles lead to a mitigation plan, consisting of measures to be taken to restore architectural consistency as far as possible. These mitigations have to be financed from the project budget. Major deviations from principles may even lead to project cancellation. Thus, EAM contributes to flexibility by facilitating change within a predefined range.

Furthermore, the company has special exception processes in place for change projects that need to deviate from architectural principles, as may happen in cases of unpredictable and urgent change. In this case, if both a project plan and a budget are defined to eventually restore consistency, exceptions can be granted. If exceptions are granted, all temporary deviations and their rationales are recorded in detail, to enable restoring consistency at a later point. The increase in design freedom has resulted in faster implementation times, and thus contributes to agility. As for restoring consistency, Company A places this responsibility with those projects that originally caused inconsistencies. There are no projects dedicated solely to improving architecture, since all projects at Company A have to define a clear business case.

Architects are also actively involved as consultants in Company A's projects. Company A provides a specific career model for architects, and typically employees in this role have previous experience with consulting-intensive tasks.

4.2 Company B

The following example is taken from Murer's [40] description of the architecture program at Company B, a large Swiss bank. Following a merger, the banking system of the acquired company was being merged into Company B's existing system. This led to a dramatic increase in overall system complexity. Eventually, the new system was no longer able to meet business requirements and suffered from heavy outages. This has led the board of company B to launch an architecture program in order to define a new IT strategy.

Instead of developing a banking system from scratch, it was decided to protect existing assets and invest in the current platform, but to provide stronger governance on the platform's evolution. The board chose an approach called "managed evolution" aimed at swiftly implementing business requirements while at the same time maintaining high levels of system availability and maintainability.

Company B has also created business object and domain models, describing required business functionalities and implementation details across architectural layers (called business, application and technical architecture). A glossary of architectural building blocks is provided in addition to as-is models in order to create a shared vocabulary between different stakeholders. This glossary specifically aims at reducing semantic ambiguity amongst stakeholders from different enterprise domains and has proven very important for shared understanding and maintaining consistency. Company B also uses to-be models communicating its architectural vision, and roadmaps to describe the transition process.

To evolve towards architectural targets, principles and standards are defined in order to guide system evolution within predefined borders (e.g., restricting the technologies to be used). This reduction of design freedom has increased interoperability between system components and decreased overall system complexity by reducing the number of interfaces to be dealt with. Under the managed evolution approach, projects conducted at Company B fall into one of three categories:

1. New change projects are required to conform to architectural principles if the available time-to-market allows. Projects of this type are considered the normal case at Company B.
2. Company B also has an exception process in place, where business projects are allowed to deviate from existing standards if required time-to-market or business requirements cannot be met within the existing borders of architectural principles. Buckl et al. [33] name the development of a mobile phone app as an example for such deviations, as the required programming language may not be covered by an existing standard limiting language selection.
3. In order to restore architectural consistency, a third type of project is defined which does not implement new business requirements, but aims solely at improving architecture by restoring consistency. Company B dedicates 20% of its IT budget on CIO level to this purpose [40]. Taking up the previous example, Buckl et al. [33] name a follow-up project replacing the mobile banking application developed in-house with an off-the-self software complying to a banking standard.

Finally, in order to anchor the managed evolution approach in the organization, architects are routinely involved as consultants in major projects. Next to bringing architectural expertise and global perspectives into projects, this also speeds up decision times on architectural issues, e.g. exceptions from principles.

4.3 Comparison of Cases

Table 4 summarizes and compares EAM as a dynamic or improvisational capability.

Table 4. EAM capabilities in Company A and B

Reconfiguration capability	EA aspect	Company A	Company B
Dynamic	descriptive	Decentralized models of partial architectures existing, integration into centralized repository pending; To-be models (scenario analysis)	As-is models as basis of shared understanding; Target architecture is captured in to-be models; Roadmaps for transition planning
	prescriptive	Standards to maintain system interoperability	Projects have to conform to architectural principles when time-to-market allows
Improvisational	descriptive	Decentralized models of partial architectures	As-is models as basis of shared understanding
	prescriptive	Exceptions from standards possible; Projects are responsible to restore architectural consistency	Exceptions from standards possible; Dedicated CIO budget to restore architectural consistency

5   Discussion

Enterprises are facing multiple levels of environmental turbulences: They might be able to (1) proactively shape their environment or they might be (2) forced to react to their environment. Therefore, the two extremes—relying exclusively on dynamic capabilities or improvisational capabilities—will lead to inefficient solutions and a loss of competitive advantage in the long run. Instead, enterprises need to reconfigure themselves by using the set of capabilities—dynamic or improvisational—that the level of environmental turbulence favors in a given situation. Enterprises may even have to simultaneously deploy both sets of capabilities in different domains.

In organizational theory, the ability to successfully deploy two apparently competing capabilities is referred to as "ambidexterity". While the interplay between operational and dynamic capabilities is given as one example of an ambidextrous organization [41], improvisational capabilities are introduced as a "third" hand to account for the different nature of dynamic capabilities in different types of environmental turbulence [17].

EAM can be regarded as one reconfiguration capability that is adapted (i.e., configured) to support ET in both types of environmental turbulence. This means that an enterprise must be able to execute EAM in two "speeds":

1. as a dynamic capability, providing a complex set of artifacts to support a planned, time-consuming reconfiguration process
2. as an improvisational capability, supporting fast, spontaneous reconfigurations with a simple set of artifacts.

Looking at the EAM instruments supporting both capabilities, we identify a set of basic elements that are required for both dynamic and improvisational capabilities. These basic elements are as-is models and their updating processes, analyses on these models (e.g., on dependencies, heterogeneity) and principles. Configured as a dynamic capability, the set of basic elements is extended with to-be models and roadmaps to support planning, and governance processes using existing principles in order to guide planned changes. Configured as an improvisational capability, the set of basic elements is extended with an exception-handling process to enable swift and creative solutions by deviating from existing principles. Planning-related instruments like to-be models and roadmaps are disregarded in this configuration. The situational EAM configurations are summarized in Fig. 2.

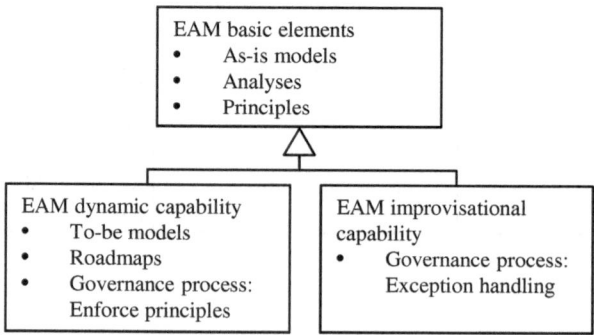

Fig. 2. Situational EAM configuration

While both reconfiguration capabilities exist in enterprises, their goals are competing and need to be balanced. In the case of EAM, this tradeoff is evident between the two goals of flexibility and agility [35]. While flexibility is consistent with the restriction of design freedom, the goal of agility requires greater leeway in reconfiguring operational capabilities. Important enablers of flexibility are standardization and consistency, as these goals provide for efficient reconfiguration within anticipated borders (as expressed via standards and their underlying principles). However, the goal of agility occasionally requires deviations from existing standards and principles and thus introduces inconsistency.

As the two case studies show, the tradeoff between agility and flexibility can be managed by an exception handling process. This process ensures that deviations from existing principles do not occur in an undocumented way (which would lead to a loss of transparency and into chaotic, ad-hoc problem solving), but in a planned way that enables restoring consistency in the long run. As a major first step, this includes documenting deviations and the associated rationales.

Managing the tradeoff between agility and flexibility and eventually restoring consistency, however, requires governance mechanisms. The two case studies show different mechanisms to govern deviations and their long-term impacts: In Company A, the responsibility for long-term consistency rests with individual change projects: Architectural exceptions are only granted when plans (time/budget) are provided to eventually restore consistency. Company B uses a different approach: centrally allocated budget with the CIO to gradually improve architecture and remove inconsistencies caused by individual projects.

Company A's approach stresses individual project responsibility and thereby puts architectural governance at a local level. This approach bears the risk of consistency-restoring projects being cancelled, for example as a consequence of management changes at project or super-ordinate levels: New managers may no longer be ready to carry out "repair" projects authorized by their predecessors. Company B's approach, on the other hand, provides centralized governance for architectural issues. This approach mitigates the risk of local managers overriding previous decisions to restore consistency by putting responsibility on a higher organizational level. On the other hand, this approach may also provide a greater incentive for local projects to disregard architectural principles, since the burden to restore consistency is not placed with them, but with a corporate unit. The interplay between dynamic and improvisational capabilities also stresses the importance of feedback mechanisms. If EAM is conducted in a unidirectional way, designed by architects and without the possibility of accounting for feedback of organizational actors, it will not be able to successfully act as any reconfiguration capability. Actors do not only need to use or "read" EA artifacts, they also need to be able to contribute to or "write" EA artifacts.

The EAM goal of transparency mandates updating EA models to reflect changes in the enterprise. These updates cannot be done by architects only in a centralized fashion, as this would in the best case lead to valid, but outdated models. Instead organizational actors have to be provided with feedback channels to forward information on changes in their respective domains to the rest of the enterprise [42]. Only then can EAM provide real-time information and contribute to shared understanding and communication between organizational actors.

In the case of principles, feedback mechanisms are equally important. By providing an exception handling process, feedback from current projects continuously challenges the validity of existing principles. This feedback can be further improved and sped up by actively involving architects in ET projects, e.g. as consultants. This scrutiny enables the ongoing refinement and validation of principles and standards—to check if the given design restrictions are still aligned with environmental demands.

Summing up our findings, we conclude with two propositions:

1. As a dynamic capability, EAM is concerned with both descriptive and prescriptive aspects of EA, while as an improvisational capability, EAM is concerned mostly with the descriptive EA aspects.
2. In order to deploy EAM as a dynamic or an improvisational capability, governance and feedback mechanisms are critical.

6   Conclusion

In this paper, we have conceptualized EAM as a capability within the dynamic capabilities framework. This framework stresses the different nature of reconfiguration capabilities based on the predictability of environmental change. Transferring these findings onto EAM, we have derived two propositions showing (1) which EA artifacts support which reconfiguration capability and (2) the mechanisms involved in alternating between the two reconfiguration capabilities or speeds of EAM, namely governance and feedback.

This distinction is the main contribution of our paper, as it shows how EAM is capable of supporting both proactive and reactive ET. The main limitation of our work is the small number of case studies: Further empirical data, focusing specifically on EAM being deployed as a dynamic or an improvisational capability, are required to improve our understanding of EAM switching between these two reconfiguration capabilities.

While this paper provides a first classification of the building blocks required for each capability, this specification needs to be worked out in greater detail in future work. Future research efforts are also needed to better understand the effects and possible designs of different EAM governance and feedback mechanisms. Especially the idea of feedback loops, with the goal of making EAM accessible to and encouraging participation from a wide audience of stakeholders seems an important research direction.

Acknowledgement. This work has been supported by the Swiss National Science Foundation (SNSF).

References

1. Rouse, W.B.: A Theory of Enterprise Transformation. Systems Engineering 8(4), 279–295 (2005)
2. Purchase, V., Parry, G., Valerdi, R., Nightingale, D., Mills, J.: Enterprise Transformation: Why Are We Interested, What Is It, and What Are the Challenges? Journal of Enterprise Transformation 1(1), 14–33 (2011)
3. Romanelli, E., Tushman, M.L.: Organizational Transformation as Punctuated Equilibrium: An Empirical Test. Academy of Management Journal 37(5), 1141–1166 (1994)
4. Orlikowski, W.J.: Improvising Organizational Transformation Over Time: A Situated Change Perspective. Information Systems Research 7(1), 63–92 (1996)

5. Safrudin, N., Recker, J., Rosemann, M.: The Emerging Management Services of Business Transformation Management. In: PACIS 2011 Proceedings, p. 160 (2011)
6. Beer, M., Eisenstat, R.A., Spector, B.: Why Change Programs Don't Produce Change. Harvard Business Review 68(6), 195–198 (1990)
7. Rouse, W.B., Baba, M.L.: Enterprise transformation. Communications of the ACM 49(7), 67–72 (2006)
8. Rouse, W.B.: Enterprises as systems: Essential challenges and approaches to transformation. Systems Engineering 8(2), 138–150 (2005)
9. Malone, T.W., Crowston, K.: The Interdisciplinary Study of Coordination. ACM Computing Surveys 26(1), 87–119 (1994)
10. Henderson, J.C., Venkatraman, N.: Strategic alignment: Leveraging information technology for transforming organizations. IBM Systems Journal 32(1), 4–16 (1993)
11. Foorthuis, R., van Steenbergen, M., Mushkudiani, N., Bruls, W., Brinkkemper, S., Bos, R.: On Course, but Not There Yet: Enterprise Architecture Conformance and Benefits in Systems Development. In: ICIS 2010 Proceedings, p. 110 (2010)
12. Radeke, F.: Toward Understanding Enterprise Architecture Management's Role in Strategic Change: Antecedents, Processes, Outcomes. In: Proceedings of the 10th International Conference on Wirtschaftsinformatik WI 2.011, pp. 497–507 (2011)
13. Barreto, I.: Dynamic Capabilities: A Review of Past Research and an Agenda for the Future. Journal of Management 36(1), 256–280 (2010)
14. Teece, D.J.: Explicating dynamic capabilities: the nature and microfoundations of (sustainable) enterprise performance. Strategic Management Journal 28(13), 1319–1350 (2007)
15. D'Aveni, R.A.: Hypercompetition: Managing the Dynamics of Strategic Management. Free Press, New York (1994)
16. Eisenhardt, K.M., Martin, J.A.: Dynamic Capabilities: What are They? Strategic Management Journal 21(10/11), 1105–1121 (2000)
17. Pavlou, P.A., El Sawy, O.A.: The "Third Hand": IT-Enabled Competitive Advantage in Turbulence Through Improvisational Capabilities. Information Systems Research 21(3), 443–471 (2010)
18. Winter, S.G.: Understanding dynamic capabilities. Strategic Management Journal 24(10), 991–995 (2003)
19. Zollo, M., Winter, S.G.: Deliberate Learning and the Evolution of Dynamic Capabilities. Organization Science 13(3), 339–351 (2002)
20. Collis, D.J.: Research note: How valuable are organizational capabilities? Strategic Management Journal 15(special issue), 143–152 (1994)
21. Niehaves, B., Plattfaut, R., Becker, J.: Does Your Business Process Management (Still) Fit the Market? – A Dynamic Capability Perspective on BPM Strategy Development. In: AMCIS 2010 Proceedings, p. 292 (2010)
22. Cohen, W.M., Levinthal, D.A.: Fortune Favors the Prepared Firm. Management Science 40(2), 227–251 (1994)
23. Wholey, D.R., Brittain, J.: Characterizing Environmental Variation. The Academy of Management Journal 32(4), 867–882 (1989)
24. Child, J.: Organizational Structure, Environment and Performance: The Role of Strategic Choice. Sociology 6(1), 1–22 (1972)
25. ISO/IEC/IEEE: Systems and software engineering – Architecture description (ISO/IEC/IEEE 42010:2011) (2011)
26. The Open Group: TOGAF Version 9.1 (2011)

27. Aier, S., Gleichauf, B., Winter, R.: Understanding Enterprise Architecture Management Design – An Empirical Analysis. In: Proceedings of the 10th International Conference on Wirtschaftsinformatik WI 2.011, Zurich, pp. 645–654 (2011)
28. Ross, J.W.: Creating a strategic IT architecture competency: Learning in stages. MIS Quarterly Executive 2(1), 31–43 (2003)
29. Rohloff, M.: Integrating Innovation into Enterprise Architecture Management. In: Proceedings of the 10th International Conference on Wirtschaftsinformatik WI 2.011, pp. 776–786 (2011)
30. Tamm, T., Seddon, P.B., Shanks, G., Reynolds, P.: How Does Enterprise Architecture Add Value to Organisations? Communications of the Association for Information Systems 28, 141–168 (2011)
31. Strano, C., Rehmani, Q.: The Role of the Enterprise Architect. International Journal of Information Systems and e-Business Management 5(4), 379–396 (2007)
32. Dietz, J.L.G., Hoogervorst, J.A.P.: Enterprise ontology in enterprise engineering. In: Proceedings of the 2008 ACM Symposium on Applied Computing, Fortaleza, Ceara, Brazil (2008)
33. Buckl, S., Matthes, F., Roth, S., Schulz, C., Schweda, C.M.: A Conceptual Framework for Enterprise Architecture Design. In: Proper, E., Lankhorst, M.M., Schönherr, M., Barjis, J., Overbeek, S. (eds.) TEAR 2010. LNBIP, vol. 70, pp. 44–56. Springer, Heidelberg (2010)
34. Alaghehband, F.K., Rivard, S.: The Strategic Role of Information Technology Sourcing: A Dynamic Capabilities Perspective. In: ICIS 2010 Proceedings, p. 107 (2010)
35. Aier, S., Schelp, J.: How to Preserve Agility in Service Oriented Architectures – An Explorative Analysis. Enterprise Modelling and Information Systems Architectures 5(2), 21–37 (2010)
36. Yusuf, Y.Y., Sarhadi, M., Gunasekaran, A.: Agile manufacturing: the drivers, concepts and attributes. International Journal of Production Economics 62(1-2), 33–43 (1999)
37. Sambamurthy, V., Bharadwaj, A., Grover, V.: Shaping Agility through Digital Options: Reconceptualizing the Role of Information Technology in Contemporary Firms. MIS Quarterly 27(2), 237–263 (2003)
38. Vera, D., Crossan, M.: Improvisation and Innovative Performance in Teams. Organization Science 16(3), 203–224 (2005)
39. Hafner, M., Winter, R.: Processes for Enterprise Application Architecture Management. In: Proceedings of the 41st Annual Hawaii International Conference on System Sciences (HICSS 41), pp. 396 (391–310). IEEE Computer Society (2008)
40. Murer, S., Bonati, B., Furrer, F.J.: Managed Evolution: A Strategy for Very Large Information Systems. Springer, Heidelberg (2010)
41. Pavlou, P.A., El Sawy, O.A.: From IT competence to competitive advantage in turbulent environments: The case of new product development. Information Systems Research 17(3), 198–227 (2006)
42. Castela, N., Zacarias, M., Tribolet, J.: PROASIS: As-Is Business Process Model Maintenance. In: Harmsen, F., Grahlmann, K., Proper, E. (eds.) PRET 2011. LNBIP, vol. 89, pp. 53–82. Springer, Heidelberg (2011)

On Enterprise Architecture Change Events

Matthias Farwick[1], Christian M. Schweda[2], Ruth Breu[1], Karsten Voges[2],
and Inge Hanschke[2]

[1] University of Innsbruck
Institute of Computer Science
Innsbruck, Austria
{matthias.farwick,ruth.breu}@uibk.ac.at
[2] iteratec GmbH
Unterhaching, Germany
{christian.schweda,karsten.voges,inge.hanschke}@iteratec.de

Abstract. In practice it is difficult to maintain a high quality enterprise architecture (EA) model with regards to its actuality and completeness. However, neither literature from practice and EA frameworks nor EA research literature provide sufficient guidance for the difficult task of maintaining EA models. Recently, researchers have presented methods to collect structured data from existing data sources, e.g. from IT operations in order to (semi-)automatically update EA models. In this paper, we make an argument for the additional use of EA change events from (management) information systems. These change events do not provide clearly mappable structured information, but can be used to trigger and guide manual EA model maintenance tasks when changes occur. We present the first classification of relevant events in EA literature, detailing on their sources and impact on the EA model. Finally, we propose a model maintenance workflow that is driven by events, explain an example usage case and point to open issues in the context of EA change events.

Keywords: enterprise architecture, model maintenance, automation, documentation, model quality, event, data collection.

1 Introduction

A major problem in Enterprise Architecture Management (EAM) practice is, according to a literature review [1] and a survey [2], to create and to maintain an EA model that is both up-to-date and of adequate quality to answer the relevant strategic questions. Complexity of the EA, the dispersed nature of EA information in organizations, and inadequate tool support are the main reasons why EA documentation is a time consuming and costly effort. Recent empirical studies have shown that these documentation efforts are still dominated by manual data collection and manual entry in EAM tools or models [3,2]. In many cases the maintenance of the models, i.e. the response to changes in the EA, is incidentally triggered due to the lack of specified data collection processes [3].

S. Aier et al. (Eds.): TEAR 2012 and PRET 2012, LNBIP 131, pp. 129–145, 2012.

To reduce effort of manual data import, today's EAM tools support the import of structured information from files or even external systems such as Configuration Management Databases (CMDBs). In addition, researchers have recently started to investigate more elaborated support mechanisms for automatically collecting EA data from runtime systems [4,5] and assuring its quality [6]. The approaches from practice and research have in common that they rely on EA data sources that are able to provide structured information which is mapped into the EAM tool.

Although these are promising approaches to reduce the manual data collection effort and to increase the data quality, we argue that the full spectrum of automation support can only be reached by also leveraging information from (management) information systems of IT operations that cannot provide structured information. Such systems can act as sources of EAM-relevant *change events*, which can be used to initiate EA model maintenance workflows at the right time, and thus increase the actuality of EA models. Examples are the events of project inception as well as project completion.

In this paper we present a first classification of such EA change events, list examples of relevant events and present a process for triggering model maintenance workflows from such events. The contribution of the paper is hence threefold. First, we establish the terminological and conceptual basis for future research on EA change events by analyzing events in organizations with regard to their granularity and their impact on the EA level. Second, we apply this basis on a non-exhaustive list of EAM-relevant events. Third, we propose a workflow that forms the basis for a tool implementation for (semi-)automatically processing events for model maintenance. Practitioners can use the presented list of events to identify and analyze potentials for leveraging event-based EA model maintenance workflows. Also, EAM tool vendors can build on the proposed workflow to include event-based model maintenance in their products. We also discuss open issues that are relevant for fellow researchers.

The following definition of an *EA change event* applies in the remainder of this paper:

Definition 1. *An EA change event is a state change pertaining to elements in the scope of the organization-specific EAM approach or to properties characterizing such elements. The state change originates from an information system of the enterprise.*

The remainder of this paper is structured as follows. In Section 2 we revisit related work on EA change, on EA model maintenance and on events in the context of EAM. Based on the insights gained, we establish our conceptualization of EA change events and provide a classification centering around *event origin* and *event impact* in Section 3. In this section we further present our non-exhaustive list of EA change events found in literature. The Sections 4 and 5 present a workflow for processing these events and give an example case for its usage, respectively. Section 6 summarizes the findings, highlights open issues in the presented workflow, and briefly outlines how these issues can be addressed in future research.

2   Related Work

A related field in EAM research is the field of EA change propagation. In [7] de Boer et al. present an approach to calculate the impact of a change in Archimate [8] models, in order to compute the ripple effect on other model elements. The primary focus of the publication is enabling simulations and not maintenance of EA models. Dam et al. [9] apply change propagation rules in their EA modeling language to calculate necessary changes to related model in elements to maintain consistency of the EA model. Both approaches focus on change events which are internal to the EA model and not on ones that happen in related information systems in the enterprise itself.

Fischer et al. present a federated approach for the maintenance of EA models [10]. The approach includes the collection of data from external sources that are integrated with maintenance processes in regular intervals. These processes may be triggered by "special events". A description of the type and origin of these events is, however, not given.

The EAM pattern catalog of Technische Universität München [11] presents several EA management patterns that apply to coarse-grained change events, resulting from or being part of projects. Projects are used as means to perform EA planning and creating a roadmap of the intended change of the EA. The patterns for EA roadmapping are furthered by Ernst and Schneider in [12], providing additional detail on the process of establishing such roadmap. While the corresponding patterns sketch how projects are modeled and project-induced transformations can be reflected, neither a refined classification of change events nor a discussion on additional sources of events is undertaken.

Sousa et al. [13] present a tool supported methodology to create time-based views on the enterprise architecture. They recognize that "IT projects are the best entity to report back the (EA) changes in some normalized form". The authors argue that IT-projects should contain concrete references to the elements of the EA they are intending to change. We agree with the authors that, if this is achieved, events indicating the inception and end of IT-projects can act as triggers for EA model maintenance processes.

The Open Group Architecture Framework (TOGAF) [14] takes a project-centric approach to EAM and does therefore not focus on maintaining an EA model. TOGAF nevertheless provides mechanisms to align the current EAM project with other running projects in dedicated phases of architecture development. In particular, phase F "migration planning" establishes a link to related projects and collects "change requests" from these projects and programs. The necessary changes are subsequently processed in the phase and incorporated as changes into the overall EA. The requirements management activity of TOGAF's architecture development method further describes steps to be taken, in case a changed requirement is detected. While these steps describe that the impacted part of the EA as well as the affected phase of architecture development has to be determined, information about the sources of such changing requirements ("can come through any route") and details about how to assess their impact on the EA are not provided.

Winter et al. [3] used a questionnaire to collect data on events that trigger EA model maintenance activities. Their findings confirm that in the majority of cases, maintenance is executed "on demand" (59,5%). This implies that maintenance processes are not well defined in many organizations. Other mentioned triggers are "when a person in charge triggers it", "when a project is finished", "when the circumstances or goals change" and "annually". This gives a range of triggers that includes fully organizational triggers ("annually", "when a project is finished") to triggers that are incidental ("on demand"). Winter et al. do not further discuss how these events can be classified or organized to better support EA model maintenance.

According to [15] Buckl, EA management is a typical management activity, which decomposes into the activities *describe & develop*, *communicate & enact*, and *analyze & evaluate*. The workflows constituting these activities are initiated by different kinds of triggers: *event triggers* and *time triggers*. Triggers of the latter type are activated, whenever a predefined amount of time has passed, i.e., they are used to define regular workflows in EA management. Event triggers in contrast link the EA management processes with each other and with related enterprise-level management processes, like project portfolio management. Such linkage is established based on the artifacts, which the different management processes create. For example, the proposal of a new project to project portfolio management can be configured as triggering event for performing an architecture analysis of the project. While Buckl et al. further provide a language for describing the workflows, the events are neither discussed nor modeled in more detail.

In [16] the authors establish a perspective on EA transformations centering around the assumption that "elements of the EA do not change accidentally", but are changed by change actions, such as projects and working packages. While the authors do not elaborate on the nature and variations of such actions, the idea is furthered by Aier et al. in [17] in discussions on EA transformation planning. The *workpackage* as the driver for EA transformation, more precisely its completion, is discussed and embedded into the context of a management method that relates to methods from neighbouring disciplines. Aier et al. further outline that while the workpackages may have impact on the EA model, depending on the level of detail at which the EA is modeled, the packages themselves may not be "visible" in the EA model. This means that the packages are too fine-grained to be subject of EAM, although their impact is EAM-relevant.

Several recent papers target the automated collection of structured data from existing data sources in organizations. In [18] we present processes for collecting such data and assuring its quality with semi-automated processes. However, this work only focuses on structured data and does not consider event sources. No specific data source implementation is described. In contrast, the works of Buschle et al. [4,5] explicitly discuss the usage of a network scanner and an enterprise service bus (ESB) as sources for structured EA data. Again, these publications focus on the direct inclusion of structured data into the EA model, without considering change events from information systems like project portfolio management tools.

In our previous work on the concept of *Living Models* [19] we have emphasized the importance of embracing change events in the management of models in the software engineering domain. In this work, however, we targeted models from the software engineering space and did not apply the event concept on EA model management.

3   Event Types

Events, in particular change events, play an important role in understanding enterprise transformation. In this section we first discuss what actually makes an event EA-relevant with respect to its granularity level of occurrence and its impact on the EA. Further, we present a list of such EA-relevant events and discuss the dimensions for this classification.

Events can be approached from two different perspectives: firstly regarding the area-of-interest in the EA, on which they have *impact*; secondly regarding the area-of-interest in the enterprise, from which they *originate*. As means to classify events according to former dimension, we apply the structuring framework outlined by Winter et al. in [20][1]. In this sense, each event whose change pertains to coarse-grained elements of the enterprise as covered by the organization-specific EAM approach, can be considered an EA change event. Such events are prevalent in the process of enterprise transformation (planning) as Aier et al. discuss in [17]. The information model supporting the process identifies the *workpackage* as constituent of a *project* as the driver of enterprise change. With the finalization of a workpackage, i.e., the completion event, the changes performed in the workpackage become effective. The completion of workpackages is relevant for EAM, if the element to which the workpackage applies, is part of the area-of-interest covered by the EA model, e.g. is an information system, business process, or infrastructure element. Change events not applying to relevant elements of the EA have an impact "below" the scope of EAM, and may hence be excluded from considerations, while other events can be categorized regarding the *EA layer* on which they impact. Figure 1 illustrates the relationship of the granularity layers in which the events occur and on which they impact. The figure shows this with examples from the infrastructure and information system EA layers. In the lower box one can see the *Technical Service Change* event that originates at the lowest granularity level and has no impact on the EA level. On the other hand the event of a *New IaaS Instance* might have impact on the EA level since it might, for example, entail the usage of a new technical platform. The second example in the figure shows events in the information system layer. Here, the event of a resolved EA-relevant change ticket and the event of a newly acquired information system license are depicted. In both cases the events stem from sources that are below the EA level but have impact on the enterprise architecture level.

---

[1] Alluding to Figure 1 in [20].

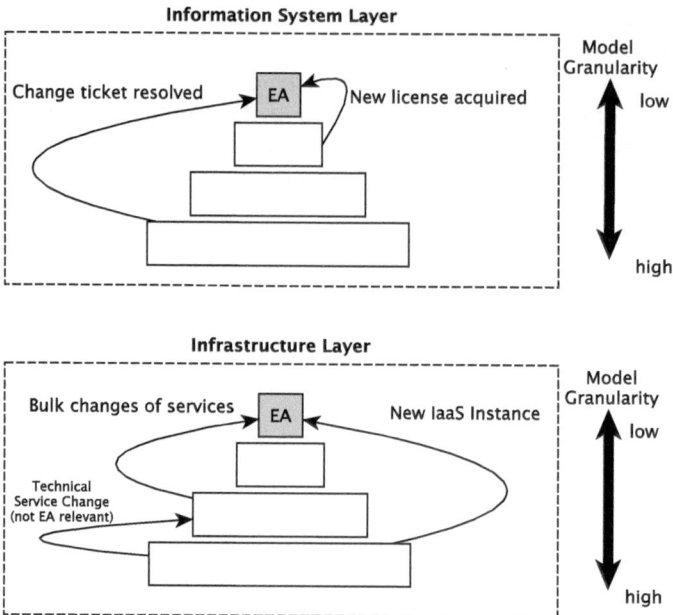

Fig. 1. Event origin and impact layers

As Aier et al. also outline in [17], even workpackages whose change impact does not pertain to the EA level, can be of interest for EA management. Ernst and Schneider detail this in [12] describing patterns for roadmapping the evolution of the EA. Change activities (called "projects" there) that do not structurally change the EA, but affect EA-relevant elements on a level "beyond" the EA-level, can be relevant for EA management, when it comes to managing the evolution of the EA. Such activities, for example long-lasting maintenance activities for information systems, have to be aligned with transformation activities in a way that they do not interfere with each other. In this sense, not only the granularity of the impact but also the *granularity* of the activity itself forms a dimension of differentiation, along which change events can be distinguished. The granularity of the activity itself is closely related to the source, from which an event originates. As stated by Hanschke in [21] EAM must be linked with neighboring enterprise-level management processes. Milestones originating from neighboring processes raise events that imply changes to the EA, either pertaining to the *current state* or to *planned states* of the EA. Typically, the neighboring processes are supported by dedicated information systems that can act as sources of events.

Latter differentiation of the state of the EA, to which the event applies, raises another dimension of differentiation for EA change events. Events targeting the current state of the EA describe changes that actually apply to the enterprise *AS-IS*. Conversely, events targeting planned states of the EA describe intended changes that shape the future enterprise, i.e. the *TO-BE* enterprise. As outlined by Aier and Gleichauf in [22] such differentiation is particularly critical in the context of enterprise transformations to distinguish between EA states, which are already confirmed and ones that may be diverted to *WILL-BE* states different from the plan. From a tooling perspective this implies that changes triggered by *TO-BE* events have to be reconciled once completion is reached.

The perspective of the events' impact further gives rise to a more technical differentiation and classification of events. Different effects can be distinguished along the *operations* which result from processing the event in a workflow. Events can be confined to operations that *add, update,* or *remove* elements of the EA, or can be *generic,* meaning that the actual effect on the EA model consists of operations of different types. As part of our conceptualization of EA change events, we further detail the operations via *implications* that provide typical statement-question sentences that can help a user in processing an event of the particular type. If, for example, a user added a new information system to the model as a result of an IS acquisition event, possible implications are described in questions like: *"You have added a new information system (IS). Are there new business services provided by this IS? Which infrastructure elements support this IS?".*

The conceptualization of events is completed with *context information* that details the event. Such information is usually not well-structured as opposed to information drawn from typical EA data sources [4,5]. Exemplary context information might be the non-normalized name of an information system, infrastructure element or business service. Information of this kind is difficult to process by machines. Humans, on the other hand, are able infer more in conjunction with the information on the data source. For example, a person might know which stakeholder to ask for more information, delegate the processing to a more appropriate stakeholder or might know where to find documentation which contains relevant information. Hence, for humans only little context information can already improve the processing of events.

3.1   Event Sources

In the following, we provide a non-exhaustive list of tool-supported neighboring enterprise-level management processes that can act as sources of EA change events. For each of the processes, we provide references to the literature, which justifies our claim of being a relevant source.

Project Management Tools. In line with Sousa et al. [13] we argue that projects are the fundamental drivers of architecture change. Hence, information systems that are used to manage projects are highly relevant sources for events. Large organizations in particular employ Project Portfolio Management (PPM) tools to manage their, often large, array of running projects. The core problem with events from such tools is the difficulty to tell which project is actually architecture relevant and thus produces relevant events. However, we argue that if the concept of architecture change projects is embedded into the project planning efforts in an organization, the needed information can be naturally integrated with project descriptions. For example, the project description of a change project should hold a list information systems that will be changed in the course of the project.

Release Management Tools. Release management tools are used to plan the delivery of new information system releases in large organizations. Hence, these tools can provide timed events which refer to the solutions that are planned or delivered. This information can be used to trigger manual update processes on the EA model. Hanschke [21] as well as Aier et al. [17] discuss the need to align planning of the enterprise IT, as part of EAM, to be aligned with release planning.

License Management Tools. Large organizations often deal with an ample amount of off-the-shelf applications for which licenses have to be acquired and renewed on a regular basis. Newly acquired licenses are an indicator of a new software product acquired by the organizations. Expired licenses on the other hand indicate that a software system is retired. This type of information can be used to produce timed events that imply changes to the EA model as stated in [23]. Note that according to [23] buying a new application possibly implies the support for new business functions and new infrastructure might be needed to be set up. This kind of reasoning can be used to suggest model changes to the user that is processing the event.

Change Management Tools. Change Management tools are used in the context of ITIL [24] in order to optimize the process of implementing change in the IT-landscape. Depending on the granularity of the managed changes, the lifecycle of the change can be a valuable source for EA change events. Change events from this source might be of advantage to track changes that are not stemming from large scale projects but rather are the result of quickly needed architecture fixes. These events are an example for events where the granularity is potentially below the EA level, but the impact might occur at the EA level.

Service Management Tools. In today's organizations IT-services are often managed in services management tools according to ITIL [24]. Changes in these tools are likely to be the result of structural changes in the EA. They can be used as EA change event triggers similar to the other tools described above.

Organizational Management Tools and Directories. Mergers and acquisitions as well as intra-organizational restructuring can have profound impact on the dependencies between the business and IT artifacts of an enterprise. Hence, the organizational structure including the major organizational units are often modeled as part of an enterprise architecture model. Changes to the organizational structure are often reflected in human resource management (HRM) tools or directories such as LDAP and can thus be used as event sources. Buckl et al. discuss in [25] how organizational restructuring rises implications in the EA and hence has to be addressed as part of EAM.

Enterprise Service Bus & SOA Registries. In today's organizations the concept of Service Oriented Architecture (SOA) is finding widespread adoption. Therein, it is common that communication between applications is mediated via service buses [5] and technical services are registered in SOA registries for re-use. If major changes occur to these runtime configuration systems, it implies a restructuring of the application landscape. Such bulk changes could be utilized to trigger an EA change event. The granularity of the changes made in these systems is another example for changes that are made below the EA-level but can have an impact on the EA-level.

EAM Tool. An EAM tool itself can be the source of EA change events. For example, as proposed in [26] expiry dates can be attached to EA model elements. This information can then be used by an EAM tool to fire events which indicate that a specific model element needs to be reviewed, because it has not been changed for a long period of time. Similarly, an EAM tool can fire scheduled events that prompt stakeholders to check the correctness of a specific range of model elements as part of scheduled EA maintenance cycles.

Note that the availability of such tools differs from organization to organization. Hence, a generic statement about the applicability of an event source is difficult to make.

3.2 Non-exhaustive List of Events

The conceptualization outlined above frames the dimensions along which a list of EA change events can be structured. Table 1 provides such list without claim to cover all relevant EA change events. The table is structured as follows: the leftmost column contains the names of the events ordered by their data sources (detailed in the second column).

The third column lists the kinds of operations that can result from an event.

Column four indicates on which areas-of-interest in the EA the operations can apply.

Column five distinguishes between AS-IS and TO-BE events. Here, it has to be noted that in some cases a clear distinction cannot be drawn, for example in the case of a new software license being acquired. This event may result in a new AS-IS model element in case it is a Software as a Software (SaaS) information system which is immediately usable. If it is a traditional system that needs to be set up and deployed, it might lead to a TO-BE model element.

Implications for the EA model and human-readable context information are described in columns six and seven of the table.

Also note, that not all of the listed event sources should be used in conjunction, since this is likely to cover overlapping areas-of-interest. Therefore, to produce overlapping events, and thus require additional work of constraining event firing (see Section 4). Hence, event sources should be implemented with this problem in mind. In addition please note, that we only listed events where we estimated a high percentage of cases where the event can be detected and appropriately used. For example, for the Technical Services we included the operations add and remove, but not the update operation. We chose to do so because we argue that updates for technical services are at such a low level of granularity that they are very unlikely to appropriately map to the EA level.

Table 1. Event listing and implications for processing user

Event Name	Source Tool(s)	Operation	Impacted Layer	EA AS-IS TO-BE	Implications for EA Model / Suggestions	Context Information
Project Start	PPM Tool	Generic	Potentially All	TO-BE	Insertion of new TO-BE elements? New project element and relations?	Names of affected elements, project name, business unit
Project End	PPM Tool	Generic	Potentially All	AS-IS	TO-BE to AS-IS of affected elements?	Names of affected elements, project name, business unit
Acquisition of new IS	Buying lists	Add	IS	AS-IS & TO-BE	New supporting infrastructure? New business functions/services covered?	Name of acquired IS
IS License Acquired	License Mgmt. Tool	Add/Update	IS	AS-IS & TO-BE	New supporting infrastructure? New business functions/services covered?	Name of acquired IS license
IS License Ended	License Mgmt. Tool	Remove	IS	AS-IS	Renew license? Which infrastructure and business units are affected?	Name of ended IS license
Change Ticket Accepted	Change Mgmt. Tool	Update/Add	IS & Infrastructure	TO-BE	New TO-BE elements and relations?	Description of requested change, names of affected elements
Change Ticket Resolved	Change Mgmt. Tool	Update/Add	IS & Infrastructure	AS-IS	TO-BE to AS-IS of affected elements?	Description of implemented change, names of affected elements
New IS Release	Release Mgmt.	Update/Add	IS & Infrastructure	AS-IS	New supporting infrastructure? New supporting infrastructure/services covered? New/removed interfaces?	Name and version of IS release
New IS Release Planned	Release Mgmt.	Update/Add	IS & Infrastructure	TO-BE	New supporting infrastructure? New business functions/services covered? New/removed interfaces?	Name and version of IS release
New Hardware Acquired	Buying lists	Add	Infrastructure	AS-IS	Which infrastructure services are provided? Which IS are supported?	Name of hardware
Organizational Restructuring Event	Directories, HRM tools	Update/Add/Remove	Business	AS-IS	Do the supporting ISs have to be remodeled?	Names of changed business units
New IaaS Instances	Cloud/Virtualization APIs	Add	Infrastructure	AS-IS	Which infrastructure services are provided? Which IS are supported?	Type of hardware/platform
IaaS Instances Removed	Cloud/Virtualization APIs	Remove	Infrastructure	AS-IS	Some IS also removed? Removed infrastructure service?	Type of hardware/platform
New Technical Services	SOA Registry	Add	IS & Infrastructure	AS-IS	Which IS make use of service? Add accordingly	Name of service, possibly name of calling systems
Technical Services Removed	SOA Registry	Remove	IS & Infrastructure	AS-IS	Which IS make use of service?	Name of service, possibly name of calling systems
New IT-services	IT service catalog	Add	Business	AS-IS	Services provided by which IS?	Responsible organizational unit
IT-services Removed	IT service catalog	Remove	Business	AS-IS	Services provided by which IS?	Responsible organizational unit
Scheduled Data Quality Check	EA Tool	Update	Potentially All	AS-IS & TO-BE	Have the target model element changed?	Range of model elements to be checked
Data Expiry Event	EA Tool	Update	Potentially All	AS-IS & TO-BE	Does the affected model element have to be aligned with the reality?	Name of expired model element

4   Event Processing

Different neighboring enterprise-level management processes and the information systems supporting them can, as discussed above, be sources of EA-relevant events. The workflow presented in this section can be used to process these events taking advantage of their description along the dimensions of our conceptualization. Event-processing is thereby considered a manual task, with users taking two key roles:

Event processors are assigned to process an event. The *event processor* can decide whether the event is relevant, whether it should be delegated to a more appropriate user or, most importantly, change the EA model in response to the event. *Event processors* can also decide that specific event types should be blacklisted in order to block future triggering of irrelevant events. The automated selection of the appropriate group of users as the processor for a specific event should be based on the context information of event source, event type (according to Table 1) and the target EA-layer. In [26] we propose an EA meta-model that provides concepts for the assignment of users or roles, to specific model element instances, model element types or a ranges of instances and types. The later we call *areas-of-interest*. We argue that these areas of interest can be used to assign task processing users or roles at the model level.

Information providers are stakeholders that have additional knowledge on the changes but are typically not involved in EA activities. These providers are contacted when additional knowledge is needed about a specific event. Typically these stakeholders are contacted outside the realm of the EAM tool task management system. In some cases events can contain the information on who is an appropriate information provider.

Users of both roles are involved in the event processing workflow, shown in Figure 2[2]. The workflow processes an EA change event received over one of three types of event triggers. A *Source Initiated Event* is pushed by the source information system to the workflow system in the EAM tool; the *EAM Tool Internal QA Event* that is fired from within the EAM tool itself, and the *Scheduled Retrieval of Events* where the workflow engine actually pulls events from external sources, e.g. by processing log-files.

In its first step an automatic analysis of the triggering event assesses whether the event type has been blacklisted. Such assessment considers the event source and context information and terminates the workflow if a blacklisting is diagnosed. Otherwise, the workflow determines suggestions for the needed model change, based on the type of event and the context information. Examples for such suggestions can be seen in Table 1. These suggestions form the basis for the manual processing of the event and for the changes to the EA model performed

---

[2] The diagram applies the BPMN [27]. The rhombi denote XOR gateways. Tasks with a cogwheel-, human- or hand-symbol denote automated, manual or offline tasks, respectively.

in later steps. Based on the same data, event processors are assigned with the task to process the potentially relevant event. In the next step the assigned user can accept the task, skip it, delegate it to another user/role, or directly put it on the blacklist. If the assigned user accepts the task, she needs to respond to the event processing task by changing the EA model manually. In parallel the user can consult information providers offline and access the information system that initiated the event or other documentation to get further information on the EA changes.

After a model change was performed by a responsible user, the workflow continues with giving recommendations on relationships in the EA model that have to be maintained in order to ensure model consistency. The recommendations are based on the actual model change performed as part of executing the task. Again, the assigned user (event processor) can delegate the task of maintaining the relationships to other roles.

5   Example Case

In this section we present an example case for the usage of EA change events in conjunction with an EAM tool that implements the workflow presented in the previous section. The case was inspired by discussions with enterprise architects of a German insurance company.

The organization uses a project management (PM) tool that allows to manage the lifecycle from planning to release of multiple development projects. During the planning phase it is of importance that information about other architecture change projects is known in order not to waste resources. This is why information about required infrastructure and to-be-changed software artifacts are captured in the tool during the planning phase.

At a point in time, the replacement of the legacy Human Resource Management (HRM) information system is planned in the PM tool. The plan consists of the replacement of the old system with a new to-be-built system at a given deadline and the allocation of new virtualized hardware. When the project plan is approved the project is changed manually from the *to-be-approved* state to the *planned* state in the PM tool. This change fires an event to the EAM tool. It contains the name of the project, the link to the project in the PM tool, context information such as the project description, the affected elements as well as the business unit that owns the project. Consecutively, the EAM tool creates a model change task in its task queue and notifies the architect (Andrea Archmeister) that is assigned to projects of the respective business unit.

Andrea opens the task via the link provided in the task notification email and is presented with the context information of the task. In order to get more detailed information on the project, she opens its description in the PM tool via the link provided in the task and begins to model the TO-BE architecture in the EAM tool. As she models a TO-BE information system, the EAM tool reminds her to think if new business services or functions are covered by the new IS and also about its connections to other IS and the infrastructure it will be

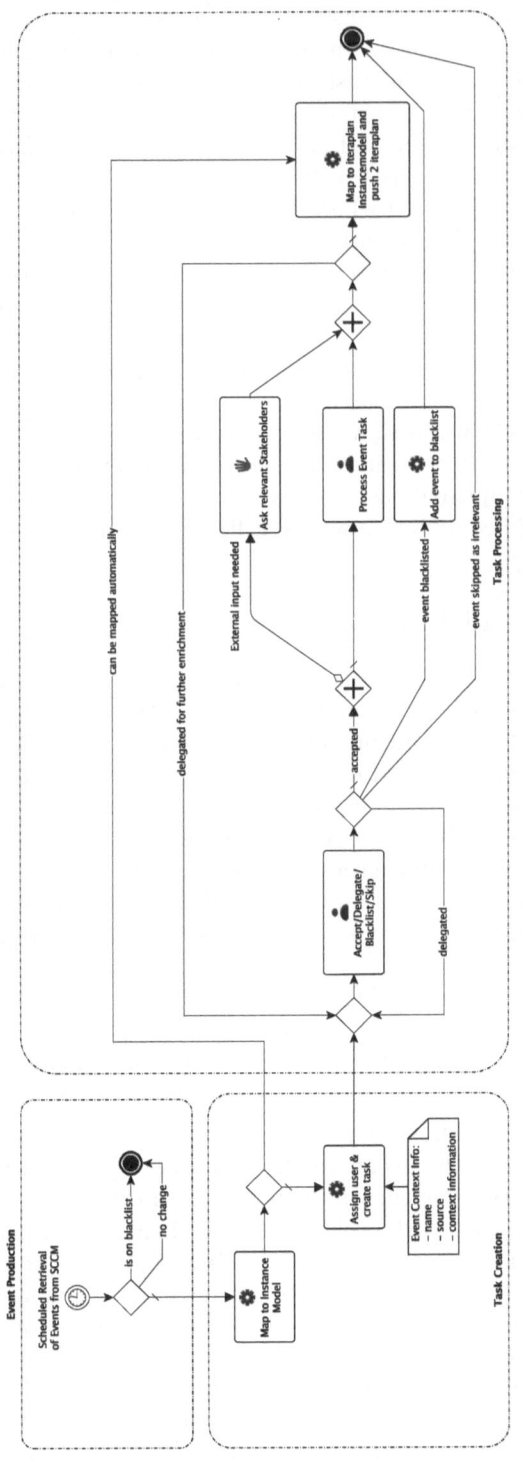

Fig. 2. Proposed process for handling EA change events

deployed on. The first two questions she can answer by the project documentation. However, the information on the infrastructure is not sufficient to model it clearly. Hence, she delegates this task to her colleague (Ines Infrastructure) that has been involved with the infrastructure planning of the project. Ines knows the architecture of the project and can thus model the TO-BE infrastructure correctly. She thereby finishes the task.

The same scheme is executed when the project moves from the planned state to the completed state eight months later. Since Andrea has already accepted a task for the same projects (matched by its name), she receives another task to transform the TO-BE elements, she modeled before, to represent the current state. In this case she does not need to further delegate the task since she has been involved with the infrastructure change management in the meantime.

Note that due to the event based nature of the system the changes to the EA model can be made when they are approved, for example at the same day, as opposed to the annual or incidental triggers discovered by Winter et al. [3]. Of course, this is the optimal case, however we argue that the specific usage of model change tasks in conjunction with notifications can enhance the EA model actuality significantly.

6   Conclusion and Future Work

In this paper we have presented the first account on using architecture change events to drive EA model maintenance processes. We highlighted that related work in the field of EA documentation focuses on the collection of structured data which is not always at hand in adequate granularity and quality. Based on this, we argued that using events from (management) information systems of IT operations can be used to initiate EA model maintenance processes more timely and provide some context information for the interpretation by stakeholders. In particular events can be used to improve activities of collecting relevant information for EA models and to increase the quality of the maintained EA models regarding actuality.

The classification and the workflow presented in the paper provide a relevant starting point for future research, but critically depend on several key issues being solved in order to realize the full benefit for EA model maintenance:

Identifying appropriate event processors: When an EA change event is processed by the workflow, it must determine a role or a user that is best suited for processing the event. In the best case a person who is the owner of the changed artifact is chosen. This person naturally has the best knowledge on the changes and the relation of the element to other EA elements. However, this is a difficult task because this mapping is not always available from events. The EA meta-model we present in [26] is a starting point for the task assignment problem by enabling the assignment of user or roles to *areas-of-interest* in the EA model.

Relating events to existing model elements: A similar problem arises when trying to relate events to already existing elements in the EA repository. In many cases only string similarity matching between the names of the changed element in the events source and existing elements in the repository may provide some automated hints.

Event overflow avoidance: Depending on the number of event sources and the sensitivity of event triggers the number of events can grow too large. A balance has to be found between which events to fire and which to blacklist in order avoid that involved persons spent too much time on blacklisting events, thus reducing acceptance.

Event after manual change: Another problem in practice occurs when events are produced for changes that have already been manually applied to the model. For example, in the case of a planned project event, a user that processes a task might have already have modeled the TO-BE hardware. If the hardware buying list is implemented as a source for events, the event of the newly acquired hardware could be fired although the respective hardware has already been modeled. Hence, the second event is superfluous.

Addition and removal events: In some cases only the event for addition or removal of an element can be detected but not always both. It should be the goal that the full lifecycle of a model element, i.e., planned, running, retired is covered by some form of automation. Such automation could be the structured data import presented in [4,5], events presented in this paper or expiry events proposed in [6].

EA modeling suggestions: A research topic that is not only relevant in the context of events, is the question of how suggestions for further modeling actions based on previous changes to the model and domain knowledge can be generated. The work of Dam et al. [9] is an interesting starting point in this direction.

We regard above issues to be best addressed with practical research. As the next step for enabling such research we plan to implement the workflow within an existing EAM tool and to evaluate the implications of workflow automation in practice.Based on the findings from the practical application, we seek to refute the practical relevance of several of the issues described above, as well as to identify solutions for relevant issues.

Acknowledgements. The authors would like to thank Waldemar Lohrer, Frederike Nickl and Rolf Wassil of Swiss Life Germany as well as Lukas Schwaiger from the University of Innsbruck for their input to this paper.

References

1. Lucke, C., München, U.D.B., Krell, S., Lechner, U.: Critical Issues in Enterprise Architecting A Literature Review. In: AMCIS 2010 Proceedings (2010)
2. Farwick, M., Agreiter, B., Ryll, S., Voges, K., Hanschke, I., Breu, R.: Requirements for automated enterprise architecture model maintenance. In: 13th International Conference on Enterprise Information Systems (ICEIS), Beijing (2011)
3. Winter, K., Buckl, S., Matthes, F., Schweda, C.: Investigating the state-of-the-art in enterprise architecture management methods in literature and practice. In: MCIS 2010 Proceedings (2010)

4. Holm, H., Buschle, M., Lagerstrm, R., Ekstedt, M.: Automatic data collection for enterprise architecture models. Software & Systems Modeling, 1–17 (2012)
5. Buschle, M., Ekstedt, M., Grunow, S., Hauder, M., Matthes, F., Roth, S.: Automating enterprise architecture documentation using an enterprise service bus. In: Proceedings of the 18th Americas Conference on Information Systems (2012), http://wwwmatthes.in.tum.de/wikis/sebis/bu12-automating-enterprise-architecture-d?confirmationMessageIds=sevp1b5i2tov
6. Farwick, M., Schweda, C.M., Pasquazzo, W., Breu, R., Voges, K., Hanschke, I.: A meta-model for Automated Enterprise Architecture Model Maintenance. In: 2012 IEEE 16th International Enterprise Distributed Object Computing Conference Workshops (2012)
7. de Boer, F., Bonsangue, M., Groenewegen, L., Stam, A., Stevens, S., van der Torre, L.: Change impact analysis of enterprise architectures. In: IEEE International Conference on Information Reuse and Integration, Conf., IRI 2005, pp. 177–181. IEEE (2005)
8. Lankhorst, M.: Enterprise Architecture at Work: Modelling, Communication and Analysis. Springer, Berlin (2005)
9. Dam, H.K., Le, L.S., Ghose, A.: Supporting change propagation in the evolution of enterprise architectures. In: 2010 14th IEEE International Enterprise Distributed Object Computing Conference, pp. 24–33. IEEE (October 2010)
10. Fischer, R., Aier, S., Winter, R.: A federated approach to enterprise architecture model maintenance. In: Reichert, M., Strecker, S., Turowski, K. (eds.) EMISA. LNI, vol. P-119, pp. 9–22. GI (2007)
11. Buckl, S., Ernst, A.M., Lankes, J., Matthes, F.: Enterprise Architecture Management Pattern Catalog (Version 1.0, February 2008). Technical report, Chair for Informatics 19 (sebis), Technische Universität München, Munich, Germany (2008)
12. Ernst, A.M., Schneider, A.W.: Roadmaps for enterprise architecture evolution. In: Engels, G., Luckey, M., Pretschner, A., Reussner, R. (eds.) 2nd European Workshop on Patterns for Enterprise Architecture Management (PEAM 2010), Paderborn, Germany, pp. 253–266 (2010)
13. Sousa, P., Lima, J., Sampaio, A., Pereira, C.: An Approach for Creating and Managing Enterprise Blueprints: A Case for IT Blueprints. In: Albani, A., Barjis, J., Dietz, J.L.G., Aalst, W., Mylopoulos, J., Rosemann, M., Shaw, M.J., Szyperski, C. (eds.) CIAO! 2009. LNBIP, vol. 34, pp. 70–84. Springer, Heidelberg (2009)
14. The Open Group: TOGAF "Enterprise Edition" Version 9 (2009), http://www.togaf.org (cited July 7, 2012)
15. Buckl, S.: Developing Organization-Specific Enterprise Architecture Management Functions Using a Method Base. PhD thesis, Fakultät für Informatik, Technische Universität München, Germany (2011)
16. Buckl, S., Matthes, F., Monahov, I., Schweda, C.M.: Modeling Enterprise Architecture Transformations. In: van Sinderen, M., Johnson, P. (eds.) IWEI 2011. LNBIP, vol. 76, Springer, Heidelberg (2011)
17. Aier, S., Buckl, S., Gleichauf, B., Matthes, F., Schweda, C.M., Winter, R.: Towards a more integrated ea planning: Linking transformation planning with evolutionary change. In: 5th International Workshop on Enterprise Modelling and Information Systems Architectures. Springer (2011)
18. Farwick, M., Agreiter, B., Breu, R., Ryll, S., Voges, K., Hanschke, I.: Automation processes for enterprise architecture management. In: 2011 IEEE 15th International Enterprise Distributed Object Computing Conference Workshops, pp. 340–349. IEEE (August 2011)

19. Breu, R., Agreiter, B., Farwick, M., Felderer, M., Hafner, M., Innerhofer-Oberperfler, F.: Living models - ten principles for change-driven software engineering. Int. J. Software and Informatics 5(1-2), 267–290 (2011)
20. Winter, R., Fischer, R.: Essential layers, artifacts, and dependencies of enterprise architecture. Journal of Enterprise Architecture, 7–18 (2007)
21. Hanschke, I.: Strategic IT Management: A Toolkit for Enterprise Architecture Management. Springer (2009)
22. Aier, S., Gleichauf, B.: Application of enterprise models for engineering enterprise transformation. Enterprise Modelling and Information System Architectures 5, 56–72 (2010)
23. Sousa, P., Martins, R., Sampaio, A.: Clarification of the Application Concept: The Caixa Geral de Depósitos Case. In: Proper, E., Gaaloul, K., Harmsen, F., Wrycza, S. (eds.) PRET 2012. LNBIP, vol. 120, pp. 1–17. Springer, Heidelberg (2012)
24. OGC: ITIL Lifecycle Publication Suite Books, 2nd impression. TSO (2007)
25. Buckl, S., Ernst, A.M., Kopper, H., Marliani, R., Matthes, F., Petschownik, P., Schweda, C.M.: Eam pattern for consolidations after mergers. In: SE 2009 – Workshopband, Kaiserslautern, Germany, pp. 67–78 (2009)
26. Farwick, M., Schweda, C., Pasquazzo, W., Voges, K., Breu, R., Hanschke, I.: A meta-model for automated enterprise architecture model maintenance. In: Enterprise Distributed Object Computing Conference, EDOC 2012. IEEE (2012)
27. Object Management Group: Business Process Model and Notation (BPMN) Version 2.0 (2011)

Enterprise Architecture for the Adaptive Enterprise – A Vision Paper

Eric Yu, Stephanie Deng, and Divyajyoti Sasmal

University of Toronto, Toronto, Canada M5S 3G6

Abstract. Dealing with change is a major concern in enterprise architecture. As organizations face increasingly fast-moving environments, systematic frameworks are needed to manage change at many levels. Recent advances in data analytics and business intelligence enable organizations to gain deep insights quickly and recognize needs for change, and to take actions in response. Current enterprise architecture approaches have limited ability to model and reason about the adaptiveness that is available or desirable in various parts of an enterprise. In this vision paper, we attempt a preliminary characterization of an adaptive enterprise, so as to stimulate debate and research towards EA frameworks that explicitly support adaptiveness as a design goal. Initial ideas to adopt and integrate modeling constructs from system dynamics and goal-oriented and agent-oriented requirements engineering are outlined.

Keywords: enterprise architecture, adaptive, system dynamics, social actors, goal-oriented requirements engineering, business intelligence, modeling.

1   Introduction

Dealing with change is a major concern in enterprise architecture [1, 2, 3, 4]. As many organizations face increasingly dynamic environments, they seek ways to become more agile and adaptive [5].

Recent advances in business intelligence and analytics technologies [6] enable organizations to gain insights into their environments as well as internal operations much more quickly and in much greater depth than before, drawing upon vast amounts of data from diverse internal and external sources. Actions resulting from these insights often require changes to IT systems that support business activities or implement business processes. However, current use of BI and analytics technologies are typically not systemically coordinated with operational IT systems to exploit the kinds of adaptive capabilities that various IT systems can or cannot provide [7].

A major opportunity exists for the field of enterprise architecture to provide methods and frameworks to assist organizations to achieve the adaptiveness that is needed for them to succeed and excel in fast-moving environments, taking advantage of the rapid and widespread adoption of BI in recent years, as well as the availability of increasingly adaptable IT system technologies – such as cloud computing, service-orientation, and adaptive software technologies.

S. Aier et al. (Eds.): TEAR 2012 and PRET 2012, LNBIP 131, pp. 146–161, 2012.

EA should not treat BI as merely another class of data-intensive applications to be managed and governed among the many other classes of applications. Its special significance in a business conception of the enterprise must be fully reflected and exploited in an EA framework. From an adaptation viewpoint, recent BI technologies vastly expand an enterprise's ability to sense and interpret its environment, thus enhancing decision making. Together with IT systems that execute business operations and processes, a BI-enabled organization can potentially achieve a high degree of adaptiveness through closed-loop monitoring and enactment.

The field of EA is well positioned to bring about such an integrated approach to the adaptive enterprise because of its explicit commitment to view IT systems in a business context. An adaptive enterprise architecture needs to coordinate and orchestrate technologies for sensing, interpreting, and decision making on the one hand, and technologies for implementation and execution on the other, while recognizing their distinct and complementary roles at the business level.

To realize the vision of an EA approach to guide the BI-enabled adaptive enterprise, we face considerable research challenges. The main objective of this paper is to attempt a preliminary characterization of the adaptive enterprise, so as to stimulate debate and research. Section 2 introduces several sample enterprise settings to illustrate and motivate the vision. Section 3 reviews existing work on enterprise adaptiveness. In section 4, we propose a number of characteristics that a framework for adaptive EA should address. Research challenges and possible directions are discussed in Section 5. We conclude by outlining future work.

2   Sample Settings

Consider first a telecom company offering mobile services. This is a highly dynamic business sector where competition is fierce, and new generations of technologies can lead to fundamental shifts in the competitive landscape. Smaller operators can target niche market segments, and offer new services or innovative pricing plans. Quality of service is often a concern [8]. Customer concerns and complaints need to be kept in check, as the reputation of the company can quickly erode from negative publicity over social media channels. Public response - from customers as well as investors – would be of great interest, for example, immediately after a product release by the company or by any of its competitors. In highly dynamic business sectors, these kinds of market dynamics can unfold over a very short time period, for example within days of a new produce release.

BI technologies today enable mobile operators to monitor sentiment on social networking sites such as Twitter and Facebook to raise early warning and observe trends, regarding specific product offerings, customer service quality, as well as overall company reputation [9]. The analytics results can be drilled down to determine the customer segment that is of interest, e.g., whether disaffection is originating from new customers, younger customers, high-value customers, and so on.

External intelligence can be correlated with internal data such as actual complaints received, new subscriptions and account cancellations, service switching, etc. Based on such internal and external intelligence, the company would formulate courses of action – e.g., to adjust product offerings or bundles, add variations to the pricing plan or terms, change the way it interacts with certain classes of customers, target particular groups with marketing campaigns and promotional offerings, etc.

Most of these response actions would involve changes to enterprise IT systems, particularly where business operations are highly automated, e.g., customer self-serve web-based systems.

From a business competitiveness and viability viewpoint, it is therefore critical to know how adaptive an enterprise is with respect to various type of change, and to have ways to achieve higher degrees of adaptiveness in areas where it is needed.

BI and analytics are also widely deployed in retail and merchandising [10]. Product variety and novelty are constantly updated to meet changing customer tastes and trends. Business practices are frequently adjusted and tuned to balance efficiency, costs, and agility. Fashion brands such as Zara and H&M are well-known for rapid design cycles, achieving several cycles within a single season. Convenience stores such as 7Eleven use data analytics to optimize product mix and shelf displays, and to improve supply chain effectiveness. Among the five groups of performance metrics (KPIs) defined in the Supply Chain Operational Reference model [11], agility and responsiveness are prominent, along with costs, reliability, and asset management.

While automation can offer dramatic gains in efficiency, they can also be obstacles to change, especially if business practices are embedded in legacy code. Recent IT infrastructures and architectures such as cloud computing [12] and SOA [13] allow a more granular trade-off among the many competing design goals.

In healthcare, data analytics are used to monitor and report on quality of care, with metrics on wait times, mortality rates, infection rates, resource utilization, and so forth. Hospitals need to frequently adapt processes to meet performance targets, to respond to regulatory and policy changes, as well as new diseases, drugs, and epidemics [14].

In all of these settings, different kinds and degrees of adaptiveness are needed in different parts of the enterprise. Adaptiveness is a desirable design goal but it must compete with other design goals. Changes may be gradual or abrupt, frequent or occasional, short-term or long-term. A systematic framework to needed to help the BI-enabled data-driven organization to model, analyze, and design its adaptiveness characteristics, in conjunction with other desirable enterprise objectives.

3   Related Work

Facilitating change and adaptiveness has been an ongoing theme in enterprise architecture. While most works in EA acknowledge the need for adaptiveness, few provide modeling and analysis support to achieving adaptiveness in specific ways.

For example, the recently updated standard for EA modeling, the Archimate 2.0 language [15], has no provision for expressing or reasoning about change or variability. The main construct for expressing dynamics is the element "business process". One cannot indicate that options are kept open at various points in the process to allow for adaptation. .In designing an adaptive enterprise, one would want to be able to reason about what variabilities to build into what processes, and at what time point or stage a commitment should be made to exclude further choices. The Architecture Development Method (ADM) in TOGAF [1] provides guidelines for major architectural change, but not for the ongoing adaptations that occur within many other kinds of time cycles.

The notion of adaptive enterprise architecture has been proposed and advocated. For example, Wilkinson [16] proposes a particular approach for designing an adaptive enterprise architecture, by exploiting the adaptability of service-oriented computing infrastructure. Hoogervorst [4] argues for the need to integrate business and IT views to enable agility and change, echoing the general EA approaches.

To the best of our knowledge, no enterprise architecture framework has been proposed that recognizes the sense-and-interpret role of business analytics to form a closed-loop with business execution, which together can be used to meet adaptiveness requirements specific to particular organizations.

In the management literature, Haeckel [17] has argued for a sense-and-respond approach to adaptive enterprise. Pantaleo [18] provides a number of case studies on agile enterprise. Lee [19] argues that the best supply chains are agile, adaptive, and aligned, and lists some methods for achieving each in the context of supply chain management – e.g., postponing design decisions to take advantage of last-minute market data, as practiced by apparel brand companies such as H&M and Zara. Concepts and principles for the agile enterprise have also originated from the manufacturing industry, e.g., [20]. A number of studies have considered the role of IT in business agility, e.g., [21], [22].

These works offer a rich body of ideas, concepts, principles, and case study illustrations to draw upon. However, they do not provide the detailed analytic support that a model-based enterprise architecture approach could.

4   Characteristics of the Adaptive Enterprise

In this section, we propose some key characteristics of the adaptive enterprise that are not easily accommodated in current EA frameworks. In doing so, we aim to characterize the problem for the EA researcher – what should an EA framework for the adaptive enterprise be able to do? What issues should it encompass? The informal description in this paper will need be formalized in future work.

To begin, an adaptive enterprise needs to recognize the dimensions and variables along which change may occur (*diversity and variability*). Since there is *uncertainty* in the anticipation of change, the architect would want to be able to choose what decisions to *commit* to at what times, and what options to leave open. While BI greatly expands the *sensing* capabilities of an enterprise, "actionable insights" from BI should be linked to the *actions and changes* that will produce desired results.

In architecting for adaptiveness, the architect will need to take into account *barriers* and obstacles to various kinds of change. Investments in adaptiveness need to be balanced and *traded-off* against competing objectives such as operational efficiency.

Different kinds of change occur at different time scales and frequencies (*levels of dynamics*). This leads to a conception of enterprise consisting of multiple *dynamic systems* (closed loop feedback systems) each with its own scope and *boundaries*. Each dynamic system is driven by its own objectives (as measured through a set of KPIs), creating tension between local *autonomy* within each system and *alignment* and coherence across the many diverse systems that make up the enterprise. This includes issues of *business-IT alignment*. Finally, since each enterprise may face unique challenges, the enterprise architect should be able to treat *adaptiveness as an explicit requirement* to be addressed using systematic methods during the architecting process.

4.1   Diversity and Variability

An adaptive enterprise needs to recognize and support change along all variables and dimensions that are relevant to that enterprise. Most complex organizations offer a range of products and/or services to a variety of clients/customers, and deal with many suppliers, channels, and payment methods, etc., all with numerous attributes. The innovative organization will explore different strategies and processes for achieving business objectives.

The architect for the adaptive enterprise will need to support not only this diversity, but also changes to this diversity. There may be frequent changes to the mix of product and services, the nature of customer relationships, and business processes and strategies. Multi-dimensional data analysis methods enabled by BI technologies greatly expand an organization's ability to slice and dice business data, triggering initiatives to rethink and restructure business operations [6].

An adaptive EA framework should provide modeling and reasoning support regarding diversity and variability along dimensions of interest, and about the implications and consequences of changes along these dimensions. Current EA frameworks have little support for reasoning about variability and diversity. Enterprise modeling languages such as Archimate [15] and UEML [23] do not have language features for modeling and reasoning about variability and adaptiveness. Research in the software produce line area (e.g., [24]) could provide inspiration for extending enterprise modeling in this direction.

4.2   Uncertainty and Commitment

An adaptive enterprise needs to anticipate specific kinds of changes, in order to have built-in provisions to allow for those changes if and when they materialize. This may include building flexible technology infrastructures, adopting configurable architectures and systems, and suitable organizational structures and training of personnel. All of these incur lead time, investments, and sunk costs. Sunk costs are expenditures that are not reversible, regardless of whether benefits were obtained.

Yet the actual trajectory of change will be hard to predict and may be highly uncertain. In an adaptive enterprise, the enterprise architect needs to decide what kinds of adaptations to be prepared for, and where in the enterprise they will be located. The preparations can be in the form of built-in provisions to handle variabilities at particular points in the enterprise (e.g. at stages along a business process). These provisions (e.g., choice of payment methods, interaction protocols) may or may not be exercised depending on the actual unfolding of circumstances. However, since there are costs in maintaining multiple options, architectural decisions must be made regarding what options to commit to at what times, and which others to leave open. BI can be used to reduce uncertainty by more timely and accurate monitoring of the environment.

Current EA frameworks do not support reasoning about where uncertainties reside and when decision commitments should be made.

4.3   Sensing and Effecting Change

The adaptive enterprise needs to able to respond quickly and effectively to various types of change. Change may be originating from outside the enterprise (e.g., a competitive threat, a technological innovation), or internally initiated (e.g., a strategic initiative). One might map a causal path, from the "source" of change, to the chains of resulting effects. The paths are not necessarily linear, as a change can propagate in multiple directions and even loop back to affect the source.

Some of the changes may be observable by the enterprise, through sensing or monitoring mechanisms (e.g., patterns, trends, and outliers in shipping costs, delays, and breakage). Others need to be inferred and require interpretation (e.g., whether a new product from a competitor is a threat).

By sensing and interpreting its environment, an enterprise (or its units) can take actions to take advantage of changes or avert undesirable effects. In so doing, the enterprise is intervening in its environment, participating in the changes to advance its own interests. In order for its actions to be effective, the enterprise needs to have some knowledge of what aspects of the environment it can exert control or influence, and the means-ends relationship between its actions and the consequences.

IT systems are powerful instruments for effecting change. By automating business processes or enabling online self-service, efficiency can often be greatly improved. In contrast, until recently, the sensing side had limited IT support. Much of the work was labor-intensive - data collection from diverse sources, reconciling inconsistencies, analyzing for trends and patterns. Today, BI platforms and analytics tools are filling this gap, enabling dramatic advances in efficiency and effectiveness in sensing and interpreting the environment.

Enterprise architecture for the adaptive enterprise needs to support both the sensing and the effecting sides of change, so that the two can work coherently to achieve the desired adaptiveness. Adaptation support includes sensing and interpreting, decision support, and then the actions to bring about the desired changes. The outcomes of the actions are monitored through the sensing and interpreting mechanisms, closing the so-called sense-interpret-decide-act (SIDA) loop [17]. The EA framework should support modeling and analysis of the propagation paths of change, mechanisms for sensing and effecting change along the paths, and properties of propagation patterns such as closed loop feedback.

4.4   Barriers to Change

In attempting to manage and exploit change in the adaptive enterprise, it is important to be aware of barriers and resistances that stand in the way of change. Some changes are more likely to occur than others. Some change initiatives succeed while others fail. Barriers to change can be technological or human organizational. Developing a new system, modifying a business rule, migrating to a new platform – each of these incur different amounts of time and costs, and present different degrees of difficulty and risks.

Human social and organizational barriers can include acquiring new knowledge and skills, and overcoming forces of habit and outdated mindsets. Resistance to change can also result from lack of trust, fear of job loss, or entrenched interests and power.

Current EAs reflect implicit understandings about such barriers. When the understanding is implicit, it is difficult for the enterprise to respond to shifts in those barriers. For an adaptive enterprise, the characteristics of barriers to change should be explicitly analyzed and managed.

New technologies may remove old barriers, though they may introduce new ones or move old ones around. For example, SOA and cloud computing allow fine-grained control over incremental functionality and capacity. Yet the initial adoption may be a steep barrier for some organizations. Business rules, scripting languages, model-driven development, and agile development methods are all examples of software innovations that shift the barriers to change. EA for the adaptive enterprise should explicitly analyze how these software practices will contribute to adaptiveness in the particular business setting. From a modeling viewpoint, barriers may be treated as preconditions that must be satisfied for particular change options to become valid.

4.5   Adaptability Trade-Offs

In adopting a technology system, one may expect a leap in productivity, a significant speed-up in some process, reductions in delays and error rates, and so forth. However, the gains are often obtained at the expense of flexibility. Most automation technologies require pre-defined activity steps. Conditional actions and exceptions can be accommodated only if the conditions are known so that responses can be pre-determined. Since the days of legacy systems, various software advances (some noted above) have emerged to provide greater flexibility and adaptability [25]. Collaboration mechanisms support interweaving of human and automated actions to accommodate even greater uncertainty (e.g., in workflow and business process management systems).

In choosing one type of technology over another, an architect is making a number of trade-offs regarding adaptability, efficiency, quality, costs, risks, etc.

In current EAs, such trade-offs are implicit. For the adaptive enterprise, there should be support for analyzing such trade-offs. An enterprise architect should know the adaptability properties of each class of technology (generically) and the actual adaptability of the systems when implemented in the particular enterprise.

4.6   Multiple Levels of Dynamics

Some changes happen within a short time interval while others occur over a longer time frame. Many changes are recurrent, so they can be thought of as occurring in cycles. Thus some types of changes have short cycle times while others have long ones. Change can be gradual or abrupt.

The enterprise architect needs to recognize different rates of change as well as cycle times for each kind of change so as to provide appropriate adaptation support. Different rates of change or timing cycles could mean different ways of using BI and different analytics techniques for the "sensing and interpreting" side, and adopting IT systems with suitable adaptability characteristic on the "action" side.

Since different kinds of changes occur along different time frames, there are changes whose entire cycles occur within a single cycle of a slower, longer time frame kind of change. For example, incremental business process improvements can occur without necessarily requiring a major system redesign. Many new system development and deployment could occur within an enterprise architecture redesign cycle.

For an adaptive enterprise, the enterprise architect needs to recognize that for each type of change and adaptation, what elements are in motion, and which ones are (relatively) static or constant. Those elements that are assumed to be constant are in fact in motion over a longer time frame, in a different kind of change cycle. However, for the purpose of managing changes within a certain range of rate of change, these other elements can be assumed to be stable or fixed, and thus omitted from the modeling and analysis of the dynamics.

To carry this perspective further, business transactions constitute a fundamental type of activity cycle in an enterprise, even though they are not normally thought of as "change". Business processes and workflows are instantiated thousands of times a day, while the process definition remains unchanged. For an incremental process improvement, one may have to assume that the software must remain largely unchanged. In designing a new system, the designer needs to work within the constraints of a given platform and enterprise architecture guidelines and rules. Common distinctions regarding operational, tactical, and strategic decision making also reflect dynamics at different time scales [26].

We may view the different types of change in an enterprise in terms of "orders of dynamics", with the longer-term slow-moving changes belonging to the higher-order dynamics. The adaptive enterprise architect needs to understand and coordinate these different orders of dynamics, enabling them to work coherently and not at cross-purposes. For example, historic data accumulating the purchase patterns of customers of a certain demographic can be used in combination with daily current sales to make promotional offers to a particular customer in a real-time BI application.

The way the various kinds of change falls into different orders of dynamics with different time cycles can vary from one enterprise to another, although there can be generic patterns – from sales transactions to product cycles to various planning cycles. As hinted at above, the rates of change and hence the cycle structures result from barriers to change. These barriers to change are themselves subject to change.

4.7   Dynamic Systems, Boundaries and Closure

The idea that there are regular patterns of change or dynamics that fall into different time scales and cycles suggests that an enterprise can be viewed as a collection of dynamic systems. For example a team responsible for the performance of a business process, with its attendant KPIs (key performance indicators), can be viewed as a dynamic system. Dynamic systems can be modeled and analyzed using well-established techniques such as causal loop analysis (e.g., reinforcing and balancing loops) and stock and flow analysis (e.g., rates of change) [27, 28]. The strategic management process would be an example of a dynamic system that operates on a longer time cycle with a broader scope.

The general availability of BI technologies across the enterprise would enable every business unit or manager to treat his/her operations as a closed-loop system – sensing the environment to make data/intelligence-based decisions, take actions, then close the loop by monitoring the results and taking further actions [17].

An adaptive EA framework should provide support for BI-enabled closed-loop management in all areas of the enterprise. An architectural description would include the boundaries and identities of the dynamic systems as well as their interrelationships. The boundary of a system is delineated by recognizing which variables are within its scope of interest and which ones are not. The scope of interest is determined by the goals and objectives of the system, some of which may be assigned by external actors (e.g., higher authorities). Each dynamic system operates within its relevant time frame, taking actions to respond to changes in its perceived environment. The sensing and interpreting mechanisms of each system filter out the "noise", extracting useful information to feed into its decisions, producing actions that are of value to that system. Irrelevant aspects would include variables that are changing too slowly (therefore can be assumed to be constant) or too quickly (e.g., individual instance data that are irrelevant for doing process redesign), as well as subject matter that is outside of its scope (e.g., the finance department not getting involved in product design, the strategic management process not intervening in daily operations). As a result, each of these systems may be said to be *bounded*.

The architecting process should support the analysis of an enterprise as a collection of interrelated bounded dynamic system. According to system dynamics thinking, dynamics systems are best understood and controlled when the need for exogenous variables is minimized [27]. This implies loose-coupling across different bounded dynamic systems.

4.8   Actor Autonomy and Alignment

In responding to change, each dynamic system is driven by goals and objectives. Ideally, the boundary of each system coincides with the division of responsibilities in an organization. For example, a business process would have a process owner responsible for its performance. Based on the goals and objectives defined for the business process, the process owner would determine what performance indicators to monitor, and how to respond to situations with appropriate actions – such as adjusting process parameters and configurations.

However, real-life enterprises are human social systems, whereas a dynamic system is an idealized abstraction. Even when a business unit (such as a team responsible for a business process) is given clear objectives and performance measures, the individuals within the team can have their own goals and objectives which are not perfectly aligned with those of the business unit.

Members of an organization are individuals with personal goals and aspirations. They collaborate to pursue collective goals to the extent that the collaboration contributes to personal goals. It is also possible for individuals to pursue personal goals at the expense of collective goals. Actors in an organization are semi-autonomous in the sense that despite assigned responsibilities, rules and regulations, they are free to act within certain social constraints [29]. They also adapt to their own perceived environments.

Alignment of interests between the idealized dynamic system and the participating actors is therefore of major concern in an enterprise architecture.

On a larger scale, since an enterprise consists of many loosely-coupled dynamic systems, they also need to be maintained in alignment with each other. Aside from the private interests of individuals, complex organizations that are divided according to functions, product lines, regions, disciplines, and time horizons have many sources of divergent and competing interests that arise naturally. These can range from competition for resources, to competing visions from different disciplines (e.g., product engineering versus marketing), to competition between long-term and short-term goals (e.g., strategic versus operational concerns) [26].

Since many kinds of adaptations on different time scales are occurring simultaneously across the enterprise, alignment needs to be thought of as ongoing processes happening in a distributed fashion. The enterprise architecture should ensure that these alignment processes can proceed effectively on an ongoing basis, and not just during major transformational change.

As the various systems have asynchronous dynamics, the alignment processes would also be asynchronous. Consequently, it would be reasonable to acknowledge that, most of the time, alignment is more of an ideal than a reality. Proper functioning of the enterprise therefore needs to tolerate a substantial amount of misalignment. BI can be used to monitor the degree of alignment to avoid major dislocations.

A framework for adaptive enterprise architecture needs to support the modeling and analysis of actors with organizational and personal goals, and varying degrees of alignment across the enterprise.

4.9   Business-IT Alignment

The bounded dynamic system is an abstraction for characterizing the adaptive behavior of an enterprise and its constituent units. In physical reality, each system will have human and technology elements, including IT systems.

The challenge of business-IT alignment is well recognized in enterprise architecture [30, 31, 32, 33, 34]. Most existing EA frameworks offer layered views which separate business elements and concerns from IT ones. Each layer is assumed to apply across the entire enterprise.

In the adaptive enterprise, if semi-autonomous units (characterized as bounded dynamic systems) must adapt at their own pace to meet their respective objectives, it would appear that business-IT alignment within each unit might take precedence over enterprise-wide alignment. For example, the requirements for business-IT alignment for an operational business process can be quite different from those for new product development. As mentioned above, BI can be used to monitor various types of misalignment and their extents. .

The distributed approach to business-IT alignment does not remove the need for interoperability among IT systems across the enterprise, as adaptability of IT systems (at the application systems level) is needed to achieve a high degree of adaptiveness at the business level (less severe barriers to change due to inflexibility in technology systems).

Terminologically and conceptually, it is useful to recognize a distinction between adaptiveness and adaptability. Adaptiveness (as used in this paper) refers to self-adaptiveness. It is the ability of an entity (an organism or system) to change its behavior to better survive or succeed in its environment. The entity senses and interprets its environment and decides what to do. Adaptiveness therefore requires all four elements of the sense-interpret-decide-act (SIDA) loop.

In contrast, we say that an artifact is adaptable if it is easy or amenable to change. The change is initiated by an external agent. An adaptable system need not be self-adaptive; and a self-adaptive system may very well not be adaptable, i.e., not receptive to an imposed change. For example, cloud and service-oriented computing are more adaptable because they offer more granular or more modular or configurable computations services and resources. However, they are not self-adaptive unless they have well-developed components for sensing, interpreting, and deciding as well as for acting.

Adaptiveness of a bounded dynamic system is therefore at a higher, business level of abstraction than that of the adaptability of technology systems, which are elements used to implement business systems. In an adaptive architecture, we want the enterprise to be adaptive, and its IT systems to be adaptable. Some IT systems have self-adaptive properties, as in autonomic systems which repair themselves [35], or intelligent agents which use reasoning and planning algorithms to guide action [36]. If such systems are not also adaptable, i.e., cannot be made to change their behaviour to meet changing business needs, then they would not be suitable for use in an adaptive enterprise.

An adaptive enterprise architecture framework needs to accommodate a distributed view of business-IT alignment. It also needs to support analysis of adaptability of IT systems, and how different mechanisms for adaptability contribute to business-level adaptiveness.

4.10   Adaptiveness as a Business Requirement

While adaptiveness is generally considered desirable, at least for enterprises in highly dynamic or turbulent environments [5], there are few specific frameworks and approaches for achieving adaptiveness. Given the above characterization, it is possible to envision adaptiveness as one of the business requirements when architecting an enterprise, along with other competing (or synergistic) requirements such as operational efficiency, costs, etc.

In characterizing an adaptive enterprise in terms of a loosely-coupled network of bounded dynamic systems (each intersecting with their respective environments, more or less in alignment, and each with mechanisms for sensing, interpreting, decision, and action), an enterprise architect can be quite specific in specifying how much and what kind of adaptiveness is desirable in which parts of the enterprise.

Adaptiveness requirements vary across different parts of an enterprise because of different rates of change in its environment, and the payoffs for being able to respond to those changes, or penalties of not being able to do so. These adaptiveness requirements will need to be weighed against upfront costs and possible loss of operational efficiency.

Adopting techniques from requirements engineering, adaptiveness requirements can be specified as goals as well as scenarios [37]. These requirements can then guide the selection of suitable approaches and mechanisms (such as BI technologies and process technologies) to meet the combination of adaptiveness and other requirements.

5   Research Challenges and Directions

The above characterization of the BI-enabled adaptive enterprise suggests a vision for an adaptive enterprise architecture framework. The vision entails a number of practical as well as technical challenges – including rethinking the scope of EA, and developing suitable modeling, analysis and design techniques and tools.

5.1   The Scope of Enterprise Architecture and the EA Team

The vision suggests an expanded scope for EA, requiring a closer collaboration between business and IT. The proposed notion of adaptive EA necessarily encompasses business architectural design, as our primary concern is the adaptiveness of the enterprise, not just the adaptability of its IT systems. Adaptiveness is one objective amongst many at the business level, as exemplified by the categories of performance metrics for supply chain management [11]. The enterprise architect therefore needs to engage fully with the business on the one hand, and with adaptability of IT systems on the other.

An adaptive EA framework should provide a systematic and coherent way for business and IT architects and strategists to understand and analyze how data analytics can contribute to adaptiveness, incorporating analytics and BI into business and IT system architectures. As well, the vision may entail a rethinking of alignment between business and IT layers.

5.2   Analysis and Tool Support

Given a conception of enterprise as a collection of dynamic systems, there are many properties of these systems that are of interest. These may include, for example, the topology of causal links between variables (where the feedback paths are, whether they are reinforcing or balancing, time delays in the loops, etc.), temporal trajectories of change (exponential growth, plateauing, oscillations, equilibrium, etc.).

Note that the actual values of the variables and the details of the behaviors of the dynamic system are of direct concern only to the business stakeholders (managers, executives, process owners) during business operations. The role of the architect is to provide enabling support - to help set up these systems and enable them to function effectively.

BI architects would work with business architects to choose data sources, data quality requirements, data analysis techniques and algorithms, visualization techniques for decision support, etc. With a well-defined bounded dynamic system as focus, they would choose indicators and metrics relevant to the goals and objectives of that system, and with an understanding of the options for action that are available in that system. The BI design would rely on lower layer support such as data warehousing, ETL, data integration with external sources, etc.

On the "action" side of the SIDA loop, IT architects would work with business process designers to choose IT systems with adaptability characteristics that facilitate or at least not adversely impact the functioning of the dynamic system. For example, barriers to change arising from inflexibilities in IT systems can introduce discontinuities or non-linearities in the dynamic system. IT architects therefore need to be fully conversant in system dynamics to understand the impact of their choices on the effectiveness of the overall dynamic system at the business level.

To assist business and IT architects in these tasks, one can envision tools for visualizing and manipulating enterprise models, analyzing for dynamic system properties, and detecting abnormalities. Simulation tools can also offer many useful insights.

Adaptiveness requirements expressed as design goals can be reasoned about using design tools that support incremental goal refinement leading to considerations of alternative operationalizations, while considering trade-offs with competing goals (e.g., employing a goal-oriented design framework such as the NFR framework [38]. Adaptiveness requirements expressed as change scenarios [39] can be used to guide design as well as to test candidate designs. There should also be tools to analyze relationships across multiple dynamic systems, such as alignment.

5.3   Modeling

Given the characterization in Section 4, developing a suitable modeling framework would be a considerable research undertaking. The collection of concepts suggests drawing upon and integrating modeling constructs from system dynamics, goal modeling, social actors modeling, and BI modeling.

The modeling and analysis of dynamic systems as applied to business is well developed [28]. System dynamics models include causal loop diagrams and stock and flow diagrams. These diagrams map out how an increase in one variable will cause which other variables to increase or decrease. Feedback paths can result in reinforcing loops (positive feedback) or balancing loops (negative feedback). There can be delays along these causal paths. A stock indicates the level (amount) of some variable. Flows in and out of the stock can be controlled by valves which vary the rate of flow.

Goal modeling [38] provides the representation for modeling and analyzing a space of alternatives. Variability and commitment can be analyzed into terms of what choices are open at what times, e.g., design time vs. run time, etc [40].

Social modeling [41] can be used to model and analyze semi-autonomous actors and their interests, as well as dependency relationships among them. Alignment can be analyzed in terms of complementary and conflicting goals.

Recent work has developed business-level modeling for BI. For example, the Business Intelligence Model (BIM) (e.g., [42], [43]) provides a modeling and query language for business users to reasoning about business objectives, strategies, situations, processes, and performance indicators, with data from BI tools. BIM models can be adapted and extended to address variability and adaptiveness in the EA context.

6   Conclusions

We have outlined a vision for enterprise architecture for the adaptive enterprise, recognizing the widespread adoption of data analytics and business intelligence to advance enterprise adaptiveness. Current EA frameworks have not specifically addressed enterprise adaptiveness – how to characterize it, and how to achieve it in particular organizations. The main contribution in this paper is to offer one possible characterization of the adaptive enterprise to stimulate discussion and debate.

We aim to use the characterization as the starting point to develop an adaptive EA framework, which would include modeling, analysis and design techniques and tools to address adaptiveness requirements specific to a particular enterprise.

This work is conducted as a research project within BIN, the Business Intelligence Network, a strategic research network of academic researchers from across Canada, and industry partners [44]. In future work, we expect to leverage research results from BIN, such as BIM [42], [43], and from other research groups,

Acknowledgments. Financial support from the NSERC Business Intelligence Network Strategic Research Network grant is gratefully acknowledged. We thank Alexei Lapouchnian, Mahsa Sadi, Sadra Abrishamkra, and David Jorjani for discussions related to this proposal.

References

1. TOGAF Version 9.1, http://pubs.opengroup.org/architecture/togaf9-doc/arch/

2. Lankhorst, M., et al.: Enterprise Architecture at Work: Modelling, Communication and Analysis (The Enterprise Engineering Series). 2nd ed. Springer, Berlin Heidelberg (2009)
3. Land, M.O., Proper, E., Waage, M., Cloo, J., Steghuis, C.: Enterprise Architecture: Creating Value by Informed Governance. (The Enterprise Engineering Series). Springer, Berlin Heidelberg (2009)
4. Hoogervorst, J.A.P.: Enterprise Architecture: Enabling Integration, Agility and Change. Int. J. Cooperative Inf. Syst., 13(3), pp. 213--233 (2004)
5. The Economist: Organisational Agility: How Business can Survive and Thrive in Turbulent Times. A report from The Economist Intelligence Unit, (2009)
   http://www.eiu.com/site_info.asp?info_name=orgagility&page=noads
6. Chaudhuri, S., Dayal, U., Narasayya, V.: An overview of business intelligence technology. Commun. ACM, 54(8), pp. 88--98 (2011)
7. Dayal, U., Wilkinson, K., Simitsis, A., Castellanos, M.: Business Processes Meet Operational Business Intelligence. IEEE Data Eng. Bull., 32(3), pp. 35--41 (2009)
8. Bolton, R.N., Drew, J.H.: A Multistage Model of Customers' Assessments of Service Quality and Value. Journal of Consumer Research, 17(4), pp. 375--384 (1991)
9. Customer Analytics in the Age of Social Media: TDWI Best Practices Report. TDWI.org, (July 2012) http://tdwi.org/research/2012/07/best-practices-report-q3-customer-analytics-in-the-age-of-social-media.aspx
10. Rosenblum, P., Rowen, S.: Twenty-first Century Merchandising Takes Hold: Benchmark Report 2011. Retail Systems Research, (2011) http://www.sas.com/resources/asset/105535_0811.pdf
11. Supply Chain Operations Reference (SCOR) Model Overview Version 10.0, http://supply- chain.org/f/SCOR-Overview-Web.pdf
12. Armbrust, M., Fox, A., Griffith, R., et. al.: A View of Cloud Computing. Communications of the ACM, 53(4), pp. 50--58 (2010)
13. Papazoglou, M.P., Traverso, P., Dustdar S., Leymann, F.: Service-Oriented Computing: State of the Art and Research Challenges. IEEE Computer, 40(11), pp. 38--45 (2007)
14. Christensen, C.M., Grossman, J., Hwang, J.: The Innovator's Prescription: A Disruptive Solution for Health Care. McGraw-Hill (2008)
15. Archimate 2.0 Specification, https://www2.opengroup.org/ogsys/jsp/publications/PublicationDetails.jsp?catalogno=c11
16. Wilkinson, M.: Designing an 'Adaptive' Enterprise Architecture. BT Technology Journal, 24(4), pp. 81--92 (2006)
17. Haeckel, S.H.: Adaptive Enterprise: Creating and Leading Sense-And-Respond Organizations. Harvard Business Press (1999)
18. Pal, N., Pantaleo, D.C.: The Agile Enterprise: Reinventing Your Organization for Success in an On-Demand World. Chp9: Agile and Adaptive: Making Organizations More Responsive to Customers — A Xerox Case Study. Springer, New York (2005)
19. Lee, H.L.: The Triple-A Supply Chain. Harvard Business Review, pp. 102--112 (October 2004)
20. Dove, R.: Response Ability - The Language, Structure, and Culture of the Agile Enterprise. Wiley, New York (2001)
21. Mathiassen, L., Pries-Heje, J.: Business Agility and Diffusion of Information Technology. Eur. J. Inf. Syst. 15(2), pp. 116--119 (2006)
22. Sambamurthy, V., Bharadwaj, A., Grover, V.: Shaping Agility through Digital Options: Reconceptualizing the Role of Information Technology in Contemporary Firms. MIS Quarterly. 27(2), pp. 237--263 (2003)

23. Anaya, V., et al.: The Unified Enterprise Modelling Language - Overview and Further Work. Computers in Industry, 61(2), pp. 99--111 (2010)
24. Dolstra, E., Florijn, G., de Jonge, M., Visser, E.: Capturing Timeline Variability with Transparent Configuration Environments. In: Bosch, J., Knauber, P. (eds.) ICSE Workshop on Software Variability Management (SVM'03). Portland, Oregon (2003)
25. Cheng, B., et al.: Software Engineering for Self-Adaptive Systems: A Research Roadmap. Software Engineering for Self-Adaptive Systems. LNCS, vol. 5525, pp. 1--26. Springer (2009)
26. Kaplan, R.S., Norton, D.P.: Alignment: Using the Balanced Scorecard to Create Corporate Synergies. Harvard Business Review Press (2006)
27. Meadows, D.H., Wright, D.: Thinking in Systems: A Primer. Chelsea Green Publishing (2009)
28. Sterman, J.D.: Business Dynamics: Systems Thinking and Modeling for a Complex World. McGraw-Hill (2000)
29. Yu, E.: Agent Orientation as a Modelling Paradigm. Wirtschaftsinformatik, 43(2), pp. 123--132 (April 2001)
30. Henderson, J.C., Venkatraman, N.: Strategic Alignment: Leveraging Information Technology for Transforming Organizations. IBM Systems Journal, 32(1), pp. 4--16 (1993)
31. Wieringa, R.J., Blanken, H.M., Fokkinga, M.M., Grefen, P.W.P.J.: Aligning Application Architecture to the Business Context. In: CAiSE'03 Proceedings of the 15th International Conference on Advanced Information Systems Engineering, pp. 209--225. Springer (2003)
32. Chen, H., Kazman, R., Garg, A.: BITAM An Engineering-Principled Method for Managing Misalignments between Business and IT Architectures. Science of Computer Programming, 57(1), pp. 5--26 (2005)
33. Bleistein, S.J., Cox, K., Verner, J.M., Phalp, K.: B-SCP: A Requirements Analysis Framework for Validating Strategic Alignment of Organizational IT based on Strategy, Context, and Process. Information & Software Technology, 48(9), pp. 846--868 (2006)
34. Ross, J., Weill, P., Robertson, D.C.: Enterprise Architecture as Strategy. Harvard Business School Press (2006)
35. Kephart, J.O., Chess, D.M.: The Vision of Autonomic Computing. IEEE Computer, 36(1), pp. 41--50 (2003)
36. Jennings, N.R., Wooldridge, M.: Applying Agent Technology. Applied Artificial Intelligence, 9(4), pp. 357--369 (1995)
37. Alexander, I., Beus-Dukic, L.: Discovering Requirements: How to Specify Products and Services. Wiley (2009)
38. Chung, L., Nixon, B., Mylopoulos, J, Yu, E.: Non-Functional Requirements in Software Engineering. Kluwer Academic Publishing (2000)
39. Kazman, R., Klein, M.H., Clements, P.C.: ATAM: Method for Architecture Evaluation (CMU/SEI-2000-TR-004). Technical report, Software Engineering Institute, Carnegie Mellon University (2000)
40. Bidian, C., Yu, E.: Towards Variability Design as Decision Boundary Placement. In: 10th Workshop on Requirements Engineering (WER'07), pp. 139--148 (2007)
41. Yu, E., Giorgini, P., Maiden, N., Mylopoulos, J. (eds.): Social Modeling for Requirements Engineering. MIT Press (2011)
42. Barone, D., Yu, E.S.K., Won, J., Jiang, L., Mylopoulos, J.: Enterprise Modeling for Business Intelligence. PoEM 2010. LNBIP, vol. 68, pp. 31--45. Springer (2010)
43. Barone, D., Topaloglou, T., Mylopoulos, J.: Business Intelligence Modeling in Action: A Hospital Case Study. In: Proceedings of the 24th Conference on Advanced Information Systems Engineering (CAiSE'12). LNCS, vol. 7328, pp. 502–517. Springer, Berlin (2012)
44. Business Intelligence Network, http://bin.cs.toronto.edu

Assessing Modifiability in Application Services Using Enterprise Architecture Models – A Case Study

Magnus Österlind, Robert Lagerström, and Peter Rosell

Industrial Information and Control Systems, KTH – The Royal Institute of
Technology, Osquldas väg 10, 10044 Stockholm, Sweden
{magnuso,robertl}@ics.kth.se

Abstract. Enterprise architecture has become an established discipline
for business and IT management. Architecture models constitute the
core of the approach and serve the purpose of making the complexities
of the real world understandable and manageable to humans. EA ideally
aids the stakeholders of the enterprise to effectively plan, design, document, and communicate IT and business related issues, i.e. they provide
decision support for the stakeholders. However, few initiatives explicitly
state how one can analyze the EA models in order to aid decision-making.
One approach that does focus on analysis is the Enterprise Architecture
Modifiability Analysis Tool. This paper suggests changes to this tool and
presents a case study in which these have been tested. The results indicate that the changes improved the tool. Also, based on the outcome of
the case study further improvement possibilities are suggested.

Keywords: Enterprise architecture, Modifiability analysis, Modeling,
Decision-making.

1 Introduction

Enterprise Architecture (EA) has become an established discipline for business
and IT management [1] with many initiatives. A few of these initiatives are
The Department of Defense Architecture Framework (DoDAF)[2], The Zachman framework [3], The Open Group Architecture Framework (TOGAF) [4]
and ArchiMate [5]. EA describes the fundamental artifacts of business and IT
as well as their interrelationships [1, 3, 4, 5]. Architecture models constitute the
core of the approach and serve the purpose of making the complexities of the
real world understandable and manageable to humans. A main concept in EA is
the metamodel which acts as a pattern for the instantiation of the architectural
models. In other words, a metamodel is a description language used when creating models [4, 5]. EA ideally aids the stakeholders of the enterprise to effectively
plan, design, document, and communicate IT and business related issues, i.e.
they provide decision support for the stakeholders [6].

A changing business environment requires IT systems which can be adapted
to new conditions. Also, systems in a modern enterprise are often connected to

S. Aier et al. (Eds.): TEAR 2012 and PRET 2012, LNBIP 131, pp. 162–181, 2012.

other systems. This, along with many other factors make it difficult to estimate the effort of modifying a system. Thus, there is a need for decision makers to be able to analyze how much effort is required to modify an enterprise IT system. Such an effort estimation could help the decision maker to assign the resources in a more efficient manner. Combining EA and modifiability analysis has the advantages of being able to analyze the IT systems in their enterprise wide context. [7] proposes The Enterprise Architecture Modifiability Analysis Tool (TEAMATe) as one way of combining EA modeling with formal analysis to solve the difficulties of estimating IT change costs in an enterprise–wide context.

TEAMATe has been tested and validated in four multiple case studies [8]. However, during these case studies it became evident that there are also numerous parts of TEAMATe that need improvements. The contribution of this paper is to present and test some of these improvements. Firstly, attributes related to modifiability analysis have been revised and further developed. Secondly, the formal analysis language used has been revised and changed. Thirdly, classes and class relationships related to modifiability analysis have been aligned with the ArchiMate modeling language . Finally, software tool support has been developed. These improvements have been employed in a case study conducted at KTH – the Royal Institute of Technology investigating nine of the software systems used by KTH University Administration division for Student Records and Information Systems. This case study indicates that the improvements made to TEAMATe was a step in the right direction towards a more usable tool for modifiability analysis using architectural modeling. The study also provided further insights for future development of the tool.

The remainder of the paper is structured as follows: In section 2 related work is presented. Section 3 presents the Enterprise Architecture Modifiability Analysis Tool. The following section goes through the improvements of this tool. Next, in section 5 the case study and its results are described. Section 6, discusses the improvements and results. Finally, section 7 summarizes the paper with conclusions and future work.

2   Related Work

2.1   Enterprise Architecture for Modifiability Analysis

Enterprise architecture has grown into a modeling discipline widely recognized with many initiatives. However, the exact procedure or algorithm for how to perform a certain analysis given an architecture model is very seldom provided by EA frameworks. Most frameworks do however recognize the need to provide special purpose models and provide different viewpoints intended for different stakeholders. Unfortunately however, most viewpoints are designed from a model entity point of view, rather than a stakeholder concern point of view. Thus, assessing a quality such as the modifiability of a system is not something that is performed in a straight forward manner. The Department of Defense Architecture Framework (DoDAF) [2] for instance, provides products (i.e. viewpoints) such as "systems communications description", "systems data exchange matrix", and "operational activity model". These are all viewpoints based on a delimitation of elements of a complete metamodel, and they are not explicitly connected to a certain stakeholder or purpose. The Zachman framework presented in [3], does connect model types describing different aspects (Data, Function, Network, People, Time, and Motivation) with very abstractly described stakeholders (Strategists, Executive Leaders, Architects, Engineers, and Technicians), but does not provide any deeper insight how different models should be used. The Open Group Architecture Framework (TOGAF) [4], explicitly states stakeholders and concerns for each viewpoint they are suggesting. However, neither the exact metamodel nor the mechanism for analyzing the stated concerns, are described. In relation to modifiability, the most appropriate viewpoints provided would, according to TOGAF, arguably be *the Software Engineering View, the Systems Engineering View, the Communications Engineering View*, and *the Enterprise Manageability View*. In the descriptions of these views one can find statements such as; "the use of standard and self-describing languages, e.g. XML, are good in order to achieve easy to maintain interface descriptions". However, the exact interpretation of such statements when it comes to architectural models or how it relates to the modifiability of a system as a whole, is left out. Moreover, these kinds of "micro theories" are only exemplary and do not claim to provide a complete theory for modifiability or similar concerns.

2.2   Modifiability Analysis Methods

The issue of dealing with modifiability is not an enterprise architecture specific problem. Managing and assessing IT system change has been addressed in research for many years. Some of the more well-known assessment approaches include the COnstructive COst MOdel (COCOMO), the Software Architecture Analysis Method (SAAM), and the Oman taxonomy.

COCOMO, COnstructive COst MOdel, was in its first version released in the early 1980's. It became one of the most frequently used and most appreciated IT cost estimation models of that time. Since then, development and modifications of COCOMO have been performed several times to keep the model up to date with the continuously evolving software development trends. Effort estimation with COCOMO is based on the size of the software, an approximate productivity constant A, an aggregation of five scale factors E (precentedness, development flexibility, architecture/risk resolution, team cohesion, and process maturity), and effort multipliers to 15 cost driving attributes [9].

Bass et al. propose the Software Architecture Analysis Method (SAAM) for software quality evaluation [10]. This method takes several quality attributes into consideration; performance, security, availability, functionality, usability, portability, reusability, testability, integrability and modifiability. Bass et al. categorize modifications as: extending or changing capabilities, deleting unwanted capabilities, adapting to new operating environments and restructuring. Based on the quality attributes presented, Bass et al. propose different architectural styles which then are employed in the SAAM. It is a scenario-based approach which intends to make sure that stakeholder quality goals are met (for instance high modifiability). According to [10] SAAM can be used in two contexts: as a validation step for an architecture being developed or as a step in the acquisition of a system.

The Definition and Taxonomy for Software Maintainability presented in [11] provides a hierarchical definition of software maintainability in the form of a taxonomy. [11] found three broad categories of factors influencing the maintainability of an IT system; management, operational environment, and the target system. Each of these top-level categories is then further broken down into measurable attributes. According to [11] the taxonomy can be useful for developers by defining characteristics affecting the software maintenance cost of the software they are developing. Hence, the developers can write highly maintainable software from the beginning by studying the taxonomy. Maintenance personnel can use the taxonomy to evaluate the maintainability of the software they are working with in order to pin point risks etc. Project managers and architects can use the taxonomy in order to prioritize projects and locate areas in need of re-design.

2.3   Related Work Summary

The available methods for modifiability analysis are not focusing on change in an enterprise architecture context. There are many problems that need to be addressed that the available methods miss, such as: the increasing number of systems affected by enterprise-wide changes, the tight integration between systems, the increasing involvement of diverse people in a company e.g. business executives, project managers, architects, developers, testers. Some methods do use models, other employ quality criteria, some have a formal analysis engine, and there are methods using scenarios in decision making situations. There is however no method having brought it all together in an EA context.

Approaching the same issue but from the other direction, the EA frameworks available do not provide any formal analysis mechanisms (especially none for modifiability analysis).

3   The Enterprise Architecture Modifiability Analysis Tool

This section presents the core of TEAMATe, namely the metamodel. The metamodel is a so called PRM (Probabilistic Relational Model), i.e. a metamodel where the attributes are related to each other by causality. These causal relations are defined as conditional probabilities. More information about the metamodel, incl. the attributes, and the PRM formalism can be found in [7]. More information on how to employ the metamodel in specific modeling scenarios, the analysis, and the results can be found in [8].

TEAMATe's metamodel for modifiability analysis, cf. Figure 1, focuses on the IT systems and the surrounding environment involved in or affected by the

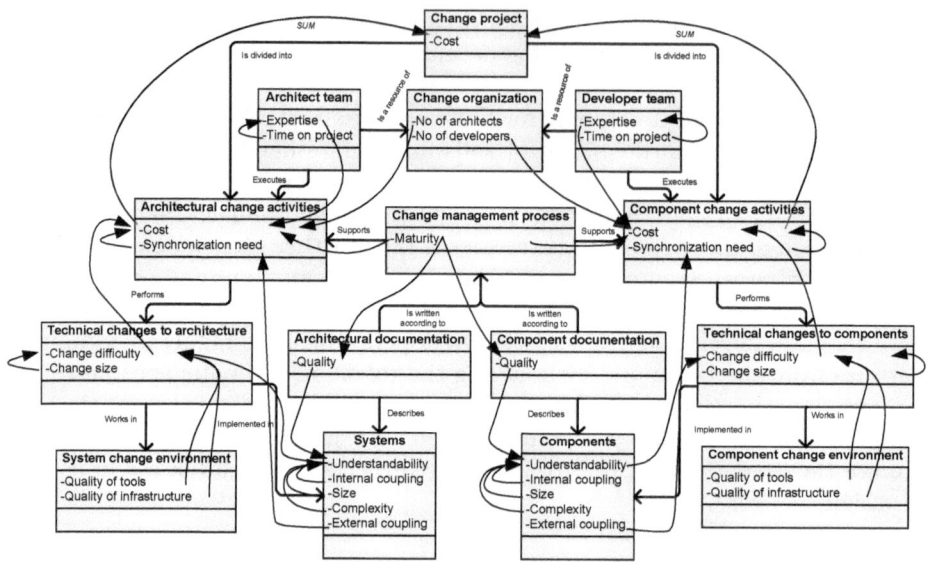

Fig. 1. The TEAMATe metamodel

modifications implemented in a change project, thus aiming at analyzing modifiability defined as change project cost (high modifiability leads to low change
costs).

TEAMATe can be divided into three viewpoints: The *architectural viewpoint*.
This viewpoint focuses on modeling the as-is and to-be architectures. The two
classes System and Component in the metamodel belong to this viewpoint. The
change management viewpoint. This viewpoint focuses on the change management process and organization. The metamodel contains the classes Change
management process, Documentation, and Change Organization which belongs
to this viewpoint. The *change project viewpoint*. This viewpoint focuses on the
specific change project being analyzed, e.g. analyzing the gap between the as-is
architecture and a to-be architecture using the resources of the change management process and organization. That is, the change project viewpoint uses an
instantiated subset of the architectural and change management viewpoints. The
classes Change project, Team, Change activities, Technical changes, and Change
environment belong to the change project viewpoint.

The focus of this paper is to present improvements to the architectural viewpoint of TEAMATe. That is, the emphasis is on the classes related to this viewpoint, System and Component, and the attributes related to these two classes,
Understandability, Size, Complexity, and Coupling.

Understandability of a system or a component is measured as the percentage
of time spent on trying to understand the system or component in question (in
relation to the total time spent on each system/component), $\{0,\ldots,100\}$. Component size is measured in number of lines of code, and system size is defined

as number of components, $\{0, \dots, \infty\}$. Complexity is measured subjectively as {Complex, Medium, Not complex}. The system external coupling attribute is defined as the number of actual relations between the systems divided by the number of possible relations between the systems, $\{0, \dots, 100\}$. System internal and component external coupling are measured as the number of actual relations between the components in the system divided by the number of possible relations between the components, $\{0, \dots, 100\}$. Component internal coupling is defined as the number of actual relations within the component divided with the number of possible relations, $\{0, \dots, 100\}$.

3.1 Previous Case Study Findings

TEAMATe has been tested in four multiple case studies (21 change projects) [8]. These cases have provided valuable input for TEAMATe in terms of showing that the approach is useful and worth further development. Some of the needed improvements found during these case studies were:

1) In the architectural viewpoint, TEAMATe contains the attributes coupling, complexity, size, and understandability. However, it was found that these needed to be reviewed in a second iteration. Complexity is only measured subjectively based on peoples experience, although there are objective complexity metrics that can be used. Size is measured as lines of code without taking the chosen programming language into consideration. The coupling measure is not based on the most well-known and tested metrics available. Understandability is defined as an a posteriori measure, which obviously limits its impact on the prediction abilities of TEAMATe. Thus, there is a need of improving the attributes in the architectural viewpoint. See section 4.1.

2) The formal analysis language used, Probabilistic Relational Models (PRMs), is based on probabilities and use Bayesian statistics to calculate estimated values for attributes in the instantiated models. This has in many cases proven useful, however in the architectural viewpoint most attributes are not related by causality and the values can be calculated based on information already available in the model. E.g. the size of a system can be calculated based on the size of its components. Thus, the architectural viewpoint would benefit from having the analysis language revised. See section 4.2.

3) ArchiMate is a commonly used modeling language and many companies can therefore relate to its concepts. Thus alignment with ArchiMate would be beneficial. See section 4.3.

4) In the multiple case studies three different tools were employed. The data collected was stored with Microsoft Excel. The architecture modeling was done with Microsoft Visio. The probabilistic analysis was carried through with GeNIe. This manual integration of tools ended up being a heavy workload for the modeler. TEAMATe would thus be more user-friendly if there was a modeling tool that could handle collected data, modeling, and analysis. See section 4.4.

4   TEAMATe: The Next Generation

This section presents the new and improved version of the architectural viewpoint in the Enterprise Architecture Modifiability Analysis Tool.

4.1   Metrics

Complexity. IEEE defines complexity as *the degree to which a system or component has a design or implementation that is difficult to understand and verify* [12]. Halstead's complexity metric was introduced in 1977 [13], it is based on the number of operators (e.g. and, or, while) and operands (e.g. variables and constants) in a software program. A drawback of Halstead's complexity metric is that it lacks predicting power for development effort since the value can be calculated first after the implementation is complete [14]. Information flow complexity, IFC, as presented in [15] is based on the idea that a large amount of information flows is caused by low cohesion, low cohesion is in turn causing a high complexity. One problem with the IFC metric is that it produces a lower complexity value for program code using global variables compared to a solution which uses function arguments when called, this is contradicting to common software design principles [16]. In this paper McCabe's Cyclomatic Complexity (MCC) metric is employed [17]. [14] has identified that MCC is useful to, identify overly complex parts of code, identify non-complex part of code, and to estimate maintenance effort. MCC is based on the control structure of the software, the control structure can be expressed as a control graph. The cyclomatic complexity value of a system with the control graph G is calculated with the following equation: $v(G) = e - n + 2$ or equivalently $v(G) = DE + 1$ where e=number of edges in the control graph, n=number of nodes in the control graph, DE=number of predicates. Considering the example code presented in Figure 2 the control graph G_{sort} can be obtained.

The MCC value of G_{sort} (cf. Figure 2) is $v(G_{sort}) = 14 - 12 + 2 = 4$. McCabe has performed a study indicating that the cyclomatic complexity value of a component should be kept below 10 [17]. MCC has been used in other studies providing additional complexity levels and guidelines on how complex a piece of software code is [14]:

- 1-4, a simple procedure.
- 5-10, a well-structured and stable procedure.
- 11-20, a more complex procedure.
- 21-50, a complex procedure, worrisome.
- 50<, an error-prone, extremely troublesome, untestable procedure.

Size. Lines of code (LOC) and function points (FP) are two ways to measure the size of an IT system. FP are based on the inputs, outputs, interfaces and databases in a system [14]. FP have the advantage of being technology independent, reasonably reliable and accurate, and they are effective from an early stage of the IT system life cycle [14]. The disadvantages of the FP size metric is

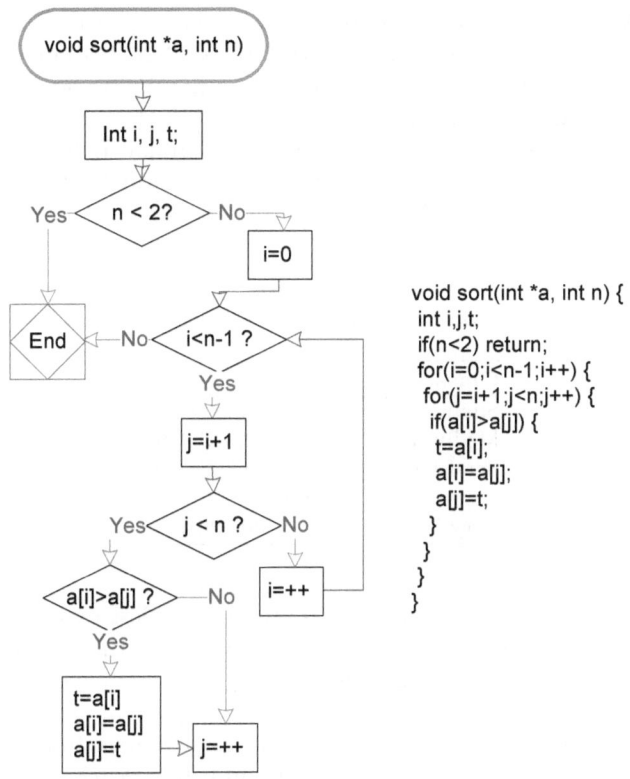

```
void sort(int *a, int n) {
int i,j,t;
if(n<2) return;
for(i=0;i<n-1;i++) {
  for(j=i+1;j<n;j++) {
   if(a[i]>a[j]) {
    t=a[i];
    a[i]=a[j];
    a[j]=t;
   }
  }
 }
}
```

Fig. 2. An example of a control graph G_{sort} with $v(G_{sort}) = 4$

that it requires significant effort to derive [14]. The LOC in a system provides the core functionality and can therefore be of importance when estimating how easy it would be to implement changes to the system. LOC in a system can be measured in different ways: Using source lines of code (SLOC) every line of code in the software implementation is counted. Non-commented lines of code (NLOC) is a subset of the previous option, where the blank lines and comments are excluded. Logical lines of code (LLOC) is another approach, where only the executable statements of the software are counted. The most popular option is NLOC, however the most important thing is to be consistent with the way you measure [14]. No matter which LOC measure is used it needs to be well specified to provide a reliable measurement [14]. A framework on how to measure lines of code has been created by the Software Engineering Institute of Carnegie-Mello University [18], with the aid of this framework the LOC measure can be specified to provide a coherent way of how to measure LOC.

Aivosto[1] suggests a classification of system size for systems coded with Visual Basic 1. The classification is based on long-time experience, but has not been

---

[1] http://www.aivosto.com/project/help/pm-loc.html

validated making it less reliable. However, given the size of the systems studied in [19], the classification seems trustworthy. Related to system size, operating systems can be much larger with over 40 million LOC [20], however an operating system would not be modeled as an application that an enterprise wishes to modify. Rumor has it that SAP[2] has over 250 million LOC in their product portfolio [3], but we believe that no enterprise would model SAP as one application. Thus, the classification of system size by Aivosto[1] still seems appropriate for our purpose.

Table 1. System size classification

Classuification	LOC
Small	0-9.999
Medium	10.000-49.999
Semi-large	50.000-99.999
Large	100.000-499.999
Very large	500.000≤

Since different programming languages are more or less expressive per line of code [14], a gearing factor can be used when comparing the lines of code of two systems if they are created in different programming languages. A high gearing factor value indicates poor expressiveness, hence a programming language with a low gearing factor require less lines of code to implement a function; given that the language is appropriate to use. [21] has published gearing factors for some programming languages of which a subset is presented in Table 2.

Table 2. Gearing factors for some commonly used programming languages

Language	Gearing factor
Assembly-Basic	320
C#	59
C++	55
Java	53
Visual Basic	52
ASP	50

Coupling. IEEE has defined coupling as *the manner and degree of interdependence between software modules. Types include common-environment coupling, content coupling, control coupling, data coupling, hybrid coupling, and pathological coupling* [12]. Fenton and Melton have developed a coupling metric based on Myers coupling levels [22], these levels are:

---

[2] SAP AG, an IT system vendor.
[3] http://judithbalancingact.com/2007/04/30/

- Content coupling relation $R_5 : (x, y) \in R_5$ if x refers to the internals of y , i.e., it branches into, changes data, or alters a statement in y.
- Common coupling relation $R_4 : (x, y) \in R_4$ if x and y refer to the same global variable.
- Control coupling relation $R_3 : (x, y) \in R_3$ if x passes a parameter to y that controls its behavior.
- Stamp coupling relation $R_2 : (x, y) \in R_2$ if x passes a variable of a record type as a parameter to y , and y uses only a subset of that record.
- Data coupling relation $R_1 : (x, y) \in R_1$ if x and y communicate by parameters, each one being either a single data item or a homogeneous set of data items that does not incorporate any control element.
- No coupling relation $R_0 : (x, y) \in R_0$ if x and y have no communication, i.e., are totally independent.

The Fenton and Melton coupling measure is pairwise calculated between components,

$$C(x, y) = i + \frac{n}{n+1}$$

where $n=$ number of interconnections between x and y. $i=$ level of highest (worst) coupling type found between x and y.

Modifiability. To evaluate the modifiability, the complexity levels by [14], the coupling levels by [22] and the size levels by Aivosto[1] are used in order to indicate how "good" a modeled architecture is. The highest level is given a value of 0, meaning that the modifiability is low, and the lowest level a value of 5, a good modifiability. The modifiability level is then evaluated as the sum of the three individual metrics. The reason to summarize the values is to create a metric that can be used in order to indicate whether a system is likely to be easy to modify or not. According to the correlations levels in [16] the three metrics used are more or less equally important when estimating the level of modifiability in an IT system. The modifiability metric gives a rough estimation, which can be of value when making decisions regarding different architecture scenarios.

The attributes in the architectural viewpoint of TEAMATe are revised based on these four metrics, cf. section 4.5 for the new metamodel description.

4.2   Analysis Language

P2AMF. The Object Constraint Language (OCL) is a formal language typically used in order to describe constraints on UML models [23]. Additionally, OCL can be applied for queries over objects described in a model [24].

The Predictive, Probabilistic Architecture Modeling Framework (P2AMF) is a probabilistic Object Constraint Language. P2AMF is an extension of OCL for probabilistic analysis and prediction, first introduced in [25] (under the name Pi-OCL). The main feature of P2AMF is its ability to express uncertainties of objects, relations and attributes in UML-models and perform probabilistic analysis incorporating these uncertainties, as illustrated in [25].

An example usage of P2AMF could be to create a model for calculating the coupling between application components, a P2AMF expression to calculate the coupling with the Fenton and Melton metric [22] might look like this:

context ApplicationComponent: attribute coupling : Real = let n : Integer = numberOfIntercon-nectionsBetweenPair(y) in getWorstCouplingTypeInPair(y) + n/(n+1)

Since the attributes in the architectural viewpoint are not related by causality, the PRM formalism seems less appropriate to use here. With P2AMF attributes can be evaluated based on information in the model and it is easy to for instance calculate the modifiability level with the definition given in the previous subsection. This would not have been possible with PRMs.

Therefore, the analysis formalism used in the architectural viewpoint of TEA-MATe has been revised and is using the P2AMF as analysis language instead of PRMs, cf. section 4.5 for the P2AMF statements defining the metamodel.

4.3   ArchiMate Alignment

ArchiMate. Lankhorst [5] has probably published the most well-known and widespread metamodel, called ArchiMate. The ArchiMate metamodel is an open, independent, and general modeling language for enterprise architecture. The primary focus of ArchiMate is to support stakeholders how to address concerns regarding their business and the supporting IT systems. ArchiMate is extensively presented in [5] and is partly based on the ANSI/IEEE 1471-2000, Recommended Practice for Architecture Description of Software-Intensive Systems, also known as the IEEE 1471 standard [26]. The Open Group accepted the ArchiMate metamodel as a technical standard[4]. The ArchiMate metamodel consists of three layers; the Business layer, the Application layer and the Technology layer. Where the technology supports the applications, which in turn support the business. Each layer consists of a number of classes and defined class relationships. The classes in each layer are categorized into three aspects of enterprise architecture: 1) The passive structure - modeling informational objects. 2) The behavioral structure - modeling the dynamic events of an enterprise. 3) The active structure - modeling the components in the architecture that perform the behavioral aspects. Figure 3 presents the application layer of the ArchiMate metamodel.

Four classes were identified as useful in the application layer, namely; Application Service, Application Function, Application Component, and Application Collaboration. These classes have thus replaced the two previously used classes System and Component. Also three new class relationships where added to the metamodel based on the relationships in ArchiMate, namely; Realization, Assignment, and Collaboration.

ArchiMate [5] defines: An *Application Service* as an externally visible unit of functionality, provided by one or more components, exposed through well-defined interfaces, and meaningful to the environment. An *Application Function* as a behavior element that groups automated behavior that can be performed by an application component. An *Application Component* as a modular, deployable,

---

[4] http://www.opengroup.org/archimate

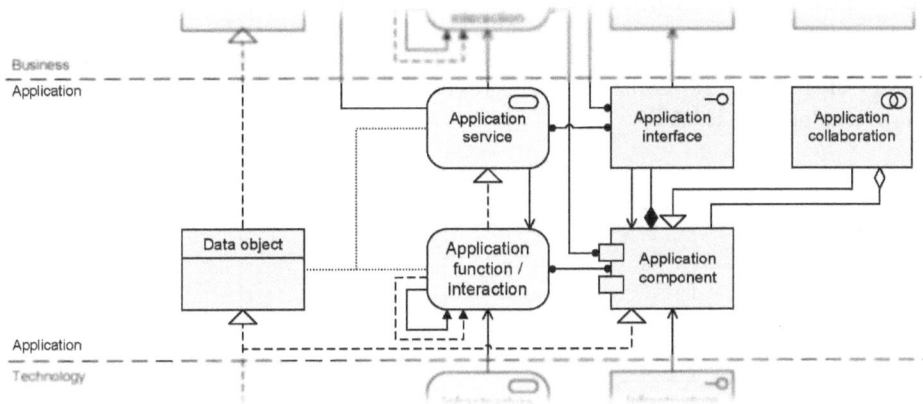

Fig. 3. The application layer of the ArchiMate metamodel

and replaceable part of a system that encapsulates its contents and exposes its functionality through a set of interfaces. An *Application Collaboration* as an aggregate of two or more application components that work together to perform collective behavior.

Realization relationship. The realization relationship links a logical entity with a more concrete entity that realizes it. In the metamodel the realization relationship is used between the application function and application service in order to model what functions realize a service. *Assignment relationship.* The assignment relationship links active elements with units of behavior that are performed by them. In the metamodel the assignment relationship is used to model the performed behavior of an application component that is an application function. *Collaboration relationship.* In the metamodel the collaboration relationship links an application collaboration with two application components. The collaboration relationship is used to model the execution dependencies between two application components or two application components charing information.

With these classes and relationships the architectural viewpoint of TEAMATe is considered to be aligned with ArchiMate, cf. section 4.5 for the metamodel description including the attributes populating these classes.

4.4   Tool Support

EAAT. The Enterprise Architecture Analysis Tool (EAAT[5]), is a software tool which supports enterprise architecture modeling and formal analysis using P2AMF. EAAT supports creation of metamodels with built in P2AMF analysis functionality. The metamodel can then be instantiated into models which are then analyzed based on the analysis code from the metamodel. One advantage of EAAT is that collected data is stored as evidence in the models. EAAT has been used in other case studies such as [25].

---

[5] http://www.ics.kth.se/eaat

4.5   The New Metamodel

This subsection presents the new and improved architectural viewpoint meta-model of TEAMATe, containing the revised metrics using P2AMF and Archi-Mate modeled in EAAT.

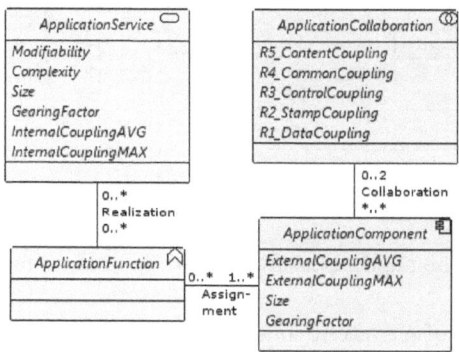

Fig. 4. The new version of the architectural viewpoint metamodel in TEAMATe

Application Service. The application service class contains the attributes Modifiability, Complexity, Size, Gearing Factor, and Coupling.

Attribute: Modifiability The modifiability metric is an aggregation of the attributes: Complexity α, InternalCouplingMAX β, and Size γ.

The complexity levels from [14] are used to give complexity c a numerical value α, where $0 \leq \alpha \leq 5$.

- If ApplicationService.Complexity is $c = 0$, then $\alpha = 5$.
- If ApplicationService.Complexity is $1 \leq c \leq 4$, then $\alpha = 4$.
- If ApplicationService.Complexity is $5 \leq c \leq 10$, then $\alpha = 3$.
- If ApplicationService.Complexity is $11 \leq c \leq 20$, then $\alpha = 2$.
- If ApplicationService.Complexity is $21 \leq c \leq 50$, then $\alpha = 1$.
- If ApplicationService.Complexity is $50 < c$, then $\alpha = 0$.

The coupling levels from [22] are used to give internal coupling (max) icm a numerical value β, where $0 \leq \beta \leq 5$.

- If ApplicationService.InternalCouplingMax is ≤ 1, then $\beta = 5$.
- If ApplicationService.InternalCouplingMax is $1 \leq icm < 2$, then $\beta = 4$.
- If ApplicationService.InternalCouplingMax is $2 \leq icm < 3$, then $\beta = 3$.
- If ApplicationService.InternalCouplingMax is $3 \leq icm < 4$, then $\beta = 2$.
- If ApplicationService.InternalCouplingMax is $4 \leq icm < 5$, then $\beta = 1$.
- If ApplicationService.InternalCouplingMax is $5 \leq icm$, then $\beta = 0$.

The size levels from Aivosto[1] are used to give size s a numerical value γ, where $0 \leq \gamma \leq 5$.

- If ApplicationService.Size is $s < 10.000$, then $\gamma = 4$.
- If ApplicationService.Size is $10.000 \leq s < 50.000$, then $\gamma = 3$.
- If ApplicationService.Size is $50.000 \leq s < 100.000$, then $\gamma = 2$.
- If ApplicationService.Size is $100.000 \leq s < 500.000$, then $\gamma = 1$.
- If ApplicationService.Size is $s \leq 500.000$, then $\gamma = 0$.

If S is an application service, then the modifiability value $= \alpha + \beta + \gamma$ with $\mathbf{V}(S.Modifiability) = \{x \in \mathbb{N} : 0 \leq x \leq 14\}$. A low modifiability value indicates that an application service is difficult to change just as a high modifiability value indicates the opposite.

Attribute: Complexity. The complexity attribute is calculated as the cyclomatic complexity by McCabe [17]. The application components are used as nodes and the values in the attributes of the application collaboration class are used as edges. This includes relations to an application component outside of the owning application service, in the case an application collaboration exists between one application component realizing the service is collaboration with a component realizing a different application service. If $I = \{i_1, ..., i_n\}$ is a list of application collaborations, S is an application service, c is an application component where $c \subseteq S.realize$ and $I \subseteq S.realize.collaboration$, then

$$f(S.Complexity) = \sum_{i=1}^{n} i_i.R5\_ContentCoupling + \sum_{i=1}^{n} i_i.R4\_CommonCoupling$$

$$+ \sum_{i=1}^{n} i_i.R3\_ControlCoupling + \sum_{i=1}^{n} i_i.R2\_StampCoupling+$$

$$\sum_{i=1}^{n} i_i.R1\_DataCoupling - \sum_{i=1}^{n} c_i + 2.$$

$$\mathbf{V}(S.Complexity) = \mathbb{N}.$$

Attribute: Size Equivalent source lines of code (ENLOC) is a size measure which uses a gearing factor to get a size measure which allows size comparison between applications written in different programing languages. If $F = \{f_1, ..., f_n\}$ is a list of application functions, S is an application service and $F \subseteq S.realizedBy$, then

$$f(S.ENLOC) = \sum_{i=1}^{n} \frac{S.GearingFactor}{f_i.assignee.GearingFactor} * f_i.assignee.NLOC.$$

$$\mathbf{V}(S.ENLOC) = \mathbb{R}.$$

Attribute: GearingFactor. If S is an application service, then $\mathbf{V}(S.GearingFactor) = \mathbb{N}$. The gearing factor is given as evidence in the model.

Attribute: InternalCouplingAVG The InternalCouplingAVG is the internal average coupling of the application service. It is calculated as the arithmetic mean of the Fenton and Melton Software Metric [22] for all pair wise coupling measures within the application service divided by the number of pairs. If $I = \{i_1, ..., i_n\}$ is a list of application collaborations, S is an application service, C is a application component where $C \subseteq S.realize$ and $I \subseteq S.realize.collaboration$, then

$$C.CouplingAVG = \frac{1}{n} \sum_{j=1}^{n} i_j.couplingInPair().$$

$$\mathbf{V}(C.CouplingAVG) = \{x \in \mathbb{R} : 0 \leq x < 6\}.$$

Attribute: InternalCouplingMAX The InternalCouplingMAX is the internal max coupling of the application service is. It gives the maximum value of all the connections pair to the application component within the application service. If $I = \{i_1, ..., i_n\}$ is a list of application collaborations, S is an application service, C is a application component where $C \subseteq S.realize$ and $I \subseteq S.realize.communication$, then $C.couplingMAX = couplingInPair(m)$ where $m \in P$ and $couplingInPair$ $(i_j) \leq couplingInPair(m)$ for all elements in P. $\mathbf{V}(C.CouplingMAX) = \{x \in \mathbb{Q} : 0 \leq x < 6\}$.

Application Component. The application component class contains the attributes Coupling, Size, and Gearing Factor.

Attribute: ExternalCouplingAVG is calculated as the arithmetic mean of the Fenton and Melton Software Metric [22] for all pair wise coupling measures divided by the number of pairs. If $I = \{i_1, ..., i_n\}$ is a list of application collaborations, C is a application component and $I \subseteq C.collaboration$, then

$$C.CouplingAVG = \frac{1}{n} \sum_{j=1}^{n} i_j.couplingInPair().$$

$$\mathbf{V}(C.CouplingAVG) = \{x \in \mathbb{R} : 0 \leq x < 6\}.$$

Attribute: ExternalCouplingMAX gives the maximum value of all the connections pair to the application component. If $I = \{i_1, ..., i_n\}$ is a list of application collaborations, C is a application component and $I \subseteq C.communication$, then $C.couplingMAX = couplingInPair(m)$ where $m \in P$ and $couplingInPair$ $(i_j) \leq couplingInPair(m)$ for all elements in P. $\mathbf{V}(C.CouplingMAX) = \{x \in \mathbb{Q} : 0 \leq x < 6\}$.

Size is measured as the number of non-commented lines of code (NLOC). If C is an application component, then $\mathbf{V}(C.NLOC) = \mathbb{N}$. The number of non-commented lines of code is given as evidence in the model.

Attribute: GearingFactor. If C is an application component, then $\mathbf{V}(C.GearingFactor) = \mathbb{N}$. The gearing factor is given as evidence in the model.

Application Collaboration. The application collaboration class contains the attribute Coupling (five different types).

If I is an application interaction, X and Y are both application components, and $\{X, Y\} \subseteq I.communicates$, then they have a:

Attribute: R5_ContentCoupling relation if X refers to the internals of Y, i.e., it branches into, changes data, or alters a statement in y. $\mathbf{V}(R5\_ContentCoupling) = \mathbb{N}$.

Attribute: R4_CommonCoupling relation if X and Y refer to the same global variable. $\mathbf{V}(R4\_CommonCoupling) = \mathbb{N}$.

Attribute: R3_ControlCoupling relation if X passes a parameter to Y that controls its behavior. $\mathbf{V}(R3\_ControlCoupling) = \mathbb{N}$.

Attribute: R2_StampCoupling relation if X passes a variable of a record type as a parameter to Y, and Y uses only a subset of that record. $\mathbf{V}(R2\_StampCoupling) = \mathbb{N}$.

Attribute: R1_DataCoupling relation if X and Y communicate by parameters, each one being either a single data item or a homogeneous set of data items that does not incorporate any control element. $\mathbf{V}(R1\_DataCoupling) = \mathbb{N}$.

The number of content, common, control, stamp, and data couplings are given as evidence in the model.

5   Case Study and Results

The revised metamodel has been applied in a case study conducted at the division for Student Records and Information Systems (VoS) at KTH – the Royal Institute of Technology, a university in Sweden. VoS is part of the university administration, their main responsibility is to provide system support for administration of courses, students and related processes. In the case study, nine application services governed by VoS have been modeled and analyzed with the metamodel. Three out of nine application services investigated are developed and maintained by VoS, two are commercially available of-the-shelf (COTS) products that are maintained by VoS, and the remaining four are developed and maintained by external service providers.

The information was collected through interviews and written correspondence. Interviews were also performed to validate the models created during the case study. The models were instantiated in the EAAT in order to make use of the P2AMF analysis language. Figure 5 shows four of the nine application services modeled. The color of the icon next to the application service name indicates the level of modifiability ranging from red to green, where green indicates high modifiability.

The nine application services modeled and analyzed indicate that the P2AMF analysis formalism is applicable to the architectural view of TEAMATe. The models also indicate that it is possible to apply the new metrics with TEAMATe. Further, the case study shows that it can be difficult to obtain coupling information regarding application component collaboration. Whereas size, programming language (for gearing factor), and complexity are easier to obtain. The complexity metric is structurally derived from the model requiring no extra effort once the model has been created. Programming language is known by the application developer and most development tools seem to have the functionality to count non-commented lines of code.

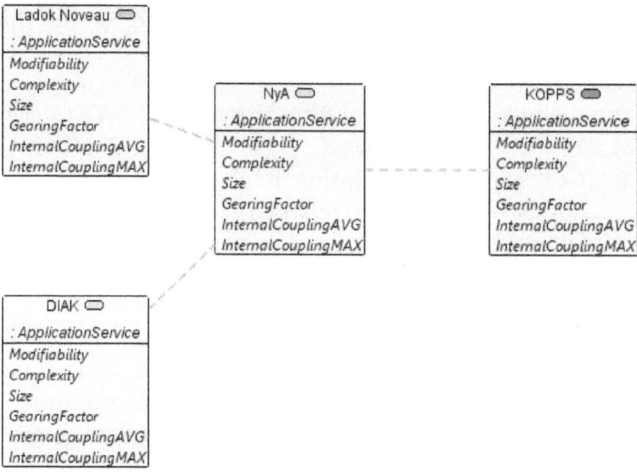

Fig. 5. A screenshot from EAAT showing four related application services. The color indicator next to the application service name illustrates the modifiability level.

Table 3. Results for the application services

Application service	Complexity	Coupling MAX	Size	Programming language	Modifiability
Alumni Community	3	3.6	23.807	C#	6
DIAK	4	3.6	N/A	ASP	9
KOPPS	7	4.6	35.156	Java	4
LadokPing	4	4.5	45.266	Java	4
LpW	6	4.9	178.758	N/A	5
Mina Sidor	10	4.6	11.323	Java	3
Nouveau	2	N/A	N/A	C++	12
NyA	0	3.6	819.341	Java	8
TimeEdit	3	4.6	N/A	C++	9

Since this paper and case study only focus on the architectural viewpoint of TEAMATe it is not as obvious how these models support decision-making, compared to when employing all viewpoints of TEAMATe including the change management and project specific classes which would provide the decision maker with information regarding the predicted cost of changing an architecture. However, only using the architectural view provides information that can be used when comparing different architecture scenarios. Also, if it is known that an application service has a modifiability value lower than others due to its complexity or high coupling, one might want to consider improving this service in order to prevent future change projects from becoming too costly. Or, when starting a new development project the information in these models can provide important input for risk analysis. E.g. if planning a change in one component, the modification's impact can be traced in the model in order to find what other components might be affected. This would prevent unknown ripple effects to occur.

6   Discussion

To measure the complexity of an IT system, the cyclomatic complexity by Mc-Cabe [17] has been used. The cyclomatic complexity is originally a software metric. Even though there are similarities of a control graph based on software source code and an architectural model displaying software components with their relations to one another, the suitability of the metric is not yet fully investigated within this context. [27] and [28] have both applied cyclomatic complexity to business process models (BPMs) indicating that the metric serves a good purpose providing general information about the complexity of a BPM.

The categorization used for the modifiability metric provides insight to whether the service is easy to modify or not. Neither the less it can be of guidance when evaluating possible architectural scenarios to one another. Here modifiability is based on the three attributes size, coupling, and complexity. These are not the only attributes that determines the modifiability of an application service. E.g. in the Definition and Taxonomy for Software Maintainability presented in [11] 140 factors are included (however some of these are related to the management process and the team involved).

The use of TEAMATe when making decisions relating to enterprise IT is beneficial due to its ability to locate potential risks concerning a system architecture. Employing TEAMATe raises awareness of the enterprise system including an understanding of how the different applications relate to each other.

Aligning TEAMATe with ArchiMate might be good for a majority of companies. However, other companies might already employ a different metamodel for their EA initiative. For the specific modeling project alignment with other metamodels might be necessary.

The Enterprise Architecture Analysis Tool is currently a research product more than a commercially available software. Hopefully it will soon be user-friendly enough for non-academic use. Unfortunately, there are no other tools available today that support the suggested type of architecture analysis.

7   Conclusions

It is feasible to combine EA models with modifiability analysis to provide support when making decisions about IT systems and their implementation. This paper has provided insight on how the enterprise architecture modeling language ArchiMate can be aligned with The Enterprise Architecture Modifiability Analysis Tool (TEAMATe). Further, well-known software metrics have been incorporated in TEAMATe in order to improve the analysis capabilities of TEAMATe regarding architecture modifiability. An improvement made possible by changing formal analysis language from the Probabilistic Relational Models and Bayesian networks to the Predictive, Probabilistic Architecture Modeling Framework (P2AMF). These improvements have been tested in a case study, where the modeling and analysis were done with the Enterprise Architecture Analysis Tool (EAAT), with good results.

7.1 Future Work and Implications

To the industrial practitioner, the present paper assists the enterprise modeling effort when the concern is focused on modifiability of application services. If the suggested metamodel is employed one can compare different architecture scenarios, find architectural improvement possibilities, and highlight risks early in change projects.

To the EA tool industry, the present paper hints to potential new features or products. Tools incorporating the suggested analysis capabilities and containing common metrics for architectural evaluation would give a more quantitative support to the user's modeling effort.

To the scientific community, the presented metamodel combines the approach of enterprise architecture modeling with modifiability metric analysis. These two, previously separate, communities can benefit from this work, as well as continue contributing in the combined area by extending/improving the metamodel and the methods utilizing it.

Of course, the different parts of TEAMATe can still be further improved. More metrics can be added. The change management viewpoint and the change project viewpoint can both be revised regarding metrics used, related modeling languages, and analysis formalism.

In order to expand this study to the broader EA context, future work will be conducted to incorporate the presented metamodel with other quality goals that are of importance when evaluating architectures. Such quality goals could be those presented in [29]; application usage, service availability, service response time, and data accuracy, as well as interoperability as presented in [25].

References

1. Ross, J., Weill, P., Robertson, D.: Enterprise architecture as strategy: Creating a foundation for business execution. Harvard Business Press (2006)
2. Department of Defense Architecture Framework Working Group: DoD Architecture Framework, version 1.5. Technical report, Department of Defense, USA (2007)
3. Zachman, J.A.: A framework for information systems architecture. IBM Systems Journal 26, 276–292 (1987)
4. The Open Group: The Open Group Architecture Framework (TOGAF) - version 9. The Open Group (2009)
5. Lankhorst, M.: Enterprise architecture at work: Modelling, communication and analysis. Springer-Verlag New York Inc. (2009)
6. Kurpjuweit, S., Winter, R.: Viewpoint-based meta model engineering. In: Enterprise Modelling and Information Systems Architectures, EMISA 2007 (2007)
7. Lagerström, R., Johnson, P., Ekstedt, M.: Architecture analysis of enterprise systems modifiability – a metamodel for software change cost estimation. Software Quality Journal 18, 437–468 (2010)
8. Lagerström, R., Johnson, P., Höök, D.: Architecture analysis of enterprise systems modifiability – models, analysis, and validation. Journal of Systems and Software 83(8), 1387–1403 (2010)
9. Boehm, B., Madachy, R., Steece, B., et al.: Software Cost Estimation with Cocomo II with Cdrom. Prentice Hall PTR (2000)

10. Bass, L., Clements, P., Kazman, R.: Software Architecture in Practice, 2nd edn. Addison-Wesley Longman Publishing Co., Inc., Boston (2003)
11. Oman, P., Hagemeister, J., Ash, D.: A definition and taxonomy for software maintainability. Technical report, Software Engineering Lab (1992)
12. IEEE Standards Board: IEEE standard glossary of software engineering technology. Technical report, The Institute of Electrical and Electronics Engineers (September 1990)
13. Halstead, M.: Elements of Software Science. Operating and programming systems series. Elsevier Science Inc. (1977)
14. Laird, L., Brennan, M.: Software measurement and estimation: a practical approach, vol. 2. Wiley-IEEE Computer Society Pr. (2006)
15. Henry, S., Kafura, D.: Software structure metrics based on information flow. IEEE Transactions on Software Engineering SE-7(5), 510–518 (1981)
16. Frappier, M., Matwin, S., Mili, A.: Software metrics for predicting maintainability. Software Metrics Study: Tech. Memo 2 (1994)
17. McCabe, T.: A complexity measure. IEEE Transactions on Software Engineering (4), 308–320 (1976)
18. Park, R.: Software size measurement: A framework for counting source statements. Technical report, DTIC Document (1992)
19. Curtis, B., Krasner, H., Iscoe, N.: A field study of the software design process for large systems. Communications of the ACM 31(11), 1268–1287 (1988)
20. Maraia, V.: The Build Master: Microsoft's Software Configuration Management Best Practices. Addison-Wesley Professional (2005)
21. Jones, C.: Applied software measurement: assuring productivity and quality. McGraw-Hill, Inc. (1991)
22. Fenton, N., Melton, A.: Deriving structurally based software measures. Journal of Systems and Software 12(3), 177–187 (1990)
23. OMG: Object constraint language, version 2.2. Technical report, Object Management Group, OMG (February 2010)
24. Akehurst, D., Bordbar, B.: On Querying UML Data Models with OCL. In: Gogolla, M., Kobryn, C. (eds.) UML 2001. LNCS, vol. 2185, pp. 91–103. Springer, Heidelberg (2001)
25. Ullberg, J., Franke, U., Buschle, M., Johnson, P.: A tool for interoperability analysis of enterprise architecture models using Pi-OCL. In: Enterprise Interoperability IV, pp. 81–90 (2010)
26. IEEE: IEEE recommended practice for architectural description of software-intensive systems. Technical report, Technical Report IEEE Std 1471-2000. IEEE Computer Society (2000)
27. Cardoso, J., Mendling, J., Neumann, G., Reijers, H.: A Discourse on Complexity of Process Models. In: Eder, J., Dustdar, S. (eds.) BPM Workshops 2006. LNCS, vol. 4103, pp. 117–128. Springer, Heidelberg (2006)
28. Gruhn, V., Laue, R.: Complexity metrics for business process models. In: 9th International Conference on Business Information Systems (BIS 2006), Citeseer, vol. 85, pp. 1–12 (2006)
29. Närman, P., Buschle, M., Ekstedt, M.: An enterprise architecture framework for multi-attribute information systems analysis. Systems and Software Modeling (accepted to be published, 2012)

New Avenues for Theoretical Contributions in Enterprise Architecture Principles - A Literature Review

Mohammad Kazem Haki and Christine Legner

Faculty of Business and Economics (HEC), University of Lausanne,
CH-1015 Lausanne, Switzerland
{kazem.haki,christine.legner}@unil.ch

Abstract. Enterprise Architecture (EA), which has been approached by both academia and industry, is considered comprising not only architectural representations, but also principles guiding architecture's design and evolution. Even though the concept of EA principles has been defined as the integral part of EA, the number of publications on this subject is very limited and only a few organizations use EA principles to manage their EA endeavors. In order to critically assess the current state of research and identify research gaps in EA principles, we focus on four general aspects of theoretical contributions in IS. By applying these aspects to EA principles, we outline future research directions in EA principles nature, adoption, practices, and impact.

Keywords: enterprise architecture (EA), EA principles, literature review.

1   Introduction

Enterprise architecture (EA) is a constantly evolving research subject that has been approached by both academia and industry [1, 2] over more than two decades. In the existing literature, most papers cite the ANSI/IEEE STD 1471-2000 and define architecture as:

- "the fundamental organization of a system, embodied in its components, their relationships to each other and the environment,
- and the principles governing its design and evolution."

According to aforementioned definition, EA artifacts include not only (1) *representation models*, which are conceptualized by means of different EA methods, meta-models and frameworks, but also (2) *principles,* which are rules guiding architecture's design and evolution [3–5]. EA principles are thus integral part of EA definition; Hoogervorst [6] even equates architecture with principles and defines EA as a set of design principles.

Even though the concept of EA principles has been defined as the essential element of EA [3–14], the number of publications on this subject is surprisingly very limited, as outlined by previous studies [3, 4, 14, 15]. This is particularly surprising if we compare the number to the vast body of literature related to the first part of the EA

S. Aier et al. (Eds.): TEAR 2012 and PRET 2012, LNBIP 131, pp. 182–197, 2012.

definition. Similarly, although principles are described in frameworks such as TOGAF [16], only few organizations use them to manage their EA efforts [3]. The EA principles are hence rather underexplored in EA research.

Given the relevance of EA principles, the main objective of this paper is to (1) critically assess the current state of research in this field, (2) identify research gaps, and (3) outline future research directions. To this aim, we suggest a research framework that applies generic IS research types and questions [17] to EA principles and identifies EA principles nature, practices, adoption, and impact as main areas of research. Based on a systematic literature review, our analysis delineates several areas that remain underserved in the existing body of knowledge and that offer researchers the opportunity to contribute to the development of the field of research on EA principles.

The remainder of this paper is structured as follows. First, we provide an overview of the research methodology and analysis framework. The subsequent section describes in detail the results of the literature review. Afterwards, based on the discussed results, we derive underserved theoretical contributions. Finally, we summarize our findings and propose further research.

2 Research Methodology and Analysis Framework

2.1 Analysis Framework

A literature review can either deal with a mature topic or an emerging issue [18]. In this paper, we use it to investigate the emerging issue of EA principles. Recognizing the suggestions of Webster and Watson [18] and Fettke [19], we use a literature review framework for guiding literature analysis and for classifying the papers based on their theoretical contributions. Our research questions are built on the research objectives. This paper aims at identifying underserved theory types in EA principles with regard to primary goals of the theory in IS i.e. description, explanation, prediction, and prescription [17]. Therefore, relying on Gregor's taxonomy of theory types in information systems [17] and in line with other studies [20], our literature review framework focuses on four rigorous research questions and applies them to EA principles (fig. 1):

- *Understanding the nature of EA principles: What are EA principles?* This research question focuses on the *"what"* and addresses the definition and characteristics of the phenomena of interest. It results in theory type I (theory for analyzing) of Gregor's taxonomy [17]. As the most basic type of theory, descriptive theories are needed when nothing or little is known about phenomena in question. This theoretical effort results in classification schema, frameworks, taxonomies, or typologies.
- *EA principles adoption: Why and to what extent are EA principles adopted?* The second research question considers the theory for understanding and explaining how and why some phenomena occur. In other words, this aspect of the analysis framework concerns different approaches of analyzing adoption and diffusion of

EA principles in different organizational context and EA designs [21]. This will ultimately lead to insights into adoption patterns and the factors that determine successful implementations of EA principles. Answering this research question requires researchers to conduct empirical studies and to collect observations from the field. It results in theory type II (theory for explaining) of Gregor's taxonomy [17].

- *EA principles practices: How to design, implement and manage EA principles?* This research question aims at specifying how organizations should develop, deploy and manage EA principles, and might be most valuable from the practitioner's point of view. It is associated with a constructivist type of research or design science, resulting in methods and justificatory theoretical knowledge in the development of the discussed phenomena. Gregor [17] classifies this type of theory as theory type V (theory for design and action).

- *EA principles impact: What are the impacts of EA principles?* The last research question considers the theoretical constructs and relationships among them. In EA principles like EA itself, measuring the impacts and organizational benefits of principles are of importance. This research question results in theory type IV (theory for explaining and predicting) of Gregor's taxonomy [17].

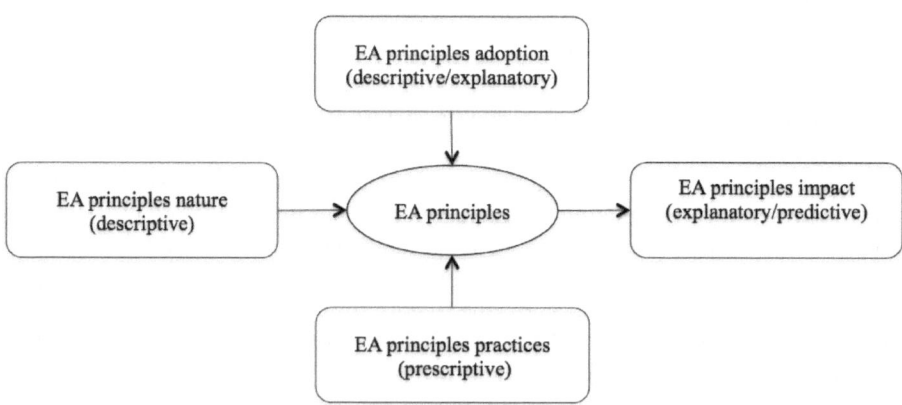

Fig. 1. Analysis framework derived from [17]

2.2   Literature Selection and Review Process

In order to analyze prior research results in the field of EA principles, we carried out a comprehensive literature review of scientific journal and conference publications based on the guideline provided by Webster and Watson [18]. We focused on peer-reviewed publications and excluded other types of publications (e.g. books, project or research reports) to ensure the quality of the contributions. A set of key terms ("principle", "architecture principle", "design principle", "guideline") was utilized to identify the related publications in EA[M] context articles. Hence, we excluded articles addressing principles in other fields (e.g. modeling [22, 23] or SOA). Owing to the paucity of publications in EA principles, we did not imply any limitation for publication date.

We identified the related articles by scanning scientific databases (AIS electronic library, ACM Digital Library, DBPL, EBSCOhost, IEEE Xplore Digital Library, Science Direct, Web of Science, and SpringerLink) as well as EA conferences (AIS supported conferences and TEAR workshop). The first step of our literature review resulted in nineteen articles investigating EA principles.

In the subsequent step, we coded and analyzed the identified articles according to a coding scheme. The coding scheme was built on the research questions of the presented analysis framework in section 2.1. In line with [14], our coding scheme also included the level of universality of proposed principles (either generic or company-specific) and emphasis on principles (either as core or among other topics). We included additional codes for research methodology based on the taxonomy of [24] (see Appendix).

3   Results

This section provides a general overview of the identified articles and their utilized research methodologies. We also provide a content classification based on our literature review framework so as to analyze their area of theoretical contributions.

3.1   Overview

We identified nineteen articles investigating EA principles, twelve of which published in conference proceedings and seven in journals. Richardson et al. [10] is the most cited paper dating back to 1990. It was the initiator of EA principles research, since it was the first to investigate EA principles as the core subject of interest. In 1999, Armour et al. [12] argued the importance of EA principles in the context of EA frameworks. As of 2004 researchers decided to concentrate on this research subject. The time-wise turning points in EA principles are 2006 and 2011, with four articles in each point. To date, twelve articles studied EA principles as the core of their research [3–5, 7–11, 14, 15, 25, 26] and seven articles investigate them among other topics [6, 12, 13, 27–30].   According to Google Scholar, the articles with focus on EA principles are mostly low cited (less than 20 citations), two average-cited (20-80 citations) and only one is high cited (more than 80 citations).

3.2   Content Classification

We coded the identified articles based on four theory types of EA principles, presented in our analysis framework. The analysis of the codes provides us with further insights into current state of theoretical contributions in EA principles.

Nature of EA Principles

All the identified nineteen papers laid emphasis on either EA principles nature or EA principles practices. They all investigated at least one of the aspects related to the nature of EA principles ("what are EA principles?"). This may be explained by the fact that EA principles are in their infancy in EA research; investing a great deal of research on fundamental concept and definitions is hence inevitable.

Since little is known about EA principles in EA research, prior work mostly concentrated on EA principles nature through: (1) suggesting an exhaustive and comprehensible definition of EA principles and shedding light on the role of principles [3–6, 8, 9, 11–15]; (2) discussing the formulation and statement of EA principles, as a set of constraints on the syntax and semantics of EA principles documentation [7, 10, 11, 26]; (3) categorizing EA principles into different areas and scope [10, 25–27]; (4) suggesting a set of EA principles, which are either generic or company (context)-specific [10, 26, 28–30]. We thus reveal four streams of research related to the nature of EA principles namely EA principles *definition and role*, EA principles *documentation*, EA principles *classification*, and EA principles *proposition*.

EA principles definition
Seven out of nineteen identified papers either provided definitions of EA principles or consolidated existing ones so as to propose a comprehensible definition [3–5, 8, 9, 14, 15]:

Architectural design vs. architectural representation: Stelzer [14] distinguishes architectural design (as the conceptual model of the system) from architectural representation (as formal description of architecture). The principles related to architectural design are so-called design principles and the principles regarding architectural representation are denoted as representation principles. Winter and Aier [3], Fischer et al. [4] and Aier et al. [5] similarly argue that EA artifacts include not only representation models, but also design principles. Representation models are described by means of different EA methods, meta-models and frameworks in baseline and target architecture. They are complemented by design principles which are guidelines and rules guiding architecture's design and evolution from baseline to target architecture. Lindström [26] makes a similar distinction by differentiating syntactical (representation) and semantic (design) principles.

Scientific principles vs. normative principles: Scientific and normative principles are distinguished by [8, 9, 15]. The scientific principles are cross-disciplinary, which are applicable in various design principles. The normative principles are based on artifacts such as strategy and environment, and influence other artifacts such as guidelines, requirements, and implementation. The EA principles are thus seen as normative principles.

Architecture principles vs. design principles: Architecture principles utilize a heuristic approach, are included in the architecture of a class of systems, and are inductive in nature. Conversely, design principles are included in the design of a specific system, and are deductive in nature [8, 9, 15].

Lindström [26] defines architecture principles from the resource management perspective, as the underlying general rules and guidelines for the use of IT resources all through the organization. Stelzer [14] investigates EA principles in a network of principles comprising IT, business, organization, application, software architecture, data, and technology principles. He also lays emphasis on "constraint" as another concept that helps assessing the principles' scope and validity. Architecture principles are also discussed in TOGAF [16]. Open Group defines architecture principle as a qualitative statement of intent that should be met by the architecture.

Although Richardson et al. [10] define the principles as guidelines and rationales for the constant examination and re-evaluation of the proposed IT target plan, Stelzer [14] and OptLand and Proper [25] found that no accepted definition of EA principles has yet emerged. Fischer et al. [4] and Aier, Fischer et al. [5] hence considered different definition notions of EA principles and consolidated them into a common understanding that we summarized them as follows:

EA principles, which can be attributed to *different architectural layers*, are based on *business and IT strategies* and refer to the *construction of an organization*. Each EA principle is described in a *principle statement*. It consists of a *rationale* that explains why the principle is helpful to attain the pre-determined goal, as well as *implications* that describe how to implement the given principle. Finally, *metrics* should be identified for each principle to measure its fulfillment.

EA principles role

Four papers argued the role of EA principles either in EA or in EA-related topics [6, 11–13]. They discuss the role of principles in EA frameworks [12] and enterprise integration and interoperability [13]. Van Bommel et al. [11] regarded EA principles as a means to realize the regulative nature of EA. They hence investigated the regulative goals and requirements of EA so as to propose a formulation structure for EA principles documentation. Hoogervorst [6] equated architecture with principles and viewed architecture as a consistent set of design principles in four areas i.e. business, organization, information, and technology.

EA principles documentation

EA principles documentation concerns the structure used for documenting and communicating principles. Each EA principle document could be made up of different sections namely statement [7, 10, 26], rational (motivation) [10, 26], implication [10, 26], measures [26], and comments [26]. Different guidelines also have been suggested to formulate and document principles. Lindström [26] argues that principles should be consistent, verifiable, unambiguous, modifiable, stable, and complete and correct. According to the TOGAF [16], understandability, robustness, completeness, consistency and stability are also of importance.

EA principles classification

Four papers covered principles classification [10, 25–27], in which researchers mostly suggested architectural layer-based approach in defining principles implications: Richardson et al. [10] defined principles in organization, application, data, and infrastructure areas; Winter and Fischer [27] placed principles in business, process, integration, software, and technology layers; OptLand and Proper [25] illustrated principles implication in enterprise engineering architectural layers namely business, informational, and datalogical. Moreover, Lindström [26] classified the proposed company-specific principles in governance, outsourcing, risk management, security, system management, environment, standardization, and infrastructure categories. Since the latter was built on a single case study, the proposed classification is not generalizable.

EA principles proposition

There are only two studies proposing a set of EA principles. They both utilized case studies and thus identified a set of detailed company-specific principles: Richardson et al. [10] explored EA principles in Texaco and Star Enterprise case. They also provided rationale for each principle and stated the practical implications that result from principles. Lindström [26] developed a set of architecture principles for the Vattenfall case.

Three other studies proposed a set of generic principles in which EA principles have been studied among other subjects (in EA context), notably e-government [29], enterprise transformations [30], and adaptive EA [28]. Wilkinson [28] is the only one proposing adaptable principles in EA, which are modularity, simplification, integration, and standardization.

EA Principles Practices

When it comes to EA principles practices, six papers [3–5, 11, 15, 25] investigated the question regarding "how to design, implement, and manage EA principles." They can be categorized into two different lenses: (1) the generic process of determining or extracting principles [3–5, 15]; (2) managing the life cycle of principles so as to turning principles into an effective means in guiding EA design [3, 11, 15, 25]. We thus reveal two streams of research in EA principles practices namely EA principles *extraction* and EA principles *management*.

EA principles extraction

This research stream investigates how to arrive at a set of principles for EA design. Greefhorst and Proper [15] examined different sources for finding principle motivations and formulated six types of drivers which are goals, values, issues, risks, potential rewards and constraints. From a practitioner survey, Winter and Aier [3] identified business strategy as the main source of extracting principles. Two other studies came to the same conclusion through one [4] or two [5] small case studies.

EA principles management

Recently Greefhorst and Proper [15] proposed a generic process to handle life cycle of architecture principles. They proposed eight sub-processes to handle architecture principles: determine drivers, determine principles, specify principles, classify principles, validate and accept principles, apply principles, manage compliance, and handle changes. Van Bommel et al. also [11] proposed three steps in managing principles, which are assessing needs, formulating principles, and preparing principles deployment. According to a survey, Winter and Aier [3] elicited the process of communicating and updating principles as the main practical issues in EA principles management.

EA Principles Adoption

Since EA principles are underexplored in EA research, there was a tendency to clarify the fundamental concept and practices, but we did not identify any research on principles adoption. This implies that we have neither empirical evidences how EA principles are adopted nor about the factors determining EA principles adoption.

EA Principles Impact

Interestingly, there is also no dedicated study investigating the impact of EA principles in prior research, but their expected impacts have been argued implicitly. Some examples are as follows.

The steering and directing role of EA is done by means of principles [7, 25, 31], which are both normative constraints (restrictions) and guidance in EA design [8, 25]. The EA principles also realize the regulative role of EA by considering EA as a set of principles to constrain the enterprise design space [11]. In other words, architecture principles bridge the gap between strategic intentions and concrete design decisions [8, 9, 26] by addressing concerns of the key stakeholders within an organization [7]. OptLand and Proper [25] also argued that EA principles impact different architectural views of enterprise engineering.

3.3   Research Methodologies

Since EA principle is an emerging topic in EA research, the majority of prior research either provided conceptual insights or utilized cases study. Nine out of nineteen papers developed conceptual descriptions [6–9, 11–13, 15, 25] relying on author's experience or thought. Case studies were preferred choice for empirical study in eight papers [4, 5, 10, 26–30]. Two out of those case studies were mostly literature reviews with one [4] or two [5] very small case descriptions. We also identified one literature review [14] as well as one survey [3] of 70 Swiss and German practitioners on the usage and management of EA principles.

4   Discussion and Findings – New Avenues of Theoretical Contributions

Based on the discussed results, the current state of research in EA principles reveals various gaps in different dimensions of our analysis framework. In this section, we derive underserved research areas in order to clarify the required research directions (table 1).

4.1   Understanding the Nature of EA Principles: What Are EA Principles?

Related to EA principles definition, prior research either provided basic definition or tried to consolidate existing definitions. There is a consensus that EA principles are integral part of EA, can be classified based on architectural layers, and should comprise statement, rationale, implication and measures. Whereas our understanding related to EA principles definition and documentation is maturing, we know very little about specific EA principles and their quality. Prior work proposed either company-specific principles, which may not be generalizable, or generic principles, which are not explicitly studied in EA context. Future research thus should propose and scientifically validate a set of generic EA principles through expert judgment, multiple-case studies or surveys. This provides a common understanding of principles and their expected level of granularity. Developing a typology of EA principles (based on e.g. EA's requirements, expected goals and outcomes) may support this endeavor. In this regard, analyzing the literature for principles in related fields, such as organizational design or software architecture could be beneficial [14].

Table 1. Current status and future research in EA principles

Fields of theoretical contributions	Current status	Future research
Nature	Consensus on EA principles definition and documentation	• Propose and validate generic EA principles and/or typologies of EA principles
Practices	Tentative or implicit processes for principles extraction and management	• Methodologies for identifying possible sources of extracting principles • Management processes to handle the life cycle of principles from extraction to assessment • Integration of EA principles in IT management and governance methodologies
Adoption	No research yet	• Understanding of the adoption process • EA principles institutionalization • EA principles embeddedness in EA design • Success factors of EA principles adoption
Impact	Implicit argumentations	• Role of EA principles in shaping the design of EA • Relationship between deploying EA principles and EA effectiveness / organizational benefits

4.2   EA Principles Practices: How to Design, Implement and Manage EA Principles?

Drawing on theory type V (theory for design and action) of Gregor's taxonomy[17], this category comprises design-oriented research related to the design, implementation, and management of EA principles.

Concerning the design of EA principles, the small portion of prior research [3–5, 15] either proposed a tentative process or implicitly looked into it. Key stakeholders must understand how the motivation behind a set of principles aligns with the organization's strategies and its micro and macro environment. Further investigation needs to be carried out in order to explore the possible sources of extracting EA principles such as higher organizational levels, industry standards, external authorities [25]. Future research should also investigate principles alignment with business and IT strategies as well as the influence of contextual and organizational factors on extracting EA principles.

Regarding the management of EA principles, a scientifically validated management process covering the entire life cycle is lacking. Owing to the relative newness of EA principles in EA research, also no research has been conducted on their implementation practices. For developing appropriate practices in EA principles, multiple-case studies are recommended to gather real-world experiences on: (1) how to translate business and IT strategies into an exhaustive set of EA principles, and (2) how to turn them into a set of rules, guidelines and standards guiding EA design.

More design-oriented research is required to engineer methodologies supporting companies in identifying EA principles as well as managing their life cycle.

When it comes to EA principles implementation, different approaches in establishing and enforcing EA principles are concerned. The EA principles implementation considers clear organizational accountability for adhering to principles so as to ensure they are used to guide design decisions. Given the nature of EA principles as governing EA design and evolution (cf. ANSI/IEEE STD 1471-2000 definition of architecture), more research is thus needed to study how EA principles complement IT management and governance methodologies.

4.3   EA Principles Adoption: Why and to What Extent Are EA Principles Adopted?

We did not identify any systematic research on EA principles adoption, which concerns acceptance, diffusion, success and influence factors, and measurement of EA principles.

Above all, we are lacking a comprehensible understanding of the adoption process of EA principles. It could be studied either as a stand-alone phenomenon or as a part of EA adoption. If EA principles adoption is considered as stand-alone phenomenon, questions related to the operationalization in organizational processes are of interest. It is recommended that future research investigates organizational adoption of EA principles through general management theories, such as institutional theory, structuration theory, or contingency theory. For understanding EA principles acceptance by organizations and individuals, different theoretical lenses, such as diffusion of innovation or technology acceptance model are useful.

When considering EA principles as inherent to EA adoption, future research needs to investigate the embeddedness of EA principles. EA adoption [21, 32, 33] is a rather new topic in EA research concerning EA institutionalization throughout the organization. Given the context-dependent nature of EA in different organizational settings [21], it is also recommended that future research propose and validate archetype-specific principles.

Winter and Aier [3] also identified that difficulties to enforce EA principles are related to the inability to *measure* EA principle implementation. In order to address this gap, metrics need to be defined to assess the measurable implementation of EA principles.

According to aforementioned discussion, we propose research streams in EA principles adoption as follows: EA principles *institutionalization*, EA principles *embeddedness in EA design*, *measurement model* for EA principles adoption, and *success and influence factors* on principles adoption.   Regarding the proposed research directions, qualitative (case studies) and large-scale quantitative research for further analysis are recommended.

4.4   EA Principles Impact: What Are the Impacts of EA Principles?

Similar to EA principles adoption, we did not identify any research on EA principles impact, but only implicit assumptions expressed by the rationale for selecting certain EA principles.

References to ANSI/IEEE STD 1471-2000 definition of architecture, EA principles govern the design and evolution of EA. The future research in EA principles impact hence could be derived from these two aspects.

The design of EA could be considered as either generic EA frameworks and patterns [32, 34–37] or situational EA designs [21, 38, 39]. Future research could use both perspectives, i.e. generic or situational EA designs, to analyze the impact of principles in ruling and guiding EA design and evolution.

Since principles are considered as an effective means to shape EA design, this brings us to the impact of principles on EA evolution and effectiveness. In effect, EA principles are used to guarantee the expected outcomes out of EA. The future research could thus study the causal relationship between deploying EA principles and EA effectiveness. This could be part of a larger causal model that also illustrates the impact of EA effectiveness on organizational benefits. Accordingly, the impact of EA principles on organizational benefits could be studies either directly or through their impact on EA effectiveness as a mediate variable.

5   Summary and Conclusion

This paper profiles the existing research on EA principles based on four research questions concerning EA principles nature, adoption, practices, and impact. Our analysis of nineteen articles has shown that existing research has mostly concentrated on EA principles definition as well as on the guidelines to document principles. Despite the fact that EA principles are highly relevant, we know relatively little about specific principles and how they should be designed, implemented, and managed. The existing research also has no illustration on how design principles are adopted and how they alter an existing architecture.

Figure 2 shows a research model representing the relationships between our proposed research directions in EA principles. According to ANSI/IEEE STD 1471-2000, EA principles are served as a means to govern the design and evolution of EA that finally lead to a set of organizational benefits. In other words, to purposefully design and manage EA and meet the expected organizational outcomes, each EA endeavor could be ruled and guided by EA principles. This also implies that EA principles only create organizational benefits, if they are properly implemented. Our research model is hence composed of four dimensions to guarantee organizational benefits.

Regarding EA principles, several topics are recommended for future research (as discussed in previous section): methodologies for identifying the possible sources of extracting EA principles, management processes to handle the life cycle of EA principles from extraction to deployment, real world experiences in principles implementation, proposing and validating a set of generic EA principles, and understanding the embeddedness of EA principles in organizational structure and processes.

Concerning the impact of principles on EA design and evolution, two topics are of interest: (1) EA design: Impact of EA principles on EA components and configuration comprising all aspects of implementing EA in the organization e.g. phases, governance, and modeling [21, 40]; (2) EA evolution: Impact of EA principles on EA effectiveness so as to foster consistency and integration between different architectural layers. The latter also describes business-IT alignment through adapting EA design to a specific organizational context.

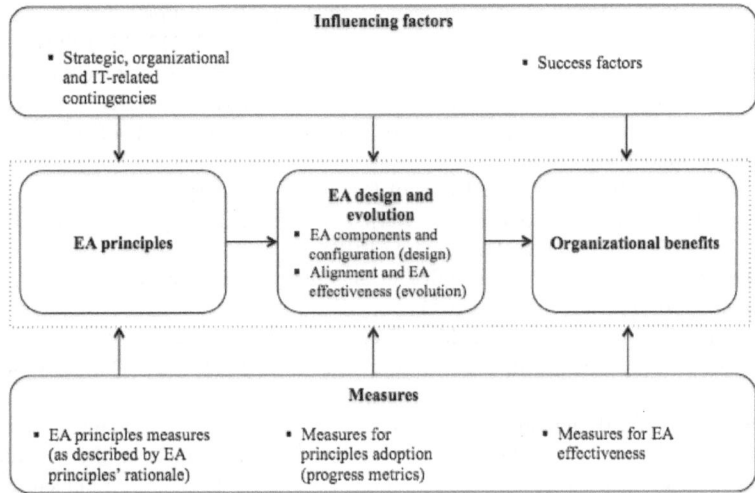

Fig. 2. General research outline in EA principles

The influencing factors consist of the success factors fostering the adoption of EA principles as well as contingency (contextual) factors influencing the effect of EA principles on EA design and evolution. In effect, EA design has to adhere to a set of contextual factors [21, 32, 40, 41]. Therefore, the effect of contextual factors could be investigated through proposing a set of EA design-specific principles for situational EA designs.

Finally, our research model suggests developing a set of measures to assess the success of EA principles adoption, the level of achievement to each of proposed generic or design-specific principles, the effectiveness of EA design, and organizational benefits resulting from EA.

References

1. Niemi, E.: Enterprise Architecture Stakeholders - a Holistic View. In: AMCIS 2007 Proceedings, vol. 41, pp. 2–9 (2007)
2. Radeke, F.: Awaiting Explanation in the Field of Enterprise Architecture Management. Presented at the Americas Conference on Information Systems (AMCIS 2010), Lima, Peru (2010)
3. Winter, R., Aier, S.: How are Enterprise Architecture Design Principles Used? Presented at the The Fifteenth IEEE International EDOC Conference Workshops, Trends in Enterprise Architecture Research (TEAR), Helsinki (2011)
4. Fischer, C., Winter, R., Aier, S.: What is an Enterprise Architecture Design Principle? In: Lee, R. (ed.) Computer and Information Science 2010. SCI, vol. 317, pp. 193–205. Springer, Heidelberg (2010)
5. Aier, S., Fischer, C., Winter, R.: Construction and Evaluation of a Meta-Model for Enterprise Architecture Design Principles. In: Wirtschaftinformatik Proceedings 2011, vol. 51, pp. 637–644 (2011)

6. Hoogervorst, J.: Enterprise Architecture: Enabling Integration, Agility And Change. International Journal of Cooperative Information Systems 13, 213–233 (2004)
7. Van Bommel, P., Hoppenbrouwers, S., Proper, H.A., Weide, T.P.: Giving Meaning to Enterprise Architectures: Architecture Principles with ORM and ORC. In: Meersman, R., Tari, Z., Herrero, P. (eds.) OTM 2006 Workshops. LNCS, vol. 4278, pp. 1138–1147. Springer, Heidelberg (2006)
8. Proper, E., Greefhorst, D.: The Roles of Principles in Enterprise Architecture. In: Proper, E., Lankhorst, M.M., Schönherr, M., Barjis, J., Overbeek, S. (eds.) TEAR 2010. LNBIP, vol. 70, pp. 57–70. Springer, Heidelberg (2010)
9. Proper, E., Greefhorst, D.: Principles in an Enterprise Architecture Context. Journal of Enterprise Architecture 7, 8–16 (2011)
10. Richardson, G.L., Jackson, B.M., Dickson, G.W.: A Principles-Based Enterprise Architecture: Lessons from Texaco and Star Enterprise. MIS Quarterly 14, 385–403 (1990)
11. Van Bommel, P., Buitenhuis, P., Hoppenbrouwers, S., Proper, E.: Architecture principles – A regulative perspective on enterprise architecture. Presented at the 1st International Workshop on Enterprise Modelling and Information Systems Architectures, EMISA (2007)
12. Armour, F.J., Kaisler, S.H., Liu, S.Y.: A big-picture look at enterprise architectures. IT Professional 1, 35–42 (1999)
13. Chen, D., Doumeingts, G., Vernadat, F.: Architectures for enterprise integration and interoperability: Past, present and future. Computers in Industry 59, 647–659 (2008)
14. Stelzer, D.: Enterprise Architecture Principles: Literature Review and Research Directions. In: Dan, A., Gittler, F., Toumani, F. (eds.) ICSOC/ServiceWave 2009. LNCS, vol. 6275, pp. 12–21. Springer, Heidelberg (2010)
15. Greefhorst, D., Proper, E.: A Practical Approach to the Formulation and Use of Architecture Principles. Presented at the 15th IEEE International Enterprise Distributed Object Computing Conference Workshops, EDOCW (2011)
16. Open Group: TOGAF Version 9 - The Open Group Architecture Framework. The Open Group (2009)
17. Gregor, S.: The Nature of Theory in Information Systems. MIS Quarterly 30, 611–642 (2006)
18. Webster, J., Watson, R.T.: Analyzing the past to prepare for the future: Writing a literature review. MIS Quarterly 26, 13–23 (2002)
19. Fettke, P.: State-of-the-Art des State-of-the-Art: Eine Untersuchung der Forschungsmethode „Review" innerhalb der Wirtschaftsinformatik. Wirtschaftsinformatik 48, 257–266 (2006)
20. Viering, G., Legner, C., Ahlemann, F.: The (Lacking) Business Perspective on SOA– Critical Themes in SOA Research. In: Tagungsband der Konferenz Wirtschaftsinformatik 2009, pp. 45–54. Österreichische Computer Gesellschaft (2009)
21. Haki, M.K., Legner, C., Ahlemann, F.: Beyond EA Frameworks: Towards an Understanding of the Adoption of Enterprise Architecture Management. In: ECIS 2012 Proceedings (2012)
22. Balabko, P., Wegmann, A.: Systemic classification of concern-based design methods in the context of enterprise architecture. Information Systems Frontiers 8, 115–131 (2006)
23. Brown, A.W.: Model driven architecture: Principles and practice. Software and Systems Modeling 3, 314–327 (2004)
24. Galliers, R.D., Land, F.F.: Viewpoint: choosing appropriate information systems research methodologies. Commun. ACM 30, 901–902 (1987)

25. OptLand, M., Proper, E.: Impact of principles on enterprise engineering. Presented at the 15th European Conference on Information Systems (2007)
26. Lindström, Å.: On the Syntax and Semantics of Architectural Principles. Presented at the 39th Annual Hawaii International Conference on System Sciences, HICSS (2006)
27. Winter, R., Fischer, R.: Essential Layers, Artifacts, and Dependencies of Enterprise Architecture. Journal of Enterprise Architecture 3, 1–12 (2007)
28. Wilkinson, M.: Designing an 'adaptive' enterprise architecture. BT Technology Journal 24, 81–92 (2006)
29. Janssen, M., Kuk, G.: A Complex Adaptive System Perspective of Enterprise Architecture in Electronic Government. Presented at the 39th Hawaii International Conference on System Sciences (HICSS), Hawaii (2006)
30. Nightingale, D.: Principles of enterprise systems. Presented at the Second International Symposium on Engineering Systems. MIT, Cambridge (2009)
31. OptLand, M., Proper, E., Waage, M., Cloo, J., Steghuis, C.: Enterprise Architecture: Creating Value by Informed Governance. Springer (2008)
32. Hjort-Madsen, K.: Institutional patterns of enterprise architecture adoption in government. Transforming Government: People, Process and Policy 1, 333–349 (2007)
33. Aier, S., Weiss, S.: An Institutional Framework for Analyzing Organizational Responses to the Establishment of Architectural Transformation. In: ECIS 2012 Proceedings (2012)
34. Buckl, E.A., Lankes, J., Schneider, K., Schweda, C.: A Pattern based Approach for constructing Enterprise Architecture Management Information Models. Internationale Tagung Wirtschaftsinformatik 2007- Band 2, 145–162 (2007)
35. Franke, U., Holschke, O., Matthes, F., Schweda, C., Sommestad, T., Ullberg, J., Buckl, S.: A Pattern-based Approach to Quantitative Enterprise Architecture Analysis. In: AMCIS 2009 Proceedings, vol. 318, pp. 3–11 (2009)
36. Ernst: Enterprise architecture management patterns. In: Proceedings of the 15th Conference on Pattern Languages of Programs, pp. 7:1–7:20. ACM, Nashville (2008)
37. Schulman, J.: Patterns Play an Essential Role in Enterprise Architecture. Gartner (2004)
38. Aier, S., Gleichauf, B., Winter, R.: Understanding Enterprise Architecture Management Design – An Empirical Analysis. Presented at the Wirtschaftinformatik Proceedings 2011 (2011)
39. Winter, R.: Design Solution Analysis for the Construction of Situational Design Methods. In: Ralyté, J., Mirbel, I., Deneckère, R. (eds.) ME 2011. IFIP AICT, vol. 351, pp. 19–33. Springer, Heidelberg (2011)
40. Schmidt, C., Buxmann, P.: Outcomes and success factors of enterprise IT architecture management: empirical insight from the international financial services industry. European Journal of Information Systems, 1–18 (2011)
41. Boh, W.F., Yellin, D.: Using Enterprise Architecture Standards in Managing Information Technology. Journal of Management Information Systems 23, 163–207 (2006)

Appendix

Table 2. Coded articles in EA principles based on theoretical contributions, level of study, universality of proposed principles, and research methodologies

| | Identified articles | | Content classification according to analysis framework | | | | | | | | | | | |
| | | | Nature | | | | | Practices | | | | | | |
Reference	Author(s)	Title	Definitions	Role	Documentation	Classification	Proposition	Extraction	Management	Adoption	Impact	Level of study	Universality of principles	Research method
[14]	Stelzer	Enterprise architecture principles: literature review and research directions	☐									1		Conceptual (LR)
[8]	Proper and Greefhorst	The roles of principles in enterprise architecture	☐									1		Conceptual
[9]	Proper and Greefhorst	Principles in an enterprise architecture context	☐									1		Conceptual
[15]	Greefhorst and Proper	A practical approach to the formulation and use of architecture principles	☐					☐	☐			1		Conceptual
[25]	OptLand and Proper	Impact of principles on enterprise engineering				☐			☐			1		Conceptual
[3]	Winter and Aier	How are enterprise architecture design principles used?	☐					☐	☐			1		Survey
[4]	Fischer et al.	What is an enterprise architecture design principle? Towards a consolidated definition	☐					☐				1		Case study
[5]	Aier et al.	Construction and evaluation of a meta-model for enterprise architecture design principles	☐					☐				1		Case study
[26]	Lindström	On the syntax and semantics of architectural principles			☐	☐	☐					1	2	Case study

Table 2. (*coninued*)

Reference	Author(s)	Title	Definitions	Role	Documentation	Classification	Proposition	Extraction	Management	Adoption	Impact	Level of study	Universality of principles	Research method
			Nature					Practices						
[7]	Van Bommel et al.	Giving meaning to enterprise architectures: Architecture principles with ORM and ORC			☐							1		Conceptual
[10]	Richardson et al.	A principles-based enterprise architecture: Lessons from Texaco and Star Enterprise			☐	☐	☐					1	2	Case study
[11]	Van Bommel et al.	Architecture principles – A regulative perspective on enterprise architecture	☐	☐					☐			1		Conceptual
[27]	Winter and Fischer	Essential layers, artifacts, and dependencies of enterprise architecture					☐					2		Case study
[6]	Hoogervorst	Enterprise architecture: Enabling integration, agility and change		☐								2		Conceptual
[28]	Wilkinson	Designing an 'adaptive' enterprise architecture					☐					2	1	Case study
[13]	Chen et al.	Architectures for enterprise integration and interoperability: Past, present and future		☐								2		Conceptual
[29]	Janssen and Kuk	A complex adaptive system perspective of enterprise architecture in electronic government					☐					2	1	Case study
[12]	Armour et al.	A big-picture look at enterprise architectures		☐								2		Conceptual
[30]	Nightingale	Principles of enterprise systems					☐					2	1	Case study

Level of study: 1. Core, 2. Among other topics
Universality of principles: 1. Generic, 2. Company-specific

A Metamodel for Web Application Injection Attacks and Countermeasures

Hannes Holm and Mathias Ekstedt

Industrial Information and Control Systems
Royal Institute of Technology
Osquldas väg 10, 100 44 Stockholm, Sweden
{hannesh,mathiase}@ics.kth.se

Abstract. Web application injection attacks such as cross site scripting and SQL injection are common and problematic for enterprises. In order to defend against them, practitioners with large heterogeneous system architectures and limited resources struggle to understand the effectiveness of different countermeasures under various conditions. This paper presents an enterprise architecture metamodel that can be used by enterprise decision makers when deciding between different countermeasures for web application injection attacks. The scope of the model is to provide low-effort guidance on an abstraction level of use for an enterprise decision maker. This metamodel is based on a literature review and revised according to the judgment by six domain experts identified through peer-review.

Keywords: Cyber security, web applications, enterprise architecture.

1   Introduction

Cyber security is a critical concern for enterprises as successful cyber attacks can result in severe economic deficits due to losses of data confidentiality, integrity or availability. Depending on the IT asset in question and the intent of the attacker, there are various cyber attacks that can be considered. For example, an attacker could try to harvest sensitive data through seemingly legitimate emails (i.e., phishing) or exploit a cross site scripting vulnerability (XSS) in a web application. A XSS vulnerability allows an attacker to execute client side script in the web browser of any visitor of the website (which could lead to a range of issues, including complete control of the visitors computer).

Of the various types of cyber attacks available, code injection is often considered the most troubling type of attack [1]. That is, to introduce code into a computer program or system by taking advantage of unchecked assumptions the system makes about its inputs. Code injection attacks can be classified into binary code injection attacks and source code injection attacks [2]. A binary code injection involves insertion of malicious code in a binary program to alter how the program behaves, and is generally carried out through a buffer overflow [3]. Source code injection attacks

S. Aier et al. (Eds.): TEAR 2012 and PRET 2012, LNBIP 131, pp. 198–217, 2012.

involve interaction with applications written in programming languages that do not require compilation, e.g., JavaScript, PHP and SQL statements. As source code injections primarily concerns Web Applications (WA) we hereafter refer to this attack type as web application injections, or WA injections.

WA injections includes a number of different attack types, for example, injections using SQL statements (i.e., SQL injections), XSS and OS Command Injection. These are highly critical software flaws according to OWASP [4] and SANS 2011 Top 25 [5] (which sample all known IT security vulnerabilities).

While large amounts of research have been committed to studying WA injections and organizations such as MITRE, SANS and OWASP have developed security awareness programs to help organizations to mitigate the issue, application developers are still unable to implement effective countermeasures to mitigate these vulnerabilities [6].

One possible reason behind the frequent occurrence of WA injection vulnerabilities is that most IT security related matters involve security tools such as specific vulnerability scanners, static code analyzers and intrusion detection systems. As the security landscape on an abstraction level of tools is rapidly changing and there are various tools available for the same purpose, it is difficult for practitioners to understand what security measures that are worth employing, given different scenarios. This is especially the case if the practitioner has a managerial position such as Chief Security Officer (CSO); this type of practitioner needs to consider the security of system-of-systems as a whole.

Enterprise architectures are typically very complex structures that involve various aspects of relevance other than web applications. Consequently, WA injections only constitute a small part of the overall "security puzzle". Thus, the effort spent to manage countermeasures for this attack type is often very limited and information on the general effectiveness of different countermeasures would be valuable to enterprises.

There are works that have attempted to quantify the general effectiveness of different types of countermeasures. However, every such study has been conducted in the presence of various assumptions that are likely to affect their validity. For example, [7] studied the effectiveness of eight WA firewalls and intrusion prevention systems but did not differentiate between what types of WA injection attacks they prevented. As such, an assumption was made that the tools would be equally effective against all types of such security flaws. Another common assumption is regarding the severity of the concerned vulnerability; most studies do not differentiate between vulnerabilities of the same category (e.g., different cross site scripting (XSS) vulnerabilities), even though vulnerabilities within the same category clearly can be of different importance in practice. For example, CVE-2010-3753 and CVE-2008-5718 are both OS Command Injection vulnerabilities; however, only one of them can provide high level privileges if successfully exploited (CVE-2008-5718).

This paper presents an Enterprise Architecture (EA) metamodel that can be used to aid enterprise decision makers deciding upon different countermeasures for WA injection attacks. A hypothesized metamodel was constructed through a literature review; this metamodel was then revised by interviews with six domain experts identified through peer-review.

The rest of the paper unfolds as follows: Section 2 describes the literature review used to construct the hypothesized metamodel and Section 3 describes its result. Section 4 presents the methodology for gathering expert judgment. Section 5 presents the findings from the expert study and the revised EA metamodel. Section 6 critically examines these findings. Finally, Section 7 concludes the paper.

2   A Literature Review of Web Application Injection Attacks

While there are several categorizations describing different areas of WA injection attacks there is no holistic work on the topic. Thus, there is a need to compile the domain theory on WA injection attacks in order to construct a valid metamodel. This chapter describes the method and result of this literature review.

2.1   A Methodology for Categorizing Variables

In order to assemble the currently available work in the field there is a need to both have a way to classify it and a way to collect it. This chapter describes these aspects.

2.1.1   Classifying Current Approaches

Hansman and Hunt [8] present a taxonomy for categorizing network and computer attacks in general that is influenced by Howard's taxonomy [9]. This well established taxonomy is constructed along a set of dimensions, which in combination gives a holistic view of the variables of interest for cyber attacks in general.

Table 1. Used categories from the taxonomy by [8]

Criterion	Description
Main means of attack	The attack vector of the cyber attack, e.g., if it is a physical attack or a brute-force password attack.
Vulnerabilities and exploits	The vulnerabilities and exploits that the attack uses are either known or unknown to the public at large (i.e., shared on the public domain such as on the US National Vulnerability Database [10]).
Result of the attack	The outcome of an attack (denial of service, corruption of information, theft of service, disclosure of information, and/or subversion)
Countermeasures	How to defend against the attack.

As this taxonomy is well established and sufficiently comprehensive to capture the whole domain of WA injections it is chosen to compare the currently available approaches. The criteria target(s) of the attack, Damage, Cost, and Propagation are however not included in the categorization utilized in this study as they significantly involve context-dependent attributes such as the actual targeted software, something which is not useful for the concept of generalizing the attack type. As such, four criteria are used when comparing current WA injection categorization approaches; these criteria are described in Table 1.

2.1.2   Collecting Current Approaches

The online databases ACM, IEEE, SCOPUS and ISI Web of Knowledge were chosen as primary sources for collecting current approaches regarding categorizing different types of WA injections. Articles published between January 2000 and March 2012 found using keywords related to the topic of the study had their titles studied. Example searches include "XSS", "SQL injection", "PHP injection", "Web Application attacks" and "XPath attacks". Through this approach a set of articles possibly related to the topic of the study were gathered. A second brief study of the abstracts of these articles delimited this set even further. The final set of papers were thoroughly read. In addition to this approach, any significant work discussed in any of the studied papers was also chosen for further study. This approach resulted in a collection of 12 works that each covers at least one of the four criteria in Table 1.

2.2   The Main Means of Attack

Six out of the 12 gathered works [2, 11–15] involves classifying different types of WA injections.

All the studied works [2, 11–15] in one way or another discuss means of attack in terms of programming languages. This paper continues this tradition, using a categorization similar to that of [2]. It is possible to inject data through two different types of languages – *domain specific languages (DSL)* and *dynamic languages (DL)*. These criteria can furthermore be more detailed in terms of actual programming languages, e.g., SQL (DSL), XPath (DSL), JavaScript (DL) or PHP (DL). For example, an SQL injection vulnerability due to an unsanitized input parameter in a PHP application can be exploited through input using a DSL (SQL command). In the same way, a vulnerable exec() variable in a PHP application can be exploited through a dynamic language (an OS command injection through a PHP script). While it certainly is possible to go into further detail, e.g., regarding SQL injection tautologies [14], this would significantly add complexity to the categorization – thus not viable for the purpose of the present study.

2.3   Vulnerabilities and Exploits

Three out of 12 studied works discuss topics related to known and unknown WA injection vulnerabilities and exploits [11–13].

Pietraszek and Berghe [11] propose that the CVE (Common Vulnerabilities and Exposures) identification number should be included in the vulnerability information, if applicable. That is, the vulnerability can be known to the public at large. This is contingent to the taxonomy of Hansman and Hunt [8]. Vorobiev and Han [13], and Sidharth and Liu [12] propose that vulnerabilities can be found through querying the WA implementation of Universal Description, Discovery and Integration (UDDI) or Web Service Description Language (WSDL). While this type of information is shared on the public domain, it still involves finding vulnerabilities in a WA, rather testing vulnerabilities known to the public at large (for instance, shared on the US National Vulnerability Database (NVD)).

The categorization used in this paper distinguish, as [11], between *known* and *unknown* vulnerabilities. A vulnerability known to the public at large is an easy target for an attacker as it often also has publicly known exploits, or at least ideas for how to conceive an exploit available. Also, a known vulnerability likely has, or is soon to have, a software patch or work-around remediating it available. This makes it an important vulnerability to manage as it (typically) requires little skill to exploit but (typically) is easily mitigated. There are numerous WA injection vulnerabilities publicly available. For example, the NVD presently describes more than 3300 SQL injection vulnerabilities and almost 3400 XSS vulnerabilities.

2.4   Result of the Attack

Four of the 12 studied articles discuss possible results of WA injection attacks [2, 11, 14, 16].

One commonly applied categorization for describing the outcome of an attack is through its impact on confidentiality, integrity and availability (CIA) [2, 16]. While the concept of CIA is somewhat holistic, it can be difficult to relate to as most attacks affect a combination of these criteria. The two remaining works [11, 14] describes attacks on significantly lower abstraction levels (e.g., SQL Union Queries and SQL PiggyBacked Queries). Employing such an abstraction level is however not useful given the purpose of the study; it would simply be too detailed.

A useful categorization for the purpose of this paper is the five criteria proposed by [8]. These criteria constitute a holistic and usable view of possible results from a WA attack. All of the studied approaches [2, 11, 14, 16] are possible to map to it. That is, theft of service, corruption of information, subversion, disclosure of information, and denial of service.

2.5   Countermeasures

Nine of the 12 studied works classify different types of countermeasures [2, 11, 12, 14, 17–21]. This section describes the classifications by these authors. Many properties of these categorizations are similar. However, no categorizations fully overlap and the used terminology is highly varied. For example, developing a software using a "secure" API is referred to as *new API's* [2], *new query development paradigms* [14], and *serialization API's* [11]. This section summarizes existing attempts to categorize countermeasures against WA injection attacks, and suggests addition of a variable that is not covered by these.

The two main types of countermeasures in the used categorization are static and runtime approaches, as discussed by [2, 14, 21]. An important distinction between static and runtime countermeasures is that runtime countermeasures do not suggest patches for vulnerabilities in the application codebase, but rather make exploitation of existing vulnerabilities more difficult. In the same fashion, static countermeasures detects (and recommends patches for) vulnerabilities in the application code base, but cannot thwart attacks against any remaining issues. Thus, static measures are often useful before deployment of a WA when code patching is reasonably simple to perform and runtime measures after deployment when code patching can be costly to perform. There is also a combination of them, hybrid approaches, which involve both static analysis for vulnerabilities and run-time analysis of incoming requests. An example of this type of tool is AMNESIA [22].

Static approaches involve measures to find and remove vulnerabilities in the application codebase. This category includes black box testing, disabling unnecessary responses, software patching, type-safe API's, and static code analysis.

Black box testing [14, 20, 21] involves running automated scanners or fuzzers on deployed WAs without viewing server-side source code. One such example is WAVES [23].

Disabling unnecessary responses [12, 14, 17, 19] involves removing any application response messages that are not needed to provide its desired service. For example, any SQL database errors should be eliminated, unnecessary WSDL and UDDI information should be removed and Web server software query responses should be limited. If this countermeasure is successfully implemented it forces the attacker to use "blind" techniques.

Software patching is not discussed by any of the studied papers. However, it is clear that it is of importance towards the success of an attack – many organizations do not aim to "reinvent the wheel" and instead deploy commercial-of-the-shelf (COTS) software. Such applications are maintained through software updates by developers which address known vulnerabilities found in their products. Typically, software patching is implemented through an automated patch management tool such as Shavlik [24].

Type-safe API's [2, 14] involves using a development environment that is built to function in a secure and reliable fashion. In essence, this countermeasure defines a rule set for allowed code and how different parts of an application exchange information. For instance, how a PHP application is allowed to communicate with an SQL database. If a developer writes code that does not comply with the rule set defined within the type-safe API an error is produced, notifying the developer of the proper syntax as defined by the API. An examples of this type of countermeasure is SQL DOM [25].

Static code analysis [2, 11, 14, 20, 21] involves detecting vulnerabilities by analyzing the application source code. That is, to learn of the control or data would flow at runtime without actually executing the code. An example static code analysis tool is Pixy [26].

Runtime approaches involve detecting and thwarting ongoing attacks through, e.g., a set of predefined signatures. This category includes content based rejection, query modification and intrusion detection systems.

Content based rejection [2, 14, 21] involves analyzing the structure of requests to see if they conform to a model of expected queries. If not, the request is considered to be malicious and as such rejected. One such approach involves creating two *grammatical representations* of input statements using finite state machines or parse trees, one with and one without user input. If the representations do not match the user input is considered to involve a malicious command. An example of this approach is SQLGuard [27]. The perhaps most common type of content based rejection countermeasure in practice is *proxy filters* [12, 14, 17–21] (e.g., application firewalls and gateways) which intercepts calls to WAs to check if requests are malicious (i.e., if they match blacklisted signatures). An example of such countermeasure is Cisco Application Velocity [28]. Thirdly, a popular approach is *dynamic taint analysis*; to mark certain input (e.g., POST) as dangerous and evaluate if it is used in a malicious fashion. An example of this approach is SecuriFly [29].

Query modification [2, 11, 14, 20, 21] involves countermeasures aimed to modify queries using predefined functions such as cryptographic keys [2, 14] or through escaping characters [11, 20, 21]. This is also the main difference from content based rejection – query modification accepts modified versions of all input. Both methods as such naturally have pros and cons. An example query modification countermeasure is SQLrand [30].

Intrusion detection systems (IDS) [14, 20, 21] involves detecting source code injection attacks. This category differs from the other runtime approaches in the sense that an IDS merely detect, and not thwart, malicious requests. As such, if an IDS is setup to thwart detected issues this categorization treats it as a content based rejection technique (or query modification technique in case it accepts modified input). Intrusion detection systems can be both signature and anomaly based [31]. A signature based IDS have a predefined set of signatures for malicious requests and alarms if a request matches such a signature. An anomaly based IDS is trained on what type of requests that are "normal" and can thus in theory differentiate regular traffic from malicious traffic. A common WA IDS is Apache Scalp [32].

3   Hypothesized Metamodel

An EA model describes an organization in terms of the artifacts of business and IT, as well as their interrelationships. An EA metamodel is a description language used when creating EA models. Various EA metamodels have been proposed, for example, general metamodels such as ArchiMate [33] and metamodels for analysis of specific properties such as modifiability [34] and data accuracy [35]. The metamodel presented in this paper is based on the concepts of an existing EA metamodel for cyber security risk analysis, namely, the Cyber Security Modeling Language (CySeMoL) [36]. This section gives a brief overview of the concepts of CySeMoL of relevance to this paper. The reader is referred to [36] for a more detailed description of CySeMoL.

3.1   The Cyber Security Modeling Language

The CySeMoL covers a variety of attacks such binary code injections, flooding attacks, abuse of obtained privileges and social-engineering attacks (it does however not cover WA injections). The main objective of CySeMoL is to allow users to create models of their architectures and make calculations on the likelihood of different attacks being successful. Security expertise is not required from the user as the model includes theory on how attributes in the object model depend on each other. In other words, users must only model their system architectures and properties.

The entities in CySeMoL includes various IT components such as `Operating System` (e.g., Windows XP) and `Firewall`, processes such as `Security Awareness Program` (i.e., IT security training) and `Zone Management` (i.e., security maintenance of network zones), and personnel (`Person`). Each entity has a set of attributes that can be either attacks or countermeasures. These attributes are related in various ways. For example, the credentials of personnel can be social engineered – but the likelihood of this attack being successful depends on whether the person has undergone security awareness training or not. Each attribute in CySeMoL has a binary range (True / False), i.e., the likelihood of an attack being successful and the likelihood of a countermeasure being functional.

3.2   A Hypothesized Metamodel

The attributes found during the literature review (cf. Section 2) can be mapped to four entities: the WA itself (`WebApplication`), the process for developing the WA (`SoftwareDevelopmentProcess`), the process for maintaining the WA (`SoftwareMaintenanceProcess`) and whether there is an intrusion detection system monitoring the WA (`IntrusionDetectionSystem`). An overview of the metamodel can be seen in Fig. 1. Each entity is associated with a set of attributes with binary ranges (i.e., true or false). An attribute can be either an attack (a means of compromising the entity) or a countermeasure (a means to counter attacks). `WebApplication` is the only entity which is associated to attacks – an attacker can achieve an intended *result* (e.g., denial of service) by exploiting a known or unknown domain-specific language or dynamic language *vulnerability*. The presence of vulnerabilities in turn depend on the presence of *countermeasures* applied during development and maintenance of the WA, and if there is an intrusion detection system present, i.e., whether `IntrusionDetectionSystem.Deployed = True`. Due to these relational dependencies, the user of the model only needs to specify the states of attributes without parents (i.e., attributes without any arrows directed towards them), which in practice means the countermeasures.

The countermeasures corresponding to `SoftwareDevelopmentProcess` and `SoftwareMaintenanceProcess` next to completely overlap. However, two measures differ between them: Type-safe API's are only used during development of a WA as they require the application codebase to be written using specific constraints. Similarly, automated patch management is a tool that only can be used for finished applications. Also, automated patch management can unlike the remainder of the countermeasures due to its nature only mitigate known vulnerabilities.

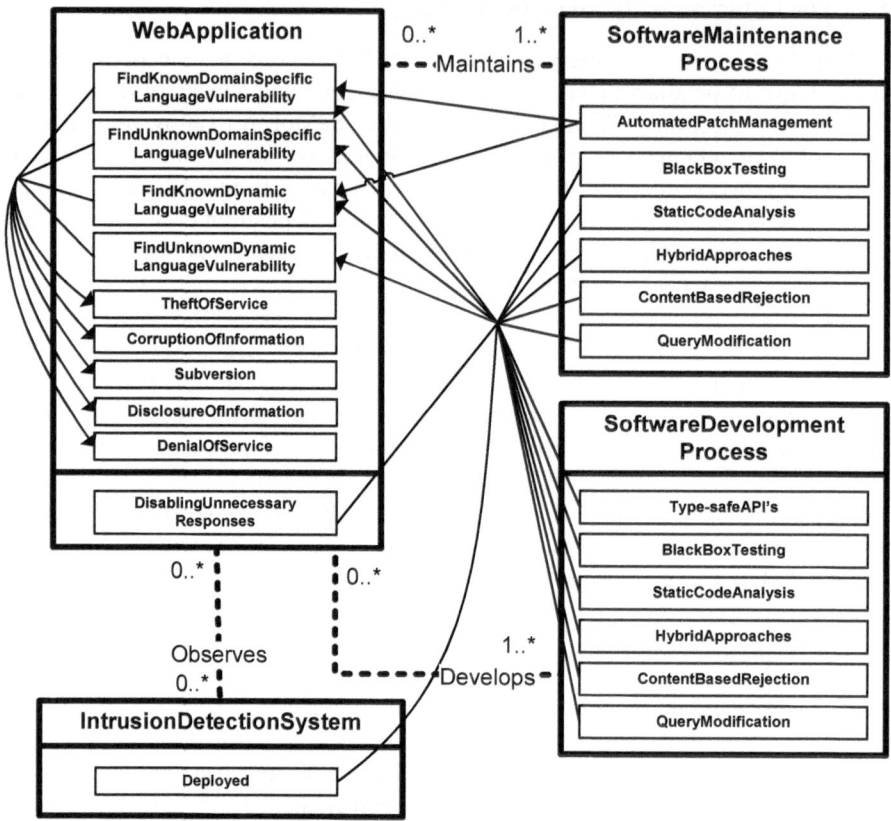

Fig. 1. A hypothesized metamodel for WA injections

4   Methodology for Revising the Hypothesized Metamodel

The complexity of this research means that it will be difficult to validate the metamodel using an experimental approach. Given such a scenario expert judgment can be justified as a means of estimation [37]. This study utilizes a combination of interviews and a workshop in order to revise the hypothesized metamodel (cf. Fig. 1).

4.1   Population and Sampling

In terms of the expert categories described in [38] individuals that are expert judges are desirable. Studies of experts' calibration have concluded that experts are well calibrated in situations with learnability and with ecological validity [39]. Learnability comes with models over the domain, the possibility to express judgment in a coherent quantifiable manner and the opportunity to learn to from historic predictions and outcomes. Ecological validity is present if the expert is used to making judgments of the type of questions they are asked. An individual that has significant and up to date professional experience from working with WA security testing should likely possess both learnability and ecological validity. This type of individual can be seen as the population of the present study.

The respondents used during the present study were identified through peer-review by prominent members of Swedish OWASP chapters. Each of the six individuals participating in the study had significant and fresh experience from professional work with WA security.

4.2   Data Collection

This study utilizes a combination of three semi-structured interviews and a workshop with three individuals, all carried out face-to-face. Due to the complexity of the matter effort was spent to enforce reliability of results. That is, the original layout and scope of the data collection was somewhat changed according to the focus area(s) of the respondents. For example, no answers were forced, the scales were allowed to be switched for a ranking system, and the respondents were allowed to traverse from the original scope if needed. For example, if they wanted to discuss a particular countermeasure in greater detail. As a consequence, more time was spent on those matters the respondents perceived to be of greater importance for the topic of the study.

The interviews and the workshop all had the same general approach. A summary of this methodology is described below. The approach consisted of two main objectives: (i) to study what aspects of the hypothesized metamodel that should be revised, and (ii) to estimate the general effectiveness of different countermeasures given the revised metamodel defined by the respondent(s), i.e., what attribute relations that should be present in the metamodel.

4.2.1   Revision of Hypothesized Metamodel

The first part of the interview or workshop concerned describing the topic of the study and the outline of the event. After this the respondents were given a graphical description of the proposed metamodel (cf. Fig. 1) and introduced to the concepts of it. The second part concerned the countermeasures of the metamodel. Effort was spent to identify if the abstraction levels of the countermeasures were reasonable given the scope of the study and if any countermeasures should have been changed, removed or added. A specific focus during this phase was placed on that the countermeasure must be applicable in practice, i.e., it must be readily available to practitioners and reasonably effortless to deploy and manage. The third part concerned the difference between known and unknown vulnerabilities; if this concept should be changed, and elicit the dependencies between countermeasures and the variables of this type. The fourth part involved if the employed types of WA injection attacks were useful (i.e., attacks for domain specific and dynamic language vulnerabilities), or if some aspects should have been revised. It also involved eliciting the dependencies between countermeasures and attack types – if any countermeasure was more competent at mitigating some attack types than others. The fifth part concerned the different categorized results of successful attacks (e.g., denial of service); if anything should be revised, and whether any countermeasure was more viable for mitigating attacks of different outputs than others.

4.2.2   Estimations of the Effectiveness of Countermeasures

The sixth part concerned identifying dependencies between the different countermeasures (using the information identified in step 1-5). That is, what combination of approaches that provide significantly greater effectiveness (and which that do not). The seventh part involved quantitatively scoring each countermeasure according to its mean effectiveness and variance (using the dependencies and information identified in the previous steps) through a scale of 1-5. In terms of mean effectiveness, 1 meant "do not increase the difficulty of successful attack" and 5 "greatly increases the difficulty of successful attack", and in terms of variation 1 meant "very small variation" and 5 "very high variation". To decrease ambiguity, the respondents were told that the variation was "if you would pick two countermeasures at random from the countermeasure category, how much would their effectiveness typically differ?". This quantitative scoring was carried out for one countermeasure at a time until all had been scored.

4.2.3   Respondents Part of the Study

The first interview (I1) lasted for 1.5 hours. The respondent of this interview had 7 years of relevant professional experience and works with software penetration testing in general; finding vulnerabilities in software written in, for example, C++, JavaScript, and PHP. Respondent 1 had also significant previous professional experience from network penetration testing.

The second interview (I2) lasted for 2.5 hours and involved a respondent with 10 years of WA security experience that works within the area of WA security. For instance, penetration tests of software written in PHP, Perl or .NET, and communications with database solutions such as SQL. This individual also performed occasional network penetration tests.

The third interview (I3) lasted for 1.5 hours and involved a respondent with 12 years experience who did not presently work, but had previously done so, with software penetration testing. This individual works as the chief technology officer of an enterprise specializing in WA security. For instance, penetration tests of WAs and security awareness training of developers. This individual is required to inhibit knowledge of all of these aspects.

The workshop (WS) lasted for 3 hours and involved three respondents whom all performed similar work as the second respondent. These individuals had 7, 3, and 3 years of professional experience from WA security. Notable is that the two respondents with 3 years of professional experience of WA injections had worked extensively for many years on the matter before having it as a main profession.

5   A Metamodel Revised by Expert Judgment

This section concerns data collected through three interviews and a workshop. To make results more pedagogical, the opinions by the three respondents of the workshop are unified at all occurrences where complete consensus was reached between them. Agreement among experts is also used as a basis for revising the hypothesized metamodel (cf. Fig. 1). Consensus was chosen for this purpose as it has been shown to outperform competing indicators of expert calibration [40].

5.1   Changes to the Metamodel Prescribed by the Experts

This section describes the revisions that the experts recommended for the hypothesized metamodel.

5.1.1   Type of Attacker

This variable is not part of the hypothesized metamodel. However, the type of attacker in question came up very early during each session – the skill level of the studied attacker was perceived to greatly affect the effectiveness of the countermeasures. Each of these discussions resulted in two basic categories of attackers: Advanced Persistent Threats (*APT*) and *Noise*. An APT is an experienced attacker that knows how to cover its tracks [41]. Noise, or a script kiddie, is an attacker that has a very limited cyber security experience and depend a lot on automated tools created by more experienced hackers [41]. It is expected that the effort required to defend against an APT is much higher than for a noise attack [41].

5.1.2   Changes to Attack Types

None of the respondents thought that the effectiveness of any of the studied countermeasures were significantly dependent on the type of attack that is conducted – at least not on a level that would suit the purpose of the current study. For example, the respondents of the workshop denoted that it can be more difficult to find dynamic language vulnerabilities (e.g., OS Command injections) than domain-specific language vulnerabilities (e.g., SQL injections) as there traditionally are no error messages provided during the probing. Such vulnerabilities are likely easier to find through white box analysis rather than black box analysis. However, given the purpose of the study, the respondents did not perceive it is useful to detail these aspects. Consequently, this category is removed from the metamodel.

5.1.3   Changes to Results of Attacks

As for the *type of attack*, all respondents thought that the variables of the *attack result* category (cf. Section 2.4) should be aggregated into a single variable. That is, the different countermeasures are not significantly more effective at preventing, for example, denial of service attacks compared to attacks which aim to corrupt information. Thus, this category is removed from the metamodel.

5.1.4   Changes to Vulnerabilities

All of the respondents perceived that there was a significant difference in effectiveness of the countermeasures depending on whether the vulnerability and exploit was known to the public at large or not. As such, the qualitative structure regarding this variable is the same as the variables presented in Section 2.3.

5.1.5   Changes to Countermeasures

The results from each data collection event are fairly similar in terms of recommended changes to the concepts of the hypothesized metamodel (cf. Fig. 1). There are however a few notable suggestions by the experts.

Table 2. Recommended revisions to countermeasures

Countermeasure	I1	I2	I3	WS
Software patching	None	None	None	None
Disabling unnecessary responses	None	None	None	Revise[a]
Black box testing	None	None	None	Revise[b]
Type-safe API's	Remove	None	None	None
Static code analysis	None	None	None	-
Hybrid approaches	Remove	Remove	Remove	Remove[c]
Content based rejection	None	Revise[d]	Revise[d]	Revise[d]
Query modification	Remove	Remove	Remove	None
Intrusion detection systems	None	Revise[e]	Revise[e]	Revise[e]
Disabling unnecessary services	Add	-	-	-
Developer security training	Add[f]	Add	Add	Add[f]
A formalized development process	-	-	Add	-

[a] Change for Configuration management.
[b] Change for Vulnerability scanning.
[c] Effective, but not used in practice.
[d] Change for Web Application Firewall (prevent).
[e] Change for Web Application Firewall (detect).
[f] Important, but difficult to estimate and categorize.

One notable recommendation was to replace Content based rejection and Intrusion Detection Systems for Web Application Firewalls (WAF), a common type of countermeasure that often is employed after deployment of a WA. A WAF can be configured to automatically prevent detected attacks or to report of their occurrence to human operators.

Another notable revision prescribed by the experts was removal of hybrid approaches. The experts believed that this would be an effective solution in the future, but not something that was practically available at the time of the study.

A third notable revision made by suggestion of the experts was replacing query modification by the broad category of developer security training. A developer that have been security trained can be perceived to both be able to produce more secure code and be able to apply countermeasures such as static code analysis in a more effective way [14, 20].

5.2   Estimates on the Significance of Relations between Attributes

This section describes the estimates made by the experts on the effectiveness of the countermeasures, both alone and in combination with others'. I.e., it analyzes the significance of the attribute relations of the metamodel.

5.2.1   Effectiveness of Individual Countermeasures

The quantitative estimates made by the respondents can be seen in Table 3. These estimates are made under the assumption that no countermeasure other than the one studied is present. The effectiveness of the countermeasures was studied based on the revised metamodel as seen by the experts (cf. Section 5.1). As the respondents prescribed removing attributes related to *the type of attack* and *the results of attacks* the hypothesized dependencies regarding these attributes were not analyzed. While the experts made estimations for both known and unknown vulnerabilities, data is only provided for known vulnerabilities. This as the experts depicted exactly the same values for them - the only difference is that software patching per definition is not effective for unknown security issues.

Table 3. Estimates on the effectiveness of countermeasures by experts

Countermeasure	Mean effectiveness (1-5)								Mean variance (1-5)							
	Noise				APT				Noise				APT			
	I1*	I2	I3	WS	I1*	I2	I3	WS	I1	I2	I3	WS	I1	I2	I3	WS
Software patching** (SP)	A	4	5	5	A	1	4	2	4	5	1	1	4	5	1	2.5
Disabling unnecessary responses (DUR)	D	2	5	4	D	2	3	4	4	5	2	4	4	5	2	4
Black box testing (BBT)	B	3	3	4	B	3	2	4	2	2	2	4.5	2	2	3	3.5
Type-safe API's (API)	-	4	5	5	-	4	3	5	-	4	1	1	-	4	2	1
Static code analysis (SCA)	E	4	5	-	E	3	4	-	2	2	2	-	2	2	3	-
Web Application firewall, reject (WAFr)	C	4	5	3.5	C	3	5	2	3	3	2	3	3	3	2	2
Web Application firewall, detect (WAFd)	F	1	5	2	F	1	4	1	3	3	3	2	3	3	3	2
Developer security training (DST)	-	4	4	-	-	4	4	-	-	4	4	-	-	4	4	-

* Ranked from A: most effective to F: least effective.
** Only effective for known vulnerabilities.

Notable is that the first interview respondent did not feel comfortable providing quantitative estimates, and thus instead ranked the countermeasures according to their effectiveness (from A: most effective to F: least effective).

The consensus is rather low regarding mean effectiveness and mean variance for most countermeasures. There is however agreement regarding some aspects: all respondents perceive software patching to be the most effective countermeasure given known vulnerabilities and noise attacks. Each respondent perceives black box testing to be fairly effective against noise attacks, and all interview respondents seemingly agree that the variance in effectiveness between tools in this category is fairly low. It is however clear that all attribute relations are required to be modeled.

5.2.2   Effectiveness of Countermeasures in Combination

Oftentimes, the effectiveness of one countermeasure can be thought of as dependent on the presence of another. None of the respondents however perceived that the dependencies between countermeasures would depend on the type of attacker in question. As a consequence, two dependence matrixes were scored during each data collection event: one for known vulnerabilities (cf. Table 4) and one for unknown vulnerabilities. As for the estimates on the effectiveness of individual countermeasures, the only difference between the two dependence matrixes analyzed by the respondents is that software patching is not applicable for unknown vulnerabilities. As a consequence, all combinations including software patching in the matrix for unknown vulnerabilities were denoted as not effective by all respondents. This is also the reason for why it is not shown in the paper.

In Table 4, a "0" means that the combination of countermeasures is not perceived to result in a significant increased effectiveness. A "+" means that the combination is perceived to result in a significantly increased effectiveness. A "*" means that a data collection event did not detail the perceived dependency, i.e., it was not part of the metamodel proposed by the respondent(s) (cf. Section 5.1). Interview 1 is the first symbol in each cell, interview 2 the second, interview 3 the third, and the workshop the fourth. For example, the combination between type-safe API's and prevention based WA firewalls has the symbols "*++0". That is, respondent 1 (I1) did not have type-safe API's in the perceived metamodel; and thus the first symbol is"*". The second and third respondents (I2 and I3) perceived a significant increased effectiveness of the combination, and thus the second and third symbols are "+". The respondents of the workshop (WS) did not perceive the combination to result in any significant increased effectiveness, and as such the fourth symbol is "0".

Table 4. Dependencies between countermeasures regarding known vulnerabilities. "+" denotes perceived increased effectiveness, "0"denotes no perceived increased effectiveness, and "*"denotes that the combination was not scored.

	SP	DUR	BBT	API	SCA	WAFr	WAFd
DUR	++++						
BBT	0+++	++++					
API	*0++	*+++	*+++				
SCA	00+*	+++*	+++*	*++*			
WAFr	+0++	++++	+++0	*++0	+++*		
WAFd	00+0	00+0	00+0	*0+0	00+*	00+0	
DT	*0+*	*++*	*++*	*++*	*++*	*++*	*++*

Most combinations are perceived to have significant increased effectiveness. However, the perceived non-significance of combinations involving WAFd could seem curious. The reason behind this is that all respondents except the third interview respondent perceived that the attack would be successful long before the eventual response by operators seeing the alarm. The third respondent viewed a WAFd as a good indicator of overall threat, something the respondent believed to be of importance.

5.3   Revised Metamodel for Web Application Injections

An overview of revised metamodel, formulated from the consensus by the six respondents, can be seen in Fig. 2. All attributes except `Attacker.Skill` and `WebApplicationFirewall.Functionality` have state-spaces of {*True, False*}. `Attacker.Skill` can take the states {*Noise, Advanced Persistent Threat*} and `WebApplicationFirewall.Functionality` can take the states {*Prevent, Detect and report*}.

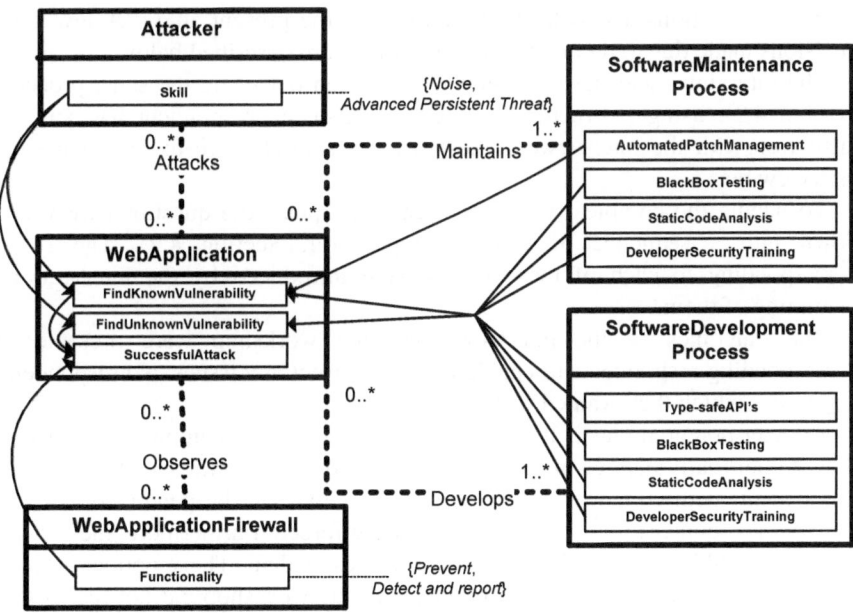

Fig. 2. A revised metamodel of WA injections

As can be seen, while the entity `Attacker` has been added, the revised metamodel is significantly smaller than the hypothesized metamodel (cf. Fig. 1). A less detailed metamodel is preferable due to two main reasons: (i) it requires less effort to manage by the modeler and (ii) it performs better when simulating attacks using the CySeMoL calculation engine (due to a smaller total state-space).

6   A Critical Discussion of Research Findings

While the hypothesized metamodel is constructed from peer-reviewed domain theory, the revised metamodel is subject to potential bias, for example, bias due to the chosen sample [42]. The findings from this study are based on assessments by a small number of individuals. Even though these individuals were selected based on recommendations by their peers and had significant experience on the topic it is difficult to say that their estimates are representative for the population at large. Nevertheless, while it is important to recognize these delimitations, the results provided by this paper give valuable input that no previous study has analyzed.

Another bias that is important to address is the bias due to the data collection methodology [42]. Moser [42] argue that there are three possible bias in terms of data collection methodology through interviews: (i) bias due to the interaction of interviewer and respondent, (ii) bias due to factors connected with the questionnaire, and (iii) bias due to factors connected with the setup and circumstances of the interview. The author describes a list of factors that are of importance in order to limit bias due to these three factors; these suggestions were consulted when formulating interview questions and collecting data during the present study. A few significant decisions made due to recommendations by [42] are described below.

The interviews and the workshop were carried out using the same procedure (cf. Section 4.2), using a structured procedure. Also, no respondent had any previous affiliation with the interviewer. These aspects should serve to reduce the threat of interview bias.

To handle the complexity of the research purpose, the questionnaire was broken down into a sequence of different topics (cf. Section 4.2). The sub-session corresponding to each of these topics were introduced by the interviewer at the beginning of them.

The outcomes of the interviews and the workshop were presented to the corresponding respondents to enable them to correct any issues. No respondent found any issues which they wanted to address.

Another potential bias is that respondents, if pressured, can provide answers which they do not really believe in [43]. This is of particular significance to a study such as the present, with complex high-level questions that can be perceived as difficult to answer. To counter this issue, no answers were forced. Furthermore, the format of the estimates could be changed to better suit the respondent. These options were utilized twice in the present study: the respondents of the workshop did not feel comfortable addressing static code analyzers, and the first respondent did not feel comfortable with the measurement scale of "mean effectiveness". As a consequence, the interview instrument was revised during these occasions to accommodate their needs.

7   Conclusions

While decision support on an abstraction level of actual security tools (e.g., WAVES or AMNESIA) is useful in the sense that it provides *accurate* information it would end up with a significant number of options which would require large amounts of resources to parse – something which rarely is available, especially as WA injection attacks only constitute one small piece of the "security puzzle". The present work presents a metamodel that can aid enterprise decision makers with a language for modeling WA injections and estimating the effectiveness of different countermeasures for the attack type. However, in order to decide upon a specific WA security solution, practitioners' are naturally in need to consider more precise and valid knowledge.

The results also indicate that some countermeasures do seem to outperform others (i.e., some attribute relations are more significant than others). The expert judgment indicate that type-safe API's is the most effective approach – given that there is a possibility to manipulate the software code base. Under other circumstances, things are a bit different. Software patching is the most effective means of handling publicly known security issues and noise attacks. Static code analysis is the most effective for known security issues and APT, and for unknown security issues for both noise and APT. Hybrid based countermeasures are not a useful method of countermeasure as of yet, but are perceived to be a more viable solution in the future. It is also often times perceived to be useful to employ combinations of different countermeasures.

Finally, it is important to acknowledge that the results presented in this paper only provide tentative findings - in order to enable sound conclusions regarding the topic of the study there is a need to perform further studies with more samples that can be perceived representative of the population.

References

1. Tsipenyuk, K., Chess, B., McGraw, G.: Seven pernicious kingdoms: A taxonomy of software security errors. IEEE Security & Privacy 3, 81–84 (2005)
2. Mitropoulos, M.D., Karakoidas, V., Louridas, P., Spinellis, D.: Countering Code Injection Attacks: A Unified Approach. Information Management & Computer Security 19, 3 (2011)
3. One, A.: Smashing the stack for fun and profit (1996), http://ezano-secu.fr/securite/Applicatif/Smashing_the_stack_for_fun_and_profit.pdf
4. OWASP: 2010 OWASP Top 10 (2010)
5. Martin, B., Brown, M., Paller, A., Kirby, D., Christey, S.: 2011 CWE/SANS Top 25 Most Dangerous Software Errors (2011)
6. Scholtea, T., Balzarottib, D., Kirdac, E.: Have things changed now? An empirical study on input validation vulnerabilities in web applications. Computers and Security (2012)
7. Suto, L.: Analyzing the Effectiveness of Web Application Firewalls (2011)
8. Hansman, S., Hunt, R.: A taxonomy of network and computer attacks. Computers & Security 24, 31–43 (2005)
9. Howard, J.D.: An analysis of security incidents on the Internet 1989-1995 (1997)
10. NVD: National Vulnerability Database, http://nvd.nist.gov/
11. Pietraszek, T., Berghe, C.: Defending Against Injection Attacks Through Context-Sensitive String Evaluation. In: Valdes, A., Zamboni, D. (eds.) RAID 2005. LNCS, vol. 3858, pp. 124–145. Springer, Heidelberg (2006)

12. Sidharth, N., Liu, J.: IAPF: A Framework for Enhancing Web Services Security. The Computer Society (2007)
13. Vorobiev, A., Han, J.: Security attack ontology for web services. In: Second International Conference on Semantics, Knowledge and Grid, SKG 2006, p. 42. IEEE (2006)
14. Halfond, W., Viegas, J., Orso, A.: A classification of SQL-injection attacks and countermeasures. In: Int'l Symp. on Secure Software Engineering, Citeseer (2006)
15. Zuchlinski, G.: The Anatomy of Cross Site Scripting (November 2003)
16. Álvarez, G., Petrovi, S.: A new taxonomy of web attacks suitable for efficient encoding. Computers & Security 22, 435–449 (2003)
17. Stamos, A., Stender, S.: Attacking Web Services: The Next Generation of Vulnerable Enterprise Apps. In: BlackHat 2005 (2005)
18. Klein, A.: Blind XPath Injection. Whitepaper from Watchfire (2005)
19. Ghourabi, A., Abbes, T., Bouhoula, A.: Experimental analysis of attacks against web services and countermeasures. In: Proceedings of the 12th International Conference on Information Integration and Web-based Applications & Services, pp. 195–201. ACM (2010)
20. Nystrom, M.: Sql injection defenses. O'Reilly Media, Inc. (2007)
21. Shin, Y., Williams, L.: Toward A Taxonomy of Techniques to Detect Cross-site Scripting and SQL Injection Vulnerabilities (2008)
22. Halfond, W.G.J., Orso, A.: AMNESIA: analysis and monitoring for NEutralizing SQL-injection attacks. In: Proceedings of the 20th IEEE/ACM International Conference on Automated Software Engineering, pp. 174–183. ACM (2005)
23. Huang, Y., Huang, S.: Web application security assessment by fault injection and behavior monitoring. In: Proceedings of the 12th International Conference on World Wide Web, pp. 148–159. ACM (2003)
24. Shavlik: Shavlik Technologies, http://www.shavlik.com/
25. McClure, R.A., Krüger, I.H.: SQL DOM: compile time checking of dynamic SQL statements. In: Proceedings of the 27th International Conference on Software Engineering, pp. 88–96 (2005)
26. Jovanovic, N., Kruegel, C., Kirda, E.: Pixy: A static analysis tool for detecting web application vulnerabilities (short paper). In: Proceedings aof the 2006 IEEE Symposium on Security and Privacy, pp. 258–263. IEEE Computer Society (2006)
27. Buehrer, G., Weide, B.W., Sivilotti, P.A.G.: Using parse tree validation to prevent SQL injection attacks. In: Proceedings of the 5th International Workshop on Software Engineering and Middleware, pp. 106–113. ACM (2005)
28. Cisco: Cisco Application Velocity System, http://www.cisco.com/en/US/products/ps6499/index.html
29. Livshits, B., Martin, M., Lam, M.S.: Securifly: Runtime protection and recovery from web application vulnerabilities (2006)
30. Boyd, S.W., Keromytis, A.D.: SQLrand: Preventing SQL Injection Attacks. In: Jakobsson, M., Yung, M., Zhou, J. (eds.) ACNS 2004. LNCS, vol. 3089, pp. 292–302. Springer, Heidelberg (2004)
31. Denning, D.E.: An intrusion-detection model. IEEE Transactions on Software Engineering, 222–232 (1987)
32. apache-scalp: Apache log analyzer for security, http://code.google.com/p/apache-scalp/
33. Lankhorst, M.: Enterprise architecture at work: Modelling, communication and analysis. Springer-Verlag New York Inc. (2009)

34. Lagerström, R.: Analyzing system maintainability using enterprise architecture models. Journal of Enterprise Architecture 3, 33–42 (2007)
35. Närman, P., Holm, H., Johnson, P., König, J., Chenine, M., Ekstedt, M.: Data accuracy assessment using enterprise architecture. Enterprise Information Systems 5, 37–58 (2011)
36. Sommestad, T., Ekstedt, M., Holm, H.: The Cyber Security Modeling Language: A Tool for Assessing the Vulnerability of Enterprise System Architectures. IEEE Systems Journal (to be available)
37. Cooke, R.: Special issue on expert judgment. Reliability Engineering & System Safety 93, 655–656 (2008)
38. Weiss, D.J., Shanteau, J.: Empirical Assessment of Expertise. Human Factors: The Journal of the Human Factors and Ergonomics Society 45, 104–116 (2003)
39. Bolger, F., Wright, G.: Assessing the quality of expert judgment: Issues and analysis. Decision Support Systems 11, 1–24 (1994)
40. Holm, H., Sommestad, T., Ekstedt, M., Honeth, N.: Indicators of expert judgment and their value: an empirical investigation in the area of cyber security. Expert Systems: The Journal of Knowledge Engineering (to be available)
41. Bodeau, D.J., Graubart, R., Fabius-Greene, J.: Improving Cyber Security and Mission Assurance Via Cyber Preparedness (Cyber Prep) Levels. In: 2010 IEEE Second International Conference on Social Computing, pp. 1147–1152. IEEE (2010)
42. Moser, C.: Interview bias. Review of the International Statistical Institute, 28–40 (1951)
43. Crespi, L.: The interview effect in polling. Public Opinion Quarterly 12, 99–111 (1948)

The Extended
Enterprise Coherence-Governance Assessment*

Roel Wagter[1,3], Henderik A. Proper[2,3], and Dirk Witte[4]

[1] Ordina, Nieuwegein, The Netherlands
[2] CRP Henri Tudor, Luxembourg
[3] Radboud University Nijmegen, Nijmegen, The Netherlands
[4] Logica, Amstelveen, The Netherlands
roel.wagter@ordina.nl, erik.proper@tudor.lu,
dirk.witte@logica.com

Abstract. The Enterprise Coherence-governance Assessment (ECA) instrument is a part of the GEA (General Enterprise Architecting) method for enterprise architecture. Based on experiences with this assessment instrument in a range of real world projects, the ECA has been improved, leading to the *extended* Enterprise Coherence-governance Assessment (*e*ECA). So far, the *e*ECA been applied in 54 organizations with a total of 120 respondents. The paper discusses the context in which the *e*ECA instrument was developed, the instrument itself, as well as the results of the assessment study in which the instrument was applied.

The ECA and *e*ECA use the term 'coherence' rather than the more common term 'Business-IT alignment', since the latter is generally associated with bringing only 'Business' and 'IT' inline. The word coherence, however, stresses the need to go beyond this. Enterprise coherence involves connections and synchronisation between *all* important aspects of an enterprise. 'IT' and 'Business' just being two of these aspects.

Keywords: business-IT alignment, enterprise coherence-governance assessment, enterprise architecture, enterprise architecture maturity model, enterprise coherence framework.

1   Introduction

As reported on in earlier work [27, 28], the Enterprise Coherence-governance Assessment (ECA) is an instrument that enables organizations to assess their ability (maturity) to effectively govern their *enterprise coherence*, where *enterprise coherence* is understood to be:

> *The extent to which all relevant aspects of an enterprise are connected, to the extend necessary to let the enterprise meet its desired results.*

The *relevant aspects* in the above definition are organization dependent. Even more, the clarity with which an organization has articulated these aspects is one of the parameters

---

* This work has been partially sponsored by the *Fonds National de la Recherche Luxembourg* (www.fnr.lu), via the PEARL programme.

S. Aier et al. (Eds.): TEAR 2012 and PRET 2012, LNBIP 131, pp. 218–235, 2012.

determining their ability/maturity to govern enterprise coherence. In [28] we have discussed the concept of the (organization specific) *coherence dashboard*, which enables organizations to precisely express the relevant aspects that need to be connected.

As argued in [27, 28], and demonstrated in terms of a report on a real world case in [29], enterprise coherence involves more than aligning 'Business' and 'IT'. Enterprise coherence involves connections and synchronisation between *all* important aspects of an enterprise. 'IT' and 'Business' just being two of these aspects. Other (practise oriented) sources also explicitly acknowledge the need for enterprise architecture methods to look well beyond the traditional Business-to-IT stack. Consider for example: [9, 12, 7].

The ECA is part of the GEA (General Enterprise Architecting) method for enterprise architecture. The development of GEA was initiated in 2006 by the consultancy firm Ordina (www.ordina.nl) as a multi-client[1] research project. The decision by Ordina to embark on the development of the GEA method originated from the observation that large scale enterprise transformations fail more often than not, while, in their experience, existing methods and frameworks for enterprise architecture failed to contribute to the success of enterprise transformation efforts [26, 25]. Furthermore, a survey held at the start of the GEA research programme, showed that the experience was not limited to Ordina alone, but was equally shared among a broad range of client organizations participating in the programme. The underlying issues were also considered grave enough for the participating client organizations to indeed co-invest in the programme in terms of time and money, in the GEA research programme. The initial survey also resulted in the driving hypothesis of the GEA programme: *the overall performance of an enterprise is positively influenced by a strong coherence among the key aspects of the enterprise, including business processes, organizational culture, product portfolio, human resources, information systems, IT support, etc.*

A first step in the GEA programme was the the development of (the first version of) an Enterprise Coherence-governance Assessment (ECA) [27] instrument to obtain a clearer understanding of the challenges to enterprise coherence, and its potential impact on organizational performance. This assessment was consequently applied at the participating client organizations. Based on the outcomes of these ECA studies the GEA research programme focussed its efforts on four research objectives:

1. *Definition of the indicators and factors influencing/defining enterprise coherence.*
2. *Identification of the impact of enterprise coherence on organizational performance.*
3. *An instrument to assess an enterprise's level of coherence.*
4. *Instruments to guard/improve the level of coherence in enterprises.*

In its current form, the GEA method comprises three core ingredients [25]. Next to the Enterprise Coherence-governance Assessment (ECA) [27] that allows organizations to

---

[1] During different stages of the GEA research programme, the members of the programme included: ABN AMRO; ANWB; Achmea; Belastingdienst – Centrum voor ICT ICTU; ING; Kappa Holding; Ministerie van Binnenlandse Zaken en Koninkrijksrelaties; Ministerie van Defensie; Ministerie van Justitie – Dienst Justitiële Inrichtingen; Ministerie van LNV – Dienst Regelingen; Ministerie van Landbouw, Natuur en Voedselkwaliteit; Nederlandse Spoorwegen; Ordina; PGGM; Politie Nederland; Prorail; Provincie Flevoland; Rabobank; Radboud University Nijmegen; Rijkswaterstaat; UWV; Wehkamp.

assess their ability to govern coherence during enterprise transformation, it contains an Enterprise Coherence Framework (ECF) [28] and a (situational) Enterprise Coherence Governance (ECG) [25] approach. The latter includes the identification of specific deliverables/results to be produced, the processes needed to produce these deliverables/results, as well as an articulation of the responsibilities and competences of the people involved. The ECF enables enterprises to set up their own *coherence dashboard*. This, enterprise specific, dashboard enables senior management to govern the coherence between key aspects of an enterprise during transformations.

As already identified in [27], there was a need to extend future versions of the ECA with a.o. characteristics from additional sources, including IT Architecture Capability Maturity Model [6], the Normalized Architecture Organization Maturity Index (NAOMI) [19], the Enterprise Architecture Score Card [21] and the NASCIO Enterprise Architecture Maturity Model [1]. Next to that, practical experiences in using the ECA is client projects, also produced feedback that called for an update/extension of the original ECA. This paper reports on the resulting new version of the ECA, the *extended Enterprise Coherence-governance Assessment (eECA)*.

The remainder of this paper is structured as follows. In Section 2 we briefly explain two other parts of the GEA method that are relevant to the discussions in this paper. More specifically, this involves the Enterprise Coherence Framework (ECF) and the Enterprise Coherence Governance (ECG) approach. In Section 3 then we continue with the presentation of the current version of the *eECA* instrument. Before concluding, Section 4 continues with a report on the application of the instrument in the context of 54 large Dutch organizations with a total of 120 respondents.

2 Relevant Elements of the GEA Method

In this section, we briefly summarize the ECF and ECG parts of the GEA method. They will be used as a basis for our discussion of the *eECA*.

2.1 The Enterprise Coherence Framework

The ECF (Enterprise Coherence Framework) [28] defines a series of cohesive elements and cohesive relationships, which together define the playing field for an enterprise's cohesion. By making the definition of these elements explicit in a specific enterprise, one gains insight in the 'state of cohesion' while also being able to assess the impact of potential transformations. This then enables a deliberate governance of enterprise coherence in terms of an organization specific *coherence dashboard* (also making the organization specific 'relevant aspects', that make up enterprise coherence, explicit). The ECF is defined in terms of two levels and their connections: the level of *purpose* and the level of *design*. At the level of purpose, the following cohesive elements have been identified, which are based on commonly known concepts from strategy formulation [15, 4, 3]:

Mission – a brief, typically one sentence, statement that defines the fundamental purpose of the organization that is enduringly pursued but never fulfilled.

Vision – a concise statement that defines the mid to long-term goals of an organization.
Core values – defines the desired behaviour, character and culture of an organization.
Goals – the visions quantified success factors, which become the reference points to
    judge the feasibility of strategies.
Strategy – forms a comprehensive master plan stating how the corporation will achieve
    its mission and goals.

The presence of a well documented enterprise mission, vision, core values, goals and
strategy are preconditions to be able to determine the content of the core factors on the
design level of the organization and they are the essential resources for this determination. The cohesive elements at the design level are:

Perspective – an angle from which one wishes to govern/steer/influence enterprise
    transformations. The set of perspectives used in a specific enterprise depend very
    much on its formal and informal power structures. Both internally, and externally.
    Typical examples are culture, customer, products/services, business processes, in-
    formation provision, finance, value chain, corporate governance, etc. In GEA's
    view, it are really these perspectives that need to be aligned, in order to achieve
    enterprise coherence on the design level.
Core concept – a concept, within a perspective, that plays a key role in governing the
    organization from that perspective. Examples of core concepts within the perspec-
    tive Finance are, for instance, "Financing" and "Budgeting".
Guiding statement – an internally agreed and published statement, which directs de-
    sirable behaviour. They only have to express a desire and/or give direction. Guiding
    statements may therefore cover policy statements, (normative) principles [10] and
    objectives.
Core model – a high level view of a perspective, based on, and in line with, the guiding
    statements of the corresponding perspective.
Relevant relationship – a description of the connection between two guiding
    statements of different perspectives.

The cohesive elements and their relationships are illustrated in Figure 1.

GEA' concept of *perspective* is related to the notion of *viewpoint* as defined in architecture standards such as TOGAF [23] and the IEEE definition of architecture [22].
The two notions are, however, not equal. A perspective is an angle from which one
wants to *govern* enterprise transformations. Given a this desire to govern transformations from a certain angle, a viewpoint can be defined that captures the way one wants
to view/contemplate from this angle. As such, one might say that GEA's notion of
perspectives could be defined as *transformation-governance viewpoints*.

The set of perspectives used by a specific enterprise on its *coherence dashboard* is
highly organization specific. This set is not likely correspond to the cells of well known
design frameworks such as Zachman [32] or TOGAF's content framework [23]. Such
frameworks, however, can indeed play an important role in the development of the core
models within the different perspectives. Based on their respective underlying "design
philosophies", these more design/engineering oriented frameworks provide a way (1)
to ensure completeness and consistency from an engineering point of view, (2) to en-
force/invite a specific line of reasoning on the design/construction of the enterprise and

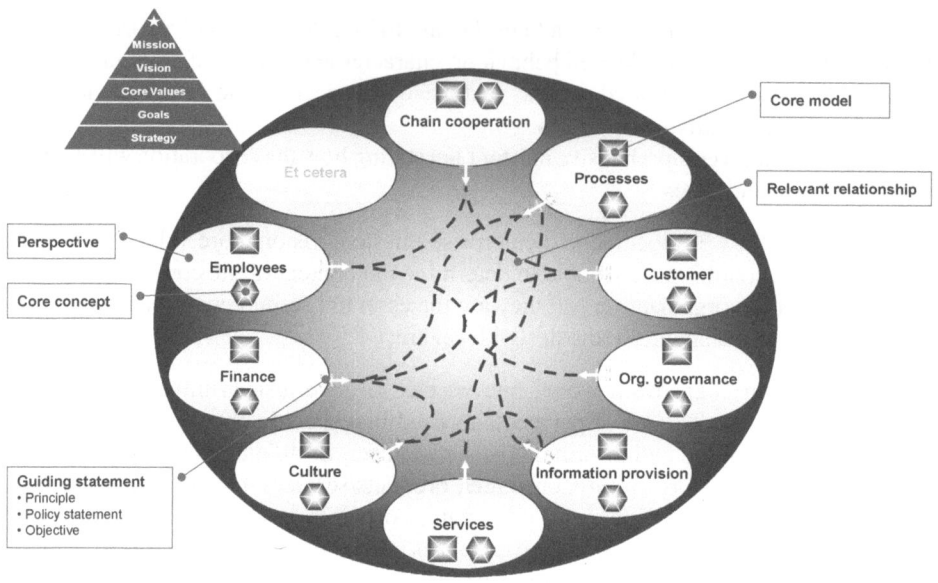

Fig. 1. The Enterprise Coherence Framework

(3) to classify/structure the different core models. In the creation of the latter models, modelling languages such as ArchiMate [13], e3Value [8], BPMN [16], or UML [17] can be used.

2.2   Enterprise Coherence Governance

As reported in [28], at the start of the GEA programme 31 requirements were formulated that should we met by the GEA method. The ECA [27] and ECF [28] only partly covered those requirements. Additional method components were needed, in particular a process to for enterprise coherence governance, the ECG. Collectively, the ECA, ECF and ECG method components cover the GEA concepts as depicted in Figure 2, where one concept builds on the other leading to a coherent whole. All the promises of the EA-vision, such as improving the coherence of the organization, should be achieved through the execution of EA-processes. The execution of the EA-processes results in EA-products that will direct change programmes and via this the enterprise coherence. EA-people are needed to carry out the EA-processes and to produce the EA-products. The EA-people need, to execute the EA-processes, allocation of means in terms of time, budgets and tools. The EA-people and the execution of EA-processes need to be governed by EA-governance. And finally to store a maintainable formal description of the formulation of the EA-Vision, EA-processes, EA-products, EA-people and EA-governance there is need for an EA-methodology. The ECG binds all these concepts together in a workable procedure for doing enterprise architecture [30, 25].

Enterprise Architecture

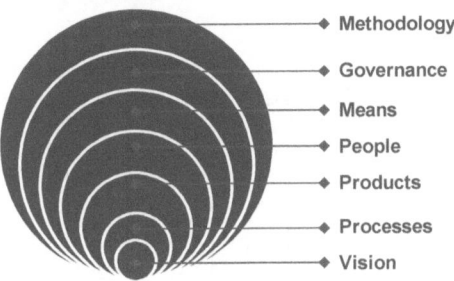

Fig. 2. Coherent set of GEA concepts

3   The Extended Enterprise Coherence-Governance Assessment

The original ECA [27] was based on the original requirements on the GEA method. The *e*ECA is based on the experiences gained from the development of the additional GEA components (ECF and ECG), as well as practical experiences in using the ECA and the GEA components in client engagements. See for example [29]. We also used additional sources to derive characteristics to assess an enterprise's coherence, e.g. from the Architecture Maturity Model embedded in the Dynamic Enterprise Architecture (DYA) method [31], the IT Architecture Capability Maturity Model [6], the Normalized Architecture Organization Maturity Index (NAOMI) [19], the Enterprise Architecture Score Card [20], and the NASCIO Enterprise Architecture Maturity Model [1].

A problem with the existing architecture maturity models, is that they have a traditional business-IT alignment focus. In our view the cause of this is that existing enterprise architecture approaches and frameworks, such as Zachman [32], DYA [31], Abcouwer et al. [2], Henderson & Venkatraman [11], TOGAF [23], IAF [24] and Archi-Mate [14], take an "engineering oriented" style of communicating with senior management and stakeholders in general. The architecture frameworks underlying each of these approaches are very much driven by "engineering principles", and as such correspond to a Blue-print style of thinking about change [5]. The requirements on the GEA method, however, suggested the need to use another style of thinking. More in terms of stakeholder interests, formal and informal power structures within enterprises, and the associated processes of creating win-win situations and forming coalitions. In terms of De Caluwé [5], this is more the Yellow-print style of thinking about change. In the GEA programme, the Yellow-print line of thinking was taken as a starting point rather than the Blue-print line of thinking. This was done by taking the perspective that the actual social forces and associated strategic dialogues within an enterprise should be taken as a starting point, rather than the frameworks of existing architecture approaches suggesting the full make ability of an organization. This is also the reason why (see Section 2) GEA's enterprise architecture framework does not have an a priori defined set of perspectives. The relevant set of perspectives is highly organization dependent.

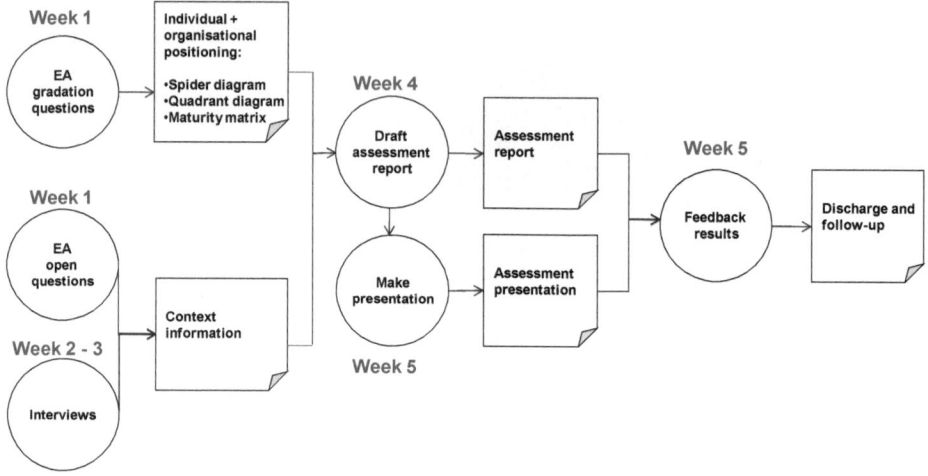

Fig. 3. Application of the *e*ECA (processes and products)

For this reason we have adopted the maturity levels used in the aforementioned architecture maturity models, but as aspects on which the maturity level should be determined we use the GEA components, including the requirements and cohesive elements which these components are based on. The *e*ECA developed by the members of the innovation programme GEA consists of three interrelated parts. See Figure 3.

These parts consists of a set of fifty gradation questions (see ++++ Appendix 1), a set of twenty three open questions (see +++ Appendix 2) and an interview based on these questions. To conduct these 3 parts including the following reporting activities takes a turnaround time of approximately 5 weeks by a given number of about 25 respondents. Each of the gradation questions must be answered by one of the following gradations: '*not at all*', '*minor*', '*sufficient*', '*largely*', '*entirely*', '*do not know*'. By choosing the latter possibility the appropriate question does not count in the calculations to determine the maturity level.

The gradation questions result in three types of reporting: a '*spider diagram*', a '*quadrant diagram*' and a '*maturity matrix*' both on individual level and on organizational level. The answers on the open questions provide the necessary context information. Also include the open questions a number of cross-reference questions with respect to the gradation questions. After receiving the answers on the gradation questions and the open questions the interviews are planned. During the interviews the interviewer can ask more detailed questions about the gradation and open questions, but may also ascertain things that respondents not initially want to write down. Through conducting the interview the interviewer completes the context information obtained through the open questions. First we discuss the above mentioned diagrams and maturity matrix.

3.1 Spider Diagram

In the spider diagram, the answers to the 50 gradation questions are plotted on a four-point scale on the seven axes representing the seven GEA components. See Figure 4. So one can quickly see how each of the maturity levels of the GEA components are measured and also the diagram gives an insight about the overall maturity level of the EA function. Is the shaded area in the spider diagram relatively small one can say that in the opinion of the respondent(s) the organization has not done enough to EA. The diagram would be completely shaded in case all the questions were answered with 'entirely'.

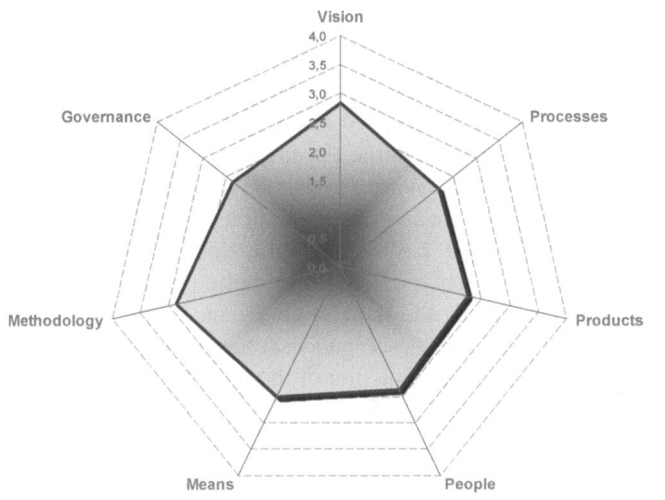

Fig. 4. Maturity score, of a single employee, on the seven GEA components

3.2 Quadrant Diagram

The results of the answers to the fifty rating questions are reflected in a quadrant model, as depicted in Figure 5. This model is composed of two axes, the horizontal axis represents the level of development of the EA Vision and the vertical axis represents the level of the application of the EA Vision. These axes represent two dimensions of the governance of enterprise coherence, which correspond to the aforementioned GEA parts that need to be developed. Each quadrant has a lavel, characterizing the hypothetical (maturity) state of the enterprise as a function of the maturity of the EA function. In short, the scores are computed as follows:

$$S^{\text{development}} \triangleq \Sigma_{i=1}^{7} W_i^{\text{development}} \cdot C_i$$

$$S^{\text{application}} \triangleq \Sigma_{i=1}^{7} W_i^{\text{application}} \cdot C_i$$

$$C_i \triangleq \Sigma_{j=1}^{50} w_{i,j} \cdot Q_j$$

where:

$W^{development}$ is a vector expressing the relative weight of a GEA component towards the development of an EA vision.

$W^{application}$ is a vector expressing the relative weight of a GEA component towards the application of an EA vision.

w is a matrix expressing the relative contribution of a question to the score of a given GEA component.

Q is a vector expressing the score that was given to a specific question, ranging from 0 ('*not at all*') to 4 ('*entirely*').

The axis 'EA vision development' describes the extent to which an organization's body of knowledge concerning the governance of enterprise coherence has been made explicit, in particular the EA-vision and the EA-methodology. Is there a vision about enterprise architecting? Has the vision been translated into a methodology and how an organization wants to use it (is there an implementation plan)? Is there a real ambition for the application of EA? The axis 'EA vision application' describes the extent to which an organization actually operates the body of thought, in particular the EA-processes, the EA-products, the EA-means and the EA-governance. The correlation between the two axes results in four quadrants. Each quadrant has a label, characterizing the hypothetical state of the enterprise as a function of the maturity of the EA function. This is illustrated for one employee in Figure 5.

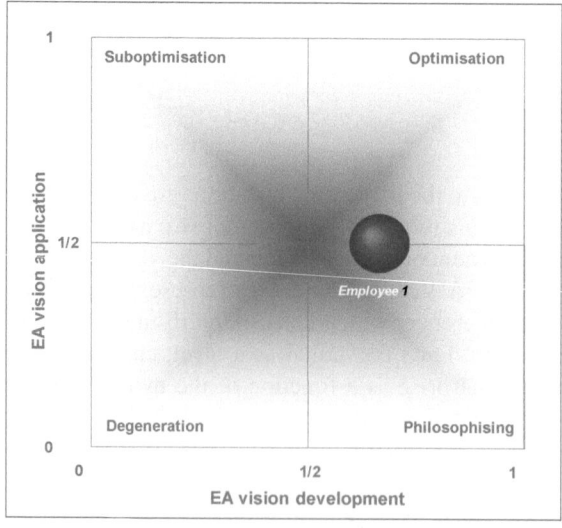

Fig. 5. Example individual (Employee₁) perception of the maturity of the EA function

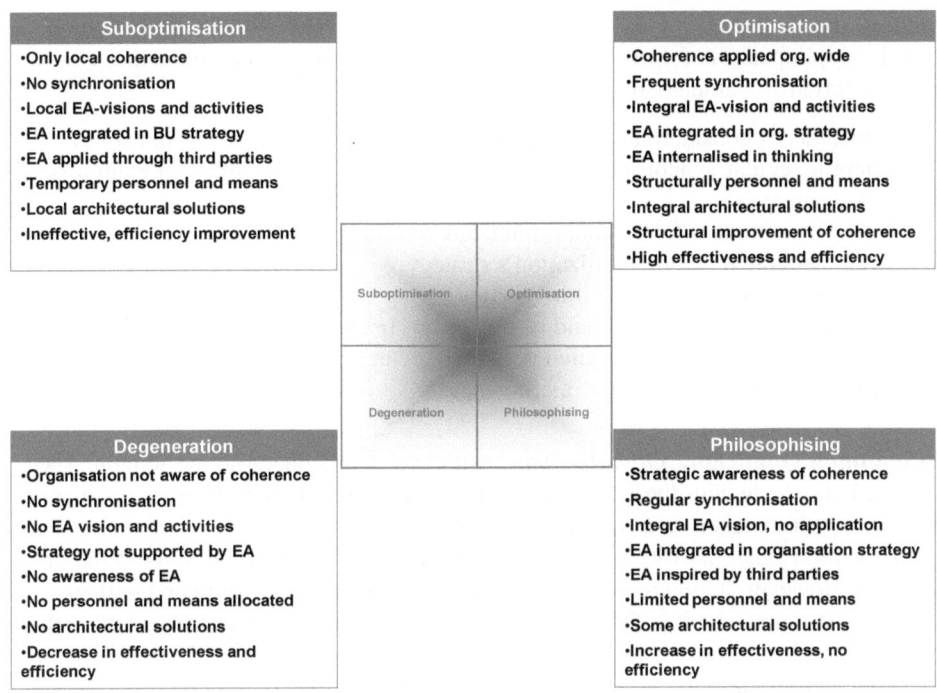

Fig. 6. Characteristics of organizations as a function of EA maturity

Figure 6 provides a brief outline of the characteristics per quadrant. Below we will discuss the quadrants in more detail, while Table 1 provides anonymized real world examples of fifty-four organizations and their positioning in relation to the quadrants.

Degenerating Quadrant. If an organization has no vision about enterprise architecting and also does not know how to apply this form of management then the organization scores in this quadrant. Coherence in the organization will continue to degenerate with proportionate effects on the organization's performance. Characteristic aspects for this quadrant are:

- Coherence is not considered an important aspect.
- There is little or no synchronisation between representatives of the important aspects of the enterprise.
- No worth mentioning EA vision or activities.
- Strategy is not supported by EA.
- There is no awareness of EA.
- No people or resources are allocated to EA.
- Solutions are designed and implemented without architecture.
- Decrease in effectiveness and efficiency.

Philosophical Quadrant. There is a vision of enterprise architecting, this is also translated into how it should be implemented, but it is not developed beyond terms of 'paper' and 'goodwill'. It is not 'exploited', let alone implemented. There may be some basic increase in effectiveness. A basic level/awareness of governance of enterprise coherence may be developed. Therefore, there is an increased likelihood that things move in 'the right direction'. Characteristic aspects for this quadrant are:

- Coherence is considered to be a strategic aspect throughout the organization.
- There is regular synchronisation between representatives of the important aspects of the enterprise.
- There is an integral EA vision, limited EA activities in the enterprise's operations.
- EA is integrated in the organization's strategy.
- EA is inspired especially by third parties.
- A limited number of people and resources has been allocated to EA.
- Some solutions are implemented with architecture.
- Increase in effectiveness, not in efficiency.

Suboptimal Quadrant. Organizations positioned in this quadrant are inhabited with do-ers, individuals with their own perception, belief and ideas about enterprise architecting, who have taken their own local actions. Models have been designed that perhaps offer the most potential for reinforcing governance of coherence throughout the organization. However, these are not synchronized/aligned and are formulated in their own jargon. The biggest flaw is that the managers, who should use these products in their decision making processes, do not know that they exist or they do not know how to understand and interpret them. A number of things are done well, but these are not good things by definition. Throughout the organization there is some increase in efficiency. Characteristic aspects of this quadrant are:

- Coherence is only experienced as an enterprise aspect locally and in different ways.
- There is no synchronisation between representatives of the important enterprise aspects.
- Local EA perceptions and interpretations and activities are on the agenda.
- EA is integrated in one or more department strategies.
- EA is applied particularly by third parties.
- Local and frequent temporary allocation of people and resources to EA.
- Local solutions are implemented with architecture.
- Not effective, increase in efficiency.

Optimization Quadrant. In this quadrant, vision and action go hand in hand. The organization has a clear understanding of enterprise architecting and knows how to use it to its advantage. The managers take strategic decisions from their integral and actual knowledge about the meaning and design of the organization. The organization works on optimising management and implementation processes that are supported by EA processes and products. The good things are done well, in other words efficiency and effectiveness go hand in hand. Characteristic aspects for this quadrant are:

- Coherence is experienced as an important aspect and governance of coherence is applied throughout the organization.
- There is frequent synchronisation between representatives of the important aspects of the enterprise.

- EA is used as a directional framework to guide decision making processes resulting in integral solutions addressing all important aspects of the enterprise on strategic, tactical and operational levels and aligning the interdependencies between them.
- EA is integrated in the organization's strategy.
- The notion of necessity of enterprise coherence is internalized in the thinking and action of its leaders and managers.
- People and resources are structurally assigned to the EA function.
- Integral solutions for major issues are implemented with architecture.
- Structural improvements in coherence within the organization is on the agenda.
- There is high effectiveness and efficiency.

When the questions from the questionnaire have been answered, then the respondents' scores offer a good starting point for follow up actions to improve the governance of enterprise coherence. In particular, by using the following questions as drivers:

- How can the (possible) differences in the positioning of the maturity of EA according to the respondents be explained?
- Which steps for improvement can be made in connection with the positioning on an aggregate level (average of the respondents' scores)?

The discussion arising from the first question may urge employees adjusting their views, which would have provided a very different score. Especially employees who are supposed to make use of EA products, but did not have the courage to do so, will find a platform to express their dissatisfaction. Or if not, it may lead to new concepts for the whole group. The organization's score is an average of the given scores from the individual respondents. However, as we will see in the next section, the average is not just computed, but rather determined in joined sessions with all the involved respondents. During such a session, individual respondents may change their scores in response to improved insights into their understanding of the actual situation in the organization and/or insight into the question itself. If the results of the organization's score are in the optimization quadrant then people will be reap the benefits of applying coherence governance. It is important to maintain this optimization and to stay alert so as not to fall back into old habits. In other words, a position in a quadrant is not a fixed state, but subject to constant change. More specific, you need to put a constant effort in keeping of improving the enterprise coherence otherwise it will gradually decline into a state of degeneration. If the positioning falls in one of the three following quadrants: degeneration, philosophising or sub-optimisation, then this offers greater possibilities for improvement. If the score falls in the degeneration quadrant this means that one must first take a step to the right as well as directly upwards, before the step can be made towards optimization (see Figure 7). These approaches correspond to organization's management styles. One organization may first want to consider it properly, as a supporter of the Design School and another organization may want to initiate experiments first, as a supporter of the Learning School [18].

3.3 Maturity Matrix

The results of the answers of the fity rating questions are reflected in a weighted, not normalized score and showed in a maturity matrix, as depicted in Figure 8. This model

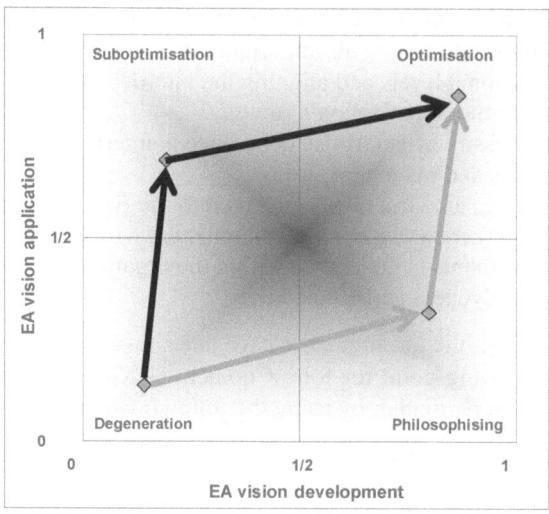

Fig. 7. EA maturity development scenarios

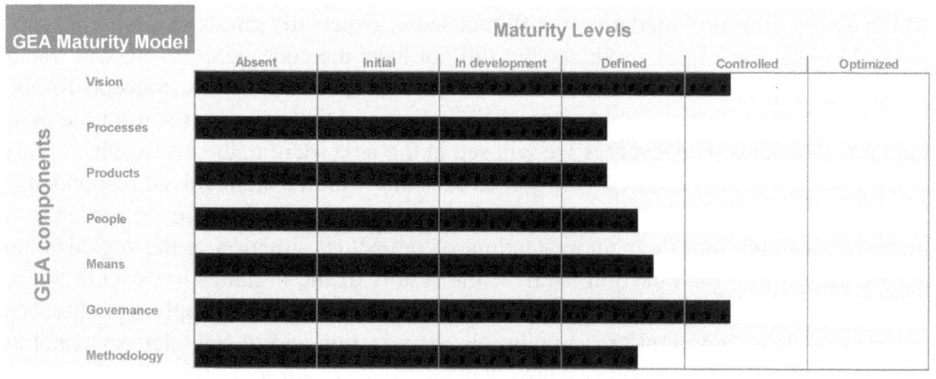

Fig. 8. Case illustration results *e*ECA plotted on the GEA Maturity Model

is composed of two axes, the horizontal axis represents the EA maturity levels and the vertical axis represents the set of GEA components. In the cells of appendix 3 'GEA Maturity Model@@ one will find the status of a GEA component on a certain maturity level as well as descriptions of on the axes presented maturity levels and GEA components. In practise, we plot the maturity scores of the GEA components as represented in Figure 8 on the figure as represented in appendix 3 ????? making the state of maturity in terms of the GEA components quickly visible.

Table 1. Participants *e*ECA in 2011

Market sector	Number of organisations	Number of respondents
Public	16	64
Finance	17	29
Industry	7	7
Rest	14	20
Total	54	120

4   Results of the Application of the *e*ECA

In 2011 we applied the *e*ECA with respect to the part of the grading questions in 54 organiza-tions with the participation of 120 respondents. We distinguished in this research four market sectors: Public, Finance, Industry and Rest. See Table 1 for the distribution of participating organizations per market and number of respondents.

In Figure 9 we show the results of the *e*ECA 2011 per market sector in a Spider Diagram. These diagrams provide the following insights. First all market sectors explores about the same efforts to enterprise coherence governance, in which the Finance sector

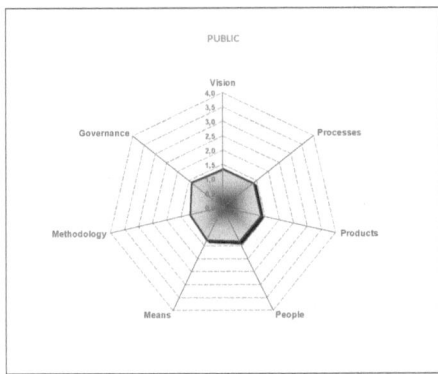
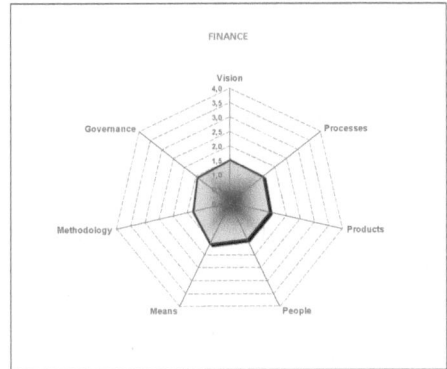
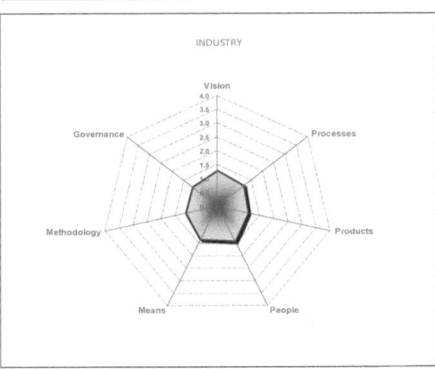
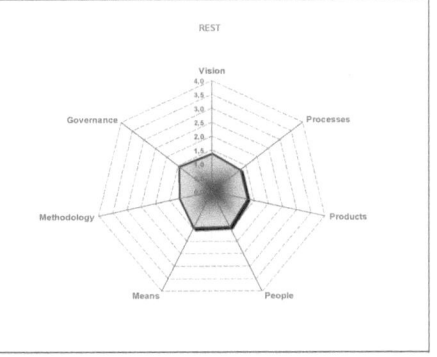

Fig. 9. Results of the *e*ECA 2011 plotted as spider diagrams

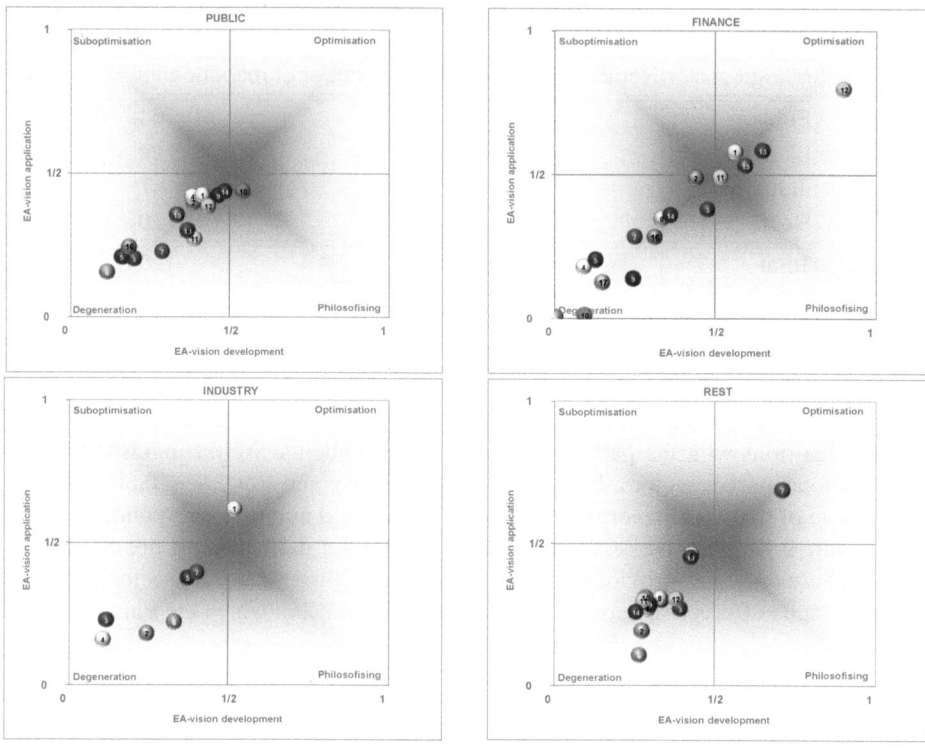

Fig. 10. Results of the *e*ECA 2011 plotted on the maturity quadrant diagram

scores a little higher. Compared to the other sectors the Finance sector scores, except for the component Means, for all GEA components on 1.5 points. Second, all market sectors do have a low score on enterprise coherence governance. If all the grading questions had been completed with 'entirely', the surfaces shown in Figure 9 would be fully shaded.

In Figure 10 we show the results of the *e*ECA 2011 per market sector on the GEA Quadrant Diagram. The numbered spheres in the quadrants represent the participating organizations. Figure 10 shows that 11.1% (6 of 54) of the organizations do have a score in the quadrant op-timisation. So 88.9% do not. A similar, but more limited study in [27], if less than 50% of the assessed organizations scores in the optimization quadrant. In that study we showed that 85.7% of the participants did not score in the optimization quadrant and that it clearly demonstrated the need for further research into the governance of enterprise coherence, in particular the development of a theory for the governance of enterprise coherence. With a similar score of 88.9% in our extended study of 2011, we confirm the aforementioned need.

In Figure 11 we show the results of the *e*ECA 2011 per market sector on the GEA Maturity Model. These maturity models provide the following insights. First, in all market sectors the GEA component 'Governance' scores lowest. Second, all market

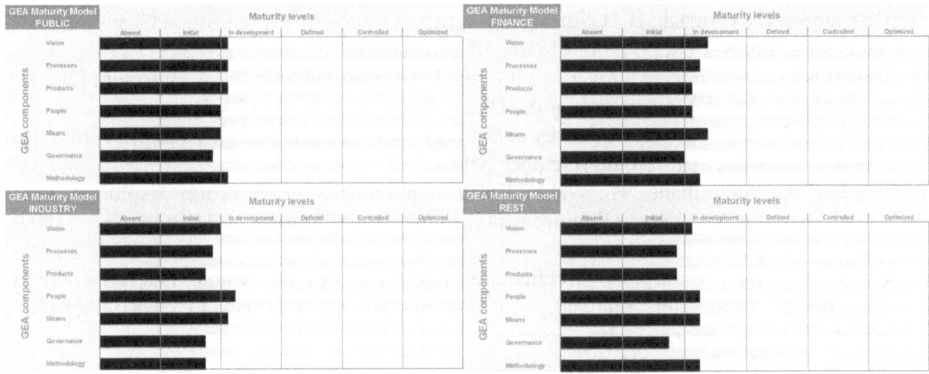

Fig. 11. Results of the eECA 2011 plotted on the GEA maturity model

sectors are at the begin-ning of the maturity level 'In development@@ in which the market sector 'Finance' is most far.

5   Conclusion

In this article we explored the Extended Enterprise Coherence-governance Assessment (eECA) instrument and the application of the eECA in 54 organizations in the Netherlands with 120 respondents in de market sectors Public, Finance, Industry and Rest. This instrument provides individual organizations with an important measure for positioning itself on a maturity scale, indicating the organization's ability to govern enterprise coherence. Also, it helps to provide the degree of maturity on the 7 components enterprise coherence governance consists of. Through this assessment, conducted in 2011, we have shown that 88.9% of the participating organizations lack enterprise coherence governance. Also we confirm with this assessment the result of a similar but more limited study carried out in 2007, which showed a corresponding percentage of 85.7%. Principles, design, procedure and backgrounds to the instrument were also discussed. The results of the assessment offer organizations useful arguments and insights for discussions, about the use of enterprise architecture as an instrument to achieve better governance of enterprise coherence.

References

1. Enterprise architecture maturity model version 1.3. Technical report, National Association of State Chief Information Officers (NASCIO), United States of America (2003), http://www.nascio.org/
2. Abcouwer, A., Maes, R., Truijens, J.: Contouren van een generiek model voor informatiemanagement. Primavera working paper, Universiteit van Amsterdam (1997) (in Dutch)
3. Chandler, A.D.: Strategy and Structure, Chapters in the History of the American Industrial Enterprise. The MIT Press, Cambridge (1969) ISBN-10: 0262530090
4. Collins, J., Porras, J.: Building Your Company's Vision. Harvard Business Review (1996)

5. De Caluwé, L., Vermaak, H.: Learning to Change: A Guide for Organization Change Agents. Sage publications, London (2003) ISBN-10: 9014961587
6. Department of Commerce, Government of the USA. Introduction - IT Architecture Capability Maturity Model. Government of the United States of America (2003)
7. Fehskens, L.: Deriving Execution from Strategy: Architecture and the Enterprise. In: Open Group Conference Amsterdam (October 2010)
8. Gordijn, J., Akkermans, H.: Value based requirements engineering: Exploring innovative e-commerce ideas. Requirements Engineering Journal 8(2), 114–134 (2003), doi:10.1007/s00766-003-0169-x
9. Graves, T.: Real Enterprise Architecture: beyond IT to the whole enterprise. Tetradian Books, Colchester, England, United Kingdom (2008) ISBN-13: 9781906681005, http://tetradianbooks.com
10. Greefhorst, D., Proper, H.A.: Architecture Principles – The Cornerstones of Enterprise Architecture. Enterprise Engineering Series. Springer, Berlin (2011) ISBN-13: 9783642202780, http://www.springer.com/business+%26+management/business+information+systems/book/978-3-642-20278-0
11. Henderson, J.C., Venkatraman, N.: Strategic alignment: Leveraging information technology for transforming organizations. IBM Systems Journal 32(1), 4–16 (1993)
12. Hoogervorst, J.A.P.: Enterprise Governance and Enterprise Engineering. Springer, Berlin (2009) ISBN-13: 9783540926702
13. Iacob, M.-E., Jonkers, H., Lankhorst, M.M., Proper, H.A.: ArchiMate 1.0 Specification. The Open Group (2009) ISBN-13: 9789087535025
14. Iacob, M.-E., Jonkers, H., Lankhorst, M.M., Proper, H.A., Quartel, D.A.C.: ArchiMate 2.0 Specification. The Open Group (2012) ISBN-10: 1937218003
15. Kaplan, R.S., Norton, D.P.: The Strategy-Focused Organization: How Balanced Scorecard Companies Thrive in the New Business Environment. Harvard Business School Press, Boston (2000) ISBN-10: 1578512506
16. Object Management Group. Business process modeling notation, v1.1. OMG Available Specification OMG Document Number: formal/2008-01-17 (January 2008)
17. OMG. UML 2.0 Superstructure Specification – Final Adopted Specification. Technical Report ptc/03–08–02 (August 2003)
18. Pettigrew, A., Thomas, H., Whittington, R.: Handbook of Strategy & Management. Sage Publications (2001) ISBN-13: 9780761958932
19. van der Raadt, B., Slot, R., Van Vliet, H.: Experience Report: Assessing a Global Financial Services Company on its Enterprise Architecture Effectiveness Using NAOMI, p. 218b (2007) ISBN-10: 0769527558, doi:10.1109/HICSS.2007.217
20. Schekkerman, J.: Enterprise Architecture Score Card. Technical report, Institute for Enterprise Architecture Developments, Amersfoort, The Netherlands (2004)
21. Schekkerman, J.: How to Survive in the Jungle of Enterprise Architecture Frameworks: Creating or Choosing an Enterprise Architecture Framework. Trafford Publishing, Victoria (2006) ISBN-13: 9781412016070
22. The Architecture Working Group of the Software Engineering Committee. Recommended Practice for Architectural Description of Software Intensive Systems. Technical Report IEEE P1471:2000, ISO/IEC 42010:2007, Standards Department. IEEE, Piscataway, New Jersey (September 2000) ISBN-10: 0738125180
23. The Open Group. TOGAF Version 9. Van Haren Publishing, Zaltbommel, The Netherlands (2009) ISBN-13: 9789087532307
24. Van't Wout, J., Waage, M., Hartman, H., Stahlecker, M., Hofman, A.: The Integrated Architecture Framework Explained. Springer, Berlin (2010) ISBN-13: 9783642115172
25. Wagter, R.: Sturen op samenhang op basis van GEA – Permanent en event driven. Van Haren Publishing, Zaltbommel, The Netherlands (2009) (in Dutch) ISBN-13: 9789087534066

26. Wagter, R., Nijkamp, G., Proper, H.A.: Overview 1th Phase - General Enterprise Architec-
    turing. White Paper GEA-1, Ordina, Utrecht, The Netherlands (2007) (in Dutch)
27. Wagter, R., Proper, H.A., Witte, D.: Enterprise Coherence Assessment Version. In: Harm-
    sen, F., Grahlmann, K., Proper, E. (eds.) PRET 2011. LNBIP, vol. 89, pp. 28–52. Springer,
    Heidelberg (2011)
28. Wagter, R., Proper, H.A., Witte, D.: A Practice-Based Framework for Enterprise Coherence.
    In: Proper, E., Gaaloul, K., Harmsen, F., Wrycza, S. (eds.) PRET 2012. LNBIP, vol. 120, pp.
    77–95. Springer, Heidelberg (2012)
29. Wagter, R., Proper, H.A., Witte, D.: Enterprise Coherence in the Dutch Ministry of Social
    Affairs and Employment. In: Huemer, C., Viscusi, G., Rychkova, I., Andersson, B. (eds.)
    Proceedings of the 7th International Workshop on Business/IT-Alignment and Interoperabil-
    ity (BUSITAL 2012). LNBIP. Springer, Berlin (2012)
30. Wagter, R., Stovers, R., Nijkamp, G., Proper, H.A.: GEA-processes and products, a closer
    examination. White Paper GEA-6, Ordina, Utrecht, The Netherlands (2007) (in Dutch)
31. Wagter, R., Van den Berg, M., Luijpers, J., Van Steenbergen, M.: Dynamic Enterprise Archi-
    tecture: How to Make It Work. Wiley, New York (2005) ISBN-10: 0471682721
32. Zachman, J.A.: A framework for information systems architecture. IBM Systems Jour-
    nal 26(3) (1987)

Designing Enterprise Architecture Management Functions – The Interplay of Organizational Contexts and Methods

Sabine Buckl[1], Florian Matthes[1], and Christian M. Schweda[2]

[1] Chair for Informatics 19, Technische Universität München
Boltzmannstr. 3, 85748 Garching, Germany
{sabine.buckl,matthes}@mytum.de
http://wwwmatthes.in.tum.de
[2] iteratec GmbH
Inselkammerstr. 4, 82008 München-Unterhaching, Germany
christian.schweda@iteratec.com
http://www.iteratec.com

Abstract. Enterprise architecture (EA) management is today a critical success factor for enterprises that have to survive in a continually changing environment. The embracing nature of the management subject and the variety of concrete goals that enterprises seek to pursue with EA management raises the need for management functions tailored to the specific demands of the using organization. The majority of existing approaches to EA management does account for the organization-specificity of their implementation, while concrete prescriptions on how to adapt an EA management function are scarce.

In this paper we present a development method for organization-specific EA management functions based on the idea of reusable *building blocks*. A building block describes a practice-proven solution to a recurring EA management problem. The theoretic exposition of the development method is complemented by a fictitious application example.

Keywords: Enterprise architecture management, enterprise architecture management function, situational method engineering, method base, building block-based design.

1 Introduction and Motivation

Alignment between business and IT is a major challenge for today's enterprises and in particular for their IT departments. In the past IT took a mere *provider role* fulfilling business requirements. In the future IT must also take an *enabler role* seeking to increase flexibility and adaptability of the provided business support. In order to facilitate the sketched transition [1, 2] and to support IT departments in taking this two-fold role, an overarching management function has to be set in place, targeting both business and IT aspects, but also accounting for *crosscutting aspects*, as strategies and projects. The latter is especially necessary

S. Aier et al. (Eds.): TEAR 2012 and PRET 2012, LNBIP 131, pp. 236–252, 2012.
© Springer-Verlag Berlin Heidelberg 2012

as a managed evolution of the organization inevitably connects to the strategies as drivers of organizational change and the projects as its vehicles. The enterprise architecture (EA) aims at such holistic understanding of "fundamental organization of the enterprise in its environment, embodied in its elements, their relationships to each other and to its environment, and the principles guiding its design and evolution" (adapted from ISO standard 42010 [3]).

Aforementioned holistic understanding forms the basis for EA management, that seeks to foster the mutual alignment of business and IT. As of today, many practitioners and researchers have formulated their particular perspective on EA management and have such promulgated the topic through enterprises (cf. [4–7]). Nevertheless, currently no broadly accepted step-by-step guideline for managing the EA exists. Some researchers doubt that a one-size-fits-them-all management approach satisfies the different EA management goals in the various organizational contexts, but that the approach has to be organization-specific (cf. [8–10]). Details on how to perform an adaptation of the EA management function are scarce. For example, The Open Group Architecture Framework [11, page 56-57] states that the *architecture development method* must be adapted, but abstains from providing information on how to perform these adaptations. This situation is similar to the one in software development, where albeit a general agreement on important activities as e.g. *requirements elicitation* or *testing*, various process models exist, which strongly differ concerning the linkages between the different activities and the level of detail in which the different activities are described. The concrete design of an EA management function varies from organization to organization (cf. [12–14]). This raises the research question of this article:

How does a development method for organization-specific EA management functions look like?

The presentation in this article continues the discussions from [15], where a method framework for EA management functions was introduced, see Figure 1. Based on the activities of this framework, we present re-usable building blocks for substantiated EA management processes. These building blocks are used in a method based on the idea of situational method engineering, as discussed in Section 2. The development method itself is discussed in detail in Section 3 and an application of the method in a real world case study is described in Section 4. Final Section 5 provides a critical reflection of the achieved results, the findings of applying the method, and hints to further areas of research.

2   Related Work – Situational Method Engineering

In [16, page 25] Harmsen introduces the idea of *situational method engineering* as an approach to "tailor and tune methods to a particular situation". The driving idea behind situational method engineering can be summarized as follows: "There is no method that fits all situations" [16, page 6]. Introducing the term *controlled flexibility* Harmsen elicits requirements for a method engineering approach, which accomplishes standardization and at the same time is flexible

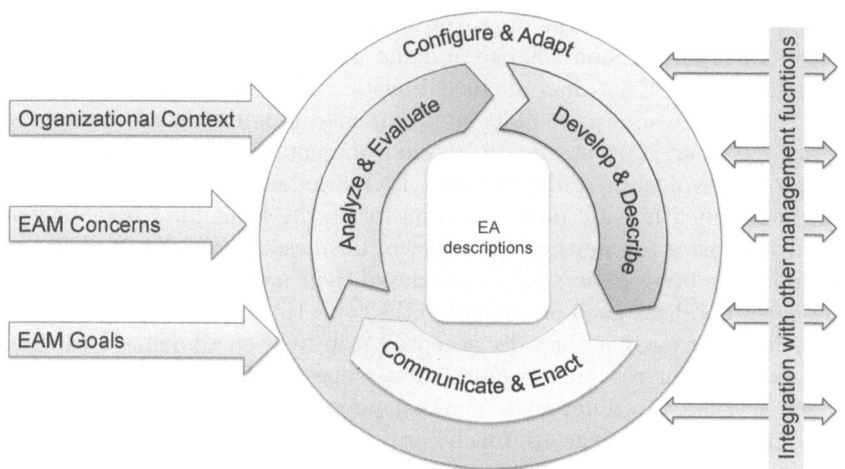

Fig. 1. Method framework for the EA management function

enough to match the situation at hand. A *situation* thereby refers to the combination of circumstances at a given point in time in a given organization [16]. In order to address these requirements, for each situation a suitable method – the so-called situational method – is *constructed*. This method takes into account the circumstances applicable in the corresponding situation. In the construction process uniform method fragments are selected, which can be configured and adapted with the help of formally defined guidelines.

The generic process to constructing situational methods consists of four steps. Input to the configuration process is the specific situation in which the method should be applied, e.g. the environment of the initiative, involved users, organizational culture, or management commitment. This situation is analyzed in the first step (*characterization of the situation*) to describe the application characteristics. The gathered information is used in the second step (*selection of method fragments*) to select suitable method fragments from the method base. Heuristics can thereby be applied to foster the selection process. In the third step (*method assembly*) the method fragments suitable for the characterized situation are combined to a situational method. During assembling method fragments, aspects like completeness, consistency, efficiency, soundness, and applicability are accounted for [16]. The actual use of the constructed situational method is performed in the last step (*project performance*). Figure 2 gives an overview on the construction process and illustrates the relationships between the different steps.

In addition to the construction process, Harmsen introduces in [16] the activity *method administration* that captures methodical knowledge, i.e. adds or updates method fragments based on feedback from the project performance step. The different method fragments in the method base are thereby characterized via criteria that facilitate the selection of fragments matching the given situation and goals. In the context of EA management we have to account for the

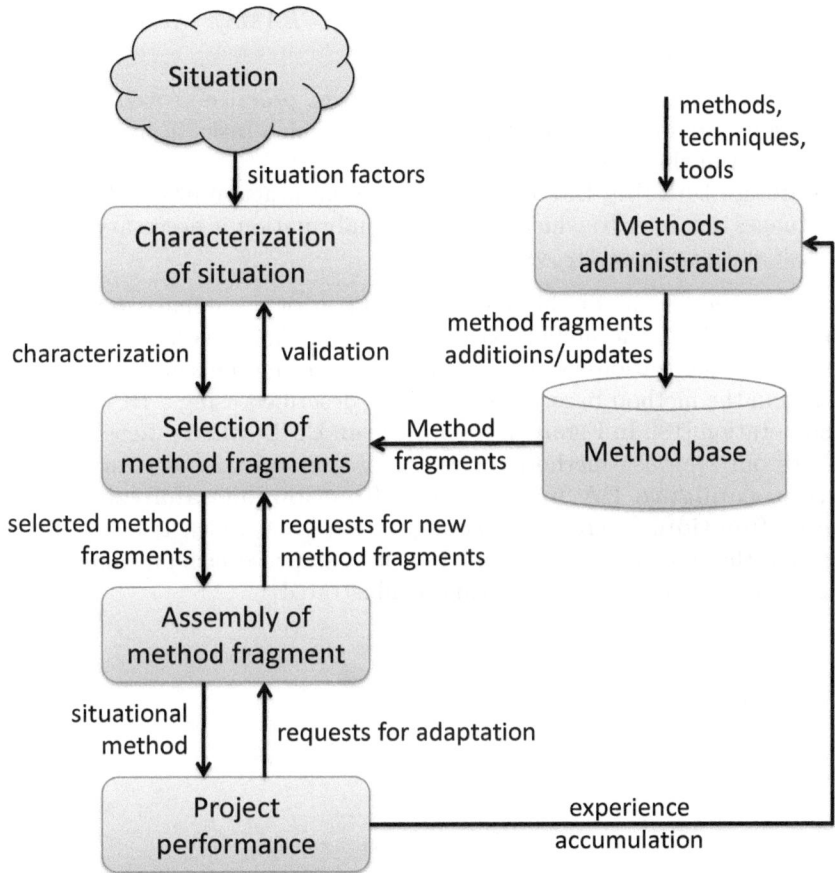

Fig. 2. The process of situational method engineering according to [16]

fact that these criteria are not *symmetrical*, i.e. that one method may target a criterion that is not applicable for another one. We reflect this peculiarity of the application field via a specific construction of the method base, resembling the structuring of a *design theory nexus* as presented by Pries-Heje and Baskerville in [17].

3   Developing an EA Management Function Using a Method Base

We present a method for developing an organization-specific EA management function based on best practices collected from literature and practice. These best practices are reflected in so-called *building blocks* that form a central contribution of our approach, a fact also reflected in the name of the approach:

building blocks for EA management solutions (BEAMS). We distinguish two types of building blocks, namely

- **Method building blocks (MBBs)** present practice-proven method prescriptions, i.e. describe who has to perform which tasks in order to address a problem in the situated context and
- **Language building blocks (LBBs)** present practice-proven EA modeling languages, i.e. refer to which EA-related information is necessary to perform a task and how it can be visualized.

With the method focus of this paper, we put critical emphasis on the MBBs which together form the *method base* of BEAMS. The **development method** for designing organization-specific EA management functions builds on the MBBs contained in the method base. The MBBs are described using a BPMN-like syntax and notation [18]. In Figure 3, we provide an UML *activity diagram* [19] that illustrates our stepwise method consisting of the activities **characterize the situation, configure EA management function**, and **analyze EA management function**. Therein, the configuration cycle which is concerned with configuring the EA management function in a stepwise fashion taking one EA management-related problem at a time is illustrated.

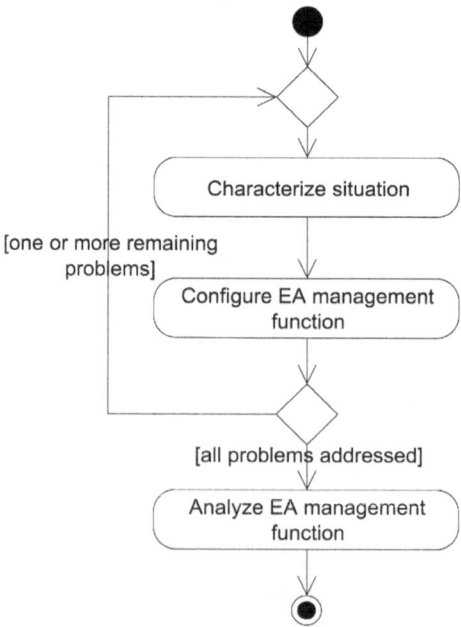

Fig. 3. Activity diagram illustrating the development method

The characterization of the situation provides the input for selecting appropriate MBBs from the method base, i.e. is concerned with a black-box perspective on MBBs. In contrast, configuring the EA management function is concerned with selection, customization, and integration of MBBs and thus takes a white box perspective. Starting with an empty EA management function, a first EA management-related problem to be addressed is selected as part of the characterization of the situation for which an appropriate EA management function is configured. This EA management function is stepwise enhanced with methods addressing further EA management-related problems, which are identified and integrated into the already configured EA management function in an iterative manner. Preliminary output during the development method is stored in an **organization-specific configuration** for the EA management function. If all identified problems are addressed, the resulting EA management function is analyzed for organizational implementability in the final activity [20].

Subsequently, we detail the single steps of the development method and designate the involved participants. While we assume the enterprise architect to be the typical user of the method other stakeholders of the EA management initiative need to be consulted during the development method in order to identify the problems that should be addressed. The development method is subsequently presented in a twofold way: an overview on parts of the method is given by an UML activity diagram and the single activities of the diagram are described textually.

3.1   Characterize Situation

The first activity of the development method **characterize situation** consists of three sub-activities, namely **determine organizational context**, **identify and operationalize EA-related problem**, and **specify existing information sources**. The outputs of the characterize situation step are a set of defined organizational contexts, an actual problem to be pursued, and information on the already existing data, i.e. EA-related content. Figure 4 shows a detailed activity diagram describing the single steps to be performed to achieve the aforementioned outcomes.

To develop an organization-specific EA management function, the enterprise architects have to characterize the situation in which the management function should be embedded in the step determine organizational context. Different factors and criteria influencing the applicability of an EA management function exist. To support the enterprise architects in characterizing the situation, a **catalog of organizational context** descriptions that impact the applicability of the MBBs in the method base is provided. The enterprise architects browse the catalog and select the organizational contexts that reflect the current situation in the organization. Output of the step is an organization-specific configuration containing first characterization of the situation with respect to the organizational context, i.e. a set of selected organizational contexts that describe the environment in which the EA management function should be embedded.

Besides the environment in which the EA management function should be embedded the enterprise architects have to identify the EA-related problems to be pursued. Therefore, the stakeholders of the EA management initiative should be

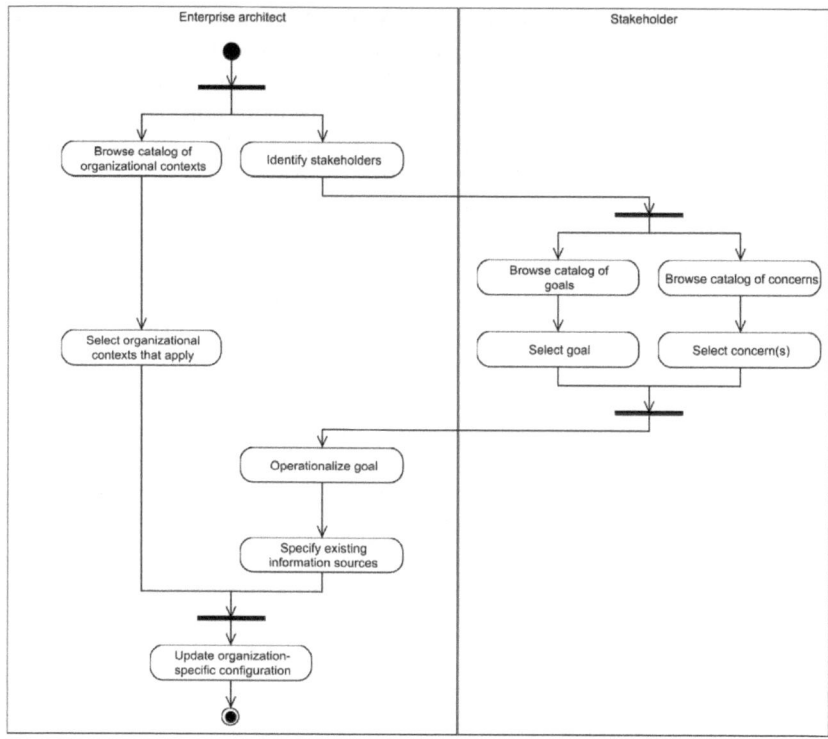

Fig. 4. Development method: Characterize situation

consulted. Typically these problems are described by the stakeholders on a rather abstract level. BEAMS provides a collection of such abstract EA management-related problems. This collection is organized in two catalogs, namely the catalog of goals defining *what* should be achieved, and the catalog of concerns specifying *where* the different goals can be applied. Based on the combination of one selected goal and one concern, a problem is defined and an information model describing the concepts relevant for the problem is determined.

Complimenting the characterization of the situation, already existing information sources that contribute to the EA management function by providing required input, need to be specified in the step **specify existing information sources**. Therefore, the concepts of the information model configured in the preceding step are analyzed and contributing sources are delineated. The organization-specific configuration is accordingly updated by the enterprise architects to include the existing information sources.

3.2   Configure EA Management Function

The activity **configure EA management function** represents an iterative activity consisting of two sub-activities. During the sub-activity **select MBB** the set of MBBs applicable in the current situation is determined based on the criteria stored in the configuration and one MBB is selected. The selected MBB is subsequently configured to the organization-specificities in the sub-activity **customize MBB**. The two sub-activities are iteratively performed until all EA management activities of the framework introduced in the motivating section are covered (cf. Figure 1).

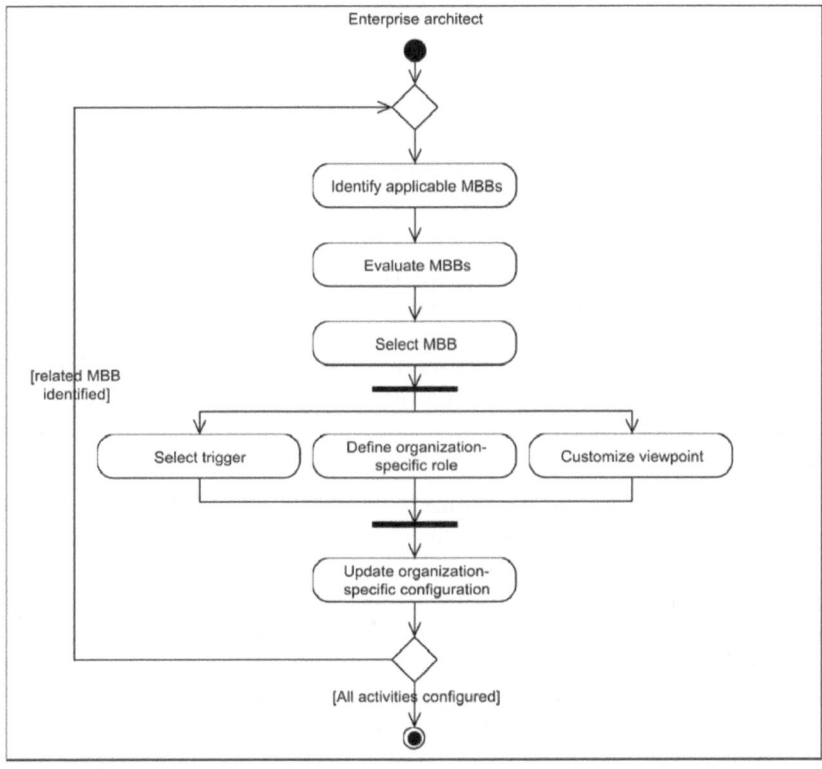

Fig. 5. Development method: configure EA management function

Entering the construction of the EA management function itself, the step **select MBB** is executed by the enterprise architects. The enterprise architects identify applicable MBBs by revisiting the admissibility requirements of all MBBs and comparing them with the information stored in the organization-specific configuration. Putting it more simply the MBBs are assessed according to

- the associated goal,
- the applicability in the defined organizational context, and
- the fulfillment of specific pre-conditions by the information already covered.

The pre-conditions are described by *meta-attributes*. Meta-attributes represent properties of associated concepts of the information model. If for instance no method is currently selected to document business processes, the business process concept has no meta-attribute defined. After selecting an MBB from the develop & describe activity to gather information on business processes, the meta-attribute "businessProcess.documented" is set to true. Different meta-attributes like *.documented*, *.communicated*, or *.published* exist.

The enterprise architects chose an admissible MBB from the set of appropriate MBBs. The choice can be supported by taking into account the participants that must be involved in executing the tasks as well as the consequences of applying an MBB.

While above step already shifts the process from an analytic one to a constructive one, the step **customize MBB** is clearly related to design and construction. Three parallel activities are performed during this step all relating to the customization of the selected MBB.

- The trigger of the MBB is detailed taking into account possible limitations that are already specified by the MBB.
- The participant variables delineated by the MBB has to be replaced by an organization-specific role.
- For each involvement of a participant in a task the used viewpoint has to be defined. While the constraints provided by the type of viewpoint have to be accounted for, the recommendations and dissuasions can optionally be considered.

After the configuration, the customized method is integrated into the set of configured methods that represent the current status quo of the organization-specific EA management function.

After the enterprise architects have finished customization of the selected MBB, the organization-specific configuration is updated to incorporate the customized method and the conditions on the information model are updated accordingly. If not all activities of the EA management function are yet covered, the development method continues with the identification of the next MBBs that are admissible. The output of the activity configure EA management function part of the method is a coherent and self-contained EA management function that addresses the defined set of problems stored in the organization-specific configuration. Otherwise, the enterprise architects can either start to characterize the next situation and problem to be addressed (configuration cycle) or continue the development method with the analysis of the EA management function.

3.3   Analyze EA Management Function

Since quick-wins and short-term benefits of EA management are sparse, a stringent implementation of the EA management function is not easy to ensure. A central challenge for enterprise architects is to ensure organizational implementability. The third phase of the development method is concerned with analyzing the organizational implementability of an EA management function. Central thereto, is a distinction between

- **stakeholder**s who own the problems to be addressed by the EA management function and
- **actor**s who are responsible for or consulted during the conduction of an EA management-related task.

The activity **analyze the EA management function** consists of three sub-activities as illustrated in Figure 6, namely **analyze stakeholder involvement, investigate stakeholder-actor-dependencies**, and **propose organizational interventions**.

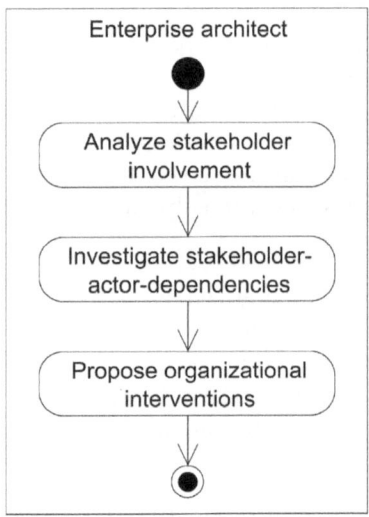

Fig. 6. Development method: analyze EA management function

In the first activity **analyze stakeholder involvement** the involvement of the stakeholders as typical stakeholders of the EA management function is investigated. To ensure long-term investments in the endeavor, we thereby ensure that a defined method fragment to inform the stakeholders on the results related to their specific problem is defined. The second activity **investigate stakeholder-actor-dependencies** the aspect of information demand and supply is analyzed. For each stakeholder, representing an information consumer, the dependencies on actors, who provide information are determined. The resulting dependencies are mapped to the organizational (control) structures. Based on the results different organizational interventions as e.g. tits-for-tats or social competition, are provided in the final activity of **propose organizational interventions**. In this vein, different mechanisms to ensure the supply of information can be established.

4   A Fictitious Case Study from Industry

In our fictitious example, we accompany the enterprise architects from a fictional organization, namely the financial service provider BS&M through their first experiences with EA management. The situation at BS&M can be characterized as follows: Over the last years BS&M has been constantly growing resulting in a heterogeneous application landscape due to a rising number of business request to IT.

To cope with the proliferating application landscape, an IT Infrastructure Library (ITIL) project was launched a year ago, that established a configuration management data base (CMDB) in which the currently used business applications and using organizational units are documented. Furthermore, the federated IT departments were centralized and a process for deciding on the project portfolio based on defined criteria as estimated project costs was set up to increase standardization of the provided IT solutions.

Browsing the catalog of organizational contexts the enterprise architects select the following characteristics that are subsequently stored in the configuration, namely

- the initiative can be characterized as *bottom-up initiative* as no official mandate from the management exists,
- the organizational structure supplies a *centralized IT department*, and
- *office tools* should be used in the initiative as no dedicated tool support for EA management yet exists and no official budget is available for the initiative.

At BS&M the enterprise architects identify the project portfolio managers as potential stakeholder of the EA management initiative. During interviews these stakeholders expressed problems with determining the impact of planned projects onto the application landscape. In particular, the impact on the business support provided by the applications is of major interest as well as interdependencies between different projects.

Browsing the catalog of goals, the enterprise architects accordingly select the goal *increasing transparency*. Furthermore, the catalog of concerns is browsed in order to identify relevant elements of the EA on which the goal should be applied. The concern "business application supports business process at organizational unit" is selected, thereby introducing the corresponding concepts and relationships to the information model. Further the cross-cutting aspects "project changes architecture elements" and "project proposal affects architectural elements" are selected and applied onto the concept business application. Figure 7 shows the information model resulting from the integration of the corresponding LBBs.

To operationalize the goal, the enterprise architects decide to use the qualitative measure *stakeholder satisfaction*, which is proposed as an operationalization for the goal *increasing transparency* by the BEAMS catalog of goals.

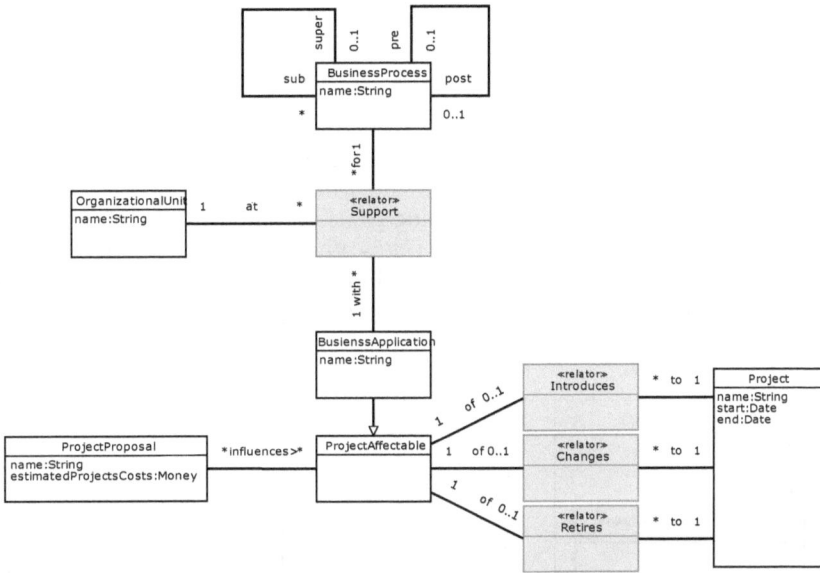

Fig. 7. An exemplary information model for the above described problem

Revisiting the concepts from the information model, the enterprise architects of BS&M identify the ITIL CMDB as information source for their EA management initiative. Therein information on the current landscape is stored covering the information demands for ORGANIZATIONAL UNITS and BUSINESS APPLICATIONS as well as their relationships. Further, information on PROJECT PROPOSALS and their impact on the application landscape can be derived from the project charter demanded as input to the project portfolio management process.

With these contributing information sources, the enterprise architects specifies the meta-attribute ".documented" to hold for the above described parts of the information model. Nevertheless, as not all information is yet available the general condition concern.documented is not yet fulfilled.

At BS&M, the input for the assess suitability technique is the information stored in the configuration, namely

- **goal:** increasing transparency,
- **context:** bottom-up initiative, centralized IT department, office tools, and
- **conditions:**

Based on above criteria the enterprise architects identify applicable MBBs. With respect to the current goal, the set of admissible MBBs can be limited to the ones associated with the activities "develop & describe" and "communicate & enact". Taking further the empty set of fulfilled conditions into account, MBBs from the activity "communicate & enact" can be excluded from the set of applicable MBBs, such that the following MBBs from the "develop & describe" activity are evaluated to be applicable based on the specified organizational context descriptions:

- describe by interview
- describe by questionnaire
- describe by workshop

The enterprise architects of BS&M decide to use the first MBB (cf. Figure 8) to gather the missing information on BUSINESS PROCESSES. The convincing argument therefore, was the possibility to individually promote the EA management initiative at the different business departments in a face-to-face interview.

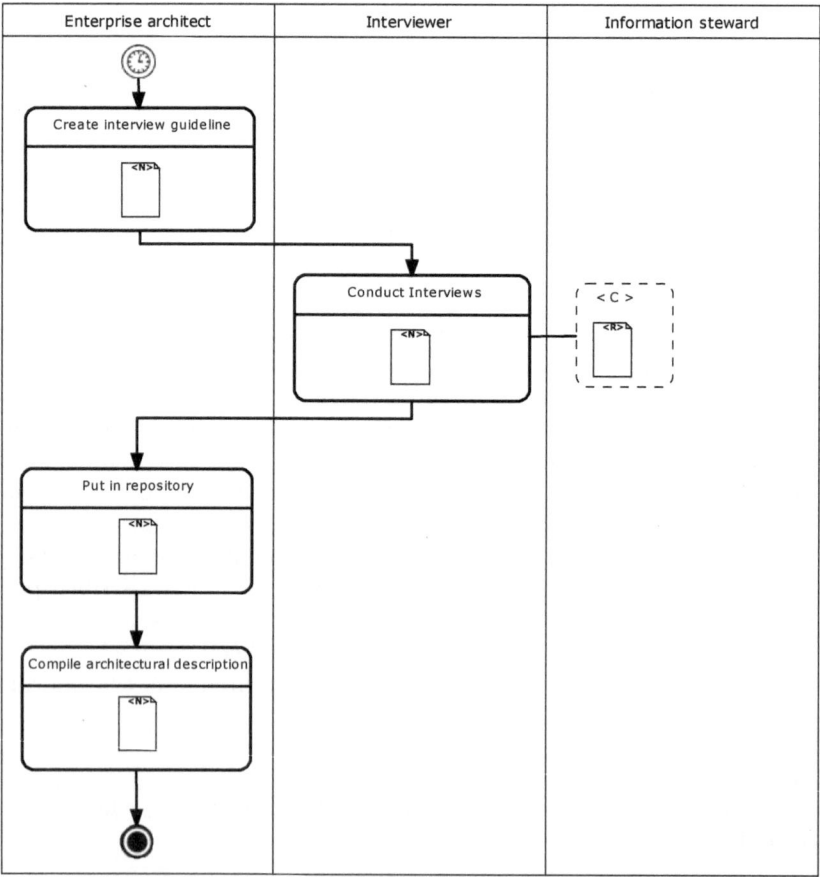

Fig. 8. MBB describe by interview

At BS&M the enterprise architects customize the selected MBB as follows. As the trigger is specified by the MBB to be of type "temporal" the enterprise architects decide to update the documentation of business processes on a yearly basis which reflects the update schedule of the CMDB from the ITIL initiative.

The participant variable INTERVIEWER is defined to be an enterprise architect to facilitate the promotion of the EA management initiative. Further, the process owners are identified as information stewards.

Complementing, the viewpoints used to involve the different participants are defined. Typical office documents are used with one exception. The architectural description used in the last step is displayed in a so-called *matrix card* that relates business processes, business applications, and organizational units.

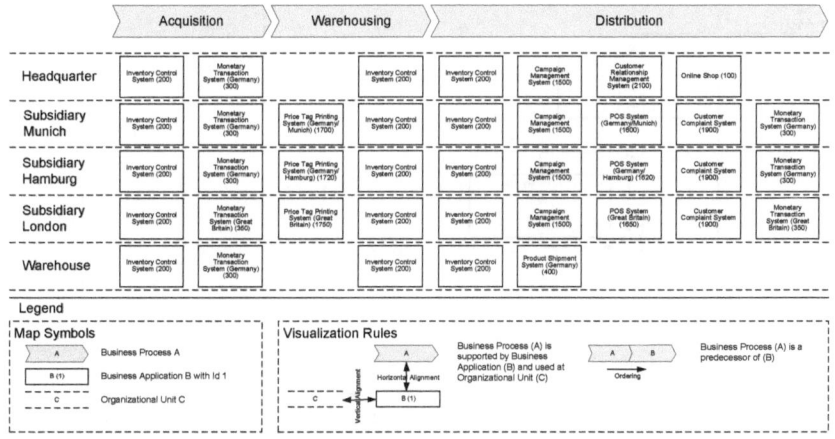

Fig. 9. A matrix visualization

The enterprise architects from BS&M update their organization-specific configuration to on the one hand incorporate the customized method and on the other hand extend the set of fulfilled conditions with the condition "concern.documented" as now all concepts specified by the information model are documented.

Based on the updated configuration a new set of admissible MBBs can be identified. The assessment technique now additionally returns MBBs from the communicate & enact activity as the minimum pre-condition concern.documented is fulfilled. Omitting the iterative steps, we present the resulting EA management function in Figure 10 that addresses the problem of "increasing transparency on the interplay of planned projects" that consists of the following MBBs

- ensure information consistency (develop & describe)
- develop planned states of the EA (develop & describe)
- perform single expert evaluation (analyze & evaluate)
- publish architectural description (communicate & enact)

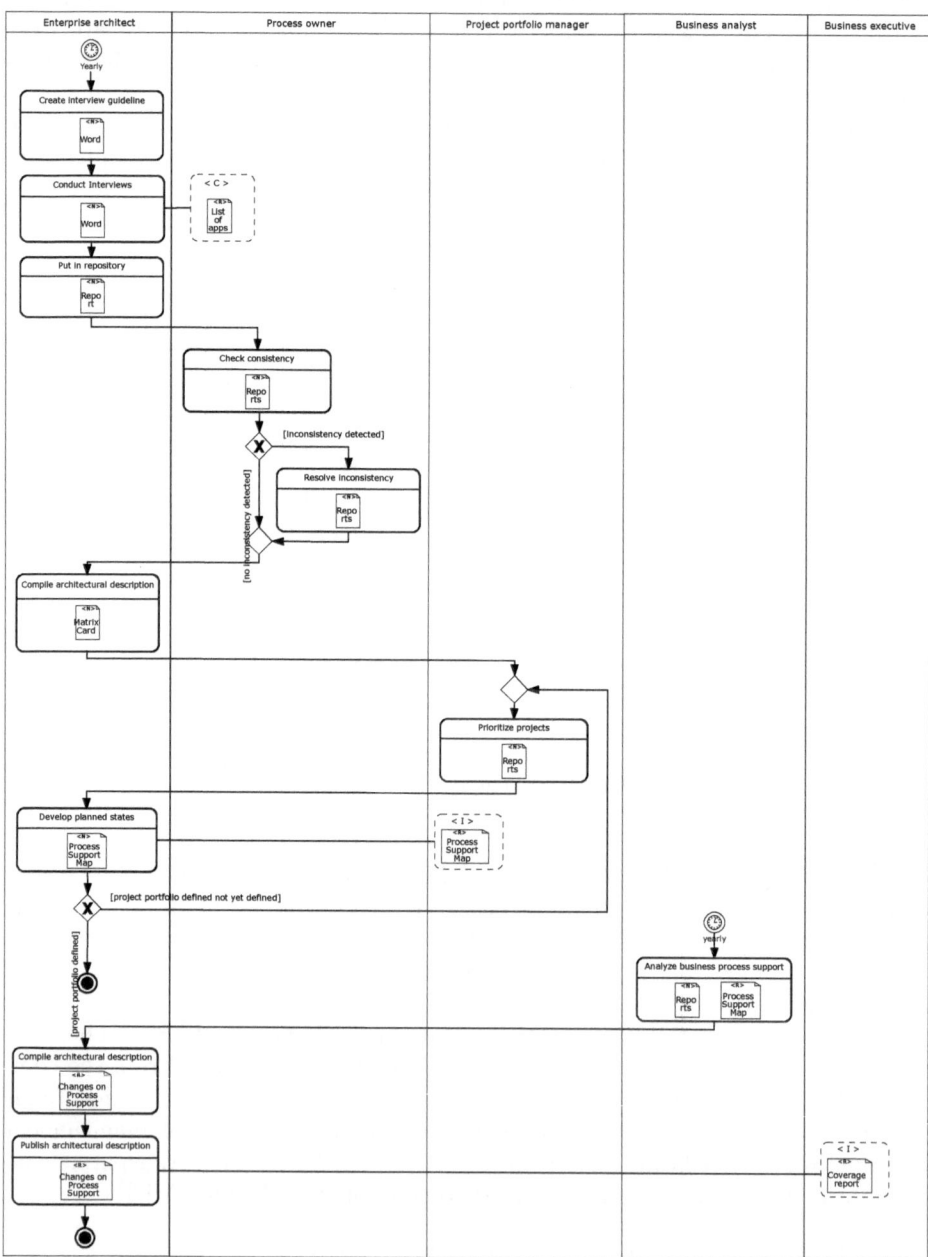

Fig. 10. An organization-specific EA management function developed using the BEAMS method base

5   Conclusion and Outlook

In this article we motivated the need for an organization-specific approach to develop an EA management function based on the idea of re-usable, practice proven building blocks. Following the idea of situational method engineering the building blocks are selected based on a characterization of the organizational context of the associated organization. While the application of the development method in this paper is only performed using a fictitious case, we are currently evaluating the development method and the EA management function resulting from its application in different cases in industry. First results from these cases hint towards the usability of the development method and prove the suitability and applicability of the resulting artifact at least from the subjective perspective of the industry partners. However, a long-term survey is necessary to demonstrate and prove the utility of the development method and the resulting EA management function.

Findings from our first applications additionally proved the need for a tool support to facilitate accessing the knowledge base as well as to support an enterprise architect during the different activities of the development method. As a first step towards a more sophisticated tool support, we plan to publish the method base, i.e. the collection of MBBs, online in a wiki system. The wiki system should be used to establish a community of researchers and practitioners with are interested in further evolving and enhancing the method base.

References

1. Luftman, J.N., Lewis, P.R., Oldach, S.H.: Transforming the enterprise: The alignment of business and information technology strategies. IBM Systems Journal 32(1), 198–221 (1993)
2. Wegmann, A., Balabko, P., Lê Regev, G., Rychkova, I.: A method and tool for business-it alignment in enterprise architecture. In: Belo, O., Eder, J., ao e Cunha, F., Pastor, O. (eds.) Proceedings of the CAiSE 2005 Forum, pp. 113–118 (2005)
3. International Organization for Standardization: ISO/IEC 42010:2007 Systems and software engineering – Recommended practice for architectural description of software-intensive systems (2007)
4. Johnson, P., Ekstedt, M.: Enterprise Architecture – Models and Analyses for Information Systems Decision Making, Studentlitteratur, Pozkal, Poland (2007)
5. Lankhorst, M.M.: Enterprise Architecture at Work: Modelling, Communication and Analysis, 2nd edn. Springer, Heidelberg (2009)
6. Niemann, K.D.: From Enterprise Architecture to IT Governance – Elements of Effective IT Management. Vieweg+Teubner, Wiesbaden, Germany (2006)
7. Ross, J.W., Weill, P., Robertson, D.C.: Enterprise Architecture as Strategy. Harvard Business School Press, Boston (2006)
8. Buckl, S., Ernst, A.M., Lankes, J., Matthes, F.: Enterprise Architecture Management Pattern Catalog (Version 1.0, February 2008). Technical report, Chair for Informatics 19 (sebis), Technische Universität München, Munich, Germany (2008)

 9. Kurpjuweit, S., Winter, R.: Viewpoint-based meta model engineering. In: Reichert, M., Strecker, S., Turowski, K. (eds.) 2nd International Workshop on Enterprise Modelling and Information Systems Architectures (EMISA 2007). LNI, pp. 143–161. Gesellschaft für Informatik, Bonn (2007)
10. van den Berg, M., van Steenbergen, M.: Building an Enterprise Architecture Practice – Tools, Tips, Best Practices, Ready-to-Use Insights. Springer, Dordrecht (2006)
11. The Open Group: TOGAF "Enterprise Edition" Version 9 (2009), http://www.togaf.org (cited February 14, 2011)
12. Leppänen, M., Valtonen, K., Pulkkinen, M.: Towards a contingency framework for engineering and enterprise architecture planning method. In: 30th Information Systems Research Seminar in Scandinavia (IRIS), pp. 1–20 (2007)
13. Riege, C., Aier, S.: A Contingency Approach to Enterprise Architecture Method Engineering. In: Feuerlicht, G., Lamersdorf, W. (eds.) ICSOC 2008. LNCS, vol. 5472, pp. 388–399. Springer, Heidelberg (2009)
14. Wagter, R., van den Berg, M., Luijpers, J., van Steenbergen, M.: Dynamic Enterprise Architecture: How to Make IT Work. John Wiley (2005)
15. Buckl, S., Matthes, F., Schweda, C.M.: Towards a method framework for enterprise architecture management – a literature analysis from a viable system perspective. In: 5th International Workshop on Business/IT Alignment and Interoperability, BUSITAL 2010 (2010)
16. Harmsen, A.F.: Situational Method Engineering. PhD thesis, University of Twente, Twente, The Netherlands (1997)
17. Pries-Heje, J., Baskerville, R.: The design theory nexus. MIS Quarterly 32(4), 731–755 (2008)
18. Object Management Group (OMG): Business process model and notation (bpmn) – version 2.0 (2010)
19. Object Management Group (OMG): Omg unified modeling language^{TM} (omg uml), superstructure – version 2.3 (formal/2010-05-05) (2010)
20. Buckl, S., Gehlert, A., Matthes, F., Schulz, C., Schweda, C.M.: Modeling the Supply and Demand of Architectural Information on Enterprise Level. In: Fifteenth IEEE International EDOC Conference (EDOC 2011). LNBIP. Springer, Heidelberg (2011)

Management of Large-Scale Transformation Programs: State of the Practice and Future Potential

Gerrit Lahrmann[1], Nils Labusch[1], Robert Winter[1], and Axel Uhl[2]

[1] Institute of Information Management, University of St. Gallen,
St. Gallen, Switzerland
{Gerrit.Lahrmann,Nils.Labusch,Robert.Winter}@unisg.ch
[2] University of Applied Sciences and Arts Northwestern Switzerland FHNW, SAP AG,
Basel, Switzerland
Axel.Uhl@fhnw.ch

Abstract. In addition to continuous, evolutionary optimizations, most enterprises also undergo revolutionary transformations from time to time. Knowledge about current corporate practice for coherent IT and business transformation is therefore very valuable. In this paper we present the results of an empirical study on the management of large-scale transformation programs that focuses on IT as much as business aspects. Companies that rate themselves as mature with regards to transformation management, assess certain transformation management components different than less mature companies. Cost reduction, revenue improvement, and agility improvement are the most relevant goals of transformation programs – all these are business goals and not IT goals. Current state of the practice transformation management can be classified into three approaches: Value-driven, ungoverned and change-driven. We found that no single management approach covers all these areas appropriately yet.

Keywords: transformation methodology, empirical study, holistic transformation management.

1 Introduction

According to Rouse [1], transformation and especially enterprise transformation (ET) is not routine but "fundamental change that substantially alters an organization's relationships with one or more key constituencies, e.g., customers, employees, suppliers, and investors". Such an ET can involve new value propositions or change the inner structure of the enterprise. Further, ET could involve old value propositions provided in fundamentally new ways [1]. Reasons can be the reaction to an insecure, permanently changing economic environment [2] or the pro-active measure to explore business potentials, e.g. those of IT innovations [3]. Further examples are mergers & acquisitions, detachment of host systems or other efforts that are reflected in strategic planning. ETs are usually implemented as programs, i.e. bundles of projects [4], while evolutionary changes are either implemented by regular projects or are even included in permanent processes.

S. Aier et al. (Eds.): TEAR 2012 and PRET 2012, LNBIP 131, pp. 253–267, 2012.

Due to the complex intertwining of IT and business in many companies [5], one challenge of ET programs is to address the often diverse worlds of business and IT coherently [6]. Examples from our survey are the introduction of a new banking platform for all units of a banking group (program duration two years, program budget 60 million Euros, 120 full time employees on average) or the world-wide standardization of business processes on the basis of a unified enterprise resource planning platform in a high tech company (program duration four years, program budget considerably more than one billion Dollars).

Thus, in the following sections we present the results of an empirical study on the management of large-scale ET programs and extend a study that was partially reported in [7]. In the paper at hand we present more details, e.g. qualitative statements concerning the experiences within the described ETs. We further provide a more detailed discussion and analysis of results and implications for corporate practice. First, we are interested in the current practice of ET programs, their extent as much as the guiding goals and key drivers. We reflect this interest in our first research question:

RQ1: What is the current corporate practice of enterprise transformation?

Managing and conducting ET is a complex issue [8]. Since many ETs fail [9], we are particularly interested in success factors for effective ET. Motivated by Robbins [10], we especially consider a holistic approach as being appropriate. We cover this aspect with our second research question:

RQ2: What are success factors for effective enterprise transformation, especially within a holistic enterprise transformation management approach?

For the successful management of ETs, many different tasks and techniques need to be executed and coordinated [11]. In the next part of our study, we aim at getting an overview of currently executed tasks and techniques concerning ET. Further we are interested in the combinations mostly present, in order to reflect these with the success factors. This leads to the third research question:

RQ3: What are prevalent approaches to conduct enterprise transformation management?

Connected to these research questions, the subject occurs, which areas of ET management offer potentials for further research and practice design solutions. Therefore, we are interested in gaps of current ET approaches and in the maturity of its components (techniques). We address the matter with a last research question:

RQ4: Which components of enterprise transformation management offer the largest improvement potential?

The remainder of the paper is structured as follows. First, we give a brief introduction to ET management. Next, we outline our research approach. Then we present the results of our study. We conclude with a discussion of our results, limitations and an outlook on future work.

2   Enterprise Transformation Management

As a formal construct, ET can be understood as a process or a sequence of activities that change an organization in its present or initial state to a future, desirable target state. Therefore, ET becomes a plan of how a firm intends to move from one position to another [6]. According to Baumoel [12], change or ET programs are unique, because they are embedded into unique contexts, i.e. the economic, technological, and social environment. As a consequence, the setup and the execution of ET programs need to refer to this unique context [12] (see figure 1).

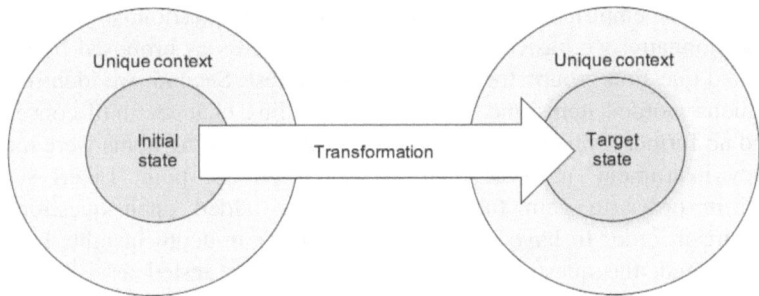

Fig. 1. Conceptual model of transformation [13]

ETs usually are comprised of technological and social components [6]. Technologies, or more specifically IT, can be both enabler and driver of ETs. Examples are knowledge management or collaboration technology [6]. The social components of ET induce certain irrationality during ET endeavors. This implies that technological and work-processes need to be developed jointly during ETs [6]. How and when ETs are conducted is mostly induced by the market environment [14] – companies conduct ET decisions in response to the situations in which they find themselves. According to Yu et al. [14] "companies will transform their enterprise by some combination of predicting better, learning faster, and acting faster, as long as the market is sufficiently predictable to reasonably expect that ET will improve the market value the company can provide".

In order to foster successful ET and to improve the gained value, a precondition is having an understanding of how to systematically manage ET programs. We understand "enterprise transformation management" as the process of goal-directed planning, implementation, and control of fundamental changes in companies. In response to the limitations of single methods and management approaches and in view of the complexity of ETs, ET management integrates and extends existing management approaches like strategic management, value management, risk management, project management, (business) process management, change management, competence management, and of course IT transformation management. An example for such an approach is Business Transformation Management Methodology (BTM^2) [15]. It is comprised of an overarching discipline called meta management that offers a cyclic and iterative phase model for ETs (envision, engage, transform and optimize), a structure including roles and disciplinary ET activities, provision of measures, skill development support and guiding principles.

At this point, there is no related work that provides an overview about current management practice of large scale ET programs. In order to document current ET management practice, to analyze improvement potentials and to close this gap, we conducted the empirical study at hand.

3   Research Methodology

3.1   Study Concept

We conducted the empirical study by means of a written questionnaire. For the design of the questionnaire, we basically adhered to the process as proposed by [16]. First, we compiled question groups for each topic of interest. Second, we identified poorly or ambiguous worded items and made minor wording changes until consensus was found and no further problems were uncovered. The remaining items were included in the survey instrument, most of them measured on a 5-point Likert scale [17]. However, in order to gain further insights, we added open questions to the questionnaire in order to have the chance for further in-depth insights [18]. Before being distributed, the questionnaire instrument was pre-tested as a whole by two participants. The final survey consisted of five parts. In part I, demographic information on the study participants, their company, and, in part II, their company's ET program was acquired. In part III, a literature-based [3, 12, 19, 20, 21] holistic ET management approach was presented to the participants, whose potential the participants were asked to assess. In part IV, the study participants were asked, how mature they would estimate their own company as regards certain components of the holistic ET management approach and as how important they would rate each component. Further questions were used to assure the completeness of the approach. In part V, further ET management aspects, e. g. enablers and inhibitors, were documented.

3.2   Data Collection

We targeted heads of current ET programs in large, multi-national companies (program managers, head of ET competency centers, regional CIOs, etc.). We consider a rather low amount of high knowledgeable informants to be more appropriate than a high amount of less knowledgeable but better accessible ones. Only high knowledgeable informants are able to view the focal phenomena from diverse perspectives [22]. We selected our informants by two major criteria: First, they needed to be located in management or positions closely related to management.

Second, they needed to have major influences and insights into the ET program. We identified the informants by having access to the customer network of a large consulting company and the university network. We further applied snowball sampling techniques in order to increase the amount of informants [23]. We contacted the informants by providing a brief management summary of the study via mail or email. We further attached the questionnaire and asked participants to send it back via mail or fax. We provided the chance to include contact data in order to allow for the provision of study results when interested. However, in general, we gave anonymity to our informants in order to receive honest answers and reduce biases [18].

3.3   Data Analysis

Depending on the type of question in the questionnaire we applied different analysis techniques. For the closed questions, we applied quantitative analysis techniques in an exploratory manner [18]. We used factor analyses in order "to summarize relationships in the form of a more parsimonious set of factor scores that can then be used in subsequent analyses" [24] and thus identify variables and questions that belong together. In order to further match cases in groups that belong together, we applied hierarchical clustering [25]. The purpose of clustering, a form of combinatorial data analysis, is to investigate "a set of objects in order to establish whether or not they fall [...] into groups [...] of objects with the property that objects in the same group are similar to one another and different from objects in other groups." [25]

Based on open questions, we asked for key deliverables, drivers, and inhibitors of successful ET programs. We analyzed the open questions in two different ways. First, in order to derive interpretable results, a standardized process for content analysis (conceptualization, codebook creation, coding, refinement, & reliability check) was applied, thereby helping to ensure the necessary rigor in the classification process [26]. First, we matched synonyms. As an example, one participant used the term "New optimized way of doing business" and another participant used the term "Process improvements", both actually addressing a similar aspect. The outcomes are three lists of key deliverables, drivers, and inhibitors of ET programs, which should cover all aspects as mentioned by the study participants. Second, we extracted interesting arguments in a qualitative manner [18] and present those within the results section.

3.4   Data Set

Both business and IT representatives participated. The study was conducted globally, certainly with a focus on Europe (Europe 68%, Americas 14%, Asia 14% and Africa 4%). Altogether, 28 companies (respectively their representatives) participated. In the data set, the primarily present industries were high tech (25%), consumer products (14%), banking and insurance (7%), and professional services (7%). Our rather elusive focus on heads of large-scale ET management programs explains the rather low number of participating organizations. However, we consider this as appropriate, since the scope of the paper at hand is rather explorative and less confirmative. Table 1 summarizes the most important measures of the data set.

Table 1. Characterization of the data set

Function		Industry		Region	
C-Level Executive	11%	High Tech	25%	Europe	68%
Director / Head of ...	32%	Consumer Products	14%	Americas	14%
(Program) Manager	25%	Banking and Insurance	7%	Asia	14%
Business or IT Architect	14%	Professional Services	7%	Africa	%
Other	18%	Other	46%		
Division		**Company Size**			
Business	29%	1-999	18%		
IT	61%	1000-9999	11%		
Business / IT	11%	10000 and above	71%		

4   Study Results

4.1   Enterprise Transformation in Current Corporate Practice

Foremost, the ET programs we investigated in the study had a program duration between two and four years and a program budget between ten and 100 million Euros. In smaller companies (< 10'000 employees), 52 full time employees (FTEs) were working on average on the ET program. In larger companies (> 10'000 employees), this number went up to 126 FTEs. Most of the programs have a clear business focus or combine elements of business and IT transformation. Our results show that cost reduction, revenue improvement, and agility improvement are the most relevant goals in ET programs. Agility improvement is the ability of being able to react fast to necessary changes. Business networking has not yet arrived. Despite the economic crisis, risk reduction still has a low priority. In table 2 the goals of ET programs are summarized. The list is sorted by relevance (= frequency of mention * priority). The list is based on and extends a classification by Baumoel [12].

As key deliverables, the study participants named business optimization, operating models, standardized processes & platform as much as roadmaps. These are all business-driven topics. Drivers of successful ET programs are top management support, stakeholder management, and clear responsibilities. Resistance to change, organizational barriers, and resource constraints are inhibitors of successful ET. Table 3 summarizes the key deliverables, drivers, and inhibitors of successful ET programs.

Table 2. Goals of ET programs

Goals	Frequency	Average Priority	Relevance
Cost reduction	82%	4.22	3.46
Revenue improvement	71%	4.50	3.21
Agility improvement	68%	4.37	2.96
Strategy adaptation	64%	4.17	2.68
Process redesign	64%	3.78	2.43
Technology-enabled growth	61%	3.47	2.11
Risk reduction	54%	3.27	1.75
Business networking	32%	2.78	0.89

Table 3. Top key deliverables, drivers, and inhibitors of ET programs

Rank	Key Deliverables	Drivers	Inhibitors
1	Business optimization	Top management support	Resistance to change
2	Operating model	Stakeholder management	Organizational barriers
3	Standardized processes & platform	Clear responsibilities	Resource constraints
4	Roadmap	- / -	- / -

4.2   Success Factors of Enterprise Transformation Management

In order to be more effective, ET management requires a comprehensive overall view of the construction and changing of an organization's structures, i.e. its organizational design [10]. As a basis for this, adequate interdisciplinary approaches should be used, which do not only concentrate on one aspect of the ET process, e.g. the role of IT, but rather include the main levers of organizational ET from all relevant disciplines (e. g. strategy making, organizational design and behavior, or business process engineering) [12].

Therefore, in order to analyze such an interdisciplinary approach and to get a more or less complete overview of ET management, we derived components of a holistic ET management approach from the literature. Based on the established Business Engineering framework [3], the approach presented in table 4 is structured into the three layers Strategy, Processes & Organization as much as Information Systems & Technology. Altogether, the holistic ET management approach contains 13 subparts or ET management components (see table 4).

Table 4. Holistic ET management

Holistic Enterprise Transformation Management	Importance in mature companies	Importance in less mature companies	Difference
Strategy	**4.33**	**3.80**	**0.53**
A joint (company and implementation partner) agreement on business objectives	4.78	3.44	1.33
Mid-term planning and continuous alignment of business requirements and IT capabilities	3.78	4.00	-0.22
Management of program value	4.38	3.56	0.81
Identifying and managing interdependencies of projects within and across programs	4.40	4.20	0.20
Processes and Organization	4.21	3.51	0.70
Business process optimization and innovation services	4.29	3.73	0.56
A joint (company and implementation partner) governance model	4.23	3.57	0.66
Organizational change management	4.33	3.71	0.62
High qualified representative of implementation partner	4.13	3.56	0.57
Professional program and project management	4.08	3.00	1.08
Information Systems & Technology	3.53	3.26	0.27
Tool-supported transparency on progress, risks, and costs of ET program activities	3.89	3.13	0.76
IT architecture services	3.30	3.44	-0.14
High qualified IT people with excellent business understanding	3.82	3.75	0.07
Monitoring of technology trends	3.10	2.71	0.39

In order to analyze if ET programs are more successful if a holistic ET management approach is used, we asked for the company representatives' estimation as regards impact on ET program execution. The study participants could chose if they wanted to estimate the impact on the basis of their own companies' ET program or an exemplary ET program. Table 5 summarizes the estimation of the company representatives as regards impact on program quality, program budget, program duration, and program risk. Program quality describes that all goals were achieved and that the ET is sustainable.

Table 5. Impact on ET programs

Impact on Enterprise Transformation Program Execution	Positive Impact	Negative Impact
Program quality	100 %	0 %
Program budget	76 %	24 %
Program duration	75 %	25 %
Program risk	92 %	8 %

Altogether, all participants expect a better program quality. More than three quarters of the participants expect that the extra costs of the components will be compensated by better quality. Only one quarter expects higher quality along with higher program budgets and higher program duration. As regards program risk, expectations of a positive impact prevail.

4.3 Approaches of Enterprise Transformation Management

In order to identify archetypal ET management approaches which are currently used in corporate practice, we conducted an exploratory analysis [27]. In order to elucidate the predominant design factors of ET management approaches, data is examined by factor analysis. The five factors consist of two to four items. Items are usually assigned to a factor if the factor loading adds up to at least 0.5 [27]. In the cases of "Mid-term planning and continuous alignment" and "Professional program and project management", the items are attributed to the factor with the highest factor loading. Based on an interpretation of the contained items, we termed the five design factors of ET management approaches as "People & Technology Governance", "Holistic Change Management", "Target-Driven Planning", "Commitment to Transformation", and "Benefits Management". See table 6 for the detailed loadings and factor items.

Table 6. Results of the Factor Analysis

Factors	Item description	F1	F2	F3	F4	F5
People & Technology Governance	High qualified IT people with excellent business understanding	0.93	0.09	0.14	-0.02	0.16
	Monitoring of technology trends	0.81	-0.06	0.04	0.37	0.24
	Joint (company and implementation partner) governance model	0.51	0.46	0.44	0.25	0.01
Holistic Change Management	Identifying and managing interdependencies of projects	-0.07	0.86	-0.01	0.07	0.18
	Organizational change management	0.10	0.76	0.23	0.27	-0.08

Table 6. (*continued*)

Factors	Item description	F1	F2	F3	F4	F5
Target-driven Planning	Joint (company and implementation partner) agreement on business objectives	-0.08	0.28	0.79	0.11	0.31
	IT architecture services	0.45	-0.11	0.72	0.31	0.03
	Mid-term planning and continuous alignment	0.29	0.18	0.56	0.21	0.53
	Professional program and project management	0.40	0.43	0.45	-0.36	0.20
Commitment to Transformation	Business process optimization and innovation services	0.10	0.12	0.10	0.81	-0.03
	High qualified representative of implementation partner	0.17	0.28	0.23	0.69	0.24
Benefits Management	Transparency on progress, risks, and costs of ET program activities	0.41	-0.17	0.30	-0.18	0.74
	Management of program value	0.10	0.44	0.12	0.38	0.70

Based on the factor scores of the factor analysis, hierarchical clustering is used, in order to determine archetypal ET management approaches. Altogether, we identified three different ET management approaches. Due to their characterizing factor scores, we termed these approaches as "Value-Driven Approach", "Un-Governed Approach", and "Change-Driven Approach" See table 7 for the clusters and the corresponding factor values.

Table 7. Impact on ET programs

Cluster	n	People & Technology Governance	Holistic Change Management	Target-driven Planning	Commitment to Transformation	Benefits Management
1	16	-0.47 1	-0.33 0	0.03 4	-0.18 0	-0.09 4
2	7	-1.21 0	-0.34 0	-0.77 0	0.09 1	-0.21 3
3	5	1.14 4	0.86 4	-0.70 0	0.60 4	-0.55 0

Cluster one, that we call the *Value-Driven Approach* is present in 57 % of the examined companies and can be characterized by a high Target-Driven Planning and a high Benefits Management. The average maturity of companies using the Value-Driven ET management approach is 3.30.

Cluster two, the *Un-Governed Approach* is present in almost 25% of the companies that have an average maturity level of 2.30. Especially a low people and technology governance can be seen in these companies.

Cluster three, the *Change Driven Approach* is present in 18% of the companies that have an average maturity of 3.43. In this cluster we can observe a high presence of people and technology governance, holistic change management and commitment to transformation.

All three approaches have in common that they place emphasis on different aspects, e. g. business value in the case of the Value-Driven Approach, but overall, a well-balanced, holistic approach is missing. Considering the potential of a holistic ET management approach, this opens room for improvement. The components which have been rated important by mature companies might be reasonable starting points for this.

4.4   Potentials for Enterprise Transformation Support Improvement

In our analysis, we asked for the maturity of companies as regards with regard to each ET management component as well as the importance attributed to each component. On a 5-point Likert scale, the company representatives were asked to estimate the maturity of their own company and the importance which is attributed to a component in their company (self-assessment). By partitioning the data set into mature (self-assessed values of four or five) and less mature (self-assessed values of one, two, or three) companies it is possible to highlight components which are critical for successful ET management. Furthermore, this analysis allows deriving development directions for single companies.

Companies, that attributed themselves to be mature, rated especially the following aspects as more important than less mature companies: Active management of ET in general (as mature companies rated almost all components to be more important than less mature companies), Operational and organizational structure in general (e. g. through a joint governance model and organizational change management) and certain strategic aspects (for example a joint agreement on business objectives).

The components which were rated with the highest importance and the lowest maturity at the same time offer the highest potential for improvement. Such components should be of particular interest for researchers as well as practitioners (see fig 2).

Based on this classification, the most important ET management components with the highest need for action are (illustrated by the black circle): "Identifying and managing interdependencies of projects within and across programs", "Management of program value" and "Business process optimization and innovation services".

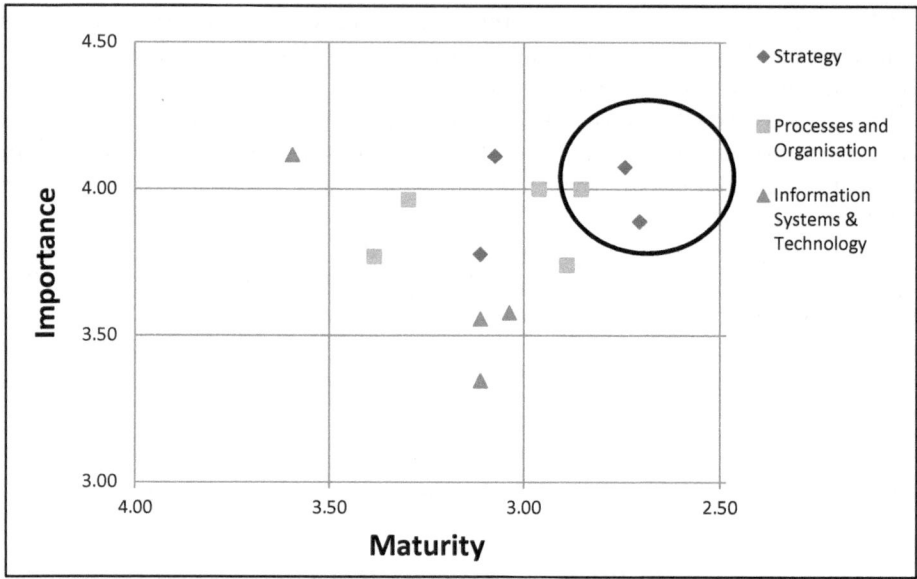

Fig. 2. ET management components with a high improvement potential

5   Discussion and Outlook

The results provide an explorative overview of ET programs currently conducted in corporate practice. Some further interesting hints about the future development of ET management approaches can be gained from direct statements the informants wrote in the questionnaires. We asked to openly provide major flaws and lessons learned from their point of view. One point that was mentioned by almost all informants is the importance of management support. Such support can be present to a different extent. While some mentioned management support in general, some directly referred to the board. However, a first challenge is to align within the Board. Like one informant stated as a critical point:

"Cross board area transformation goals were not defined and not aligned"

Therefore, in order to provide support as a board, first internal, cross-responsibility alignment needs to be achieved. After such alignment has been achieved, top-management support can be communicated credibly to the involved employees.

Further important are cultural aspects. Like one informant mentioned, knowledge, experience and courage concerning the relational aspects are very important. An example would be new ways of conducting work. Another informant mentioned, that the whole culture during an ET needs to shift away from a "it`s their fault" towards a "we are all responsible and need to be a role-model". A third informant provided an interesting catch phrase for the importance of culture:

"Culture eats strategy for breakfast"

Another often mentioned aspect is communication. Many informants claim that communicating information to the people involved or affected by the ET is crucial to ensure its success. Like one informant claimed:

"Communicate, Communicate, Communicate"

However, such claim might go not fully cover the communication aspect since another informant claimed:

"Intense communication can result in information overload"

Therefore, communication during an ET is a matter that needs to be planned intensively and conducted in a meaningful but controlled fashion.

Our results and the statements above show that management of ET programs is an important topic – especially in large organizations. Currently, different approaches to ET management exist in corporate practice, but a holistic approach is not there yet. Nonetheless, all study participants attribute a high potential to such an approach: All participants agree that a holistic ET management approach will improve the quality of the ET and will thereby lead to a more sustainable goal achievement. Such an approach needs to be capable of aligning and coordinating the different stakeholders and disciplines that are involved in ETs. However, from our point of view such an approach also needs to be able to differentiate different situations in order to achieve a certain fit with the context at hand.

Some limitations occur in the design of the study at hand. The study targets at a high level of abstraction that needs to be detailed and developed towards a more operative solution in further research. The study cannot claim general and overall coverage, however, we claim that because of the high knowledgeable informants, relevant data could be collected and the study contributes to the body of ET knowledge.

Concluding, the following points should be kept in mind in order to foster successful ET management:

First, Companies, that rate themselves as mature with regards to ET management, assess certain ET management components differently than less mature companies. Especially the active management of ET, the operational and organizational structures and certain strategic aspects receive higher attention in mature companies.

Second, Cost reduction, revenue improvement, and agility improvement are the most relevant goals of ET programs. It is worth to mention that these are all business and not IT-related goals. Information systems and supporting technology seem to be considered as a general precondition for successful ET management. Quite surprising in view of the recent financial and economic crisis is the fact that risk reduction has a low priority only.

Third, drivers and inhibitors of successful ET are dominated by soft factors. A key insight is that ET should be driven by business content and strategic aspects.

The findings of the study provide a foundation for further research in the field and the design of applicable artifacts like methods or reference frameworks. Based on the presented study, we plan to develop such artifacts especially in the areas identified in section 4.4. Identified gaps are "Identifying and managing interdependencies of projects within and across programs", "Management of program value" and "Business process optimization and innovation services". For the first identified gap, approaches like enterprise architecture can provide valuable support and should be researched and developed with a focus on transformation. The second gap needs to be addressed by work that focuses on the value of the program itself and the applied methods. Although already lots of research is present in the area of process optimization, further work with a focus on ET is necessary in that area. We further consider situational differentiation as appropriate, e.g. distinguishing complex service industries vs. volume operations, distinguishing different industries or further contextual factors.

References

1. Rouse, W.B.: A Theory of Enterprise Transformation. Systems Engineering 8(4), 279–295 (2005)
2. Moreton, R.: Transforming the organization: the contribution of the information systems function. Journal of Strategic Information Systems 4(2), 149–163 (1995)
3. Österle, H., Winter, R.: Business Engineering. Springer, Heidelberg (2003)
4. De Reyck, B., Grushka-Cockayne, Y., Lockett, M., Calderini, S.R., Moura, M.: The impact of project portfolio management on information technology projects. International Journal of Project Management 23(7), 524–537 (2005)
5. Henderson, J.C., Venkatraman, N.: Strategic Alignment: Leveraging Information Technology for Transforming Organizations. IBM Systems Journal 38(2/3), 472–484 (1999)
6. Rouse, W.B., Baba, M.L.: Enterprise transformation. Communications of the ACM 49(7), 67–72 (2006)
7. Lahrmann, G., Winter, R., Uhl, A.: Transformation Management Survey - Current State of Development and Potential of Transformation Management in Practice. 360° - The Business Transformation Journal 1, 29–37 (2011)
8. Purchase, V., Parry, G., Valerdi, R., Nightingale, D., Mills, J.: Enterprise Transformation: Why Are We Interested, What Is It, and What Are the Challenges? Journal of Enterprise Transformation 1(1), 14–33 (2011)
9. Ward, J., Uhl, A.: Success and Failure in Transformation – Lessons from 13 Case Studies. 360° – The Business Transformation Journal 3, 30–38 (2012)
10. Robbins, S.P.: Organization Theory: Structure, Design, and Applications. Prentice-Hall, Englewood Cliffs (1987)
11. Radeke, F.: Toward Understanding Enterprise Architecture Management's Role in Strategic Change: Antecedents, Processes, Outcomes. In: Wirtschaftinformatik Proceedings 2011, p. 62 (2011)
12. Baumöl, U.: Strategic Agility through Situational Method Construction. In: Proceedings of the European Academy of Management Annual Conference 2005, München (2005)

13. Bucher, T., Klesse, M., Kurpjuweit, S., Winter, R.: Situational Method Engineering - On the Differentiation of "Context" and "Project Type". In: Situational Method Engineering - Fundamentals and Experiences, pp. 33–48. Springer, Geneva (2007)
14. Yu, Z., Rouse, W.B., Serban, N.: A computational theory of enterprise transformation. Systems Engineering 14(4), 441–454 (2011)
15. Stiles, P., Uhl, A.: Meta Management: Connecting the Parts of Business Transformation. 360° – The Business Transformation Journal 3, 24–29 (2012)
16. Moore, G.C., Benbasat, I.: Development of an Instrument to Measure the Perceptions of Adopting an Information Technology Innovation. Information Systems Research 2(3), 192–222 (1991)
17. Likert, R.: A Technique for the Measurement of Attitudes. Archives of Psychology 22(140), 1–55 (1932)
18. Flick, U.: An Introduction to Qualitative Research. Sage, London (2006)
19. Winter, R.: Organisational Design and Engineering - Proposal of a Conceptual Framework and Comparison of Business Engineering with other Approaches. International Journal of Organizational Design and Engineering 1(1&2), 126–147 (2010)
20. Aier, S., Kurpjuweit, S., Saat, J., Winter, R.: Business Engineering Navigator – A "Business to IT" Approach to Enterprise Architecture Management. In: Bernard, S., Doucet, G., Gøtze, J., Saha, P. (eds.) Coherency Management – Architecting the Enterprise for Alignment, Agility, and Assurance, pp. 77–98. Author House, Bloomington (2009)
21. Baumöl, U.: Change Management in Organisationen: SituativeMethodenkonstruktionfür flexible Veränderungsprozesse. Gabler, Wiesbaden (2008)
22. Eisenhardt, K.M., Graebner, M.E.: Theory Building from Cases: Opportunities and Challenges. Academy of Management Journal 50(1), 25–32 (2007)
23. Noy, C.: Sampling Knowledge: The Hermeneutics of Snowball Sampling in Qualitative Research. International Journal of Social Research Methodology 11(4), 327–344 (2007)
24. Thompson, B.: Exploratory and Confirmatory Factor Analysis: Understanding Concepts and Applications. American Psychological Association, Washington, DC (2004)
25. Gordon, A.D.: Hierarchical Classification. In: Arabie, P., Hubert, L.J., De Soete, G. (eds.) Clustering and Classification, pp. 65–121. World Scientific Publishing, River Edge (1996)
26. Neuendorf, K.A.: The content analysis guidebook. SAGE Publications, Thousand Oaks (2002)
27. Härdle, W., Simar, L.: Applied Multivariate Statistical Analysis. Springer, Heidelberg (2007)

Development of Measurement Items
for the Institutionalization of Enterprise Architecture
Management in Organizations

Simon Weiss and Robert Winter

University of St. Gallen, Institute of Information Management
Mueller-Friedberg-Strasse 8, 9000 St. Gallen, Switzerland
{simon.weiss,robert.winter}@unisg.ch

Abstract. While elaborate enterprise architecture management (EAM) methods
and models are at architects' disposal, it remains an observable and critical
challenge to actually anchor, i.e. institutionalize, EAM in the organization and
among non-architects. Based on previous work outlining design factors for
EAM in light of institutional theory, this work discusses the theoretical grounding of respective design factors and proposes measurement items for assessing
the institutionalization of EAM in organizations. The work identifies measurement items for the factors legitimacy, efficiency, stakeholder multiplicity, organizational grounding, goal consistency, content creation, diffusion and trust,
contributing to evaluate and inform EAM design from several, partially new
perspectives.

Keywords: Measurement items, Institutionalization, Enterprise Architecture
Management.

1   Introduction

At the core of this research lies the observable issue that an effective anchoring of
EAM within the organization and in particular among non-architects remains a major
challenge. This challenge is also well reflected in Gartner's recent reasoning for the
finding that most analyzed organizations are still at a rather low EA maturity level [1].
This is despite the fact that EAM has become a maturing discipline in research as well
as in practice, and a wide set of EAM methods, tools and best practices have been
researched, developed and applied [2, 3]. However, unless these methods are broadly
supported and become operative, envisioned EA benefits will be limited or, for that
matter, take much longer time for realization. One reason for the difficulties of such
an anchoring of EAM may be that the immediate context of EAM, i.e. the way how
and why the organization responds to the EAM approach on a normative level, is only
little understood [4].

The paper at hand addresses this issue based on an institutional theory perspective,
as it may be well applicable to inform and conceptualize an anchoring of EAM.
Institutional theory is among other aspects concerned with the questions of how

S. Aier et al. (Eds.): TEAR 2012 and PRET 2012, LNBIP 131, pp. 268–283, 2012.

organizations and individuals respond to pressures and what factors influence their conformance [5-7]. In our case we ask which design factors are important to anchor EAM and foster its acceptance, or said differently, which design factors should be obeyed in order to institutionalize EAM. Institutionalization can be defined as the process of establishing a practice as a norm thus giving it a "rulelike status in social thought and action" [8]. Under the assumption that EAM is being useful and adequately implemented such that it provide a positive contribution to the organizational development [9], this is what we should try to achieve. The term *design factor* is used to indicate our ultimate goal, namely the design of EAM. We are thus interested in factors that can actually be influence by the design of EAM as opposed to wider influencing factors which may also be important (e.g. world economy fluctuations), but which cannot be controlled nor be reasonably respected as part of our intraorganizational EAM context.

Fig. 1 illustrates the line of thought underlying this work: The upper bubbles represent directing functions that exert pressures onto the rest of the focal organization. A pressure can be a guideline, rule, norm or regulation, for example. Depending on the pressure's characteristics, the organization's response may range from acquiesce to defiance and manipulation of the pressure or the pressure exerting entity itself [7]. Clearly, obligations such as the necessity to keep track of financial spending coming from the controlling function, for example, are much more accepted and institutionalized than e.g. architecture principles coming from EAM. The focus of this research lies on the very left of the figure, asking which design factors are important to institutionalize EAM, i.e. to essentially foster positive rather than defying organizational responses.

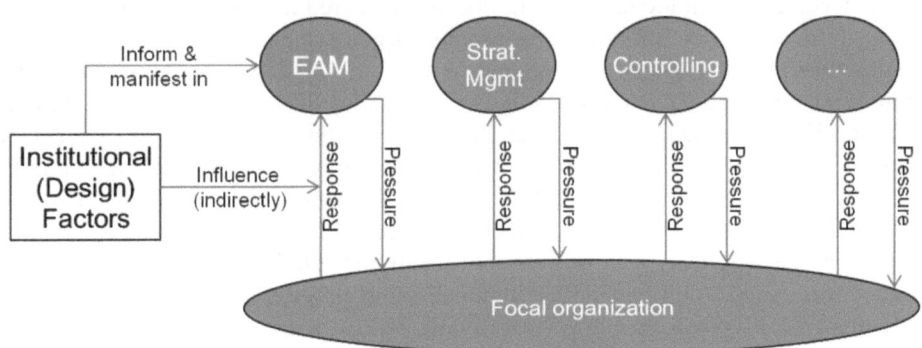

Fig. 1. Design Factors for EAM

The paper reports on research in progress towards an instrument providing guidance on how to institutionalize EAM in organizations. To that end, the work addresses in general two research gaps: From an institutional theory point of view, it applies the institutional perspective to the organization as level of analysis, thus aiming at understanding *intra*-organizational behavior. While previous institutional research at this level of analysis is very limited, it is believed to go far in adding to institutional theory [10]. From an EAM point of view, this work's perspective should contribute to better EAM design and an empowerment of existing EAM methods. Hjort-Madsen notes that an institutional perspective addressing economic, political and contextual factors as opposed to technical ones, is underrepresented in EA research so far [11, 12].

In conclusion, the goal of the paper at hand is to construct *measurement items* towards a theoretically grounded model of design factors for an institutionalization of EAM. These items should be the foundation of a model providing the utility to be able to analyze an organization's EAM approach and to subsequently derive important fields of action for improvement. The measurement item creation is based on previous work about relevant design factors. Following thorough methodological procedures for construct measurement, the paper (1) conceptualizes the constructs and (2) identifies measurement items based on reviews of the literature, deduction from the theoretical definition of the constructs and previous empirical research on the focal constructs [13-15].[1]

The remainder of the paper is structured as follows. Chapter two outlines the theoretical and methodological foundations. Chapter three conceptualizes our design factors and discusses each factor and related measurement items. Chapter four concludes the paper with a discussion, limitations, and an outlook on evaluation procedures for the herein presented work.

2   Theoretical Foundations and Relevant Factors

2.1   An Institutional Perspective on EAM

In an IS context, institutional theory has been considered in many facets. Boudreau & Robey [16], Markus & Robey [17] for example argue that and how theories, including institutional theory, can contribute to questions of information technology and organizational change. In a similar vein, Orlikowski & Barley [18] elaborate on the interplay between IT and organizational research, suggesting that transformations cannot be understood without considering their institutional contexts. Also, from a macro perspective, it has been analyzed which institutions influence (IT) innovations and how institutional pressures influence the adoption of respective systems [19, 20]. Another stream of research deals with processes of institutionalization of IT in organizations, with institutionalization and de-institutionalization processes and respective forces that drive such endeavors [21]. While being far from complete, this brief review shows that an institutional perspective is being considered important in the context of IS and (strategic) management.

Focused on the relationship between institutional theory and EAM the work by Hjort-Madsen stands out. Hjort-Madsen investigates how EA implementation [11] and adoption [12] is dependent upon and shaped by institutional forces, noting that this issue is underrepresented in EA research so far. Looking at public sector

---

[1]   Methodologically-wise so called *constructs* are in our case instantiated by the aforementioned *design factors*, which can be regarded to embody our application domain and the deeper purpose. Both terms may be used interchangeably throughout this work, though.

organizations, Hjort-Madsen points out that interoperability and IS planning, which can be facilitated through EAM, is not only a technical issue, but economic, political and contextual factors are just as important. Related to different institutional settings, he identifies adoption patterns that describe how EA is adopted by agencies. By considering formerly ignored institutional pressures, he contributes to understanding and advancing EA as a transformation approach. However, his work stays on a descriptive-explorative level and focuses on pressures coming from the outside of the focal organization. In contrast to this, we intend to look at how institutional factors relate to an intra-organizational anchoring and acceptance of EAM, and how resulting insights can inform EAM design. Overall, we found that a concrete structuring of institutional factors influencing EAM in an intra-organizational context is lacking so far.

2.2   Adopted Methodology

For scale development, we adopt a combination of the approaches from Moore & Benbasat [22], which can be regarded as a revised version of the methodological procedures from Davis [14], and the construct measurement and validation procedures from MacKenzie et al. [13]. The reason for a combination of both methods lies in the intention to utilize the strengths of both: Moore & Benbasat's so called Instrument Development Process consists of three stages, which are well comprehensible and have gained wide acceptance among IS researchers, who adopted (and adapted) the approach to various contexts (e.g. [23]). The three stages are Item Creation, Scale Development and Instrument Testing. MacKenzie et al.'s "construct measurement and validation procedures" in turn represent a revised, complementary and more detailed guideline. They split the whole scale development process into ten steps and propose additional techniques for accomplishing certain steps. The paper at hand mainly deals with the Item Creation stage, which corresponds to step two ("Generate Items to Represent the Construct") of MacKenzie et al.'s [13] updated scale development procedure. The essence of the three stages is outlined in the following.

Item Creation is concerned with establishing a pool of items that can potentially describe a construct. An item is typically a statement that respondents can indicate their degree of agreement to. The goal of the phase is to ensure content validity, i.e. the intended content of a construct shall be adequately addressed, or represented, by the pool of measurement items. Adequately in this context means that the items shall be focused on the construct's domain, but fully capture all of the essential aspects of the construct while at the same time trying to minimize overlaps with other constructs. The items may come from a variety of sources such as literature, deduction from construct definition, empirical research or expert suggestions [13]. However, generated items should always be tailored to the research issue in question and thus follow Ajzen & Fishbein's [24] suggestions to not only include the actual behavior (e.g. using EA), but also to respect the target at which the behavior is directed (e.g. EAM function), the context for the behavior (e.g. intra-organizational use of EAM services for transformation support), and a time frame (e.g. current, previous and planned EAM initiatives). Overall, we follow these guidelines, while trying to adopt measurement items that were rigorously derived and successfully applied in previous research as far as possible and feasible. The time frame is not explicitly included in our item specifications though, as we intend to examine the current situation in organizations only.

Scale Development aims at so called construct validity (cf. [22]). Using a certain technique, previously generated items are assessed by a group of (targeted) experts in order to achieve the following goals: 1) Convergent validity and discriminant validity, i.e. an item is consistently attributed to only one particular construct; 2) Appropriate coverage, i.e. removal or refinement of ambiguous, too similar or less relevant items. Many techniques have been developed to achieve construct validity, while two of them appear to have gained most prominence. The first technique resembles a "card sorting" exercise: Judges are asked to sort the various items into construct categories and rank how well the items fit the construct definitions. The procedure allows for multiple rounds and the option to present the definition of intended constructs upfront or to have the participants create their own labels for the constructs [14, 22]. In the second technique, the researcher creates a matrix with construct definitions at the top of the columns and items listed at the rows. Judges are then asked to rate in each cell how well an item fits the construct, typically using a five point Likert scale. The ratings are then evaluated using statistical means [13, 25].

Instrument Testing is then the last step towards a valid theoretical model. It is concerned with testing the developed scales (and potential construct relationships) at a higher sample size. However, provided that the previous phases are conducted rigorously, this phase should a) be limited to data gathering and evaluation, and b) be likely to yield good and significant results.

3   Development of Measurement Items

3.1   Conceptualization of Constructs

Prior to the aforementioned measurement item generation and scale development procedure, conceptual definitions of the constructs of interest have to be developed. A construct is a rather abstract, more general and latent variable that is not or hardly directly observable or measurable. A solid conceptualization of constructs has gained increased attention in literature. While Moore and Benbasat's frequently cited three stages instrument development process does not explicitly address construct conceptualization, MacKenzie et al. dedicate a detailed first step to it, noting that an adequate construct definition was a critical limitation of current scale development procedures and measurement model specifications. They critically note that "the failure to adequately specify the conceptual meaning of a study's focal constructs…triggers a sequence of events that undermines construct validity (primarily due to measure deficiency), statistical conclusion validity (due to the biasing effects of measurement model misspecification), and ultimately internal validity (due to a combination of factors)" [cf. 26]. In our attempt to avoid these problems, **Table 1** portrays the design factors and their respective specification following respective conceptualization recommendations [13].

Our constructs have been developed in previous research [4] based on case study assessments and informed by the institutional framework from Oliver [7]. The constructs are to represent factors that influence stakeholders', i.e. in particular non-architects', perception and acceptance of EAM. Together, the factors can therefore be regarded as indicators for a successful institutionalization of EAM.

As previously mentioned, our long-term goal is to develop design principles that address these constructs and inform the design of EAM (according to the design science research paradigm [27]), which is why we refer to our constructs as design factors.

Table 1. Conceptualization of Design Factors

EAM Design Factor	Specification
Legitimacy	Entity: Person; General property: Perceived social rationale for participation (in EAM); Themes: Management acknowledgement, reputation, social acceptance; Definition: The degree to which a stakeholder gains social fitness when supporting EAM.
Efficiency	Entity: Person; General property: Perceived economic rationale for participation (in EAM); Themes: Decision making speed, project time, project sustainability, implementation quality, utilization of available infrastructure/information; Definition: The degree to which a stakeholder becomes more efficient when following EA guidelines.
Coordination of Pressure Multiplicity	Entity: Organization; General property: Potential for inconsistencies/conflicts with other directing entities depending upon the amount of coordinating action; Themes: Alignment with other coordinating functions (e.g. process management), alignment of different EAM divisions/levels, centrality of EA decision making; Definition: The degree to which the focal EAM is aligned with other pressure exerting entities.
Grounding	Entity: Organization; General property: Organizational anchor points (for EAM); Themes: Stakeholder demand, strategic importance, hierarchical position; Definition: The degree to which EAM is grounded at different anchor points within the organization
Goal Consistency	Entity: Person; General property: Characteristics of goal system; Themes: Stakeholders' knowledge about others' transformation activities, design of stakeholder goal systems, raise/promotion; Definition: The degree to which EA goals are in line with / supported by stakeholders' goals.

Table 1. (*continued*)

EAM Design Factor	Specification
Content Creation	Entity: Process; General property: Stakeholder-orientation in EA content creation activities; Themes: Availability of stakeholder-involving processes, participation of stakeholders, contribution channels, approval of stakeholders; Definition: The degree to which EA content creation processes cater for stakeholder involvement.
Diffusion	Entity: Process/Team; General property: Communication and diffusion activities; Themes: Propagation of the EA idea, availability of showcases, communication procedures; Definition: The degree to which (voluntary) EA participation is fostered by communication.
Trust	Entity: Person; General property: Attitude / Trustworthiness (of the EAM function); Themes: Trust in EAM as instrument, trust in EAM team; Definition: The degree to which stakeholders have trust in EAM.

Besides a label (column1), column two specifies the construct with respect to four dimensions. The entity is the object that is in focus of the construct, i.e. it is the object to which the general property applies and that is eventually addressed by measurement items. The general property refers to the conceptual domain of the construct. This should be specified, because it may make a considerable difference whether the construct is to represent a (subjective) perception or an as far as possible objective outcome, for example [13, citing 28]. In our case, we may differentiate two major groups of constructs. On the one hand, we have constructs addressing *personal* perceptions or feelings towards EAM such as the potential to gain legitimacy, become more efficient, or one's personal trust towards EAM. On the other hand, we have constructs which address the wider EAM setup and are attributed the entities organization, process, or team, accordingly. Examples are coordination activities, grounding, as well as content creation or diffusion activities. Goal consistency may be regarded to be a special case as it is to some extent concerned with clearly defined, job-related performance goals. However, the extent to which EAM goals are intrinsically or extrinsically supported by an individual is a personal matter, which is why we have attributed the construct to the entity person. The themes then portray the line of thought and the aspects of the construct, which will subsequently be captured by the measurement items. At last, the definition is intended to wrap up all these aspects in a short and understandable manner. Based on this construct conceptualization, the following section will have a closer look at how each construct can be measured.

3.2   Generation of Measurement Items

Items were created based on literature and domain knowledge. Starting from a search for measurement scales in the IS domain, the search was continued in an explorative fashion including a wider range of other research domains such as business administration, management, psychology and politics. The search was conducted using EBSCO and google scholar using key words from the construct descriptions and the terms "measurement", "scale" or "model". The search was limited to title, keywords and abstract. The more explorative approach taken appeared reasonable as our primary goal was to first of all generate feasible items rather than validate them [21]. The last column (Adoption Type (AT)) of the measurement item tables below indicates to which extent a scale could be adopted:

1. Construct and context fit – Items fit to our factor's purpose, and the context is (closely) related to EAM and/or an intra-organizational institutional perspective.
2. Construct fits – Items fit to our factor's purpose, but the context is different.
3. Analogy – Items can be adapted based on our construct's conceptualization.

Legitimacy in our case refers to the amount of social fitness or acceptance that an individual gains when contributing to an advancement of the enterprise architecture. Addressing personal social benefit expectancy, the items for this factor can be well drawn from Venkatesh et al.'s work, which in turn already consolidates previous measurement items. Of particular relevance appear items from performance expectancy and social influence (see Table 2) [15]. Legitimacy in general is acknowledged as an important concept for explaining a wide range of effects such as desirability, credibility and appropriateness [29]. We hypothesize this to be relevant for EAM, too [30].

Table 2. Measurement Items for (Social) Legitimacy

No	Item definition	Source(s)	AT
LE1	People who are important to me think that I should mind EAM.	[15]	2
LE2	Minding EA is acknowledged by my superiors.	[15, 31]	2
LE3	Senior management supports me in advancing EA.	[15, 31]	2
LE4	In general, the organization supports EAM.	[15, 31]	2
LE5	People minding EAM have more prestige than those who do not.	[15, 22]	2
LE6	People minding EAM have a high profile.	[15, 22]	2

Efficiency is related to economic accountability and rationalization on a personal perceptional level. In a similar fashion, this factor is also regularly part of eventual EA benefit measurement, representing a main rationale to run EAM programs in the first place [cf. 32, 33]. However, in our case the factor is targeted at stakeholder perception (entity=person). As such, we may again draw some items from Venkatesh et al. [15]. The last two items though are novel and intended to address specific EAM concerns (**Table 3**).

Table 3. Measurement Items for Efficiency

No	Item definition	Source(s)	AT
EF1	Minding EAM allows accomplishing decision making for transformation projects more quickly.	[14, 15, 22]	2
EF2	Minding EAM allows completing transformation projects more quickly.	[14, 15, 22]	2
EF3	Minding EAM increases the quality of output of transformation projects.	[15, 31]	2
EF4	Minding EAM increases the sustainability of project outputs.	[15, 31]	3
EF5	Using EAM reduces the time needed for data gathering required for transformation projects.	[15, 31]	2
EF6	Minding EAM takes too long.	[15, 31]	2
EF7	Using EAM allows making use of available infrastructure efficiently.		
EF8	Using EAM allows making use of available transformation knowledge efficiently.		

Multiplicity refers to directions, strengths, and synergies of interacting stakeholder claims [34]. We apply this thought to EAM. Besides EAM, constituents like strategic management, controlling, HR, and IT exert pressures on each other and the focal organization as a whole with respect to requirements, releases, project portfolios, business development etc. A major challenge of EAM operating at the nexus of Business and IT is to coordinate and line up with all these pressure exerting entities in order to become more effective and to increase its penetration. We hypothesize that if such coordination is low, EA development will be less aligned and in consequence, EAM's voice will also be less heard among non-architects and project managers (e.g. due to conflicting development objectives). After all, the latter aspect appears to be critical but a major challenge, as EAM is a rather young (and thus less institutionalized) enterprise function as opposed to controlling, for example. Not surprisingly then, we could so far hardly find measurement scales that fit our construct (**Table 4**).

Table 4. Measurement Items for Multiplicity

No	Item definition	Source(s)	AT
MU1	EAM is coordinated with other management functions.		
MU2	Different EAM units are aligned to each other.		
MU3	EAM decision making is done centrally, involving a multiplicity of stakeholders / business units.	[33]	1
MU4	Bodies for the coordination of EAM concerns (e.g. EAM board) are formally established.		
MU5	Considerable differences exist between the EA function and other business units with respect to EA development.		

Grounding refers to the anchoring points of EAM within the organization, which can be decomposed into two distinguishable facets or sub-dimensions (**Table 5**): GR1-3 refer to the demand side of EAM. They intend to elicit who the demanders of EAM in the organization are, i.e. who is actually interested in and makes use of EAM services.

To that end, we differentiate between three classical EAM stakeholder groups - (1) business units, (2) IT and (3) senior management. GR4-6 then relate to some extent to governance issues, asking how possibly restricting guidelines EAM may impose are grounded. Like the previous factor (multiplicity), grounding appears to be very EAM-specific by relating to cross-functional and cross-level issues.

Table 5. Measurement Items for Grounding

No	Item definition	Source(s)	AT
GR1	EAM is called for by business units.		
GR2	EAM is called for by the IT function.		
GR3	EAM is called for by senior management.		
GR4	EAM is positioned high in the organizational hierarchy (organigram).		
GR5	EAM guidelines are grounded in the overall business strategy.		
GR6	EAM guidelines are grounded in the IT strategy.		

Goal Consistency refers to the congruence of EA goals and individual stakeholders' goals, such as project managers. This, ideally, also includes awareness between stakeholders about their respective goals and transformation intentions, as this may provide opportunities to consult EAM to help leverage synergies - for instance by coordinating (joint) projects of multiple business units. The last two items address personal career goals more directly (**Table 6**). In previous research, goal congruence has in varying settings been identified as a significant thruster for goal achievement [35, 36]. Overall, goal consistency is very relevant for EAM, as a major goal of EAM is to leverage synergies across projects. However, even if the top management directive was to maximize the benefit for the whole organization, this will be difficult to achieve without additional incentives. As repeatedly experienced with industry partners, a project manager will be reluctant to spend $10 M more, even if it would save another unit $20 M.

Table 6. Measurement Items for Goal Consistency

No	Item definition	Source(s)	AT
CO1	Stakeholders know about other units' goals.		
CO2	Stakeholders know about other units' transformations.		
CO3	EAM goals are supported by non-architects' goal system formulation.		
CO4	EAM goals are explicitly addressed in non-architects' goal system formulation.		
CO5	Non-architects have incentives to pursue cross-project or cross-departmental goals.		
CO6	Minding EAM will increase stakeholders' chances of obtaining a promotion.	[15, 37]	2
CO7	Minding EAM will increase stakeholders' chances of getting a raise.	[15, 37]	2

Content Creation items are intended to capture two related issues, namely if defined processes exist for content creation and whether stakeholder participation is explicitly part of these processes. For one, we ask whether stakeholders participate in content creation and approval, which is also addressed in related literature (**Table 7**). Overall though, we relate this to the question of whether participation processes are properly defined (entity=process). This link is based on the observation that participation (or at least approval) is frequently catered for and appreciated, but defined processes and EAM reviews as part of which participation happens may be lacking. In consequence to the latter, (proactive) contributions from non-architects are limited, handled non-transparently and may eventually come to an end, which in turn is contra-productive to the outset objective, namely fostering an institutionalization of EAM.

Table 7. Measurement Items for Content Creation

No	Item definition	Source(s)	AT
CR1	EA content is developed with all relevant stakeholders.		
CR2	EA content is approved (signed off) by all relevant stakeholders.	[33]	1
CR3	Adequate stakeholder participation is ensured as part of EAM processes.	[33]	1
CR4	Stakeholder participation (e.g. making architectural suggestions) is facilitated through defined channels and processes.		
CR5	EAM guidelines are regularly reviewed.		
CR6	Exceptions to EAM guidelines are discussed through defined channels and processes.		

Diffusion is to address what is done to make stakeholders aware of EAM services in order to foster their diffusion. Due to the challenges that a) EAM is oftentimes a rather young function within the organizations, b) EAM is concerned with partially abstract issues, and c) Architects are often occupied with operative work or project work, EAM communication is frequently lacking. However, making non-architects aware of EAM is an important antecedent to EAM demand and EAM penetration. The last two items capture a particular sub-aspect, namely the extent to which 'allied' *non*-architects signify that EAM is a good idea.

Table 8. Measurement Items for Diffusion

No	Item definition	Source(s)	AT
DI1	EA documents are communicated to all relevant stakeholders.	[33]	3
DI2	EA documents can be accessed easily by all relevant stakeholders.	[33]	3
DI3	Showcases demonstrating the necessity for EAM are available.		
DI4	Showcases demonstrating the necessity for EAM are effectively communicated.		
DI5	Showcases demonstrating success stories of EAM are available.		
DI6	Showcases demonstrating success stories of EAM are effectively communicated.		
DI7	It is defined how and which EA documents are communicated.		
DI8	Non-architects promote the EA idea.		
DI9	Non-architects promote EA content.		

Trust has been added as dedicated factor even though one may argue that trust is indirectly reflected by all other factors. However, this factor shall in particular capture non-architects' attitude towards EAM as instrument and the architecture team behind it, which may for example also include personal trust relationships not explicitly addressed in previous factors. In consequence, the construct is clearly comprised of two sub-dimensions. The first (TR1 & TR2) addresses trust in EAM as an instrument in general, whereas the second (TR3-17) is more related to interpersonal trust and trust in the EAM team, respectively. With respect to the second sub-dimension, many measurement items could be adopted from two major sources. Weatherford's work is actually concerned with political legitimacy, which, however, comprises several briefly and well-worded measurement items that appear to 'hit the nail on the head' - also in our setting (see TR3-8) [38]. Serva et al. investigated trust between interacting teams, i.e. between management and development teams. Their scales cover the facets of ability (here TR9-11), benevolence (here TR12-14), and integrity (here TR15-17) [39, 40]. Analogously, we intend to examine trust between the EAM team and affected non-architects. All potential measurement items are presented in **Table 9** for completeness and integrity purposes. We are aware though that this large amount of items has to be condensed considerably in order to be manageable for future probing. However, we decided to do that in conjunction with industry input as part of further research rather than limiting results in this work upfront.

Table 9. Measurement Items for Trust

No	Item definition	Source(s)	AT
TR1	Non-architects trust EAM to be a reasonable instrument for the organization		
TR2	Non-architects believe that EAM wastes a lot of money.	[38]	2
TR3	Non-architects believe that Architects do not care much about what non-architects think.	[38]	2
TR4	Non-architects trust EAM to do what is right.	[38]	2
TR5	Non-architects believe that EAM is just looking out for itself.	[38]	2
TR6	Non-architects believe that EAM is run for non-architects' benefit.	[38]	2
TR7	Non-architects believe that the people running EAM are competent and know what they do.	[38]	2
TR8	Non-architects feel taken seriously by the EAM team.	[38]	3
TR9	Non-architects feel that the EAM team is very capable of performing its job.	[39]	2
TR10	Non-architects have confidence in the skills of the EAM team.	[39]	2
TR11	Non-architects believe that the EAM team is well qualified.	[39]	2
TR12	The EAM team really looks out for what is important to non-architects.	[39]	2
TR13	Non-architects' needs and desires are very important to the EAM team.	[39]	2
TR14	The EAM team goes out of its way to help non-architects.	[39]	2
TR15	Non-architects believe that the EAM team tries to be fair in dealings with others.	[39]	2
TR16	The EAM team has a strong sense of justice.	[39]	2
TR17	Non-architects like the values of the EAM team.	[39]	2

4   Discussion and Outlook

Reflecting on the up to this point established measurement items yields two findings. Firstly, it was hardly possible to find constructs or a set of measurement items in literature that perfectly fit our purposes. This may among other things be related to the history of research of the two research domains the paper at hand builds upon: With respect to EAM research, in-depth assessments of success and acceptance factors for EAM using sophisticated measurement scales still appears to be in its infancy. While first results to that end exist [32, 33], previous research was primarily focused on technical, methodological and governance issues from a rather managerial perspective. Institutional theory in turn was rarely applied to an intra-organizational context, and quantitative assessments of institutional constructs appear to be limited. As a consequence for the presented measurement items, these issues meant that also in cases where constructs were semantically similar (e.g. legitimacy or efficiency), items had to be reasonably selected rather than being able to adopt a whole construct conceptualization including its items at once. Secondly, items may overlap with other constructs. While trying to develop items through appropriate planning and rigorous procedures rather than through ex post testing in order to increase convergent and discriminant validity and coverage up front, this cannot be excluded yet, but has to be developed through further research including practice evaluations, using one of the techniques described in chapter two. At last, we would like to note that we make no claim for completeness with respect to identified measurement items, which would appear to be a bold and hardly provable claim given the wickedness of the problem at hand. We may have missed literature to provide further measurement items for our constructs, in particular because appropriate measurement items adoptable to our purpose may appear in a wider range of research fields. Also, the conceptualization of our constructs and the related search procedure may have limited our results. However, we are confident to have covered a thorough spectrum of important constructs and items, and to be able resolve ambiguities and increase the stability of our items when iteratively developing final scales.

Despite these limitations, the paper at hand contributes to stakeholder-oriented EAM research and to institutional theory. The paper advances research of how an institutional perspective can be concretized and inform another discipline. Especially an organization-internal application of institutional theory is so far very limited in previous research [10]. To that end, we hope to have contributed to this level of institutional analysis' body of knowledge. For practitioners and the EAM knowledge base, we think that our approach provides a differentiated and worthwhile perspective, namely addressing in particular normative factors and perceptions of EAM stakeholders. Concerning the utility for practitioners, the identified design factors should allow for a differentiated reflection of norms and values attributed to EAM by stakeholders, notwithstanding the fact that final and validated measurement scales, or, for that matter, a complete theoretical model, are still pending. However, despite of this lack of validation of the proposed constructs and measurement items, the herein presented perspective may be relevant and worth a discussion at this stage.

This being said, future research needs to first of all assess the proposed items and constructs with respect to construct validity, i.e. stage two of Moore & Benbasat's procedure has to be conducted. As described in chapter two, good methodological reference literature on how and with which potential techniques to proceed exist to that end. As part of ongoing research, the development of scales as well as a theoretical model is currently in progress in an iterative fashion, using the 'matrix technique' and results from a first questionnaire-based survey. Concerning the former, a matrix is being created with construct definitions at the top of the columns and items listed at the rows. Judges consisting of academic scholars as well as professionals are then asked to rate in each cell how well an item fits the construct, using a five point Likert scale ranging from 1 (not at all) to 5 (completely). A one-way repeated measures ANOVA should then be used to assess whether an item's mean rating on one design factor differs from its ratings on other design factors [cf. 13]. In a related, parallel stream of research, we asked professionals about their status of establishing EAM. The survey comprised questions pertaining to institutional factors, stakeholder responses, organizational culture and the realized utility of EAM. Results from this survey are expected to triangulate and inform scale development for the herein discussed institutional design factors. First results from 90 respondents look promising. Based on resulting insights from these two approaches, we will then develop design principles for EAM that address the critical design factors such that EAM may become more operative within organizations.

Acknowledgement. This work has been supported by the Swiss National Science Foundation (SNSF).

References

1. Gartner, I.: ITScore Overview for Enterprise Architecture. Gartner, Inc., Stamford (2012)
2. Mykhashchuk, M., Buckl, S., Dierl, T., Schweda, C.M.: Charting the Landscape of Enterprise Architecture Management. In: The 10th International Conference on Wirtschaftsinformatik WI 2.011, Zurich, pp. 570–577 (2011)
3. Buckl, S., Schweda, C.M.: On the State-of-the-Art in Enterprise Architecture Management Literature. Munich (2011)
4. Aier, S., Weiss, S.: An Institutional Framework for Analyzing Organizational Responses to the Establishment of Architectural Transformation. In: The 20th European Conference on Information Systems, Barcelona (2012)
5. Zucker, L.G.: Institutional Theories of Organization. Annual Review of Sociology 13, 443–464 (1987)
6. Scott, W.R.: Institutions and Organizations: Ideas and Interests. Sage Publications, London (2008)
7. Oliver, C.: Strategic Responses to Institutional Processes. Academy of Management Review 16, 145–179 (1991)
8. Meyer, J.W., Rowan, B.: Institutionalized Organizations: Formal Structure as Myth and Ceremony. American Journal of Sociology 83, 340–363 (1977)

9. Aier, S., Gleichauf, B., Winter, R.: Understanding Enterprise Architecture Management Design – An Empirical Analysis. In: The 10th International Conference on Wirtschaftsinformatik WI 2.011, Zurich, pp. 645–654 (2011)

10. Greenwood, R., Oliver, C., Suddaby, R., Sahlin-Andersson, K. (eds.): The SAGE Handbook of Organizational Institutionalism. Sage Publications, London (2008)

11. Hjort-Madsen, K.: Enterprise Architecture Implementation and Management: A Case Study on Interoperability, p. 71c. IEEE Computer Society Press, Hawaii (2006)

12. Hjort-Madsen, K.: Institutional patterns of enterprise architecture adoption in government. Transforming Government: People, Process and Policy 1, 333–349 (2007)

13. MacKenzie, S.B., Podsakoff, P.M., Podsakoff, N.P.: Construct Measurement and Validation Procedures in MIS and Behavioral Research: Integrating New and Existing Techniques. MIS Quarterly 35, 293–334 (2011)

14. Davis, F.D.: Perceived Usefulness, Perceived Ease of Use, and User Acceptance of Information Technology. MIS Quartely 13, 318–340 (1989)

15. Venkatesh, V., Morris, M.G., Davis, G.B., Davis, F.D.: User Acceptance of Information Technology: Toward A Unified View. MIS Quarterly 27, 425–478 (2003)

16. Boudreau, M.-C., Robey, D.: Coping with contradictions in business process re-engineering. Information Technology & People 9, 40–57 (1996)

17. Markus, M.L., Robey, D.: Information Technology and Organizational Change – Causal Structure in Theory and Research. Management Science 34, 583–598 (1988)

18. Orlikowski, W.J., Barley, S.R.: Technology and Institutions: What Can Research on Information Technology and Research on Organizations Learn From Each Other? MIS Quarterly 25, 145–165 (2001)

19. King, J.L., Gurbaxani, V., Kraemer, K.L., McFarlan, F.W., Raman, K.S., Yap, C.S.: Institutional Factors in Information Technology Innovation. Information Systems Research 5, 139–169 (1994)

20. Teo, H.H., Wei, K.K., Benbasat, I.: Predicting intention to adopt interorganizational linkages: an institutional perspective. MIS Quarterly 27, 19–49 (2003)

21. Baptista, J.J.: Institutionalisation as a process of interplay between technology and its organisational context of use. Journal of Information Technology 24, 305–319 (2009)

22. Moore, G., Benbasat, I.: Development of an instrument to measure the perceptions of adopting an information technology innovation. Information Systems Research 2, 192–222 (1991)

23. Recker, J., Rosemann, M.: Understanding the Process of Constructing Scales Inventories in the Process Modelling Domain. In: European Conference on Information Systems (ECIS), p. 8. St. Gallen, Switzerland (2007)

24. Ajzen, I., Fishbein, M.: Understanding Attitudes and Predicting Social Behavior. Prentice-Hall, Englewood Cliffs (1980)

25. Hinkin, T.R., Tracey, J.B.: An Analysis of Variance Approach to Content Validation. Organizational Research Methods 2, 175–186 (1999)

26. MacKenzie, S.B.: The Dangers of Poor Construct Conceptualization. Journal of the Academy of Marketing Science 31, 323–326 (2003)

27. Hevner, A.R., Chatterjee, S.: Design Research in Information Systems: Theory and Practice, vol. 22. Springer US, Heidelberg (2010)

28. Schwab, D.P.: Construct Validity in Organizational Behavior. In: Staw, B.M., Cummings, L.L. (eds.) Research in Organizational Behavior, pp. 3–43. JAI Press, Greenwich (1980)

29. Suchman, M.C.: Managing Legitimacy: Strategic and Institutional Approaches. Academy of Management Review 20, 571–610 (1995)

30. Aier, S., Weiss, S.: Facilitating Enterprise Transformation Through Legitimacy – An Institutional Perspective. In: Multikonferenz Wirtschaftsinformatik 2012, Gito, Braunschweig, pp. 1073–1084 (2012)
31. Thompson, R.L., Higgins, C.A., Howell, J.M.: Personal Computing: Toward a Conceptual Model of Utilization. MIS Quarterly 15, 125–143 (1991)
32. Foorthuis, R., van Steenbergen, M., Mushkudiani, N., Bruls, W., Brinkkemper, S., Bos, R.: On Course, but Not There Yet: Enterprise Architecture Conformance and Benefits in Systems Development (2010)
33. Schmidt, C., Buxmann, P.: Outcomes and success factors of enterprise IT architecture management: empirical insight from the international financial services industry. European Journal of Information Systems 20, 168–185 (2011)
34. Neville, B.A., Menguc, B.: Stakeholder Multiplicity: Toward an Understanding of the Interactions between Stakeholders. Journal of Business Ethics 66, 377–391 (2006)
35. Jauch, L.R., Osborn, R.N., Terpening, W.D.: Goal Congruence and Employee Orientation: The Substitution Effect. Academy of Management Journal 23, 544–550 (1980)
36. Kristof-Brown, A.L., Stevens, C.K.: Goal congruence in project teams: Does the fit between members' personal mastery and performance goals matter? Journal of Applied Psychology 86, 1083–1095 (2001)
37. Compeau, D., Higgins, C.A., Huff, S.: Social Cognitive Theory and Individual Reactions to Computing Technology: A Longitudinal Study. MIS Quarterly 23, 145–158 (1999)
38. Weatherford, M.S.: Measuring Political Legitimacy. The American Political Science Review 86, 149–166 (1992)
39. Serva, M.A., Fuller, M.A., Mayer, R.C.: The reciprocal nature of trust: a longitudinal study of interacting teams. Journal of Organizational Behavior 26, 625–648 (2005)
40. Mayer, R.C., Davis, J.H., Schoorman, F.D.: An Integrative Model of Organizational Trust. The Academy of Management Review 20, 709–734 (1995)

Towards a Unified and Configurable Structure for EA Management KPIs

Florian Matthes, Ivan Monahov,
Alexander W. Schneider, and Christopher Schulz

Technische Universität München (TUM)
Chair for Informatics 19 (sebis)
Boltzmannstr. 3, 85748 Garching bei München, Germany
{matthes,ivan.monahov,alexander.w.schneider,christopher.schulz}@in.tum.de

Abstract. The discipline Enterprise Architecture (EA) management aims to align business and IT, foster communication, and support the everlasting transformation of the organization. Thereby, EA management initiatives are driven by respective EA management goals, whose degree of achievement must be measurable. This calls for the definition of corresponding Key Performance Indicators (KPIs) enabling enterprise architects to plan, forecast, benchmark, and assess the goal fulfillment. As recent literature in the field shows, there are only few KPIs dedicated to validate EA management goal achievement. Moreover, existing indicators are differently structured, selective regarding the specific EA management goals, too general and vague with respect to the required data, and do not provide any adoption techniques for the enterprise context. In this paper we present a structure enabling the unified and configurable description of EA management KPIs. While the artifact ensures consistency among documented KPIs, it further provides guidance during their introduction and organization-specific adaptation. As first evaluation results prove, EA management domain experts consider the artifact on the whole as being helpful and applicable while simultaneously confirming the relevance of its constituents.

Keywords: EA management, key performance indicator, measurement, structure, goal.

1 Introduction

Today's globalized and highly competitive business environments are characterized by an increasing frequency of changes. The drivers for these changes are manifold. In a nutshell, they can be categorized as follows: newly evolving business demands, continuous technological progress, and new laws and regulations. Very often these changes tie in with a growing internal complexity of the socio-technical system of the enterprise.

Rooted in the domain of information systems architecture [34], Enterprise Architecture (EA) management represents a commonly accepted discipline to deal with this complexity. In this context, an EA can be understood as the

S. Aier et al. (Eds.): TEAR 2012 and PRET 2012, LNBIP 131, pp. 284–299, 2012.
© Springer-Verlag Berlin Heidelberg 2012

"fundamental organization of a system [enterprise] embodied in its components, their relationships to each other, and to the environment, and the principles guiding its design and evolution" as proposed by the ISO Standard 42010 [16]. As this definition suggests, EA management considers the system 'enterprise' from a holistic stance. Furthermore, the discipline covers all elements of an enterprise from business and organizational via application and information to infrastructure and data aspects [38]. Among others, the following three important advantages offered by EA management are (cf. [1], [36]):

- create a holistic perspective on the enterprise, comprising business and IT elements,
- foster communication by defining a common language for multidisciplinary stakeholders, and
- gather information from differing sources and provisioning of consistent decision base.

As part of the term EA management, the word management generally refers "to the process of assembling and using resources - human, financial, material, and information - in a goal directed manner to accomplish tasks in an organization" [4]. Concerned with the present and the expected and desired future [10], management functions are usually described by a planning, leading, organizing, and controlling dimension [4]. In EA management, the objective-directed character is realized through the definition and pursuit of specific EA management goals. Regarded as the basic purpose of any EA management initiative, each individual EA management goal represents an abstract objective ideally supporting at least one business goal [5]. Examples for typical goals are increase homogeneity or provide transparency [5]. According to a well-known quote of Tom DeMarco "you can't control what you can't measure" [9]. When focusing on the controlling dimension of EA management it becomes obvious that dedicated performance measurements present a quantitative approach to check the degree a particular EA management goal is currently fulfilled. Such measures are commonly referred to as Key Performance Indicators (KPIs). Thereby, a KPI can be defined as "an item of information collected at regular intervals to track the performance of a system [enterprise]" [12]. Literature applies also the terms metrics [25] or performance indicators [17] to refer to an identical concept.

As current literature highlights, there is a general lack of meaningful KPIs for EA management [19]. In particular this holds true for the application landscape as the sum of interconnected and continuously evolving business applications [25]. More importantly, there exists no common structure tailored to define, document, and retrieve EA management KPIs to the best knowledge of the authors. Against this background, the present article addresses subsequent research questions:

1. What are typical elements, as proposed by recent related work in the domain of economics and IT controlling, as well as IT management, to be part of a KPI description structure?
2. How could a structure, focusing on the documentation, definition, and retrieval of EA management KPIs look like?

3. Is the developed KPI structure in line with the expectations of industry experts and academics active in the field of EA management?

The remainder of this article is structured as follows: in Section 2 we describe the research approach which was put into action when developing a unified structure for documenting EA management KPIs. Based on studied literature, a KPI description structure is explained in the course of Section 3. Afterwards, the underlying literature itself is presented, revealing those elements of the designed structure which have been already proposed by sources in the field of EA managementand KPIs or which have been added based on our experience (Section 4). In Section 5, we present the results of two evaluation steps comprising an online survey and the instantiation of the structure. Finally, Section 6 summarizes our findings and lists topics we consider the most pressing for future research.

2   Research Approach

The development of a unified and configurable structure to describe EA management KPIs will result in a new Information System (IS) design artifact. Therefore, we adhere to the guidelines for IS design science proposed by Hevner et al. [15]. In the contribution section of this paper (Section 3), we present a construct which provides a vocabulary and enables the development of concrete KPI solutions (guideline 1). The relevance of the respective problem has already been described in Section 1 (guideline 2). Our research process is designed following the three phases research process of Offermann et al. [29].

Figure 1 visualizes our research approach as well as yielded (intermediate) results. In this sense, the structured and systematic approach we applied contributes to the rigor of our research (guideline 5). Since we have been embarking on a few examined domain we started the problem identification phase with an extensive literature study as proposed by [37]. Thereby, available sources from different fields, including EA management, economics and IT controlling, and IT management have been analyzed according to recommended elements of KPI descriptions. The resulting set of suitable structure elements has been iteratively extended and validated to account for EA management specific aspects (guideline 6). After a first design, primarily based on literature study and

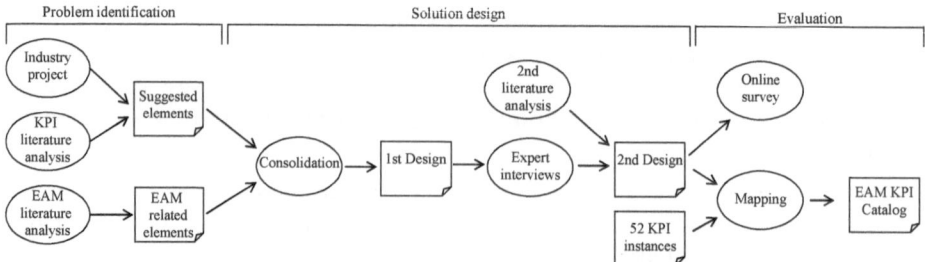

Fig. 1. Research approach for the KPI structure

our EA management knowledge, a second version of the artifact has been developed including qualitative feedback given by domain experts of a German car manufacturer. Next, the refined design artifact has been evaluated in two steps (guideline 3). First, we successfully mapped 52 measures we previously observed in industry projects and literature to the designed structure. The results [26]) have been communicated to an EA management audience and already sparked interest among Swedish practitioners [24] (guideline 7).

3   A Uniform and Configurable EA management KPI Structure

The continuously growing interest of both - practitioners and academics in the area of EA management KPIs lead us to start our research activities in this field by September of 2010. Based on literature and our experience in the area of EA management, we developed a novel structure to define, document, and retrieve EA management KPIs. The resulting artifact consists of ten elements and is introduced in this section.

3.1   EA Management KPI Structure

Figure 2 shows the arrangement of the ten elements. Each element is filled with values of an exemplary KPI which we applied in the context of a project with a large German engineering company in spring 2011. Please notice that some of these values contain bogus data due to confidentiality reasons. Fitting on a DIN A4 page, the elements are placed according to their estimated space required and significance to support quick overview and facilitate printing. In general, we distinguish between two types of KPI structure elements: **general** and **organization-specific**.

3.2   General Structure Elements (GSEs)

GSEs are understood as independent from any enterprise context. For example, the name and the calculation of a KPI are independent from the enterprise employing this KPI.

The first general structure element is a short and unique **title** as suggested by [35, 27, 13, 14, 7, 31] and also promoted by the pattern community [2]. The title is a short description providing a very general overview of the purpose of the KPI. In our experience, the title length should not exceed five words. In this vein, the title can be easily memorized and acts as a means of communication.

Next to the title, the developed structure offers a comprehensive textual **description** of the KPIs as suggested by [18, 35, 17, 30, 33, 27, 13, 23, 14, 22, 20, 3, 7, 31]. Containing not more than three phrases, the description supports interested readers in quickly deciding whenever the KPI is relevant for their purposes.

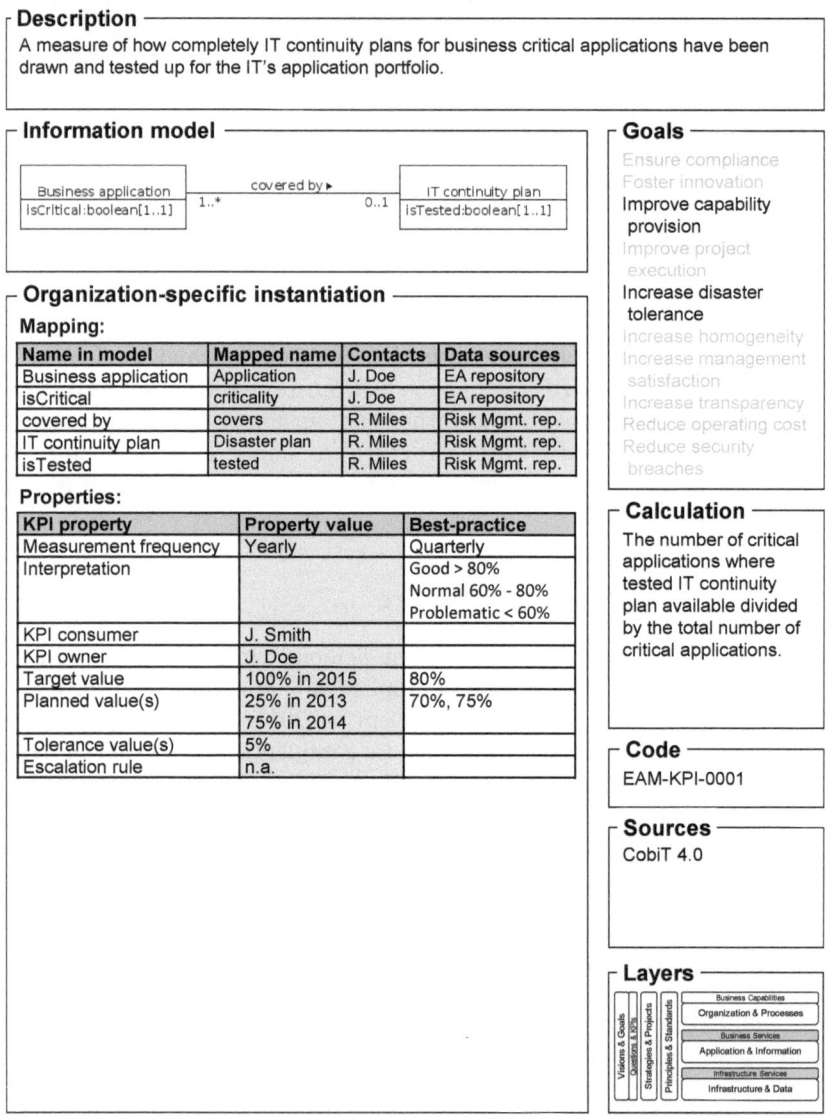

Fig. 2. Example of a concrete EA management KPI based on [26]

The **goals** element contains a list of ten common EA management goals based on the findings of Buckl et al. [5]. Thereby, each of these goals is either highlighted (black) indicating that their achievement can be measured by the underlying KPI or not (gray). A direct link between goals and KPIs measuring their achievement is been considered important also by [18, 17, 33, 13, 22, 20, 3, 7].

The **calculation** element gives a comprehensive description of the employed calculation rule. Such description is also advocated by [18, 35, 17, 30, 33, 27, 13, 23, 14, 22, 3, 7, 31].

In line with [18, 27], the **source** section is concerned about the origin of the underlying calculation. We differentiate between KPIs rooting in practice and literature. Referring to literature sources bears two advantages: first, further KPI information can be found in the corresponding source. Second, integration is facilitated in case the organization, intending to use the KPI, already applies the framework. Whenever a calculation originates from practice, two aspects are demonstrated: first, it is relevant and second, its application in an organizational context is feasible.

The **layers and cross-cutting aspects** can be understood as a static view on an organization [6] categorizing it into different parts. In the context of a KPI structure, all those parts are highlighted, whose input is required for the calculation of the KPI. This allows the enterprise to quickly decide if the KPI can be employed at all. Documenting this aspect is also suggested by [18, 35].

The **information model** describes the entities, their relationships, and their minimal properties required as input to compute the KPI [5]. Since the focus is put on data, we employ the class diagram type of the Unified Modeling Language (UML) [28]. Alternatively, the Entity Relationship Model (ERM) [8] or crow's foot notation [32] can be employed for this purpose. A documentation of required KPI data by means of an (information) model is also suggested by [18, 13].

Last but not least, a **code** element is used to uniquely define a KPI. Such identifiers are also recommended by [35, 23, 14].

3.3 Organization-Specific KPI Structure Elements (OSSEs)

As acknowledged by existing EA managementliterature, each EA management endeavor depends on the specific organizational context [5, 6]. Consequently, OSSEs depend on the context of the enterprise employing the corresponding KPI. For example, the person's name of the KPI consumer (i.e., stakeholder interested in the KPI value) and the organization-specific data sources used for the calculation. We distinguish between following two tables: (information model) **mapping** and (KPI) **properties**.

The **mapping** table supports the linking of all information model elements to the organization-specific concepts. In line with the information model, the column **name in model** provides a full listing of all concepts, their properties, and their relationships. The column **mapped name** contains the corresponding organization-specific concepts. Even though we have not found this explicit mapping in literature, this is crucial for an organization, which is committed to its own terminology. As recommended by [23], the column **contacts** documents the data owner, hence the person providing information about the specific EA element. Finally, the column **data sources** specifies the technical organization-specific data storage. The documentation of data sources, used for the computation of KPIs in enterprises, is considered important by [27, 23, 14, 31].

The **properties** table provides eight further parameterization variables (column **KPI properties**), organization-specific values (**property value**), and property values observed in practice (**best-practices**). While the first column is suggested by different sources, e.g., [23, 35], property value as well as **best-practices** have not been found during our literature study. According to [17, 23] it is important to document the actual **KPI consumer**. While the **KPI owner** (i.e., a stakeholder in the enterprise responsible for the achievement of a defined the KPIs) is proposed also by [35, 17, 23, 31], these and other authors [35, 33, 13, 23, 31] recommend the documentation of a **target value**. Furthermore, only [23] proposes the elements **planned values** and **tolerance values**. The **escalation rules** provide guidance for the KPI owner. They describe how the owners should respond to events which are are beyond their control but relevant for the achievement of their KPI target value (cf. [23, 31]).Depending on [35, 13, 23, 31] it is important to document the **measurement frequency** for every KPI. Finally, a KPI structure should also provide a clear definition on the **interpretation** of the possible KPI values [13, 22].

4   Related Work

In addition to the initial literature study we conducted a second in-depth study between March, 01st and May, 31st 2012 by using the following three search engines: Google, Google scholar, and the search engine of our university library. We applied the key words "EA", "Enterprise Architecture", "EAM", "EA management", "KPI", "indicator", "metric", "structure", and "template" in different combinations. The search was performed using these English terms and their German translations. Thereby, we identified 15 relevant books and publications providing substantial statements regarding our research questions. These search results are described in more depth within the next paragraphs. The remainder of this section is clustered with respect to the origin of the examined sources: IT management literature, EA management literature, economics and IT controlling literature.

4.1   IT Management Literature

The framework CobiT 4.1 considers itself as the de facto standard for IT management and IT Governance in the industry [17]. Focusing on IT processes, the framework distinguishes between three goals types: IT goals, process goals, and activities goals. For each of this goal types, the framework outlines a huge number of recommended calculation rules (in the terms of CobiT called metrics). However, the metrics are formulated by a short textual description only, there exists no uniformed and configurable structure.

The Information Technology Infrastructure Library (ITIL) [30] is a framework contains a set of best-practices for IT service management. The renowned and widely applied framework focuses on the adjustment of IT services to the needs of business. The framework contains detailed IT processes, corresponding critical success factors, and a list of KPIs for the measurement of these factors. However, the listed KPIs are documented only by a short textual description. Similar to CobiT, no description structure is given.

4.2 EA Management Literature

The Open Group is a vendor and technology-neutral consortium developing and publishing their well known EA framework TOGAF [36]. Based on the terminology of the ISO Standard 42010 [16], TOGAF provides a Architecture Development Method (ADM), supporting models, and techniques for the development of enterprise architectures. Furthermore, it states in the phase A of the ADM cycle, more precisely in step 9 "Define the Target Architecture Value Propositions and KPIs", that KPIs are required "to meet the business needs" . However, no further information regarding KPIs and their documentation are contained. Therefore, the first column of the results overview table 1 remains empty.

Johnson et. al. describe in [18] a EA decision making process supported by influence diagrams. They introduce three domains of goals: business goals, information system goals, and IT organization goals. The latter category is refined by sub goals originating from the COBIT framework [17]. These sub goals are mapped to concrete information models to measure their achievement by employing Bayesian analysis as suggested by the authors as well as COBIT's calculation rules. However, Johnson et. al. do not provide further information regarding additional KPI structure elements like frequency of measurement, target, and planned values.

Stutz presents in his PhD thesis [35] a development method for EA KPIs based on the idea of the balanced score card. He introduces also a KPI description structure for documenting KPIs consisting of twelve elements. However, the author does not provide any further information regarding the design and evaluation of this KPI description structure. Furthermore, the presented structure disregards EA management goals and data required.

In [27] Murer et. al. highlight the importance of measuring progress when coping with very large application landscapes. To measure the achievement of predefined application landscape goals of a large Swiss bank the authors provide a list of concrete KPIs. However, these KPIs are described only on a textual basis with varying level of detail.

In [13] Frank et. al. describe a method to model and use indicator systems. To describe concrete indicators, they firstly introduce a domain specific modeling language called SCORE-ML. Furthermore, KPIs are linked to concrete organizational goals. However, the authors do not introduce a KPI structure. Even though the SCORE-ML meta model provides a good starting point for designing a KPI structure, it lacks important elements like planned and target values as well as KPI owner and KPI consumer information.

Caputo et. al. focus in [7] on the definition of KPI in Model Driven Architectures (MDAs) to enable automatic calculation. The authors suggest thereby different languages for the formal definition of KPIs. In addition, they recommend languages for the mathematical representation of these KPIs aiming to support automation. Unfortunately, the authors do not provide further details regarding KPI structure.

Gringel focuses in his master's thesis [14] on metrics for the EA. Next to the introduction of related frameworks and metric sources, he also introduces a structure for documenting EA KPIs and provides a list of several concrete KPIs in the appendix of his work. However, he refrains from providing any information with regards to evaluation of this KPI description structure.

Keuntje et. al. present in their book [22] typical challenges for the EA managementin industry and present respective practice-proven solutions. Among others, the authors claim the importance of KPI to measure the achievements and to steer the EA management initiative. Furthermore, they provide a small set of concrete KPIs, which do not have a common structure.

4.3   Economics and IT Controlling Literature

Siegwart et al. deliver in [33] a detailed overview on the field of enterprise controlling KPIs from an economics perspective. Next to many concrete calculation rules from this area, the authors emphasize the importance of measuring the achievement of enterprise goals by using appropriate KPIs. However, they do not introduce a structure for defining and documenting (organization-specific) enterprise controlling KPIs.

Parmenter describes in his book [31] KPIs from the economics point of view. The author also provides a list of elements required for the description of KPIs. He further introduces a collection of concrete KPIs covering different parts of an enterprise. However, his concrete KPI structure examples do not take all of his suggested description elements into account. Furthermore, no additional information is provided about the selection and origin of these description elements.

In his book [23], Kütz presents eleven IT controlling frameworks (e.g. [17, 30, 21]), focusing thereby on the contribution they make regarding KPIs. Next to these frameworks, the author provides a generic IT controlling KPI profile consisting of 20 elements. However, the proposed structure is not tailored to EA management, but rather IT controlling in general. Consequently, important EA management structure elements like goals, information model, as well as layers and cross-cutting aspects are not covered. The idea to apply the profile for the EA management is spawned by Feldschmid in his master's thesis [11]. Neither he does describe an adaptation process, nor he does present the result of this adaptation.

Kaplan et. al. present in [20] the renowned concept of the Balanced Scorecard (BSC). It is used for the identification of a small number of multi-perspective metrics (e.g., financial, customer) and attaching target values to them. The results are used to check if the current performance actually meets the predefined expectations. However both - the goals and the metrics are described only by a short textual statements. Moreover, no uniform and configurable KPI structure is presented.

Basili et al. present in [3] the Goal Question Metric (GQM) approach as a mechanism for defining software measurements. First, questions concerned

Table 1. KPI structure elements as discussed by related literature

		[36]	[18]	[35]	[17]	[30]	[33]	[27]	[13]	[23]	[14]	[22]	[20]	[3]	[7]	[31]
GSE	Title			✓				✓	✓		✓	✓			✓	✓
	Description	✓	✓	✓	✓	✓	✓	✓	✓	✓	✓	✓	✓		✓	✓
	Information model	✓							✓							
	Goals	✓		✓		✓			✓		✓	✓	✓	✓		
	Calculation	✓	✓	✓	✓	✓	✓	✓	✓	✓	✓				✓	✓
	Code			✓							✓	✓				
	Sources	✓							✓							
	Layers	✓	✓													
Mapping	Name in model															
	Mapped name															
	Contacts											✓				
	Data sources						✓			✓	✓					✓
Properties	Measurement frequency			✓						✓	✓					✓
	Interpretation									✓			✓			
	KPI consumer						✓			✓						
	KPI owner		✓	✓						✓						✓
	Target value			✓		✓				✓	✓					✓
	Planned value(s)									✓						
	Tolerance value(s)									✓						
	Escalation rule									✓						✓

about specific goal aspects are posed. Then, corresponding metrics are defined. However, all three levels - conceptual level (goals), operational level (questions), and the quantitative level (metrics) are described only in textual form. A general structure for defining and documenting of measurement developed by employing the GQM method is not provided by the authors.

Table 1 depicts a detailed summary of our findings. For each element of our proposed KPI structure (table row) the table indicates whether a certain author group covers this item (by means of a check mark symbol).

5   Evaluation

As pointed out in the research approach section 2, we applied a two-step approach to evaluate the designed structure for EA management KPI descriptions. First, we mapped KPI descriptions found in literature to the proposed KPI structure. Second, we evaluated the added value of each description element by means of an online expert survey.

5.1   Solution Design Application

The basis of the design's application is made up of 52 KPIs derived from literature [17] in the course of an industry project. The main goal of this EA management project was to introduce project, staff, and architecture KPIs supporting changes within the industry partner's IT organization. Based on a literature (e.g., [17, 30]) research as well as interactions with one consulting research institution, we were asked to design and document organization-specific measurements.

These mere textual KPI documentations have been mapped to the designed KPI description structure. Afterwards, all information not included in the textual documentation but required by the structure was complemented. Very often, this was the case for the information model, EA management goals, and the mapping tables containing the organization-specific details. As pointed out in Section 2, the outcome of this completion activity can be found in [26][1]. The catalog demonstrates the theoretical applicability of the proposed structure and provides a facility to evaluate the artifact's usability with industry domain experts.

5.2   Solution Design Assessment

We started the assessment of the KPI description structure's applicability by a 2h group discussion with six enterprise architects from a German car manufacturing company in December 2011. As result, the experts approved the general idea behind our concept. Furthermore, they suggested the renaming of some elements, i.e., 'contacts' instead of 'contact' and 'data sources' instead of 'data source' allowing for the documentation of multiple entries. In addition, they came up with several ideas about how the structure can be extended. This included, for example, a mechanism to ensure that the same data base is used for similar calculations and to add a (mathematical) calculation formula.

After implementing the suggested changes, an online expert survey was conducted to evaluate the relevance of the artifact on an elemental level. The survey took place from April, 10th 2012 to May, 21th 2012 and comprised 35 questions. Of this set, 24 were closed questions using a strict five-point Likert scale. Targeting at an academic as well as practitioner audience, we estimated a survey completion time of 17min. To ensure familiarity with the underlying concepts, only those experts were eligible to participate in the survey who had previously downloaded the EAM KPI catalog [26].

In total the survey has been completed by 29 experts working in seven different European countries while . At the time we collected the data, the experts were employed in the industry of consulting (9), finance (7), manufacturing (3), education (2), telecommunication (2), IT services (2), energy (1), and government (1). 45% of the participants defined their professional occupation as enterprise architect. In total, 45% have more than six years of experience in the field of EA management. Also, 20 respondents stated to have at least one year of experience with KPIs of which 6 indicated to have been working with KPIs for more than six years. The experience of the respondents was determined by the numbers of KPIs they have designed and were currently using. In average, the experts have

---

[1] An excerpt of the resulting KPIs is given in the appendix section of this paper.

conceived 23 KPIs and were in actually charge of 5 KPIs at the time the survey took place (median: 10, 2.5).

Within the survey, each single element of the proposed KPI structure has been evaluated separately. The respective group of questions has been answered by 22 respondents and the respective evaluation results are depicted in Table 2. While the column "acceptance rate" indicates the percentage to which experts (strongly) agreed that an element should be part of the structure, "remarks" contain the comments made. One can easily see that for each GSE a majority of respondents agrees with its usage. This also holds for the OSSEs grouped into the organization-specific mapping (59% acceptance rate) and properties section (81% acceptance rate) given that for each individual OSSE 10% or less respondents would exclude the proposed OSSE.

Table 2. Evaluation results

GSE	Acceptance rate	Remarks
Title	82%	
Description	91%	
EAM Goals	82%	Too unspecific to be helpful Free reign for redundancy Too general
Calculation description	95%	KPI's should only show added business value Use i* Use BPMN
Unique id	86%	Should reflect the type of KPI
EAM layers	68%	
Information model	71%	
Sources	76%	
OSSE (mapping)	**Acceptance rate**	**Remarks**
Name in Model	100%	
Mapped name	100%	
Contacts	100%	
Data source	100%	Add location for multiple instances
OSSE (properties)	**Acceptance rate**	**Remarks**
Measurement frequency	100%	
Interpretation	100%	
KPI consumer	100%	
KPI owner	97%	
Target value	93%	self fulfilling prophecy
Planned value(s)	97%	self fulfilling prophecy
Tolerance value(s)	90%	self fulfilling prophecy
Escalation rule	97%	

Remarkably, some respondents reported that certain EA management goals used in the KPI documentation structure are too general or vague and that business goals are missing. Moreover, suggestions for additional goals (e.g., improve resource utilization, increase standardization, increase time-to-market) were given and one expert even called for a free-text field allowing to specify newly evolved goals. Furthermore, one participant pointed out that planned and target values are "self fulfilling prophecies", meaning that calculation rules and underlying data are purposefully adjusted in order to meet these targets. Lastly, the survey respondents recommended the inclusion of additional elements, for instance, a cost field providing details on operating a certain KPI.

Beside the relevance of each element the added value of the KPI documentation structure has also been evaluated as a whole. 15 out of 18 respondents (strongly) agreed with the statement that the presented KPI structure is helpful for communicating about organization-specific KPIs. In addition, 10 out of 18 respondents (strongly) agreed with the statement that the presented KPI structure could become the standard form for describing EAM KPIs in their company.

In summary, the results indicate that the proposed elements of the KPI description structure are useful when documenting EA management KPIs. While this result is not unexpected for the predominantly literature-related GSEs, it is especially surprising for the OSSEs which are very rarely discussed by current sources.

6   Conclusion

In this article, we designed and evaluated a KPI structure which eases the definition, documentation, and retrieval of EA management KPIs. Thereby, the indicators defined by this structure represent one option to ensure the achievement of predefined EA management goals. Starting our research with the examination of the status quo in the field, we quickly found out that there exists no KPI structure so far which would allow architects to measure their actual EA management goal fulfillment while taking organization-specific conditions into account. With current literature forming the foundation, we devised a configurable and uniform structure suitable for EA management KPI description. Thereby, uniform refers to an identical representation of different EAM KPIs abd configurable signifies that the the structure's content as well as the structure itself can be tailored to the organizational context. Afterwards, we evaluated the designed artifact by means of a group discussion and an online survey. The first results of our design science based research confirm the validity and usability of our structure and provide substantial feedback for further enhancements.

It is particular the evaluation where we see the need for future research. The structure should be validated within EA management initiatives where a set of goals necessitates the establishment of new or adjustment of existing KPIs. In this regard, a design method to select, instantiate, and configure an organization-specific structure needs to be devised advancing the groundwork made in [26]. Complementing the methodological aspect, future research could focus on dedicated tool support. As a start, the structure should be made publicly available on a website, for instance a Wiki space. Gradually, functionalities like KPI configuration or a collection of applied KPIs should be made available. Finally, we consider the enactment of EA management KPIs as an intriguing field of research. Once a measure is established within an enterprise, it needs to be continuously adapted to the ever-changing organizational context.

References

1. Aier, S., Riege, C., Winter, R.: Classification of enterprise architecture scenarios – an exploratory analysis. Enterprise Modelling and Information Systems Architectures 3, 14–23 (2008)
2. Alexander, C., Ishikawa, S., Silverstein, M., Jacobson, M., Fiksdahl-King, I., Angel, S.: A Pattern Language. Oxford University Press, New York (1977)
3. Basili, V.R., Caldiera, G., Rombach, H.D.: The Goal Question Metric Approach. Wiley, New York (1994)
4. Black, J., Porter, L.: Management: meeting new challenges. Prentice Hall (2000)
5. Buckl, S., Dierl, T., Matthes, F., Schweda, C.M.: Building Blocks for Enterprise Architecture Management Solutions. In: Harmsen, F., Proper, E., Schalkwijk, F., Barjis, J., Overbeek, S. (eds.) PRET 2010. LNBIP, vol. 69, pp. 17–46. Springer, Heidelberg (2010)
6. Buckl, S.M.: Developing Organization-Specific Enterprise Architecture Management Functions Using a Method Base. PhD thesis, Technische Universität München, München, Germany (2011)
7. Caputo, E., Corallo, A., Damiani, E., Passiante, G.: KPI Modeling in MDA Perspective. In: Meersman, R., Dillon, T., Herrero, P. (eds.) OTM 2010. LNCS, vol. 6428, pp. 384–393. Springer, Heidelberg (2010)
8. Chen, P.P.-S.: The entity-relationship model – toward a unified view of data. ACM Transactions on Database Systems (TODS) 1(1), 9–36 (1976)
9. DeMarco, T.: Controlling Software Projects: Management, Measurement, and Estimates: Management, Measurement and Estimation. Prentice Hall (1982)
10. Drucker, P.F.: The Practice of Management. reissue edition. Harper Paperbacks, Oxford (2006)
11. Feldschmid, A.: Konzeption und prototypische Implementierung eines Steuerungscockpits im Kontext des Managements von Unternehmensarchitektur. Master's thesis, Hochschule Rosenheim (2009)
12. Fitz-Gibbon, C.: Performance Indicators. Bera Dialogues. Multilingual Matters (1990)
13. Frank, U., Heise, D., Kattenstroth, H., Schauer, H.: Designing and utilising business indicator systems within enterprise models – outline of a method. In: Modellierung Betrieblicher Informationssysteme (MobIS 2008) – Modellierung Zwischen SOA und Compliance Management, Saarbrücken, Germany, November 27-28 (2008)
14. Gringel, P.: Metriken zur Bewertung von Anwendungslandschaften. Master's thesis, Universität Oldenburg (2009)
15. Hevner, A.R., March, S.T., Park, J., Ram, S.: Design science in information systems research. MIS Quarterly 28(1), 75–105 (2004)

16. International Organization for Standardization. ISO/IEC 42010:2007 Systems and software engineering – Recommended practice for architectural description of software-intensive systems (2007)
17. ITGI. CobiT 4.1. Technical report, IT Governance Institute, Rolling Meadows, IL, USA (2009)
18. Johnson, P., Ekstedt, M.: Enterprise Architecture – Models and Analyses for Information Systems Decision Making, Studentlitteratur, Pozkal, Poland (2007)
19. Kaisler, S., Armour, F., Valivullah, M.: Enterprise Architecting: Critical Problems. In: Proceedings of the Proceedings of the 38th Annual Hawaii International Conference on System Sciences (HICSS 2005), track 8, vol. 08. IEEE Computer Society, Washington, DC (2005)
20. Kaplan, R.S., Norton, D.P.: The balanced scorecard – measures that drive performance. Harvard Business Review 70(1), 71–79 (1991)
21. Kargl, H., Kütz, M.: IV-Controlling. Arvato DMR (2007)
22. Keuntje, J.H., Matthes, F., Buckl, S., Schweda, C.M.: Eam-werkzeuge. In: Keuntje, J.H., Barkow, R. (eds.) Enterprise Architecture Management in der Praxis – Wandel, Komplexität und IT-Kosten im Unternehmen Beherrschen. Symposium, Düsseldorf, Germany, pp. 189–214 (2010)
23. Kuetz, M.: Kennzahlen in der IT. Werkzeuge für Controlling und Management, 4th edn. dpunkt.verlag, Heidelberg (2010)
24. Lagerström, R.: KPI:er för EA (2012), http://www.idg.se/2.1085/1.434625/kpier-for-ea (cited June 14, 2012)
25. Lankes, J.: Metrics for Application Landscapes – Status Quo, Development, and a Case Study. PhD thesis, Technische Universität München, Fakultät für Informatik, Munich, Germany (2008)
26. Matthes, F., Monahov, I., Schneider, A., Schulz, C.: EAM KPI Catalog v1.0 (2012), http://wwwmatthes.in.tum.de/wikis/sebis/eam-kpi-catalog (cited June 15, 2012)
27. Murer, S., Bonati, B., Furrer, F.J.: Managed Evolution: A Strategy for Very Large Information Systems. Springer (2010)
28. Object Management Group (OMG). Omg unified modeling language^{TM}(omg uml), infrastructure – version 2.3 (formal/2010-05-03) (2010)
29. Offermann, P., Levina, O., Schönherr, M., Bub, U.: Outline of a design science research process. In: DESRIST 2009: Proceedings of the 4th International Conference on Design Science Research in Information Systems and Technology, pp. 1–11. ACM, New York (2009)
30. Office of Government Commerce (OGC). ITIL – Service Delivery. IT Infrastructure Library (ITIL). The Stationery Office, Norwich, UK (2000)
31. Parmenter, D.: Key Performance Indicators: Developing, Implementing,and Using Winning KPIs. Wiley (2007)
32. Peter, R., Coronel, C., Rob, P.: Database Systems: Design, Implementation, and Management. Crisp Learning (2006)
33. Siegwart, H., Reinecke, S., Sander, S.: Kennzahlen für die Unternehmungsführung, Haupt (2010)
34. Sowa, J.F., Zachman, J.A.: Extending and formalizing the framework for information systems architecture. IBM Systems Journal 31(3), 590–616 (1992)

35. Stutz, M.: Kennzahlen für Unternehmensarchitekturen: Entwicklung einer Methode zum Aufbau eines Kennzahlensystems für die wertorientierte Steuerung der Veränderung von Unternehmensarchitekturen: Univ., Diss.–St. Gallen, 2009, vol. 31. Schriftenreihe Studien zur Wirtschaftsinformatik, Kovac (2009)

36. The Open Group. TOGAF "Enterprise Edition" Version 9 (2009), http://www.togaf.org (cited June 08, 2011)
37. Webster, J., Watson, R.T.: Analyzing the Past to Prepare for the Future: Writing a Literature Review. MIS Quarterly 26(2), xiii–xxiii (2002)
38. Wittenburg, A.: Softwarekartographie: Modelle und Methoden zur systematischen Visualisierung von Anwendungslandschaften. PhD thesis, Fakultät für Informatik, Technische Universität München, Germany (2007)

The Enterprise Architecture Realization Scorecard: A Result Oriented Assessment Instrument

Leo Pruijt[1], Raymond Slot[1], Henk Plessius[1], Rik Bos[2], and Sjaak Brinkkemper[2]

[1] HU University of Applied Sciences
Information Systems Architecture Research Group,
Nijenoord 1, 3552 AS Utrecht, The Netherlands
{leo.pruijt,raymond.slot,henk.plessius}@hu.nl
[2] University Utrecht
Department of Information and Computing Sciences,
Princetonplein 5, 3584 CC Utrecht, The Netherlands
{r.bos,s.brinkkemper}@uu.nl

Abstract. Enterprise Architecture (EA) is a well-accepted, but relatively young discipline. Since most practices are in the early stages of maturity, our research is aimed to develop an assessment instrument to measure and improve the EA management function's ability to realize its goals. In this paper, we propose the Enterprise Architecture Realization Scorecard (EARS) and an accompanying method to discover the strengths and weaknesses in the realization process of an EA management function. During an assessment, representative EA goals are selected, and for each goal, the results, delivered during the different stages of the realization process, are analyzed, discussed and valued. The outcome of an assessment is a numerical EARScorecard, explicated with indicator-values, strengths, weaknesses, and recommendations. The concept and composition of the EARS is primarily inspired by the principles of CobiT and TOGAF's Architecture Development Method. Two cases are discussed to illustrate the use of the instrument.

Keywords: Enterprise Architecture, Assessment, CobiT, TOGAF.

1 Introduction

The Enterprise Architecture (EA) management function forms a means to enhance the alignment of business and IT and to support the managed evolution of the enterprise [4]. EA can be defined, according to the ISO/IEC 42010 [11], as "the fundamental organization of [the enterprise] embodied in its components, their relationships to each other, and to the environment, and the principles guiding its design and evolution". A number of enterprise architecture frameworks have been proposed, including The Open Group Architecture Framework [26], DoDaf [6], GERAM [10], the Zachman Framework [30], and many more, as described by Chen, Doumeingts and Vernadat [5].

Over the last decades, EA management is introduced in many large organizations, but most practices are in the early stages of maturity, and the introduction and

S. Aier et al. (Eds.): TEAR 2012 and PRET 2012, LNBIP 131, pp. 300–318, 2012.
© Springer-Verlag Berlin Heidelberg 2012

elaboration often do not proceed without problems ([3], [25]). Moreover, the performance of the EA management function typically is not measured [29]. Existing research aimed at evaluating the maturity and performance level of EA (e.g., [17], [16], [19], [24]) and improving the effectiveness of EA (e.g., [7], [15]) holds promise of practical uses.

Our study builds on this line of research and contributes to it by the development of the Enterprise Architecture Realization Scorecard (EARS), a result oriented assessment instrument, focused on measuring and improving the effectiveness of an EA practice in realizing its goals. Our research aims to deliver a product with practical relevance and focuses on the research question: How can we measure the EA management function's ability to realize its goals? Two core concepts call for some elaboration: 'EA management function' and 'effectiveness of EA'.

The EA (management) function is extensively defined by van der Raadt and van Vliet [20]: "The organizational functions, roles and bodies involved with creating, maintaining, ratifying, enforcing, and observing Enterprise Architecture decision-making – established in the enterprise architecture and EA policy – interacting through formal (governance) and informal (collaboration) processes at enterprise, domain, project, and operational levels."

The effectiveness of EA management can be viewed, defined and measured in many different ways [16]. The EARS approach states that an EA management function is effective, when it is able to transform a given baseline situation into a target situation as specified by one or more goals, set out to the EA management function. These EA goals, or in terms of TOGAF [26] "requests for architecture work", should be aligned with the corporate strategy, as shown in Fig. 1. There is a huge variety in type and scope of goals set to different EA management functions. An example of an EA goal of a governmental organization is, "The organization should be able to implement a change in legislation within three months".

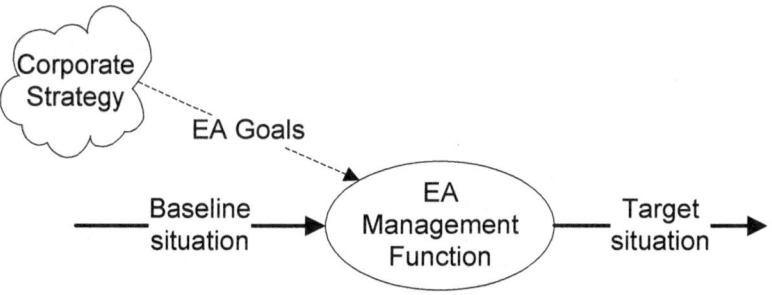

Fig. 1. The role of the EA management function

The objective of the EARS approach is to assess how well an EA management function is able to realize its goals; independent of the type of goals. The approach aims to do this by selecting some representative goals, by successively investigating the results produced in the context of an EA goal, and by scoring the results on different aspects. An EARS assessment may be used for awareness and improvement, but also for governance with respect to the progress and quality regarding an EA goal.

A number of instruments with similar objectives is developed and proposed, like EA balanced scorecard [23], EA maturity models ([9], [17], [21], [24]), and EA analysis approaches ([4], 14]). The main difference between the balanced scorecard approach and the EARS approach is that the balanced scorecard approach is concerned only with the outcome (added value) of EA management, while the EARS approach is also concerned with how the outcome is reached. The main difference with the maturity approach is that this approach aims to measure the effectiveness of the EA realization process indirectly (assuming that when a certain maturity level is reached for each key area, the EA function will operate effectively), while the EARS approach aims to measure the effectiveness of each step in the EA realization process directly, by assessing the results. The main difference with the EA analysis approaches is that, expressed in terms of Buckl's classification schema [4], most of them have a specific Analysis Concern, have a related specific Body of Analysis, and are not Self-Referential, while in the EARS approach the Analysis Concern and the Body of Analysis will vary per EA goal, and the approach is Self-Referential. Furthermore, the EARS approach is not only focused on EA artifacts, but on all activities and results of the EA realization process, including acceptance of the architectural decisions, outcome of architecture conformance checks, etc.

The research approach applied to develop the EARS is that of design-science research ([8], [18]), since the research was intended to deliver artefacts relevant to the professional practice. The applied approach conformed to the seven guidelines of Hevner et al [8]. For instance, the design of the EARS was evaluated with experts from the professional and scientific fields, and EARS assessments were conducted at large organizations to evaluate its applicability.

In this paper, the EARS instrument is presented in section 2, where the major decisions regarding the design of the EARS are explained as well. Section 3 describes the method and section 4 the application of the EARS at two organizations. Section 5 discusses the strengths and weaknesses of the EARS approach and the research so far, while section 6 presents the conclusions and an outlook to future work.

2   The Enterprise Architecture Realization Scorecard (EARS)

2.1   Concept of the EARS

The research question "How can we measure the EA management function's ability to realize its goals?" can be answered in different ways. One option is to measure the final result (changes in business operation) only and answer the question: To which extent is the operational performance matching with the target values of the EA goal?

The advantage of this approach is that it seems to be straightforward and relative simple. However, there are a number of disadvantages. Only goals that are realized completely will be eligible for a measurement. Additionally, it is not made plausible that the final results may be attributed to EA management. Moreover, the resulting score does not give any grips for the causes and so for improvement. Therefore the option 'measuring the final result only' was rejected and the alternative option was chosen: measure at a more detailed level. To find the best way to do this, the body of knowledge of (IT) governance was used, since measuring the organizational and IT performance is a well-established practice within this field. CobiT [12] appeared to be especially useful for this study. It is an open standard for IT Governance, well accepted both in practice and in the academic world. The CobiT framework is based on the following principles: business-focused, process-oriented, controls-based and measurement-driven. These principles are extensively explained in the CobiT 4.1 Excerpt [13]. Transfer of these CobiT-principles to the field of EA resulted in a metamodel, shown in Fig. 2, and a set of principles. Together they form a concept, which enables measurement of the EA management function in achieving its goals, at a detailed level.

- *EA goals* are derived from the business goals and enterprise strategy. *EA goals* should best be specific, measurable, actionable, realistic, results-oriented and timely.
- *EA goals* are realized through a (repeatable) *EA realization process*.
- The *EA realization process* is composed of a logical sequence of *EA activities*.
- Per *EA activity* an *activity goal* and related *metrics* are specified. The metrics are primarily focused on the *result* of the *EA activity*.

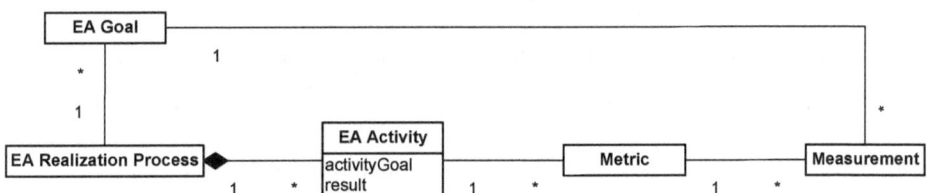

Fig. 2. Metamodel of the EARS concept

2.2   EA Activities and Results

After the concept of the EARS was established, the following sub-question became relevant: Which EA activities and results should be distinguished? Since no commonly accepted reference process exists, one could evaluate the EA management against [4], we designed an EA realization process suitable for the EARS concept. Five EA activities, depicted by rectangles, with their results were identified, which are shown in Fig. 3 and further explained in Table 1.

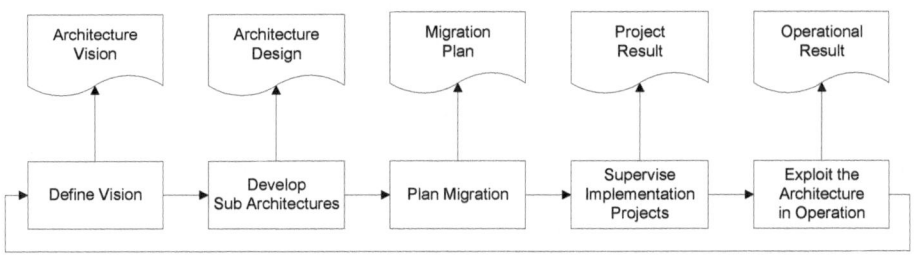

Fig. 3. The five EA activities with their results distinguished in the EARS

The EA activities were primarily derived from the Architecture Development Method (ADM) of TOGAF 9 [26], because it offers an architecture development cycle that covers all life cycle aspect as required by GERAM [22]. Furthermore, TOGAF is "probably the most well-known framework for EA management" [29]. To ensure completeness of the set of EA activities, other sources (e.g., [20], [27], [28]) were also studied and the proposals were validated during expert meetings.

Although EARS is based on TOGAF, its EA realization process differs from TOGAF's ADM. EARS distinguishes five EA activities while ADM recognizes nine phases, so the mapping (shown in Table 1) is not one to one. The first two EARS EA activities simply can be linked to four ADM phases. For the last three EA activities, coupling is more complex. The reason is that ADM often defines different types of output for a phase, while these types of output should be measured and assessed separately according the EARS approach. For instance, within ADM Phase G, Implementation Governance, the architecture is implemented within the solution under development and afterwards the solution is implemented in the operational environment. However, these two results are considered as very different within the EARS and consequently they are measured separately.

Table 1. The characteristics of the five activities distinguished in the EARS

Id	EA Activity	EA Activity Goal	Result	ADM Phase
#1	Define Vision	Determine the EA goals within scope of the architecture iteration, develop a high level, integrated and approved solution direction towards matching these goals and create a concise plan to realize them.	Architecture Vision	A
#2	Develop Sub Architectures	Develop the required subsets of architectures to support the agreed architecture vision.	Architecture Design	B, C, D
#3	Plan Migration	Search for opportunities to implement the architecture and plan the migration.	Migration Plan	E, F
#4	Supervise Implementation Projects	Ensure conformance to the architecture during the development and implementation projects.	Project Result	F, G
#5	Exploit the Architecture in Operation	Assess the performance of the architecture in operation, ensure optimal use of the architecture, and ensure continuous fit for purpose.	Operational Result	G, H

2.3   Valuing the Results: Aspects and Indicators

During an assessment a few representative EA goals are selected. For each goal is determined to which extent the EA management function was able to realize the goal (up to the moment of the assessment). This is done by valuing the results so far. EARS distinguishes five results, one per EA activity, as shown in Table 1. Furthermore, three aspects (product, acceptance, scope) of a result are distinguished to enable an objective way of measuring and scoring. This is done, because an architect can design a top quality solution (product aspect), but if it is not accepted (acceptance aspect), nothing is gained. On the other hand, if the solution is limited (scope aspect) to one architectural domain, e.g. technology, the goal may never be realized. The three aspects with their focus, question and scale are defined in Table 2.

Table 2. The aspects to be valued per result

Result Aspect	Description/Question	Scale
Product	Focus: The completeness, in terms of depth, and the quality of the outputs. Question: To which extent will the EA-goal be realized with it?	1-10
Acceptance	Focus: The acceptance and commitment of the stakeholders. Question: To which extent do they know, understand and agree with the product, and do they act committed?	1-10
Scope	Focus: The completeness, in terms of width, of the outputs. Question: Is the output width sufficient to realize the goal?	1-10

For each EA activity result, the three aspects are scored separately, and these scores are recorded at the EARScorecard. An EARScorecard summarizes the assessment result. An example of a scorecard (with the scores of case 2 in section 4) is shown in Table 3. Most scores are at a scale of 1-10, where 1 stands for low and very incomplete, and 10 for high and complete. The totals in the scorecard are calculated, based on the aspect scores of product, acceptance and scope. The derivation of the totals is described in the next sub section.

Table 3. EARS scorecard of the EA goal of Case 2

Id	Result	Aspect	Aspect score	Scope score	Aspect total	Result total
#1	Architecture Vision	Product	8	8	6	5
		Acceptance	5		4	
#2	Architecture Design	Product	3	6	2	2
		Acceptance	2		1	
#3	Migration Plan	Product	5	2	1	1
		Acceptance	5		1	
#4	Project Result	Product	7	1	1	1
		Acceptance	6		1	
#5	Operational Result	Product	4	1	1	1
		Acceptance	3		1	
	Goal total				19	

The different scores represent the collected evidence, and should enable reasoning about the strengths and weaknesses of the EA management's realization process:

- Aspect score and Aspect total express the contribution of an aspect to a result of a specific EA activity;

- Result total expresses the contribution of the EA activity to the realization of the goal;
- Goal total expresses the extent, creditable to EA management, to which the EA goal is realized. The goal total is the most abstract, and the least precise score of all. It is influenced by many factors and consequently, comparison of the goal totals of different EA management functions is not useful. However the goal total can be used to track the progress in time, regarding a goal.

During the judgment of a result, a number of considerations should be taken into account, like the EA-goal, the activity goal and the three aspects with their questions. To support the assessors and to objectify the rating, indicators were developed for each combination of result and aspect. The indicators for the aspects *Product* and *Scope* were mainly derived from TOGAF's ADM [26], since it provides elaborate descriptions of objectives, intent, approach, activities, artifacts, inputs and outputs for each phase [22]. The technique of scaled coverage percentage [31] was used to classify and prioritize the indicators. As an example, the set of indicators with their relative weights (W) for result *Architecture Vision* is shown in Table 4. For reasons of space, the indicator sets of the other EA activity results are not included in this paper, but a manual with all the indicators can be requested from the first author. The process of evidence collection and scoring (based on indicators and arguments) is explained in section 3 and illustrated in section 4.

Table 4. Set of indicators of result #1, Architecture Vision

Aspect	Id	Indicator	W
Product	1	The EA-goal is related to the business strategy and included in the vision.	0,2
	2	The EA-goal is SMART and (if needed) decomposed into high level stakeholder requirements.	0,2
	3	A high level solution direction is described and the solution direction to the goal is correct and realistic/realizable.	0,2
	4	The solution direction to the goal is integrated with the solution directions of the other goals (integrated vision).	0,3
	5	A comprehensive plan exist to realize the solution direction.	0,1
Acceptance	1	The architecture vision is well known by the stakeholder.	0,2
	2	The stakeholders understand the vision, the solution direction to the goal and its implication.	0,2
	3	The stakeholders agree with the solution direction to the goal and its implications.	0,3
	4	The stakeholders feel committed to (this part of) the vision.	0,3
Scope	1	The architecture vision covers the business, data, application and technology domains, related to the goal.	1,0

2.4   Formal Description of EARS

The EARS instrument is composed of the instantiations of *EA Realization Process*, *EA Activity*, *Aspect*, *Metric* and *Indicator* in the final metamodel, shown in Fig. 3. There is only one *EA Realization Process* and its processGoal is, to realize an *EA goal*, regardless of what the goal may be.

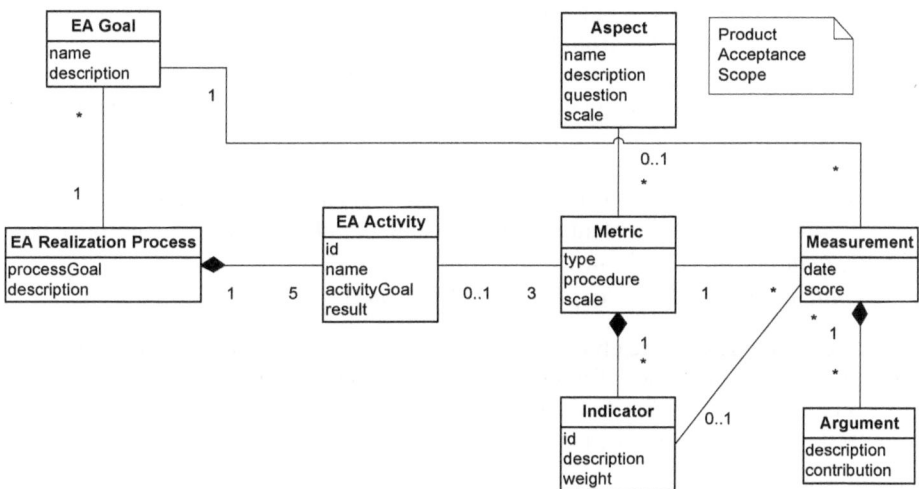

Fig. 4. Final EARS metamodel

Instantiations of *EA Goal*, *Measurement* and *Argument* are specific to an assessment. The Goal Question Metric approach [2] was taken into account, but no separate entity Question is included, because the questions at Aspect do satisfy in combination with the activity goals and the EA goal. The terms metric and measurement are often used in a quantitative approach, but in CobiT [12] they are also used for qualitative usage, which is also the usage within the EARS approach.

Most metrics within the EARS describe how an aspect of a result of an EA activity can be measured. The metrics, needed to calculate the totals of the EARS scorecard, are described below.

First, the notations are introduced:

- Let $G = \{g_1, g_2, ..., g_n\}$ be the set of EA goals.
- Let $R = \{r_1, r_2, ..., r_5\}$ be the set of Results of the EA Activities of the EA Realization Process.
- Let $A = \{product, acceptance, scope\}$ be the set of Aspects.
- Let $PA = \{pa_1, pa_2\}$ be the subset of A containing *product* (pa_1 and *acceptance* (pa_2 only.

Subsequently, the scores and totals can be defined as follows:

- The aspect score expresses the score for the product or acceptance aspect for a result of a goal:
  aspect_score is a function from $G \times R \times PA$ to $\{1, \ldots, 10\}$
- The scope score expresses the score for the scope aspect for a result of a goal:
  scope_score is a function from $G \times R$ to $\{1, \ldots, 10\}$
- The aspect total can be calculated as the multiplication of the aspect score (product or acceptance) with the scope score for a result of a goal, divided by 10:
  aspect_total is a function from $G \times R \times PA$ to $[1, 10]$
  $$aspect\_total(g, r, pa) = (aspect\_score(g, r, pa) \times scope\_score(g, r))/10$$
- The result total can be calculated as the average of the aspect totals for a result of a goal:
  result_total is a function from $G \times R$ to $[1, 10]$
  $$result\_total(g, r) = (aspect\_total(g, r, pa_1) + aspect\_total(g, r, pa_2))/2$$
- The goal total can be calculated as the sum of all the aspect totals of a goal:
  goal_total is a function from $G \rightarrow [1, 100]$
  $$goal\_total(g) = \sum_{i=1, j=1}^{5,2} aspect\_total(g, r_i, pa_j)$$

The scales of the EARS are chosen as specified, because decimal scales are often used and quite understandable. Therefore, they enhance correct valuing and correct interpretation of the scores. Since the scores do represent substantiated opinions and not exactly measured data, the numbers are rounded off to integers.

3   Method

The purpose of an EARS assessment is to provide an analysis of the strengths and weaknesses of the EA management function's realization process. Furthermore, to provide recommendations to the responsible manager and his team. The process to execute an EARS assessment is summarized below. The main line corresponds with the main line of Johnson's et al. [14] "overall process of enterprise architecture analysis".

1. Prepare the assessment with the responsible manager.
   a. Determine the objective of the assessment.
   b. Determine the position of the EA function within the organization.
   c. Select the EA goal(s).
   d. Select the architect(s) and stakeholders, suitable to the selected goal(s). Include at least one relevant stakeholder per EA activity. A typical set interviewees contains a business manager, information manager, enterprise architect, portfolio manager, solution architect, software engineer, expert from the business.
   e. Plan the assessment.
2. Collect evidence.
   a. Study relevant documents (strategy, goals, architecture, roadmaps, project portfolios ...).

    b.   Interview the architects and stakeholders.

    c.   Process the findings into arguments per indicator.

3.   Interpret the evidence and set up a report.

    a.   Process the arguments into scores within the scorecard.

    b.   Set up an assessment report with strengths and weaknesses, and recommendations.

4.   Present the outcomes of the assessment.

    a.   Discuss the report and the findings with the responsible manager.

    b.   Present the results to the architects and stakeholders.

Some topics related to step 2 and 3 do need some elaboration. During these steps, the assessor searches for information, interprets the information, and processes the information into arguments and scores. Scores within the EARScorecard will often represent substantiated opinions. The substantiation of the score of an aspect of a result is constituted by the weighted average of the related indicator scores. The indicators aid the assessor, but nevertheless have a high level of abstraction, since they should be useful for very different types of EA goals. Consequently, an indicator score needs substantiation as well, which is enabled by arguments and its contribution. The arguments per indicator are assembled in step 2 and recorded in tables, preferably with their source (interviewee or document). An example set of arguments is shown in Table 5. The arguments are not exclusively used for scoring, since they also form the basis for the description of the strengths and weaknesses, which explain the scores, and the recommendations in the assessment report.

Table 5. Example set of arguments belonging to result #2, Architecture Design

Aspect	Indic.	Contr.	Argument description
Product	1	+	Baseline Application architecture is described.
		-	Baseline Business, Data and Technology architectures are not described.
	2	...	...

    To score the results, the assessor should be able to determine and value the artifacts (depth and width) required to realize a specific goal. Questionnaires and indicators are available to support the assessors, but since the indicators have a high level of abstraction, other sources should be used as well. The EARS-indicators are derived from the TOGAF ADM input and output descriptions per phase [26], so detailed knowledge of ADM is desirable. Besides, TOGAF contains an "Enterprise Content Metamodel" that describes the core classes, properties and relationships that make up an EA model. Furthermore, other sources, like 'Essential layers, artifacts, and dependencies of EA' [28] and 'An engineering approach to EA design' [1], are useful as well.

    No goal specific expertise is expected from the assessor, because an EARS assessment is a retrospective study. The effectiveness of the architectural choices and solutions is revealed by the opinions and the information of the interviewees.

4   Application

To evaluate and improve EARS, the instrument was used in various organizations, located in the Netherlands. One assessment was conducted at a governmental organization and another at a financial organization. These assessments will be discussed below. A third assessment was conducted at an industrial company. It contributed to the research, but will not be discussed here, as EA management was not functioning long enough for a complete assessment.

Case 1: A Large Governmental Organization

This governmental organization is practicing enterprise architecture for some years. The study focused on the EA management function responsible for a large organizational domain with more than 10,000 employees. The case study aimed to deliver the organization an assessment focused on awareness and improvement of the EA function.

Two goals were selected in dialog with the client, namely 'Provide clarity to customers more quickly' and 'Reduce the complexity of the processes'. These goals were selected because they were representative for the complete set of EA goals, and because the organization was well on its way achieving these goals. Thereafter, the responsible architect was consulted, documents relevant to the goals were collected and studied, and ten architects and stakeholders were interviewed. Finally, a report was prepared, which was discussed with, and approved by the responsible manager and some key stakeholders. The EARScorecard of the EA goal 'Provide clarity to customers more quickly' is shown in Table 6, and a graphical representation of the aspect totals and result totals is shown in Fig. 5.

Table 6. EARS scorecard of the EA goal: 'Provide clarity to customers more quickly'

Id	Result	Aspect	Aspect score	Scope score	Aspect total	Result total
#1	Architecture Vision	Product	9	10	9	10
		Acceptance	10		10	
#2	Architecture Design	Product	4	10	4	4
		Acceptance	4		4	
#3	Migration Plan	Product	10	10	10	10
		Acceptance	10		10	
#4	Project Result	Product	4	10	4	5
		Acceptance	6		6	
#5	Operational Result	Product	1	5	1	1
		Acceptance	1		1	
	Goal total				39	

The EARS scorecard shows large differences between the five results. The scores for the *Architectural Vision* are very high, because there is an approved, high-level description of what is necessary to realize the goal. Additionally, the impact of the changes is known. The high acceptance score is due to the fact that the architects work in close cooperation with the decision makers.

The score for the *Architectural Design* is relatively low. At the moment of the assessment, the architecture was focused on the baseline architecture, which sufficed to perform a proper impact analysis of the intended changes. An integrated target architecture, needed to realize all EA goals for the coming years, was mostly missing, while considerable changes were expected. Consequently, the projects related to the goal could not anticipate on the target architecture, which will result in higher than necessary transition cost in the near future.

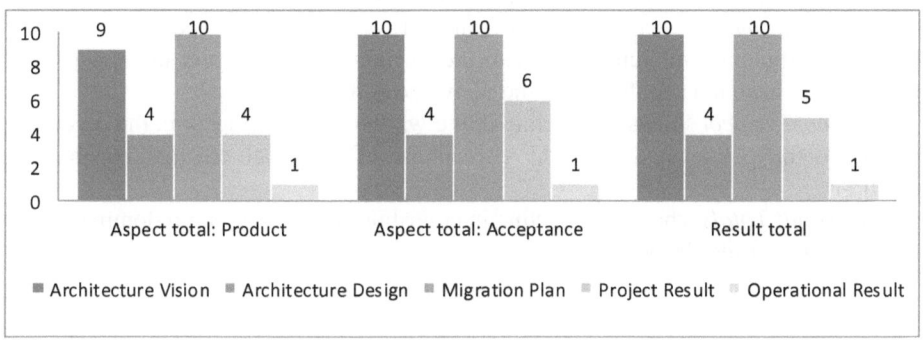

Fig. 5. The result totals of the EA goal 'Provide clarity to customers more quickly'

Migration Plan scores high, because a realistic roadmap was developed and acceptance and commitment of the stakeholders was high and remained high. All four projects, needed to realize the selected goal, were included in the project portfolio, and were already under development or beyond.

The low score for *Project Result* is partly related to the missing target architecture, as discussed under Architecture Design. Consequently, the projects were not provided with architectural definitions and requirements. Positive was the collaboration with the project architects in the early stages of the project. Negative was the lack of checking of the conformance of the implementation to the architecture.

Finally, the low score for *Operational Result* is because the most important implementations were not yet operational. Positive returns were expected in the next calendar year.

Case 2: A Large Financial Organization

This financial service provider is in transition from a decentralized organization, composed of more than ten companies and brands, to one centralized company, striving for one way of working and for operational excellence. For this assessment, the following EA goal was selected, "Implement a corporate data warehouse". Sub goals included not only corporate wide business intelligence, but also the provision of integrated production data to portal and output service. This goal was part of an architecture master plan, which was approved approximately three years before. Evidence collection included a total of two days of document study and ten interviews, which mostly lasted 30-60 minutes. The scores in Table 3 and Fig. 6, 7 show the outline of the assessment outcome.

The *Product aspect* of *Architecture Vision* and *Project Result* contribute most to the goal. It shows the focus of the EA management's attention.

Architecture Design was largely skipped as part of a bottom-up strategy. The deficiency of the *Architecture Design* is probably one of the reasons why the first projects in the roadmap encountered huge problems in various areas. Complexity appeared much greater than anticipated. Consequently, the initial projects ran out of time, trust disappeared and follow-up projects were not approved.

The *Acceptance aspect* scores significantly low, compared to the *Product aspect*, due to insufficient communication with the business. Furthermore, the end users in the business were not satisfied with the delivered solution.

The *Scope aspect* shows the decline in the width of the architecture, the percentage of the roadmap executed, and the percentage of the goal covered by the final solutions.

The *Result Totals*, shows the decline in contribution to the goal, predominantly due to the decline of the *Scope aspect*.

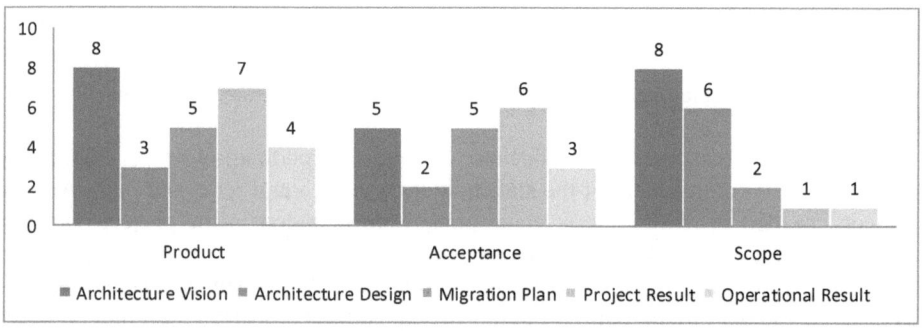

Fig. 6. Product, Acceptance and Scope scores per EA activity result

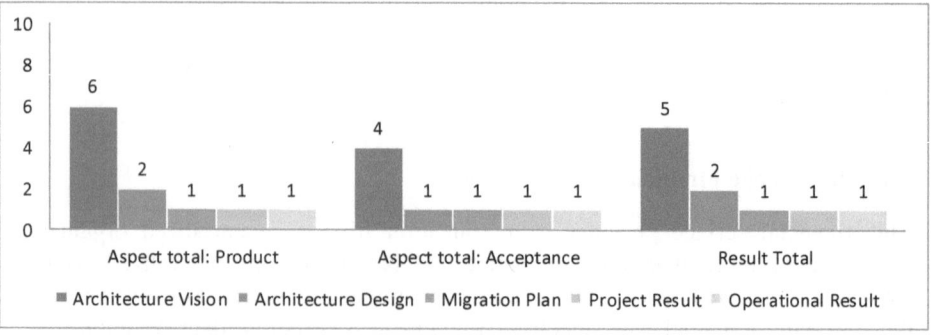

Fig. 7. Aspect totals and Result totals per EA activity result

The three aspect-scores per EA activity result were each constituted by the weighted average of the related indicator scores. As an illustration, Table 7 shows how the product score, acceptance score and scope score of the result #1 Architecture Vision are composed of the indicator scores. Per indicator, the indicator score (S), valued by the assessor on a scale of 1-10, is multiplied with the indicator's weight (W) to the indicator total (T).

Table 7. Aspect and indicator scores of result #1, Architecture Vision

Aspect	Id	Indicator	W	S	T
Product	1	The EA-goal is related to the business strategy and included in the vision.	0,2	10	2,0
	2	The EA-goal is SMART and (if needed) decomposed into high level stakeholder requirements.	0,2	6	1,2
	3	A high level solution direction is described and the solution direction to the goal is correct and realistic/realizable.	0,2	7	1,4
	4	The solution direction to the goal is integrated with the solution directions of the other goals (integrated vision).	0,3	8	2,4
	5	A comprehensive plan exist to realize the solution direction.	0,1	7	0,7
		Product score			**7,7**
Accep-tance	1	The architecture vision is well known by the stakeholder.	0,2	8	1,6
	2	The stakeholders understand the vision, the solution direction to the goal and its implication.	0,2	4	0,8
	3	The stakeholders agree with the solution direction to the goal and its implications.	0,3	5	1,5
	4	The stakeholders feel committed to (this part of) the vision.	0,3	4	1,2
		Acceptance score			**5,1**
Scope	1	The architecture vision covers the business, data, application and technology domains, related to the goal.	1	8	8,0
		Scope score			**8,0**

The indicator values were substantiated by means of arguments collected during the assessment. E.g., with regard to result #1 Architecture Vision, twenty five arguments were gathered, varying from two to seven arguments per indicator. Approximately 60% of these arguments originated from the study of architectural artifacts, while the remaining 40% did arise during the interviews. Table 8 shows examples of arguments. Arguments are described in case specific terms and may include references to the sources of the information. To ensure anonymity, table 8 contains the condensed arguments of only a few indicators.

Table 8. Arguments regarding two indicators of the product aspect of result #1

Aspect	Indicator	Contribution	Argument description
Product	1	+	The goal "Implement a corporate data warehouse" is based on the corporation's strategy and target operating model.
		+	Conformance is confirmed by several interviewees.
	2	-	The goal is not formulated explicitly, it is not SMART and no sub-goals were specified.
		+	Sub-goals can be derived from the architecture master plan.
		+	Stakeholder requirements are described in the master plan as business and ICT issues to be solved by the data warehouse.
		-	No objectives were set for the EA management function, when the function was initiated.

The assessment report describes the strengths and weaknesses of the realization process of the EA management function and recommendations for improvements. The strengths and weaknesses were based on the indicator scores and were described in case specific terms, in line with the corresponding arguments.

The recommendations were derived from the strength and weaknesses. The recommendations summarized the most important improvements to work on and included references to relevant literature. Some main lines from the recommendations of this case are:

- Identify explicit goals to the EA management function in collaboration with the stakeholders. Set realistic and SMART (sub) goals and work from these goals.
- Do not combine major goals and complex projects with a bottom-up strategy regarding the development of the EA management function and EA artifacts.
- Develop architectural artifacts to substantiate and verify the accuracy, impact and feasibility of the goals and solution directions. Do this for both the baseline and target situation and use these as a base for roadmaps.

5   Discussion

The EARS assessments, described above in the case studies, proceeded without problems and provided interesting analysis outcomes and recommendations to the organizations involved. The two described cases show great differences in the EA management's goals and approaches, and the assessments delivered very different outcomes. However, some similarities were identified as well. Both EA functions scored low on Architecture Design, especially the target architecture. This was partly compensated, by a shared effort to draw up solution architectures within the projects. Another similarity is that both EA functions failed to check on conformance during the implementation. These findings match with research on the maturity level of 56 EA management cases [25], where the focus areas 'Development of architecture' and 'Monitoring' scored respectively low and very low on the maturity scale.

The case studies were also focused on the evaluation of the EARS approach itself. During the interviews and meetings of the case studies, additional information was gathered to gain insight in the applicability, effectiveness and efficiency of the instrument.

The EARS approach appeared to be effective, since the scorecard, indicator values and assembled arguments proved to be an adequate base to identify the strengths and weaknesses of the realization process and to provide recommendations. Moreover, the responsible managers and key stakeholders approved the outcome of the assessments, and interviewees who were asked whether the main aspects of the architecture function were covered during the interview, responded positively. As additional revenue, a responsible manager observed that the assessment stimulated the internal discussion regarding the focus, method and effectiveness of the architecture function.

Some doubts in advance about the applicability of the EARS approach were answered. E.g., some findings in the case studies were:

- The EA goals were well identifiable and selecting representative goals did not cause problems.
- EA activities and the results were sufficiently distinctive and recognizable and could be found in practice.
- The aspects product, acceptance and scope were generally well identifiable for the results. However in some cases two aspects are closely linked. Such as in # 3 Migration Plan, where product and acceptance are not well distinguishable and thus are given the same value.
- The indicators were developed during the first case study and refined afterwards. During the following applications, they appeared to be useful and were not challenged.

The outcomes of the case studies give us reasons to believe that the EARS can be applied conveniently and is quite effective as an assessment instrument with awareness and improvement purposes.

However, there are some limitations to our research so far. Although three assessments in different types of organizations were conducted in the Netherlands, our research findings are not inevitably valid for other companies, sectors or countries. Furthermore, our study could not provide a valid conclusion regarding the efficiency of the assessment method, since it did not include a comparison with other assessment approaches. The EARS approach appeared to be quite efficient to the research team, because after five to six interviews, the image was sufficiently sharp and the results could be rated. Subsequent interviews did add little new knowledge to the assessment, but were useful to confirm findings.

6   Conclusions and Further Research

In this paper, we presented a novel instrument to assess and rate how well an EA management function is able to realize its goals, the Enterprise Architecture

Realization Scorecard (EARS). During the assessment of an EA goal, five types of results, delivered during the EA realization process, are analyzed and discussed in interviews with relevant stakeholders. Arguments are assembled and, by means of indicators, translated to scores. For each result, three aspects are scored: product, acceptance and scope. The scores are recorded at a scorecard and subsequently, totals at result level and goal level can be calculated. Finally, an assessment report is prepared, with a scorecard, strengths and weaknesses of the EA realization process (based on the scores in the scorecard, indicator scores and arguments), and recommendations.

We used two case studies to illustrate how the EARS instrument is used in practice. The application at a large governmental organization and a large financial organization delivered interesting outcomes: strengths and weaknesses were detected and substantiated and recommendations were given. Since the selected goal and EA management function itself were quite different from the first case, the outcome of the assessment and the recommendations differed significantly. The EARS approach appeared to be effective in these cases. The scorecard, indicator values and assembled arguments proved to be an adequate base to identify the strengths and weaknesses of the realization process and to provide recommendations. Furthermore, the assessment stimulated the internal discussion regarding the focus, method and effectiveness of the architecture function.

The EARS instrument contributes to the professional practice by adding an assessment instrument that can be used to evaluate the effectiveness of the EA management function's realization process. To connect to the professional practice, the instrument is based on two well-accepted open standards CobiT [12] and TOGAF [26].

The EARS instrument contributes to the research on architecture effectiveness by focusing on the EA realization process and its results.

Distinctive characteristics of the EARS approach are:

- the focus on goals specific to the organization;
- the focus on the realization process, its activities and results;
- aspects and indicators support the evaluation of the results;
- numerical values in a scorecard give an overview of and support reasoning about the strengths and weaknesses.

Interesting topics for future work emerged during this study. Research is needed to determine whether the assessment results of one or two representative goals can be generalized to general statements about the EA function. Furthermore, comparative research on EARS and other EA assessments approaches could be interesting. It could contribute to the further development of the set of indicators. In addition, it might reveal and explain correlations between focus areas of maturity models and high scores in the EARScorecard.

Acknowledgement. This paper results from the ArchiValue project, a collaboration between Novay, APG, the Dutch Tax and Customs Administration, BiZZdesign, University of Twente, and HU University of Applied Sciences Utrecht.

References

1. Aier, S., Kurpjuweit, S., Schmitz, O., Schulz, J., Thomas, A., Winter, R.: An Engineering Approach to Enterprise Architecture Design and its Application at a Financial Service Provider. In: Modellierungbetrieblicher Informations Systeme (MobIS 2008), Saarbrücken, GI/Köllen, pp. 115–130 (2008)
2. Basili, V., Caldeira, G., Rombach, H.D.: The Goal Question Metric Approach. In: Marciniak, J. (ed.) Encyclopedia of Software Engineering. Wiley (2004)
3. Bucher, T., Fischer, R., Kurpjuweit, S., Winter, R.: Enterprise Architecture Analysis and Application - An Exploratory Study. In: EDOC Workshop TEAR 2006, Hong Kong (2006)
4. Buckl, S., Schweda, C.M.: Classifying Enterprise Architecture Analysis Approaches. In: Poler, R., van Sinderen, M., Sanchis, R. (eds.) IWEI 2009. LNBIP, vol. 38, pp. 66–79. Springer, Heidelberg (2009)
5. Chen, D., Doumeingts, G., Vernadat, F.B.: Architectures for Enterprise Integration and Interoperability: Past, Present and Future ‖ . Computers in Industry 59(7), 647–659 (2008)
6. Department of Defense: The Department of Defense Architecture Framework (DoDAF), version 2.0 (2009)
7. Foorthuis, R., van Steenbergen, M., Mushkudiani, N., Bruls, W., Brinkkemper, S., Bos, R.: On course, but not there yet: Enterprise architecture conformance and benefits in systems development. In: ICIS 2010 Proceedings (2010)
8. Hevner, A., March, S., Park, J., Ram, S.: Design Science in Information Systems Research. MIS Quarterly 28(1), 75–105 (2004)
9. Hoffman, M.: Analysis of the Current State of Enterprise Architecture Evaluation Methods and Practices. In: The European Conference on Information Management and Evaluation (ECIME 2007), Montpellier, France, Academic Conferences Limited, pp. 237–246 (2007)
10. IFIP-IFAC Task Force: GERAM: Generalized Enterprise Reference Architecture and Methodology. IFIP-IFAC Task Force on Architectures for Enterprise Integration, Tech. Rep.(1999)
11. International Organization for Standardization:Iso/iec 42010:2007 systems and software engineering recommended practice for architectural description of software-intensive systems (2007)
12. IT Governance Institute: CObIT 4.1 (2007), http://www.itgi.org
13. IT Governance Institute: CObIT 4.1 Excerpt, Executive Summary (2007), http://www.itgi.org
14. Johnson, P., Johansson, E., Sommestad, T., Ullberg, J.: A tool for enterprise architecture analysis. In: 11th IEEE International Enterprise Distributed Object Computing Conference (EDOC 2007), Annapolis, USA (2007)
15. Lankhorst, M.: Enterprise Architecture at Work. Springer, Heidelberg (2005)
16. Morganwalp, J.M., Sage, A.P.: Enterprise architecture measures of effectiveness. International Journal of Technology, Policy and Management 4(1), 81–94 (2004)
17. Luftman, J.: Assessing Business Alignment Maturity. Communications of AIS 4, Article 14 (2000)
18. Peffers, K., Tuunanen, T., Rothenberger, M.A., Chatterjee, S.: A Design Science Research Methodology for Information Systems Research. Journal of Management Information Systems 24(3), 45–78 (2008)

19. van der Raadt, B., Slot, R., van Vliet, H.: Experience Report: Assessing a Global Financial Services Company on its Enterprise Architecture Effectiveness Using NAOMI. In: Proceedings of the 40th Annual Hawaii international Conference on System Sciences, HICSS 2007 (2007)
20. van der Raadt, B., Vliet, H.: Designing the Enterprise Architecture Function. In: Becker, S., Plasil, F., Reussner, R. (eds.) QoSA 2008. LNCS, vol. 5281, pp. 103–118. Springer, Heidelberg (2008)
21. Ross, J.: Creating a Strategic Architecture Competency: Learning in Stages. MISQ Executive 2(2) (2003)
22. Saha, P.: Analyzing The Open Group Architecture Framework from the GERAM Perspective. The Open Group, Tech. Rep (2004)
23. Schelp, J., Stutz, M.: A Balanced Scorecard Approach to Measure the Value of Enterprise Architecture. Journal of Enterprise Architecture 3(4), 8–14 (2007)
24. van Steenbergen, M., van den Berg, M., Brinkkemper, S.: A Balanced Approach to Developing the Enterprise Architecture Practice. In: Filipe, J., Cordeiro, J., Cardoso, J. (eds.) Enterprise Information Systems. LNBIP, vol. 12, pp. 240–253 (2007)
25. van Steenbergen, M., Schipper, J., Bos, R., Brinkkemper, S.: The Dynamic Architecture Maturity Matrix: Instrument Analysis and Refinement. In: Workshop on Trends in Enterprise Architecture Research (TEAR), Stockholm (2010)
26. The Open Group: The Open Group Architecture Framework: Version 9, Enterprise Edition (2009), http://www.opengroup.org/togaf
27. Wagter, R., van den Berg, M., Luijpers, L., van Steenbergen, M.: Dynamic Enterprise Architecture: How to Make it Work. Wiley, Hoboken (2005)
28. Winter, R., Fischer, R.: Essential layers, artifacts, and dependencies of enterprise architecture. In: Workshop on Trends in Enterprise Architecture Research, TEAR (2006)
29. Winter, K., Buckl, S., Matthes, F., Schweda, C.: Investigating the state-of-the-art in enterprise architecture management method in literature and practice. In: MCIS 2010, paper 90 (2010)
30. Zachman, J.A.: A framework for information systems architecture. IBM Syst. J. 26(3), 276–292 (1987)
31. van Zeist, B., Hendriks, P., Paulussen, R., Trienekens, J.: Kwaliteit van software producten. Kluwer Bedrijfsinformatie, Deventer (1996)

Author Index